America Firsthand

FIFTH EDITION

America Firsthand

FIFTH EDITION

Volume One
Readings from Settlement to Reconstruction

Robert D. Marcus
State University of New York College at Brockport

and

David Burner
State University of New York at Stony Brook

BEDFORD/ST. MARTIN'S
Boston ♦ New York

FOR BEDFORD/ST. MARTIN'S

History Editor: Katherine E. Kurzman
Developmental Editor: Molly E. Kalkstein
Production Editor: Arthur Johnson
Production Supervisor: Catherine Hetmansky
Director of Marketing: Karen Melton
Copyeditor: Rosemary Winfield
Cover Design: Donna Lee Dennison
Cover Art: Photograph taken near Coleville, 1866, by Charles W. Carter. © by
Intellectual Reserve, Inc. Courtesy of Historical Department. Used by permission.
Composition: Pine Tree Composition, Inc.
Printing and Binding: RR Donnelley & Sons Company

President: Charles H. Christensen
Editorial Director: Joan E. Feinberg
Director of Editing, Design, and Production: Marcia Cohen
Managing Editor: Elizabeth M. Schaaf

Library of Congress Control Number: 00–103106

Acknowledgments

Bracketed numbers indicate selection numbers.

[1] "Announcing the Discovery" from Stephen Greenblatt, ed., *New World Encounters*, University of California Press. Copyright © 1993 The Regents of the University of California.
Reprinted by permission.
[5] "Testimony of Pueblo Indians" from Charles Wilson Hackett, *Revolt of the Pueblo Indians
of New Mexico and Otermín's Attempted Reconquest, 1680–1682.* Copyright © 1942. Reprinted by permission of the University of New Mexico Press.
[14] "Leaving an Abusive Husband" from Ann Taves, ed., *Religion and Domestic Violence in
Early New England: The Memoirs of Abigail Abbot Bailey.* Copyright © 1989. By permission
of Indiana University Press.
[18] "Secret Correspondence of a Loyalist Wife" from H. O. H. Vernon-Jackson, ed., "A
Loyalist's Wife: Letters of Mrs. Phillip Van Cortlandt, December 1776–February 1777,"
History Today 14 (1964): 574–80. Reprinted with the permission of *History Today.*
[21] "Hemings Family Accounts" from Annette Gordon-Reed, *Thomas Jefferson and Sally
Hemings: An American Controversy.* Copyright © 1997 by the University Press of Virginia.
Reprinted by permission of the University Press of Virginia.

*Acknowledgments and copyrights are continued at the back of the book on page 332, which constitutes an
extension of the copyright page. It is a violation of the law to reproduce these selections by any means whatsoever without the written permission of the copyright holder.*

Preface

This fifth edition of *America Firsthand* continues to pursue the goal of previous editions: to supplement United States history survey textbooks in two volumes that give center stage to ordinary Americans who speak directly of their own lives. These include people from many groups whose experience has been, until recently, largely lost in mainstream history. As much as possible, individuals speak in their own words and in selections long enough to be memorable, personal, and immediate. The accounts of indentured servants, Southern aristocrats, runaway slaves, factory workers, Western explorers, civil rights activists, immigrants, and many others expose students to a wide range of human experience.

This new edition adds important features that aid in the pursuit of its pedagogical goals. It retains the Points of View selections introduced in the fourth edition that characterize the theme of each section by presenting differing angles of vision, thereby offering opportunities for critical thinking. Each volume has two new Points of View sections. In Volume One are presented Columbus's and Amerigo Vespucci's contrasting views of the New World and documents on the relationship of Thomas Jefferson and Sally Hemings. Volume Two offers views of Reconstruction from former slaves and white Southerners and two different perspectives on the effects of industrialism on workers from the 1882 Senate investigation into the relationship of capital and labor.

Also new to the fifth edition are several visual portfolios directly connected to a number of the readings and carefully annotated with background information and questions that link the images presented with the selections. One of our goals for these portfolios is that when students ask the inevitable question, instructors can easily answer that yes, they will be on the exam.

New as well is a carefully constructed Instructor's Manual prepared by Melissa Weinbrenner of the University of Montevallo and Robert Marcus. The manual includes interpretations of the main themes of each part, summaries of articles, discussion questions, active learning exercises, and essay examination questions. We have tried to make the manual useful both to experienced teachers and to graduate assistants teaching their first course or running discussion sections.

America Firsthand has been extensively revised in the fifth edition. We have retained readings that users wanted to continue teaching and have dropped less successful ones. Among many new readings in the first volume, students will find a recently rediscovered letter of Christopher Columbus interpreting his discoveries to his royal patrons, an eighteenth-century woman's account of dealing with an abusive husband, documents from the Jefferson and the Hemings families on the relationship between Thomas Jefferson and Sally Hemings, and a vivid account of the New York draft riots by a young woman trapped in the middle of the violence. Fresh selections in the second volume include a brass worker's lament over the decline of independent craftsmen, Theodore Roosevelt's version of his adventures in the Spanish-American War, a stirring account of the sit-down strike at the General Motors plant in Flint, Michigan, in December 1936, recollections of the Woodstock music festival of 1969, and eyewitness accounts of the Oklahoma City bombing of 1995 and memories of its aftermath.

Carefully written headnotes before the selections prepare students for each reading and help place personalities in their times. Questions immediately after the headnotes enable students and instructors to give attention to specific passages and issues that can provide points for discussion as well as material for testing or essays.

America Firsthand, Fifth Edition, presents the American experience through the perspectives of diverse people who have in common a vivid record of the world they inhabited and of the events they experienced. We hope that the readings will serve as fertile ground in which students can begin to root their own interest in history and deepen their understanding of the times in which they live.

ACKNOWLEDGMENTS

Many fine teachers provided thoughtful criticism and good suggestions for the fifth edition of *America Firsthand*.

Our thanks to Jeffrey S. Adler, University of Florida; Holly Baggett, Southwest Missouri State University; Margaret L. Brown, Brevard College; Susan Curtis, Purdue University; Tom Dicke, Southwest Missouri State University; Nicole Etcheson, University of Texas at El Paso; Janette T. Greenwood, Clark University; C. L. Higham, Texas A&M University; Andrew Hurley, University of Missouri–St. Louis; Ted Karamanski, Loyola University; Benjamin Larabee Jr., St. Alban's School; Anne Laszlo, Northern Essex Community College; Mark Newman, University of Illinois at Chicago; Karen Parsons, Loomis Chaffee School; Lawrence A. Peskin, Morgan State University; Nicolas W. Proctor, Simpson College; Linda Przybyszewski, University of Cincinnati; Jonathan Rees, Southwest Missouri State University; Penne L. Restad, University of

Texas at Austin; Richard Scheidenhelm, Colorado State University; Rebecca S. Shoemaker, Indiana State University; Kenneth B. Shover, University of Texas at El Paso; Gene A. Smith, Texas Christian University; Melissa Weinbrenner, University of Montevallo; and Virginia S. Wilson, North Carolina School of Science and Mathematics.

We owe gratitude as well to the many people whose editorial work and judgment improved this edition. Molly Kalkstein skillfully oversaw the evolution of the fourth edition into the fifth and helped us organize the important new features of this venture. Others at Bedford/St. Martin's who played major roles have our thanks as well: Charles Christensen, Joan Feinberg, Katherine Kurzman, Elizabeth Schaaf, Donna Dennison, and Arthur Johnson. Outside the Bedford organization, Barbara Wachob did fine service in managing many details of the manuscript. Bill Johnson's massive knowledge of American photography and visual history added a vital new dimension to the project. And, as ever, Tom West remains for both of us the editors' editor.

Contents

PART ONE

Indians and Europeans

New World Encounters

The age of exploration added the scientific and humanist ambitions of the Renaissance to the older hopes of discovering the lost tribes of Israel, reconquering Jerusalem from Islam, and gaining a westward sea route to the rich trade of the Orient. Accounts such as Christopher Columbus's first description of the New World to his sovereigns mixed the lofty dreams of the age with the grounded realities of exploration. Not for another decade would Amerigo Vespucci demonstrate that Columbus's New World was not the East Indies, as the great admiral thought, but a wholly different land, as yet unmarked by European travelers.

The people of this new land were named "Indians" by explorers who mistook the Americas for the East Indies. These Native Americans had their own complex cultures, which rapidly came into conflict with those of white explorers and settlers. And, much like the Europeans, they survived among shifting allies and enemies, territorial disputes, and cultural borrowings. European settlers, soldiers, missionaries, and their plants, animals, technologies, and especially germs disrupted and fundamentally transformed this world, finally destroying most of it. Bartolomé de Las Casas's report of the Spanish conquest of the Indies captures the full horrors of that first encounter. Yet for three centuries after Columbus, various Indian nations played independent and sometimes powerful roles in the diplomacy of the Western Hemisphere, their adaptations and cultural exchanges—now including encounters with white civilizations—continued, and, however much diminished, many tribes have maintained their identity into the present. The visual portfolio "New World Contact" (page 43) illustrates some of the earlier transformations Native Americans underwent as well as how they were viewed by Europeans and Anglo-Americans.

The Pueblo Indians' accounts of their revolt of 1680 illustrate the Spanish empire's uneasy mix of Indian and European religions and interests. John Smith's description of Virginia's Indians shows cultural conflicts similar to those of the Spanish conquest working themselves out in the colonies of the

British empire. And Father Paul Le Jeune, representing the French empire in the New World, suggests how little understanding existed even between friendly whites and receptive Native Americans.

Indians throughout the colonial era and well into the nineteenth century provoked fear and a sense of mystery. Stories about what happened when whites were captured by Indians, beginning perhaps with John Smith's account of his supposed rescue by Pocahontas, remained popular for more than two centuries, making captivity narratives among the first best sellers produced in this country. Mary Jemison's account of her captivity among the Seneca illustrates how Anglo-Americans domesticated their anxieties about Indians and wrapped them in the aura of romance.

POINTS OF VIEW

Old Dreams and New Worlds (1493–1502)

1

Announcing the Discovery

Christopher Columbus

When Christopher Columbus sighted land on October 12, 1492, he was convinced he had achieved his goal of reaching Asia—a belief he clung to even after three more voyages in 1493, 1498, and 1502. By what one scholar has described as "a giant geological trick [played] upon the admiral before historical time began," the Caribbean islands he discovered were positioned much like the islands off the coast of Asia that appeared on the medieval maps he had long studied. These maps, based on both the Bible and reports by such European travelers to Asia as Marco Polo, led him to identify Cuba first with Cipangu (Japan) and then with Cathay (China). Similarly, he erroneously identified Hispaniola and Jamaica with the islands in the China Sea. Some of the landscapes and climates Columbus encountered conformed as well to the geography of Asia firmly fixed in his mind. And many religious prophecies confirmed his various interpretations of his whereabouts. For instance, in a later voyage he believed that part of the coast of South America was the portal to the terrestrial paradise assumed in medieval theology and geography. He would go to his grave in 1505 without ever having been aware that he had reached a New World not described in any of the geographies or drawn on any of

Margarita Zamora, "Christopher Columbus's 'Letter to the Sovereigns': Announcing the Discovery," in Stephen Greenblatt, ed., *New World Encounters* (Berkeley: University of California Press, 1993), pp. 3–8.

his maps. Columbus's descriptions of the New World, as in his "Letter to the Sovereigns" in 1493, were heavily colored by the expectations of Asia that had propelled his journey.

Columbus (1451–1506) seems the most representative of Renaissance men with his scientific interests in navigation and cosmology, fascination with ancient texts, urge for power and domination, and truly overwhelming lust for gold, honors, and fame. Yet he was even more complex than that—a medieval man, as well, and an intensely religious mystic. He emphasized with special symbols in his writings that his first name, Christopher, meant "Christ-bearer." Although he never took vows, he would sometimes dress in the severe robes and rope belt of a Franciscan monk. He led his various crews through innumerable religious observances and struggled constantly to justify his behavior toward the Indians in Christian terms. He wrote extensively about the location of the earthly paradise, argued in a letter of 1498 that the earth was not round but pear-shaped, and wrote of the earthly paradise "which no one can enter except by God's leave . . . [lying] at the summit of what I have described as the stalk of a pear."

Columbus's first letter to Ferdinand and Isabella was written when Columbus feared that his ship was going down in a storm. Sealed in a barrel and tossed into the sea, it was never found. The "Letter to the Sovereigns," excerpted here, arrived at its destination by more normal means but then was apparently suppressed by the royal court and lay lost in Spanish archives for almost five centuries. A revision of this letter, doubtlessly the work of court officials, circulated in two similar versions all over Europe, providing educated readers their first glimpse of the new discoveries. In the original letter, wholly removed from the announcement to the world that defined the historic voyage for half a millennium, was the goal Columbus never abandoned: financing a crusade to reconquer Jerusalem from the Arabs, "for which purpose," Columbus reminds his sovereigns, "this enterprise was undertaken."

BEFORE YOU READ

1. How accurate is Columbus's account of the lands he discovered? What do you find convincing and what doubtful?

2. What does this letter indicate about Columbus's motives for his journey? Do you find any contradictions among his motives?

3. The royal court, in publishing a revised version of Columbus's letter, suppressed his discussion of using the riches of the world he had discovered to finance the reconquest of Jerusalem from the Muslims. Why do you think the court omitted this part of the letter?

LETTER TO THE SOVEREIGNS OF 4 MARCH 1493 ANNOUNCING THE DISCOVERY

Most Christian and lofty and powerful sovereigns:

That eternal God who has given Your Highnesses so many victories now gave you the greatest one that to this day He has ever given any prince. I come from the Indies with the armada Your Highnesses gave me, to which [place] I traveled in thirty-three days after departing from your kingdoms; after fourteen of the thirty-three there were light winds in which I covered very little ground. I found innumerable people and very many islands, of which I took possession in Your Highnesses' name, by royal crier and with Your Highnesses' royal banner unfurled, and it was not contradicted. To the first [island] I gave the name of San Salvador, in memory of His Supreme Majesty [Jesus Christ], to the second Santa María de la Concepción, to the third Fernandina, to the fourth Isabela, [and] to the fifth Juana. . . . After I arrived at Juana I followed its coast to the west and found it to be so large that I thought it was probably not an island, but rather a mainland, and most likely the province of Cathay; but I could not verify this because everywhere I arrived the people fled and I could not speak with them. And because I was unable to find a notable settlement, I thought that by hugging the coast I could not fail to find some town or great city, such as those who have gone to that province overland tell it. And after following this land for a long while, I found that I was veering away from the west and it was leading me to the north . . . , and so I turned back. In the meantime I already understood something of the speech and signs of certain Indians I had taken on the island of San Salvador, and I understood [from them] that this was still an island. And thus I came to a very good harbor, from which I sent two men inland, three days' journey, with one of the Indians I brought, who had become friendly with me, so that they could see and determine if there were any cities or large settlements, and which land it was, and what there was in it. They found many settlements and innumerable people, but no government of any importance. And so they returned, and I departed and took certain Indians at the said harbor so that I could also hear or learn from them about said lands. And thus I followed the sea coast of this island toward the east one hundred and seven leagues to where it ended. And before leaving it, I saw another island to the east, eighteen leagues out from this one, which I later named Española. And then I went to it and followed its coast on the north side, just as in the case of Juana, due east for one hundred and eighty-eight very long leagues. And I continued to enter very many harbors, in each of which I placed a very large cross in the most appropriate spot, as I had done in all the other [harbors] of the other islands, and in many places I found promontories sufficient [for this purpose]. So I went on in this fashion until the sixteenth of January, when I determined to return to Your Highnesses, as much because I had already found most of what I sought as because I had only one caravel left. . . .

Besides the above-mentioned islands, I have found many others in the Indies, of which I have not been able to tell in this letter. They, like these others, are so extremely fertile, that even if I were able to express it, it would not be a marvel were it to be disbelieved. The breezes [are] most temperate, the trees and fruits and grasses are extremely beautiful and very different from ours; the rivers and harbors are so abundant and of such extreme excellence when compared to those of Christian lands that it is a marvel. All these islands are densely populated with the best people under the sun; they have neither ill-will nor treachery. All of them, women and men alike, go about naked as their mothers bore them, although some of the women wear a small piece of cotton or a patch of grass with which they cover themselves. They have neither iron nor weapons, except for canes on the end of which they place a thin sharp stick. Everything they make is done with [stone tools]. And I have not learned that any of them have any private property, because while I was spending a few days with this king in the village of La Navidad, I saw that all of the people, and the women in particular, would bring him *agís* [hot red pepper], which is the food they eat, and he would order them to be distributed. . . .

Nowhere in these islands have I known the inhabitants to have a religion, or idolatry, or much diversity of language among them, but rather they all understand one another. I learned that they know that all powers reside in heaven. And, generally, in whatever lands I traveled, they believed and believe that I, together with these ships and people, came from heaven, and they greeted me with such veneration. And today, this very day, they are of the same mind, nor have they strayed from it. . . . And then, upon arriving at whatever settlement, the men, women, and children go from house to house calling out, "Come, come and see the people from heaven!" Everything they have or had they gave for whatever one gave them in exchange, even taking a piece of glass or broken crockery or some such thing, for gold or some other thing of whatever value. One sailor got more than two and a half *castellanos* [in gold] for the ends of leather latchets. There are ten thousand like occurrences to tell.

The islands are all very flat and low-lying, except for Juana and Española. These two are very high lands, and there are mountain chains and very high peaks, much higher than those of the island of Tenerife. The mountains are of a thousand different shapes and all [are] most beautiful, and fertile and walkable and full of trees; it seems they touch the sky. And both the one and the other of the said islands are very large. . . . Juana has many rivers, and great mountains, and very large valleys and meadows and fields, and it is all full of trees and huge palms of a thousand varieties, such as to make one marvel. [Española] has the advantage in every respect; the trees are not so tall or of the same kind, but rather very fruitful and broad; and [they are] delectable lands for all things, and for sowing and planting and raising livestock, of which I have not seen any kind on any of these islands. This island has marvelously temperate breezes, and marvelous meadows and fields incomparable to those of Castile; and the same can be said of the rivers of great and good waters, most of which are gold-bearing. There are so many and such good sea harbors that it has to be seen to be believed. I have not tarried in these islands or the others for many reasons, as I said above, but especially because it was winter when I sailed these coasts, which did not allow me to go south because I was on their north side and the [winds] were almost always easterly, which were contrary to continuing my navigation. Then I did not understand those people nor they me, except for what common sense dictated, although they were saddened and I much more so, because I wanted to have good information concerning everything. And what I did to remedy this was the Indians I had with me, for they learned our language and we theirs, and the next voyage will tell. So, there was no reason for me to tarry at any harbor wasting time when the opportunity came to set sail. Moreover, as I have said, these vessels I brought with me were too large and heavy for such a purpose, especially the [larger and heavier *Santa*

Maria], about which I was quite troubled before leaving Castile. I would much have preferred taking small caravels, but since this was the first voyage and the people I brought were afraid of running into high seas and uncertain about the voyage, and there was and has been so much opposition, and anybody dared to contradict this route and ascribe to it a thousand dangers without being able to give me any reasons, they caused me to act against my own judgment and do everything that those who were to go with me wanted, in order to get the voyage finally under way and find the land. But Our Lord, who is the light and strength of all those who seek to do good and makes them victorious in deeds that seem impossible, wished to ordain that I should find and was to find gold and mines and spicery and innumerable peoples . . . I left in [Española], in possession of the village of La Navidad, the people I brought on the [*Santa Maria*] and some from the caravels, stocked with provisions to last over a year, [with] much artillery and quite without danger from anyone, but rather with much friendship from the king of that place, who prided himself in calling me and having me for a brother; who [also] appeared to accept everything as the greatest boon in the world, as I said. And the others [feel] just as the king does, so that the people I left there suffice to subjugate the entire island without danger. This island is in a place, as I have said, signaled by the hand of Our Lord, where I hope His Majesty will give Your Highnesses as much gold as you need, spicery of a certain pepper [to fill] as many ships as Your Highnesses may order to be loaded, and as much mastic[1] as you may order to load, which today can be found only on the island of Chios, in Greece. . . . And . . . as much cotton as you may order to be loaded, and so many slaves that they are innumerable; and they will come from the idolaters. And I believe there are rhubarb and cinnamon. All this I found on this hasty trip, but I have faith in God that upon my return the people I left there will have found a thousand other things of importance, because that is the charge I left them with. And I left them a boat and its equipment and [the tools] to make boats, and masters in all the nautical arts. And above all I consider all the above-mentioned islands as belonging to Your Highnesses and you may command them as you do the kingdoms of Castile, and even more completely, especially this one of Española.

I conclude here: that through the divine grace of Him who is the origin of all good and virtuous things, who favors and gives victory to all those who walk in His path, in seven years from today I will be able to pay Your Highnesses for five thousand cavalry and fifty thousand foot soldiers for the war and conquest of Jerusalem, for which purpose this enterprise was undertaken. And in another five years another five thousand cavalry and fifty thousand foot soldiers, which will total ten thousand cavalry and one hundred thousand foot soldiers; and all of this with very little investment now on Your Highnesses' part in this beginning of the taking of the Indies and all that they contain, as I will tell Your Highnesses in person later. And I have reason for this [claim] and do not speak uncertainly, and one should not delay in it, as was the case with the execution of this enterprise, may God forgive whoever has been the cause of it.

---

1. **mastic:** tree resin used in making varnish.

Most powerful sovereigns: all of Christendom should hold great celebrations, and especially God's Church, for the finding of such a multitude of such friendly peoples, which with very little effort will be converted to our Holy Faith, and so many lands filled with so many goods very necessary to us in which all Christians will have comfort and profits, all of which was unknown nor did anyone speak of it except in fables. . . . Your Highnesses should order that [many] praises should be given to the Holy Trinity . . . because of the great love [the Holy Trinity] has shown you, more than to any other prince.

Now, most serene sovereigns, remember that I left my woman and children behind and came from my homeland to serve you, in which [service] I spent what I had. And I spent seven years of my time and put up with a thousand indignities and disgrace and I suffered much hardship. I did not wish to deal with other princes who solicited me, although Your Highnesses' giving of your protection to this voyage has owed more to my importuning [you] than to anything else. And not only has no favor been shown to me, but moreover nothing of what was promised me has been fulfilled. I do not ask favors of Your Highnesses in order to amass treasure, for I have no purpose other than to serve God and Your Highnesses and to bring this business of the Indies to perfection, as time will be my witness. And therefore I beseech you that honor be bestowed upon me according to [the quality of] my service.

The Church of God should also work for this: providing prelates and devout and wise religious; and because the matter is so great and of such a character, there is reason for the Holy Father to provide prelates who are very free of greed for temporal possessions and very true to the service of God and of Your Highnesses. And therefore I beseech you to ask the Church, in the letter you write regarding this victory, for a cardinalate for my son, and that it be granted him although he may not yet be of sufficient age, for there is little difference in his age and that of the son of the Medicis of Florence, to whom a cardinal's hat was granted without his having served or having had a purpose so honorable to Christianity, and that you give me the letter pertaining to this matter so that I [myself] may solicit it.

Furthermore, most serene sovereigns, because the sin of ungratefulness was the first one to be punished, I realize that since I am not guilty of it I must at all times try to gain from Your Highnesses the following [favor], because, without a doubt, were it not for [my friend and crew member] Villacorta, who every time it was necessary persuaded and worked on [the enterprise's] behalf, because I was already sick of it and everyone who had been and was involved in the matter was tired, [the enterprise would not have succeeded]. Therefore, I beseech Your Highnesses that you do me the favor of making him paymaster of the Indies, for I vouch that he will do it well.

Wherefore Your Highnesses should know that the first island of the Indies, closest to Spain, is populated entirely by women, without a single man, and their comportment is not feminine, but rather they use weapons and other masculine practices. They carry bows and arrows and take their adornments from the copper mines, which metal they have in very large quantity. They call this island Matenino. . . . Here are found those people which all those of the other islands of the Indies fear; they eat human flesh, are great bowmen, have many [large] canoes . . . in which they travel all over the islands of the Indies, and they are so feared that they have no equal. They go about naked like the others, except that they wear their hair very full, like women. I think the great cowardice . . . [of the] peoples of the other islands, for which there is no remedy, makes them say that these of Caribe are brave, but I think the same of them as of the rest. And when Your Highnesses give the order for me to send slaves, I hope to bring or send [you] these for the most part; these are the ones who have intercourse with the women of Matenino, who if they bear a female child they keep her with them, and if it is a male child, they raise him until he can feed himself and then they send him to Cardo. Between the islands of Cardo and Española there is another island they call Borinque, all of it is a short distance from the other region of the island of Juana that they call Cuba. In the westernmost part [of Cuba], in one of the two provinces I did not cover, which is called Faba, everyone is born with a tail. Beyond this island of Juana, still within sight, there is another that these Indians assured me was larger than Juana, which they call Jamaica, where all the people are bald. On this one there is gold in immeasurable quantities; and now I have Indians with me who have been on these [islands] as well as the others and they know the language and customs. Nothing further, except that may the Holy Trinity guard and make Your Highnesses' royal estate prosper in Its service. Written in the Sea of Spain, on the fourth day of March in the year fourteen ninety-three. At sea.

2

Mundus Novus

Amerigo Vespucci

"Strange," wrote the great American man of letters, Ralph Waldo Emerson, in 1856, "that broad America must wear the name of a thief. Amerigo Vespucci, the pickle dealer at Seville . . . whose highest naval rank was boatswain's mate in an expedition that never sailed, managed in this lying world to supplant Columbus and baptize half of the earth with his own dishonest name." Even though Emerson was echoing what historians had by then been writing for 350 years, virtually every word of this statement is wrong. Neither a thief nor dishonest, neither a pickle dealer nor a boatswain's mate, the explorer Vespucci was instead trusted by bankers, sailors, kings, conquerors, and the great Columbus himself. Vespucci had nothing to do with naming the hemisphere he had played a modest but significant role in exploring.

Amerigo Vespucci's (1454–1512) low reputation through much of the past five centuries is apparently the reverse of the glorification of his greater contemporary, Christopher Columbus. The two men are a remarkable study in contrasts. Columbus,

Letter to Lorenzo Pietro di Medici, trans. George Tyler Northup (Princeton: Princeton University Press, 1916), pp. 1–13.

born into obscurity, was a romantic figure who hungrily sought wealth and fame and yet considered himself the instrument of divine providence; Vespucci, born into a noble family in Florence, Italy, in 1454 and educated in Renaissance humanism, was, writes a modern biographer, of a "subtle, ironic, balanced, rational spirit," a man of science and practical affairs who, as an explorer, "put all his faith in maps." Vespucci's writings scarcely mention the search for gold, which makes him astonishingly rare for an explorer of this era. Columbus was a daring navigator leading a perilous expedition; Vespucci traveled as an observer and a scientist, collecting data about the phenomena around him and the stars over his head. Columbus aroused fierce devotion and bitter enmity in his pursuit of the enterprise of the Indies and achieved both great wealth and withering disappointment in his life as explorer and colonizer; Vespucci's stance was ever both modest and discreet, whether as a merchant, banker, explorer, or senior servant to kings, always retaining the trust of his employers, the Medici family of Florence and the governments of Spain and Portugal.

Historians are not sure how many voyages Vespucci made across the Atlantic. Most important, though, was the one he made in 1501 and 1502. Sailing from Portugal as an observer and navigator, he explored far down the eastern coast of what we now call South America. A brief account of that journey, entitled Mundus Novus, *is one of the most important documents in the history of exploration. Translated into many languages with its text doubtlessly altered in the process, this letter to Lorenzo Pietro di Medici, whose famous merchant family Vespucci had previously served, announced the discovery not of a part of Asia but of a New World* (Mundus Novus *in Latin) unknown to ancient geographers. Vespucci's sensational news—including accounts of Native Americans (see Plate 1 in the visual portfolio "New World Contact," which begins on page 43)—began to transform European views of the world, a process completed a few years later with Magellan's circumnavigation of the world.*

In 1507, German cartographer and cosmologist Martin Waldseemuller revised the ancient geographies by using the new data from explorers in his publication of Cosmographiae Introductio. *Noting that "It is only after Amerigo's . . . voyages that [this] land and its people are clearly understood for what they are," he gave the name* America *to the continent that Vespucci had partially mapped. In 1538, the great Flemish cartographer Gerhard Kremer, better known by his Latin name Mercatorei (Mercator), published a map of the entire Western Hemisphere with Vespucci's name printed across both continents: the letters* AME *in the north and* RICA *in the south. Historical partisans of Columbus have never forgiven this decision so quickly ratified by convention. But the New World is full of sites—even an entire country—named after Columbus, and monuments to him abound. Two continents commemorate the name of Amerigo Vespucci, but his most recent biographer claims that "in this whole hemisphere, from Alaska to Tierra del Fuego, not one statue has been erected to him."*

BEFORE YOU READ

1. What observations convinced Vespucci that he was exploring a new continent rather than Asia, as previously determined?

2. How accurate is Vespucci's account of the lands he saw, do you suppose? What do you find convincing and what doubtful?

3. How accurate is Vespucci's portrayal of the people of the New World? What do you find convincing and what doubtful?

ALBERICUS VESPUCIUS OFFERS HIS BEST
COMPLIMENTS TO LORENZO PIETRO DI MEDICI

On a former occasion I wrote to you at some length concerning my return from those new regions which we found and explored with the fleet, at the cost, and by the command of this Most Serene King of Portugal. And these we may rightly call a new world. Because our ancestors had no knowledge of them, and it will be a matter wholly new to all those who hear about them. For this transcends the view held by our ancients, inasmuch as most of them hold that there is no continent to the south beyond the equator, but only the sea which they named the Atlantic; and if some of them did aver that a continent there was, they denied with abundant argument that it was a habitable land. But that this their opinion is false and utterly opposed to the truth, this my last voyage has made manifest; for in those southern parts I have found a continent more densely peopled and abounding in animals than our Europe or Asia or Africa, and, in addition, a climate milder and more delightful than in any other region known to us, as you shall learn in the following account wherein we shall set succinctly down only capital matters and the things more worthy of comment and memory seen or heard by me in this new world, as will appear below.

On the fourteenth of the month of May, one thousand five hundred and one we set sail from Lisbon under fair sailing conditions in compliance with the commands of the aforementioned king, with these ships for the purpose of seeking new regions toward the south; and for twenty months we continuously pursued this southern course. The route of this voyage is as follows: Our course was set for the Fortunate Isles, once so called, but which are now termed the Grand Canary Islands; these are in the third climate and on the border of the inhabited west. Thence by sea we skirted the whole African coast and part of Ethiopia as far as the Ethiopic Promontory, so called by Ptolemy, which we now call Cape Verde and the Ethiopians Beseghice. And that region, Mandingha, lies within the torrid zone fourteen degrees north of the equator; it is inhabited by tribes and nations of blacks. Having there recovered our strength and taken on all that our voyage required, we weighed anchor and made sail. And directing our course over the vast ocean toward the Antarctic we for a time bent westward, owing to the wind called Vulturnus; and from the day when we set sail from the said promontory we cruised for the space of two months and three days before any land appeared to us. But what we suffered on that vast expanse of sea, what perils of shipwreck, what discomforts of the body we endured, with what anxiety of mind we toiled, this I leave to the judgment of those who out of rich experience have well learned what it is to seek the uncertain and to attempt discoveries even though ignorant. And that in a word I may briefly narrate all, you must know that of the sixty-seven days of our sailing we had forty-four of constant rain, thunder and lightning—so dark that never did we see sun by day or fair sky by night. By reason of this such fear invaded us that we soon abandoned almost all hope of life. But during these tempests of sea and sky, so numerous and so violent, the Most High was pleased to display before us a continent, new lands, and an unknown world. At sight of these things we were filled with as much joy as anyone can imagine usually falls to the lot of those who have gained refuge from varied calamity and hostile fortune. It was on the seventh day of August, one thousand five hundred and one that we anchored off the shores of those parts, thanking our God with formal ceremonial and with the celebration of a choral mass. We knew that land to be a continent and not an island both because it stretches forth in the form of a very long and unbending coast, and because it is replete with infinite inhabitants. For in it we found innumerable tribes and peoples and species of all manner of wild beasts which are found in our lands and many others never seen by us concerning which it would take long to tell in detail. God's mercy shone upon us much when we landed at that spot, for there had come a shortage of fire-wood and water, and in a few days we might have ended our lives at sea. To Him be honor, glory, and thanksgiving.

We adopted the plan of following the coast of this continent toward the east and never losing sight of it. We sailed along until at length we reached a bend where the shore made a turn to the south; and from that point where we first touched land to that corner it was about three hundred leagues, in which sailing distance we frequently landed and had friendly relations with those people, as you will hear below. I had forgotten to write you that from the promontory of Cape Verde to the nearest part of that continent is about seven hundred leagues, although I should estimate that we sailed more than eighteen hundred, partly through ignorance of the route and the ship-master's want of knowledge, partly owing to tempests and winds which kept us from the proper course and compelled us to put about frequently. Because, if my companions had not heeded me, who had knowledge of cosmography, there would have been no ship-master, nay not the leader of our expedition himself, who would have known where we were within five hundred leagues. For we were wandering and uncertain in our course, and only the instruments for taking the altitudes of the heavenly bodies showed us our true course precisely; and these were the quadrant and the astrolabe, which all men have come to know. For this reason they subsequently made me the object of great honor; for I showed them that though a man without practical experience, yet through the teaching of the marine chart for navigators I was more skilled than all the ship-masters of the whole world. For these have no knowledge except of those waters to which they have often sailed. Now, where the said corner of land showed us a southern trend of the coast we agreed to sail beyond it and inquire what there might be in those parts. So we sailed along the coast about six hundred leagues, and often landed and mingled and associated with the natives of those regions, and by them we were received in brotherly fashion; and we would dwell with them too, for fifteen or twenty days continuously, maintaining amicable and hospitable relations, as you shall learn below. Part of this new continent lies in the torrid zone beyond the equator toward the Antarctic pole, for it begins eight degrees beyond the equator. We sailed along this coast until we passed the tropic of Capricorn and found the Antarctic pole fifty degrees higher than that horizon. We advanced to within seventeen and a half degrees of the Antarctic circle, and what I there have seen and learned concerning the nature of those races, their manners, their tractability and the fertility of the soil, the salubrity of the climate, the position of the heavenly bodies in the sky, and especially concerning the fixed stars of the eighth sphere, never seen or studied by our ancestors, these things I shall relate in order.

First then as to the people. We found in those parts such a multitude of people as nobody could enumerate (as we read in the Apocalypse), a race I say gentle and amenable. All of both sexes go about naked, covering no part of their bodies; and just as they spring from their mothers' wombs so they go until death. They have indeed large square-built bodies, well formed and proportioned, and in color verging upon reddish. This I think has come to them, because, going about naked, they are colored by the sun. They have, too, hair plentiful and black. In their gait and when playing their games they are agile and dignified. They are comely, too, of countenance which they nevertheless themselves destroy; for they bore their cheeks, lips, noses and ears. Nor think those holes small or that they have one only. For some I have seen having in a single face seven borings any one of which was capable of holding a plum. They stop up these holes of theirs with blue stones, bits of marble, very beautiful crystals of alabaster, very white bones, and other things artificially prepared according to their customs. But if you could see a thing so unwonted and monstrous, that is to say a man having in his cheeks and lips alone seven stones some of which are a span and a half in length, you would not be without wonder. For I frequently observed and discovered that seven such stones weighed sixteen ounces, aside from the fact that in their ears, each perforated with three holes, they have other stones dangling on rings; and this usage applies to the men alone. For women do not bore their faces, but their ears only. They have another custom, very shameful and beyond all human belief. For their women, being very lustful, cause the private parts of their husbands to swell up to such a huge size that they appear deformed and disgusting; and this is accomplished by a certain device of theirs, the biting of certain poisonous animals. And in consequence of this many lose their organs which break through lack of attention, and they remain eunuchs. They have no cloth either of wool, linen or cotton, since they need it not; neither do they have goods of their own, but all things are held in common. They live together without king, without government, and each is his own master. They marry as many wives as they please; and son cohabits with mother, brother with sister, male cousin with female, and any man with the first woman he meets. They dissolve their marriages as often as they please, and observe no sort of law with respect to them. Beyond the fact that they have no church, no religion and are not idolaters, what more can I say? They live according to nature, and may be called Epicureans rather than Stoics. There are no merchants among their number, nor is there barter. The nations wage war upon one another without art or order. The elders by means of certain harangues of theirs bend the youths to their will and inflame them to wars in which they cruelly kill one another, and those whom they bring home captives from war they preserve, not to spare their lives, but that they may be slain for food; for they eat one another, the victors the vanquished, and among other kinds of meat human flesh is a common article of diet with them. Nay be the more assured of this fact because the father has already been seen to eat children and wife, and I knew a man whom I also spoke to who was reputed to have eaten more than three hundred human bodies. And I likewise remained twenty-seven days in a certain city where I saw salted human flesh suspended from beams between the houses, just as with us it is the custom to hang bacon and pork. I say further: they themselves wonder why we do not eat our enemies and do not use as food their flesh which they say is most savory. Their weapons are bows and arrows, and when they advance to war they cover no part of their bodies for the sake of protection, so like beasts are they in this matter. We endeavored to the extent of our power to dissuade them and persuade them to desist from these depraved customs, and they did promise us that they would leave off. The women as I have said go about naked and are very libidinous; yet they have bodies which are tolerably beautiful and cleanly. Nor are they so unsightly as one perchance might imagine; for, inasmuch as they are plump, their ugliness is the less apparent, which indeed is for the most part concealed by the excellence of their bodily structure. It was to us a matter of astonishment that none was to be seen among them who had a flabby breast, and those who had borne children were not to be distinguished from virgins by the shape and shrinking of the womb; and in the other parts of the body similar things were seen of which in the interest of modesty I make no mention. When they had the opportunity of copulating with Christians, urged by excessive lust, they defiled and prostituted themselves. They live one hundred and fifty years, and rarely fall ill, and if they do fall victims to any disease, they cure themselves with certain roots and herbs. These are the most noteworthy things I know about them. The climate there was very temperate and good, and as I was able to learn from their accounts, there was never there any pest or epidemic caused by corruption of the air; and unless they die a violent death they live long. This I take to be because the south winds are ever blowing there. . . . They are zealous in the art of fishing, and that sea is replete and abounding in every kind of fish. They are not hunters. This I deem to be because there are there many sorts of wild animals, and especially lions and bears and innumerable serpents and other horrid and ugly beasts, and also because forests and trees of huge size there extend far and wide; and they dare not, naked and without covering and arms, expose themselves to such hazards.

The land in those parts is very fertile and pleasing, abounding in numerous hills and mountains, boundless valleys and mighty rivers, watered by refreshing springs, and filled with broad, dense and wellnigh impenetrable forests full of every sort of wild animal. Trees grow to immense size without cultivation. Many of these yield fruits delectable to the taste and beneficial to the human body; some indeed do not, and no fruits there are like those of ours. Innumerable species of herbs and roots grow there too, of which they make bread and excellent food. They have, too, many seeds altogether unlike these of ours. They have there no metals of any description except gold, of which those regions have a great plenty, although to be sure we have brought none thence on this our first voyage. This the natives called to our attention, who averred that in the districts remote from the coast there is a great abundance of gold, and by them it is in no respect esteemed or valued. They are rich in pearls as I wrote you before. If I were to seek to recount in detail what things are there and to write concerning the numerous species of animals and the great number of them, it would be a matter all too prolix and vast. . . . There all trees are fragrant and they emit each and all gum, oil, or some sort of sap. If the properties of these were known to us, I doubt not but that they would be salutary to the human body. And surely if the terrestrial paradise be in any part of this earth, I esteem that it is not far distant from those parts. Its situation, as I have related, lies toward the south in such a temperate climate that icy winters and fiery summers alike are never there experienced.

The sky and atmosphere are serene during the greater part of the year, and devoid of thick vapors. The rains there fall finely, last three or four hours, and vanish like a mist. The sky is adorned with most beautiful constellations and forms among which I noted about twenty stars as bright as we ever saw Venus or Jupiter. I have considered the movements and orbits of these, I have measured their circumferences and diameters by geometric method, and I ascertained that they are of greater magnitude. . . .

I observed many other very beautiful stars, the movements of which I have diligently noted down and have described beautifully with diagrams in a certain little book of mine treating of this my voyage. But at present this Most Serene King has it, which I hope he will restore to me. In that hemisphere I saw things incompatible with the opinions of philosophers. A white rainbow was twice seen about midnight, not only by me but by all the sailors. Likewise we have frequently seen the new moon on that day when it was in conjunction with the sun. Every night in that part of the sky innumerable vapors and glowing meteors fly about. . . .

Therefore, as I have said from Lisbon whence we started, which is thirty-nine and a half degrees distant from the equator, we sailed beyond the equator through fifty degrees, which added together make about ninety degrees, which total inasmuch as it makes the fourth part of a great circle according to the true system of measurement transmitted to us by our ancients, it is evident that we sailed over a fourth part of the world. . . . And these things I have mentioned are sufficient as regards cosmography.

. . . I kept a diary of noteworthy things that if sometime I am granted leisure I may bring together these singular and wonderful things and write a book of geography or cosmography, that my memory may live with posterity and that the immense work of almighty God, partly unknown to the ancients, but known to us, may be understood. Accordingly I pray the most merciful God to prolong the days of my life that with His good favor and the salvation of my soul I may carry out in the best possible manner this my will. The accounts of the other two journeys I am preserving in my cabinet and when this Most

Serene King restores to me the third, I shall endeavor to regain my country and repose. There I shall be able to consult with experts and to receive from friends the aid and comfort necessary for the completion of this work. . . .

Jocundus, the translator, is turning this epistle from the Italian into the Latin tongue, that Latinists may know how many wonderful things are daily being discovered, and that the audacity of those who seek to scrutinize heaven and sovereignty and to know more than it is licit to know may be held in check. Inasmuch as ever since that remote time when the world began the vastness of the earth and what therein is contained has been unknown.

For Critical Thinking

1. Compare the accounts of the New World of Christopher Columbus and Amerigo Vespucci. What might a literate European perceive to be the significance of the two discoveries?

2. If you were an official in the Spanish court, how would you edit Columbus's letter before having it published?

3. What case can you make for naming the New World *America* after Amerigo Vespucci rather than, for example, *Columbia* after Christopher Columbus?

4. What differences in personality, ambitions, and views of the world can you detect between Columbus and Vespucci?

3

Destruction of the Indies

Bartolomé de Las Casas

Bartolomé de Las Casas (1474–1566) saw Columbus in 1493 when the explorer passed through Seville returning home from his first voyage. His father and two uncles sailed in that year on Columbus's second voyage. Then in 1502 Las Casas himself traveled to the New World to serve as an officer of the king. But Las Casas was a most unusual colonialist and by 1523 had become a Dominican friar, condemning his former colleagues' treatment of the New World's natives.

Las Casas spent the rest of his long life attempting to protect the Native Americans against the massacres, tortures, slavery, and forced labor imposed on them by their Spanish conquerors. His powerful writings created the image of Spanish conquest often called the "Black Legend," a vision of destruction and cruelty until that time unparalleled. Modern scholars generally accept the accuracy of Las Casas's shocking portraits of devastation, many of which he personally witnessed. Today, however, many view these horrors not as the outcome of some peculiar Spanish cruelty but as characteristic of the bloody "Columbian encounter" between Europeans and other cultures in the age of exploration and conquest.

BEFORE YOU READ

1. Do you think Las Casas's view of the Native Americans was accurate?
2. Do you judge his criticism of the Spanish empire to have been fair and accurate?
3. Throughout his life Las Casas remained fiercely loyal to both the Spanish monarch and the Catholic Church and retained great respect for Columbus. Can you reconcile these feelings with his condemnation of the Spanish empire's actions in the New World?

SHORT REPORT OF THE DESTRUCTION
OF THE WEST INDIES

The Indies were discovered in the year fourteen hundred and ninety-two. The year following, Spanish Christians went to inhabit them, so that it is since forty-nine years that numbers of Spaniards have gone there: and the first land, that they in-

Francis Augustus MacNutt, *Bartholomew de Las Casas: His Life, His Apostolate, and His Writings* (New York: G. P. Putnam's Sons, 1909), pp. 314–21.

vaded to inhabit, was the large and most delightful Isle of Hispaniola [present-day Dominican Republic and Haiti], which has a circumference of six hundred leagues.

2. There are numberless other islands, and very large ones, all around on every side, that were all—and we have seen it—as inhabited and full of their native Indian peoples as any country in the world.

3. Of the continent, the nearest part of which is more than two hundred and fifty leagues distant from this Island, more than ten thousand leagues of maritime coast have been discovered, and more is discovered every day; all that has been discovered up to the year forty-nine is full of people, like a hive of bees, so that it seems as though God had placed all, or the greater part of the entire human race in these countries.

4. God has created all these numberless people to be quite the simplest, without malice or duplicity, most obedient, most faithful to their natural Lords, and to the Christians, whom they serve; the most humble, most patient, most peaceful, and calm, without strife nor tumults; not wrangling, nor querulous, as free from uproar, hate and desire of revenge, as any in the world.

5. They are likewise the most delicate people, weak and of feeble constitution, and less than any other can they bear fatigue, and they very easily die of whatsoever infirmity; so much so, that not even the sons of our Princes and of nobles, brought up in royal and gentle life, are more delicate than they; although there are among them such as are of the peasant class. They are also a very poor people, who of worldly goods possess little, nor wish to possess: and they are therefore neither proud, nor ambitious, nor avaricious.

6. Their food is so poor, that it would seem that of the Holy Fathers in the desert was not scantier nor less pleasing. Their way of dressing is usually to go naked, covering the private parts; and at most they cover themselves with a cotton cover, which would be about equal to one and a half or two ells square of cloth. Their beds are of matting, and they mostly sleep in certain things like hanging nets, called in the language of Hispaniola *hamacas.*

7. They are likewise of a clean, unspoiled, and vivacious intellect, very capable, and receptive to every good doctrine; most prompt to accept our Holy Catholic Faith, to be endowed with virtuous customs; and they have as little difficulty with such things as any people created by God in the world.

8. Once they have begun to learn of matters pertaining to faith, they are so importunate to know them, and in frequenting the sacraments and divine service of the Church, that to tell the truth, the clergy have need to be endowed of God with the gift of pre-eminent patience to bear with them: and finally, I have heard many lay Spaniards frequently say many years ago, (unable to deny the goodness of those they saw) certainly these people were the most blessed of the earth, had they only knowledge of God.

9. Among these gentle sheep, gifted by their Maker with the above qualities, the Spaniards entered as soon as they knew them, like wolves, tigers, and lions which had been starving for many days, and since forty years they have done nothing else; nor do they otherwise at the present day, than outrage, slay, afflict, torment, and destroy them with strange and new, and divers kinds of cruelty, never before seen, nor heard of, nor read of, of which some few will be

told below: to such extremes has this gone that, whereas there were more than three million souls, whom we saw in Hispaniola, there are to-day, not two hundred of the native population left.

10. The island of Cuba is almost as long as the distance from Valladolid to Rome; it is now almost entirely deserted. The islands of San Juan [Puerto Rico], and Jamaica, very large and happy and pleasing islands, are both desolate. The Lucaya Isles lie near Hispaniola and Cuba to the north and number more than sixty, including those that are called the Giants, and other large and small Islands; the poorest of these, which is more fertile, and pleasing than the King's garden in Seville, is the healthiest country in the world, and contained more than five hundred thousand souls, but to-day there remains not even a single creature. All were killed in transporting them, to Hispaniola, because it was seen that the native population there was disappearing.

11. A ship went three years later to look for the people that had been left after the gathering in, because a good Christian was moved by compassion to convert and win those that were found to Christ; only eleven persons, whom I saw, were found.

12. More than thirty other islands, about the Isle of San Juan, are destroyed and depopulated, for the same reason. All these islands cover more than two thousand leagues of land, entirely depopulated and deserted.

13. We are assured that our Spaniards, with their cruelty and execrable works, have depopulated and made desolate the great continent, and that more than ten Kingdoms, larger than all Spain, counting Aragon and Portugal, and twice as much territory as from Seville to Jerusalem (which is more than two thousand leagues), although formerly full of people, are now deserted.

14. We give as a real and true reckoning, that in the said forty years, more than twelve million persons, men, and women, and children, have perished unjustly and through tyranny, by the infernal deeds and tyranny of the Christians; and I truly believe, nor think I am deceived, that it is more than fifteen.

15. Two ordinary and principal methods have the self-styled Christians, who have gone there, employed in extirpating these miserable nations and removing them from the face of the earth. The one, by unjust, cruel and tyrannous wars. The other, by slaying all those, who might aspire to, or sigh for, or think of liberty, or to escape from the torments that they suffer, such as all the native Lords, and adult men; for generally, they leave none alive in the wars, except the young men and the women, whom they oppress with the hardest, most horrible, and roughest servitude, to which either man or beast, can ever be put. To these two ways of infernal tyranny, all the many and divers other ways, which are numberless, of exterminating these people, are reduced, resolved, or sub-ordered according to kind.

16. The reason why the Christians have killed and destroyed such infinite numbers of souls, is solely because they have made gold their ultimate aim, seeking to load themselves with riches in the shortest time and to mount by high steps, disproportioned to their condition: namely by their insatiable avarice and ambition, the greatest, that could be on the earth. These lands, being so happy and so rich, and the people so humble, so patient, and so easily subjugated, they have had

no more respect, nor consideration nor have they taken more account of them (I speak with truth of what I have seen during all the aforementioned time) than, — I will not say of animals, for would to God they had considered and treated them as animals, — but as even less than the dung in the streets.

17. In this way have they cared for their lives—and for their souls: and therefore, all the millions above mentioned have died without faith, and without sacraments. And it is a publicly known truth, admitted, and confessed by all, even by the tyrants and homicides themselves, that the Indians throughout the Indies never did any harm to the Christians: they even esteemed them as coming from heaven, until they and their neighbours had suffered the same many evils, thefts, deaths, violence and visitations at their hands.

OF HISPANIOLA

In the island of Hispaniola—which was the first, as we have said, to be invaded by the Christians—the immense massacres and destruction of these people began. It was the first to be destroyed and made into a desert. The Christians began by taking the women and children, to use and to abuse them, and to eat of the substance of their toil and labour, instead of contenting themselves with what the Indians gave them spontaneously, according to the means of each. Such stores are always small; because they keep no more than they ordinarily need, which they acquire with little labour; but what is enough for three households, of ten persons each, for a month, a Christian eats and destroys in one day. From their using force, violence and other kinds of vexations, the Indians began to perceive that these men could not have come from heaven.

2. Some hid their provisions, others, their wives and children: others fled to the mountains to escape from people of such harsh and terrible intercourse. The Christians gave them blows in the face, beatings and cudgellings, even laying hands on the lords of the land. They reached such recklessness and effrontery, that a Christian captain violated the lawful wife of the chief king and lord of all the island.

3. After this deed, the Indians consulted to devise means of driving the Christians from their country. They took up their weapons, which are poor enough and little fitted for attack, being of little force and not even good for defence. For this reason, all their wars are little more than games with sticks, such as children play in our countries.

4. The Christians, with their horses and swords and lances, began to slaughter and practise strange cruelty among them. They penetrated into the country and spared neither children nor the aged, nor pregnant women, nor those in child labour, all of whom they ran through the body and lacerated, as though they were assaulting so many lambs herded in their sheepfold.

5. They made bets as to who would slit a man in two, or cut off his head at one blow: or they opened up his bowels. They tore the babes from their mothers' breast by the feet, and dashed their heads against the rocks. Others they seized by the shoulders and threw into the rivers, laughing and joking, and when they fell into the water they exclaimed: "boil body of so and so!" They

spitted the bodies of other babes, together with their mothers and all who were before them, on their swords.

6. They made a gallows just high enough for the feet to nearly touch the ground, and by thirteens, in honour and reverence of our Redeemer and the twelve Apostles, they put wood underneath and, with fire, they burned the Indians alive.

7. They wrapped the bodies of others entirely in dry straw, binding them in it and setting fire to it; and so they burned them. They cut off the hands of all they wished to take alive, made them carry them fastened on to them, and said: "Go and carry letters": that is; take the news to those who have fled to the mountains.

8. They generally killed the lords and nobles in the following way. They made wooden gridirons of stakes, bound them upon them, and made a slow fire beneath: thus the victims gave up the spirit by degrees, emitting cries of despair in their torture.

9. I once saw that they had four or five of the chief lords stretched on the gridirons to burn them, and I think also there were two or three pairs of gridirons, where they were burning others; and because they cried aloud and annoyed the captain or prevented him sleeping, he commanded that they should strangle them: the officer who was burning them was worse than a hangman and did not wish to suffocate them, but with his own hands he gagged them, so that they should not make themselves heard, and he stirred up the fire, until they roasted slowly, according to his pleasure. I know his name, and knew also his relations in Seville. I saw all the above things and numberless others.

10. And because all the people who could flee, hid among the mountains and climbed the crags to escape from men so deprived of humanity, so wicked, such wild beasts, exterminators and capital enemies of all the human race, the Spaniards taught and trained the fiercest boar-hounds to tear an Indian to pieces as soon as they saw him, so that they more willingly attacked and ate one, than if he had been a boar. These hounds made great havoc and slaughter.

11. And because sometimes, though rarely, the Indians killed a few Christians for just cause, they made a law among themselves, that for one Christian whom the Indians killed, the Christians should kill a hundred Indians.

4

Description of Virginia

John Smith

Before he became one of the original settlers of Jamestown in 1607, Captain John Smith (1580–1631) was already experienced as a soldier and diplomat, fighting the Spanish in the Netherlands and the Turks in Hungary. At Jamestown he took part in governing the colony—leading it from 1608 to 1609—and in managing relations with the Native Americans. His story, told years later, of being saved from death by the friendly intervention of Pocahontas, the daughter of Chief Powhatan, has a secure place in American legend. Historians and ethnographers continue to disagree about whether it happened and, if it did, whether Smith correctly understood its meaning in the context of the indigenous Indian culture. Some suspect that it was part of a ritual inducting Smith into the tribe rather than a rescue.

Smith returned to England in 1609. His later years were given over to promoting both himself and the settlement of the New World he had helped to colonize. His descriptions in numerous writings both of British America and of its Native American inhabitants set patterns that continued for centuries.

BEFORE YOU READ

1. How would you describe Smith's account of the New World? What kind of modern writing or communication does it suggest?

2. What adjectives would you apply to Smith's description of the Native Americans? How reliable does his account of the Indians seem to you?

THE COMMODITIES IN VIRGINIA
OR THAT MAY BE HAD BY INDUSTRY

The mildness of the air, the fertility of the soil, and the situation of the rivers are so propitious to the nature and use of man as no place is more convenient for pleasure, profit, and man's sustenance. Under that latitude or climate, here will live any beasts, as horses, goats, sheep, asses, hens, etc. The waters, islands, and shoals are full of safe harbors for ships of war or merchandise, for boats of all sorts, for transportation or fishing, etc.,

The Bay and rivers have much marketable fish and places fit for salt works, building of ships, making of iron, etc.

Captain John Smith of Willoughby by Alford, Lincolnshire; President of Virginia and Admiral of New England. Works: 1608–1631, ed. Edward Arber, The English Scholar's Library, No. 16 (Birmingham, 1884), pp. 63–67. The text has been modernized by Elizabeth Marcus.

Muscovia and Polonia yearly receive many thousands for pitch, tar, soap ashes, rosin, flax, cordage, sturgeon, masts, yards, wainscot, furs, glass, and suchlike; also Swethland for iron and copper. France, in like manner, for wine, canvas, and salt, Spain as much for iron, steel, figs, raisins and sherry. Italy with silks and velvets, consumes our chief commodities. Holland maintains itself by fishing and trading at our own doors. All these temporize with others for necessities, but all as uncertain as to peace or war, and besides the charge, travel and danger in transporting them, by seas, lands, storms and pirates. Then how much has Virginia the prerogative of all those flourishing kingdoms for the benefit of our lands, when as within one hundred miles all those are to be had, either ready provided by nature or else to be prepared, were there but industrious men to labor. Only copper might be lacking, but there is good probability that both copper and better minerals are there to be had if they are worked for. Their countries have it. So then here is a place a nurse for soldiers, a practice for mariners, a trade for merchants, a reward for the good, and that which is most of all, a business (most acceptable to God) to bring such poor infidels to the true knowledge of God and his holy Gospel.

OF THE NATURAL INHABITANTS
OF VIRGINIA

The land is not populous, for the men be few, their far greater number is of women and children. Within 60 miles of Jamestown there are about some 5,000 people, but of able men fit for their wars scarce 1,500. To nourish so many together they have yet no means, because they make so small a benefit of their land, be it never so fertile.

Six or seven hundred have been the most that have been seen together, when they gathered themselves to have surprised Captain Smyth at Pamaunke, having but 15 to withstand the worst of their fury. As small as the proportion of ground that has yet been discovered, is in comparison of that yet unknown. The people differ very much in stature, especially in language, as before is expressed.

Since being very great as the Sesquaesahamocks, others very little as the Wighcocomocoes: but generally tall and straight, of a comely proportion, and of a color brown, when they are of any age, but they are born white. Their hair is generally black, but few have any beards. The men wear half their heads shaven, the other half long. For barbers they use their women, who with 2 shells will grate away the hair in any fashion they please. The women are cut in many fashions agreeable to their years, but ever some part remain long.

They are very strong, of an able body and full of agility, able to endure, to lie in the woods under a tree by the fire, in the worst of winter, or in the weeds and grass, in ambush in the summer.

They are inconstant in everything, but what fear constrains them to keep. Crafty, timorous, quick of apprehension and very ingenious. Some are of disposition fearful, some bold, most cautious, all savage. Generally covetous of copper, beads and such like trash. They are soon moved to anger, and so malicious, that they seldom forget an injury: they seldom steal from one another, lest their conjurors should reveal it, and so they be pursued and punished. That they are thus feared is certain, but that any can reveal their offenses by conjuration I am doubtful. Their women are careful not to be suspected of dishonesty without leave of their husbands.

Each household knows their own lands and gardens, and most live off their own labors.

For their apparel, they are some time covered with the skins of wild beasts, which in winter are dressed with the hair but in summer without. The better sort use large mantles of deerskin not much different in fashion from the Irish mantles. Some embroidered them with beads, some with copper, others painted after their manner. But the common sort have scarce to cover their nakedness but with grass, the leaves of trees or suchlike. We have seen some use mantles that nothing could be discerned but the feathers, that was exceedingly warm and handsome. But the women are always covered about their middles with a skin and are ashamed to be seen bare.

They adorn themselves most with copper beads and paintings. Their women have their legs, hands, breasts and face cunningly embroidered with diverse works, as beasts, serpents, artificially wrought into their flesh with black spots. In each ear commonly they have three great holes, from which they hang chains, bracelets or copper. Some of their men wear in those holes a small green and yellow colored snake, near half a yard in length, which crawling and lapping herself around his neck oftentimes familiarly would kiss his lips. Others wear a dead rat tied by the tail. Some on their heads wear the wing of a bird or some large feather, with a rattle; those rattles are somewhat like the chape of a rapier, but less, which they take from the tails of a snake. Many have the whole skin of a hawk or some strange fowl, stuffed with the wings abroad. Others a broad piece of copper, and some the hand of their enemy dried. Their heads and shoulders are painted red with the root Pocone pounded to a powder mixed with oil; this they hold in summer to preserve them from the heat and in winter from the cold. Many other forms of paintings they use, but he is the most gallant that is the most monstrous to behold.

Their buildings and habitations are for the most part by the rivers or not far distant from some fresh spring. Their houses are built like our arbors of small young springs bowed and tied, and so close covered with mats or the barks of trees very handsomely, that notwithstanding either wind, rain or weather, they are as warm as stoves, but very smokey; yet at the top of the house there is a hole made for the smoke to go into right over the fire.

Against the fire they lie on little mounds of reeds covered with a mat, borne from the ground a foot and more by a mound of wood. On these round about the house, they lie heads and points one by the other against the fire, some covered with mats, some with skins, and some stark naked lie on the ground, from 6 to 20 in a house.

Their houses are in the midst of their fields or gardens; which are small plots of ground, some 20, some 40, some 100, some 200, some more, some less. Sometimes from 2 to 100 of these houses are together, or but a little separated by groves of trees. Near their habitations is a little small wood, or old trees on the ground, by reason of their burning of them for fire. So that a man may gallop a horse among these woods anyway, but where the creeks or rivers shall hinder.

Men, women and children have their several names according to the particular whim of their parents. Their women (they say) are easily delivered of child, yet do they love children dearly. To make them hardy, in the coldest mornings they wash them in the rivers, and by painting and ointments so tan their skins that after a year or two no weather will hurt them.

The men bestow their times in fishing, hunting, wars, and such manlike exercises, scorning to be seen in any woman like exercise, which is the cause that the women be very painful and the men often idle. The women and children do the rest of the work. They make mats, baskets, pots, mortars, pound their corn, make their bread, prepare their victuals, plant their corn, gather their corn, bear all kinds of burdens and suchlike.

5

Testimony of Pueblo Indians
Pedro Naranjo and Josephe

Once Cortés conquered Tenochtitlán in 1519, the Spanish quickly gained control over the entire Aztec empire. Indians accustomed to tribute and forced labor simply adapted to new masters. But as Spanish soldiers, settlers, and missionaries moved northward in search of precious metals and outposts to secure their empire from European and Indian enemies, they found that the methods that had worked farther south failed among the more independent tribes that had never been conquered by their Aztec predecessors. Franciscan and Jesuit missionaries struggled mightily to convert Native Americans as settlement inched northward; by 1670, about twenty-eight hundred Spaniards populated the valley of the Rio Grande.

The country was generally poor, punctuated only by an occasional silver mine; the population lived largely by farming and raising livestock. Needed supplies from Mexico arrived infrequently and at great cost. Governors and missionaries battled for preeminence, while settlers, there at the king's command, were disgruntled. And the Indians, however sincere their conversion to Catholicism, were at the bottom of society bearing the brunt of these harsh circumstances. Nor were the old religions dead. The valley was a true frontier with Apache, Hopi, and Navaho, all beyond Spanish power, threatening the Pueblo Indians while providing a powerful example of freedom.

The uprising of the Pueblo Indians in 1680 drove the Spanish out of Santa Fe and all the surrounding settlements. Four hundred Spaniards died during the conflict, and the rest retreated south to El Paso. Efforts at reconquest in 1681 had only temporary success. A number of the converted Indians who made peace at La Isleta moved south for Spanish protection against their tribal enemies. But others remained independent and returned to the practice of their native religions. In the 1690s, a new Spanish commander, Don Diego de Vargas, through skillful diplomacy and a few carefully limited military campaigns, brought most of the Pueblo tribes back under Spanish rule. In the meantime, however, the Indian capture of Spanish horses had begun a momentous transformation. Within a generation, this superweapon of the age had spread far northward among the Indians. When it met the other superweapon—the rifle—carried westward by English and French frontiersmen and traders, the plains Indian brave who has dominated the American imagination was born.

BEFORE YOU READ

1. How did Pedro Naranjo explain the revolt? To what extent do you think he was tailoring his answer to his Spanish questioners?

Charles Wilson Hackett, *Revolt of the Pueblo Indians of New Mexico and Otermín's Attempted Reconquest, 1680–1682* (Albuquerque: University of New Mexico Press, 1942), pp. 238–42, 245–49.

2. How did Josephe explain the revolt? What differences do you notice between his account and Pedro Naranjo's?

3. What according to Josephe were the strategic objectives of the leaders of the revolt? How did they inspire the Pueblo Indians to revolt?

DECLARATION OF PEDRO NARANJO OF THE QUERES NATION

December 19, 1681

In the said plaza de armas on the said day, month, and year, for the prosecution of the judicial proceedings of this case his lordship caused to appear before him an Indian prisoner named Pedro Naranjo, a native of the pueblo of San Felipe, of the Queres nation, who was captured in the advance and attack upon the pueblo of La Isleta. He makes himself understood very well in the Castilian language and speaks his mother tongue and the Tegua. He took the oath in due legal form in the name of God, our Lord, and a sign of the cross. . . .

Asked whether he knows the reason or motives which the Indians of this kingdom had for rebelling, forsaking the law of God and obedience to his Majesty, and committing such grave and atrocious crimes, and who were the leaders and principal movers, and by whom and how it was ordered; and why they burned the images, temples, crosses, rosaries, and things of divine worship, committing such atrocities as killing priests, Spaniards, women, and children, and the rest that he might know touching the question, he said that since the government of Señor General Hernando Ugarte y la Concha they have planned to rebel on various occasions through conspiracies of the Indian sorcerers, and that although in some pueblos the messages were accepted, in other parts they would not agree to it; and that it is true that during the government of the said señor general seven or eight Indians were hanged for this same cause, whereupon the unrest subsided. Some time thereafter they [the conspirators] sent from the pueblo of Los Taos through the pueblos of the custodia two deerskins with some pictures on them signifying conspiracy after their manner, in order to convoke the people to a new rebellion, and the said deerskins passed to the province of Moqui, where they refused to accept them. The pact which they had been forming ceased for the time being, but they always kept in their hearts the desire to carry it out, so as to live as they are living to-day. Finally, in the past years, at the summons of an Indian named Popé, who is said to have communication with the devil, it happened that in an estufa of the pueblo of Los Taos there appeared to the said Popé three figures of Indians who never came out of the estufa. They gave the said Popé to understand that they were going underground to the lake of Copala. He saw these figures emit fire from all the extremities of their bodies, and that one of them was called Caudi, another Tilini, and the other Tleume; and these three beings spoke to the said Popé, who was in hiding from the secretary, Francisco Xavier, who wished to punish him as a sorcerer. They told him to make a cord of maguey fiber and tie some knots in it which would signify the number of days that they must wait before the rebellion. He said that the cord was passed through all the pueblos of the kingdom so that the ones which agreed to it [the rebellion] might untie one knot in a sign of obedience, and by the other knots they would know the days which were lacking; and this was to be done on pain of death to those who refused to agree to it. As a sign of agreement and notice of having concurred in the treason and perfidy they were to send up smoke signals to that effect in each one of the pueblos singly. The said cord was taken from pueblo to pueblo by the swiftest youths under the penalty of death if they revealed the secret. Everything being thus arranged, two days before the time set for its execution, because his lordship had learned of it and had imprisoned two Indian accomplices from the pueblo of Tesuque, it was carried out prematurely that night, because it seemed to them that they were now discovered; and they killed religious, Spaniards, women, and children. This being done, it was proclaimed in all the pueblos that everyone in common should obey the commands of their father whom they did not know, which would be given through El Caydi or El Popé. This was heard by Alonso Catití, who came to the pueblo of this declarant to say that everyone must unite to go to the villa to kill the governor and the Spaniards who had remained with him, and that he who did not obey would, on their return, be beheaded; and in fear of this they agreed to it. Finally the señor governor and those who were with him escaped from the siege, and later this declarant saw that as soon as the Spaniards had left the kingdom an order came from the said Indian, Popé, in which he commanded all the Indians to break the lands and enlarge their cultivated fields, saying that now they were as they had been in ancient times, free from the labor they had performed for the religious and the Spaniards, who could not now be alive. He said that this is the legitimate cause and the reason they had for rebelling, because they had always desired to live as they had when they came out of the lake of Copala. Thus he replies to the question.

Asked for what reason they so blindly burned the images, temples, crosses, and other things of divine worship, he stated that the said Indian, Popé, came down in person, and with him El Saca and El Chato from the pueblo of Los Taos, and other captains and leaders and many people who were in his train, and he ordered in all the pueblos through which he passed that they instantly break up and burn the images of the holy Christ, the Virgin Mary and the other saints, the crosses, and everything pertaining to Christianity, and that they burn the temples, break up the bells, and separate from the wives whom God had given them in marriage and take those whom they desired. In order to take away their baptismal names, the water, and the holy oils, they were to plunge into the rivers and wash themselves with amole, which is a root native to the country, washing even their clothing, with the understanding that there would thus be taken from them the character of the holy sacraments. They did this, and also many other things which he does not recall, given to understand that this mandate had come from the Caydi and the other two who emitted fire from their extremities in the said estufa of Taos, and that they thereby returned to the state of their antiquity, as when they came from the lake of Copala; that this was the better life and the one they desired, because the God of the Spaniards was worth nothing and theirs was very strong, the Spaniards' God being rotten wood. These things were observed and obeyed by all except some who, moved by the zeal of Christians, opposed it, and such persons the said Popé caused to be killed immediately. He saw to it that they at once erected and rebuilt their houses of idolatry which they call estufas, and made very ugly masks in imitation of the devil in order to dance the dance of the cacina; and he said likewise that the devil had given them to understand that living thus in accordance with the law of their ancestors, they would harvest a great deal of maize, many beans, a great abundance of cotton, calabashes, and very large watermelons and cantaloupes; and that they could erect their houses and enjoy abundant health and leisure. As he has said, the people were very much pleased, living at their ease in this life of their antiquity, which was the chief cause of their falling into such laxity. Following what has already been stated, in order to terrorize them further and cause them to observe the diabolical commands, there came to them a pronouncement from the three demons already described, and from El Popé, to the effect that he who might still keep in his heart a regard for the priests, the governor, and the Spaniards would be known from his unclean face and clothes, and would be punished. And he stated that the said four persons stopped at nothing to have their commands obeyed. Thus he replies to the question.

Asked what arrangements and plans they had made for the contingency of the Spaniards' return, he said that what he knows concerning the question is that they were always saying they would have to fight to the death, for they do not wish to live in any other way than they are living at present; and the demons in the estufa of Taos had given them to understand that as soon as the Spaniards began to move toward this kingdom they would warn them so that they might unite, and none of them would be caught. He having been questioned further and repeatedly touching the case, he said that he has nothing more to say. . . . His declaration being read to him, he affirmed and ratified all of it. He declared himself to be eighty years of age, and he signed it with his lordship and the interpreters and assisting witnesses. . . .

DECLARATION OF JOSEPHE, SPANISH-SPEAKING INDIAN

December 19, 1681

In this said place and plaza de armas of this army on the 19th day of the month of December, 1681, for the said judicial proceedings of this case, his lordship caused to appear before him an Indian prisoner named Josephe, able to speak the Castilian language, a servant of Sargento Mayor Sebastián de Herrera who fled from him and went among the apostates. . . . Being asked why he fled from his master, the said Sargento Mayor Sebastián de Herrera, and went to live with the treacherous Indian apostates of New Mexico, where he has been until he came among us on the present occasion, he said that the reason why he left was that he was suffering hunger in the plaza de armas of La Toma [del Río del Norte], and a companion of his named Domingo urged this declarant to go to New Mexico for a while, so as to find out how matters stood with the Indians and to give warning to the Spaniards of any treason. They did not come with the intention of remaining always with the apostate traitors and rebels, and after they arrived they [the Indians] killed the said Domingo, his companion, because of the Pecos Indians having seen him fighting in the villa along with the Spaniards. He said that because his comrade was gone he had remained until now, when he saw the Spaniards and came to them, warning them not to be careless with the horses, because he had heard the traitors say that although the Spaniards might conclude peace with them, they would come to attack them by night and take away the horses. Thus he responds to this question.

Asked what causes or motives the said Indian rebels had for renouncing the law of God and obedience to his Majesty, and for committing so many kinds of crimes, and who were the instigators of the rebellion, and what he had heard while he was among the apostates, he said that the prime movers of the rebellion were two Indians of San Juan, one named El Popé and the other El Taqu, and another from Taos named Saca, and another from San Ildefonso named Francisco. He knows that these were the principals, and the causes they gave were alleged ill treatment and injuries received from the present secretary, Francisco Xavier, and the maestre de campo, Alonso García, and from the sargentos mayores, Luis de Quintana and Diego López, because they beat them, took away what they had, and made them work without pay. Thus he replies.

Asked why, since the said rebels had been of different minds, some believing that they should give themselves up peacefully and others opposing it, when the Spaniards arrived at the sierra of La Cieneguilla de Cochití, where the leaders of the uprising and people from all the nations were assembled, they had not attempted to give themselves up and return to the holy faith and to obedience to his Majesty—for while they had made some signs, they had done nothing definite—he said that although it is true that as soon as the Spaniards arrived some said that it was better to give up peaceably than to have war, the young men were unwilling to agree, saying that they wished to fight. In particular one Spanish-speaking Indian or coyote named Francisco, commonly called El Ollita, said that no one should surrender in peace, that all must fight, and that although some of his brothers were coming with the Spaniards, if they fought on the side of the Spaniards he would kill them, and if they came over to the side of the Indians he would not harm them. Whereupon everyone was disturbed, and there having arrived at this juncture Don Luis Tupatú, governor of the pueblo of Los Pecuríes, while they were thus consulting, news came to the place where the junta was being held from another Indian named Alonso Catití, a leader of the uprising, believed to be a coyote, in which he sent to notify the people that he had already planned to deceive the Spaniards with feigned peace. He had arranged to send to the pueblo of Cochití all the prettiest, most pleasing, and neatest Indian women so that, under pretense of coming down to prepare food for the Spaniards, they could provoke them to lewdness, and that night while they were with them, the said coyote Catití would come down with all the men of the Queres and Jemez nations, only the said Catití attempting to speak with the said Spaniards, and at a shout from him they would all rush down to kill the said Spaniards; and he gave orders that all the rest who were in the other junta where the said Don Luis and El Ollita were present, should at the same time attack the horse drove, so as to finish that too. This declarant being present during all these proceedings, and feeling compassion because of the treason they were plotting, he determined to come to warn the Spaniards, as he did, whereupon they put themselves under arms and the said Indians again went up to the heights of the sierra, and the Spaniards withdrew. Thus he replies to the question. . . .

. . . He said that what he has stated in his declaration is the truth and what he knows, under charge of his oath, which he affirms and ratifies, this, his said declaration, being read to him. He did not sign because of not knowing how, nor does he know his age. Apparently he is about twenty years old. . . .

6

Encounter with the Indians

Father Paul Le Jeune

In the sixteenth and seventeenth centuries the Society of Jesus of the Roman Catholic Church, more commonly known as the Jesuits, energetically proselytized in virtually every Portuguese, Spanish, and French colony. The first Jesuit missionaries arrived in French Canada in 1632 determined to bring Christianity to the Indians by living with them, learning their languages, educating their children, and demonstrating (sometimes at the cost of their lives) that they were as brave as the Native American warriors. The Jesuits played a major role in cementing French alliances with many Native American nations across Canada and into the Ohio Valley. This gave France a strategic position in the New World, hemming the colonies of British North America against the eastern seaboard until French power was destroyed in the mid-eighteenth century. The Jesuits in Canada reported regularly on their ministry. These reports form an important account of American Indian life and greatly influenced the European perception of the New World.

Father Paul Le Jeune, born in France in 1591, became a Jesuit in 1613. He had been a professor of rhetoric as well as Superior of the Jesuit House at Dieppe before he radically changed his activities by going to French North America in 1632. Le Jeune found much to admire in the Native Americans, as well as much that he could neither understand nor accept. The report included here was written from Quebec in August 1634. Le Jeune worked among the Indians until 1649. He died in Paris in 1664.

BEFORE YOU READ

1. What were Father Le Jeune's impressions and assessment of Native American religion?
2. What did he consider the Indians' virtues?
3. What did he consider their main vices?

CHAPTER IV. ON THE BELIEF, SUPERSTITIONS, AND ERRORS OF THE MONTAGNAIS SAVAGES

I have already reported that the Savages believe that a certain one named Atahocam had created the world, and that one named Messou had restored it. I have questioned upon this subject the famous Sorcerer and the old man with

Reuben Gold Thwaites, ed., *The Jesuit Relations and Allied Documents: Travels and Explorations of the Jesuit Missionaries in New France* (Cleveland: Burrows Brothers, 1987).

whom I passed the Winter; they answered that they did not know who was the first Author of the world,—that it was perhaps Atahocam, but that was not certain; that they only spoke of Atahocam as one speaks of a thing so far distant that nothing sure can be known about it. . . .

As to the Messou, they hold that he restored the world, which was destroyed in the flood; whence it appears that they have some tradition of that great universal deluge which happened in the time of Noë. . . .

They also say that all animals, of every species, have an elder brother, who is, as it were, the source and origin of all individuals, and this elder brother is wonderfully great and powerful. . . . Now these elders of all the animals are the juniors of the Messou. Behold him well related, this worthy restorer of the Universe, he is elder brother to all beasts. If any one, when asleep, sees the elder or progenitor of some animals, he will have a fortunate chase; if he sees the elder of the Beavers, he will take Beavers; if he sees the elder of the Elks, he will take Elks, possessing the juniors through the favor of their senior whom he has seen in the dream. . . .

Their Religion, or rather their superstition, consists besides in praying; but O, my God, what prayers they make! In the morning, when the little children come out from their Cabins, they shout, *Cacouakhi, Pakhais Amiscouakhi, Pakhais Mousouakhi, Pakhais,* "Come Porcupines; come, Beavers; come, Elk;" and this is all of their prayers.

When the Savages sneeze, and sometimes even at other times, during the Winter, they cry out in a loud voice, *Etouctaian miraounam an Mirouscamikhi,* "I shall be very glad to see the Spring."

At other times, I have heard them pray for the Spring, or for deliverance from evils and other similar things; and they express all these things in the form of desires, crying out as loudly as they can, "I would be very glad if this day would continue, if the wind would change," etc. I could not say to whom these wishes are addressed, for they themselves do not know, at least those whom I have asked have not been able to enlighten me. . . .

These are some of their superstitions. How much dust there is in their eyes, and how much trouble there will be to remove it that they may see the beautiful light of truth! I believe, nevertheless, that anyone who knew their language perfectly, in order to give them good reasons promptly, would soon make them laugh at their own stupidity; for sometimes I have made them ashamed and confused, although I speak almost entirely by my hands, I mean by signs. . . .

CHAPTER V. ON THE GOOD THINGS
WHICH ARE FOUND AMONG THE SAVAGES

If we begin with physical advantages, I will say that they possess these in abundance. They are tall, erect, strong, well proportioned, agile; and there is nothing effeminate in their appearance. Those little Fops that are seen elsewhere are only caricatures of men, compared with our Savages. I almost believed, heretofore, that the Pictures of the Roman Emperors represented the ideal of the painters rather than men who had ever existed, so strong and powerful are their heads; but I see here upon the shoulders of these people the heads of Julius Caesar, of Pompey, of Augustus, of Otho, and of others, that I have seen in France, drawn upon paper, or in relief on medallions.

As to the mind of the Savage, it is of good quality. I believe that souls are all made from the same stock, and that they do not materially differ; hence, these barbarians having well formed bodies, and organs well regulated and well arranged, their minds ought to work with ease. Education and instruction alone are lacking. Their soul is a soil which is naturally good, but loaded down with all the evils that a land abandoned since the birth of the world can produce. I naturally compare our Savages with certain villagers, because both are usually without education, though our Peasants are superior in this regard; and yet I have not seen any one thus far, of those who have come to this country, who does not confess and frankly admit that the Savages are more intelligent than our ordinary peasants.

Moreover, if it is a great blessing to be free from a great evil, our Savages are happy; for the two tyrants who provide hell and torture for many of our Europeans, do not reign in their great forests,—I mean ambition and avarice. As they have neither political organization, nor offices, nor dignities, nor any authority, for they only obey their Chief through good will toward him, therefore they never kill each other to acquire these honors. Also, as they are contented with a mere living, not one of them gives himself to the Devil to acquire wealth.

They make a pretence of never getting angry, not because of the beauty of this virtue, for which they have not even a name, but for their own contentment and happiness, I mean, to avoid the bitterness caused by anger. The Sorcerer said to me one day, speaking of one of our Frenchmen, "He has no sense, he gets angry; as for me, nothing can disturb me; let hunger oppress me, let my nearest relation pass to the other life, let the Hiroquois, our enemies, massacre our people, I never get angry." What he says is not an article of faith; for, as he ·is more haughty than any other Savage, so I have seen him oftener out of humor than any of them; it is true also that he often restrains and governs himself by force, especially when I expose his foolishness. I have only heard one Savage pronounce this word, *Ninichcatihin,* "I am angry," and he only said it once. But I noticed that they kept their eyes on him, for when these Barbarians are angry, they are dangerous and unrestrained.

Whoever professes not to get angry, ought also to make a profession of patience; the Savages surpass us to such an extent, in this respect, that we ought to be ashamed. I saw them, in their hardships and in their labors, suffer with cheerfulness. My host, wondering at the great number of people who I told him were in France, asked me if the men were good, if they did not become angry, if they were patient. I have never seen such patience as is shown by a sick Savage. You may yell, storm, jump, dance, and he will scarcely ever complain. I found myself, with them, threatened with great suffering; they said to me, "We shall be sometimes two days, sometimes three, without eating, for lack of food; take courage, *Chihiné,* let thy soul be strong to endure suffering and hardship; keep thyself from being sad, otherwise thou wilt be sick; see how we do not cease to laugh, although we have little to eat." One thing alone casts them down,—it is when they see death, for they fear this beyond measure; take away this apprehension from the Savages, and they will endure all kinds of degradation and discomfort, and all kinds of trials and suffering very patiently. . . .

They are very much attached to each other, and agree admirably. You do not see any disputes, quarrels, enmities, or reproaches among them. Men leave the arrangement of the household to the women, without interfering with them; they cut, and decide, and give away as they please, without making the husband angry. . . .

CHAPTER VI. ON THEIR VICES
AND THEIR IMPERFECTIONS

The Savages, being filled with errors, are also haughty and proud. Humility is born of truth, vanity of error and falsehood. They are void of the knowledge of truth, and are in consequence, mainly occupied with thought of themselves. They imagine that they ought by right of birth, to enjoy the liberty of Wild ass colts, rendering no homage to any one whomsoever, except when they like. They have reproached me a hundred times because we fear our Captains, while they laugh at and make sport of theirs. All the authority of their chief is in his tongue's end; for he is powerful in so far as he is eloquent; and, even if he kills himself talking and haranguing, he will not be obeyed unless he pleases the Savages. . . .

I have shown in my former letters how vindictive the Savages are toward their enemies, with what fury and cruelty they treat them, eating them after they have made them suffer all that an incarnate fiend could invent. This fury is common to the women as well as to the men, and they even surpass the latter in this respect. I have said that they eat the lice they find upon themselves, not that they like the taste of them, but because they want to bite those that bite them.

These people are very little moved by compassion. When any one is sick in their Cabins, they ordinarily do not cease to cry and storm, and make as much noise as if everybody were in good health. They do not know what it is to take care of a poor invalid, and to give him the food which is good for him; if he asks for something to drink, it is given to him, if he asks for something to eat, it is given to him, but otherwise he is neglected; to coax him with love and gentleness, is a language which they do not understand. As long as a patient can eat, they will carry or drag him with them; if he stops eating, they believe that it is all over with him and kill him, as much to free him from the sufferings that he is enduring, as to relieve themselves of the trouble of taking him with them when they go to some other place. I have both admired and pitied the patience of the invalids whom I have seen among them.

The Savages are slanderous beyond all belief; I say, also among themselves, for they do not even spare their nearest relations, and with it all they are deceitful. For, if one speaks ill of another, they all jeer with loud laughter; if the other appears upon the scene, the first one will show him as much affection and treat him with as much love, as if he had elevated him to the third heaven by his praise. The reason of this is, it seems to me, that their slanders and derision do not come from malicious hearts or from infected mouths, but from a mind which says what it thinks in order to give itself free scope, and which seeks grat-ification from everything, even from slander and mockery. Hence they are not troubled even if they are told that others are making sport of them, or have in-jured their reputation. All they usually answer to such talk is, *mama irinisiou*, "He has no sense, he does not know what he is talking about"; and at the first opportunity they will pay their slanderer in the same coin, returning him the like.

Lying is as natural to Savages as talking, not among themselves, but to strangers. Hence it can be said that fear and hope, in one word, interest, is the measure of their fidelity. I would not be willing to trust them, except as they would fear to be punished if they had failed in their duty, or hoped to be re-warded if they were faithful to it. They do not know what it is to keep a secret, to keep their word, and to love with constancy, — especially those who are not of their nation, for they are harmonious among themselves, and their slanders and raillery do not disturb their peace and friendly intercourse. . . .

CHAPTER XII. WHAT ONE MUST SUFFER IN WINTERING WITH THE SAVAGES

In order to have some conception of the beauty of this edifice, its construction must be described. I shall speak from knowledge, for I have often helped to build it. Now, when we arrived at the place where we were to camp, the women, armed with axes, went here and there in the great forests, cutting the framework of the hostelry where we were to lodge; meantime the men, having drawn the plan thereof, cleared away the snow with their snowshoes, or with shovels which they make and carry expressly for this purpose. Imagine now a great ring or square in the snow, two, three or four feet deep, according to the weather or the place where they encamp. This depth of snow makes a white wall for us, which surrounds us on all sides, except the end where it is broken through to form the door. The framework having been brought, which consists of twenty or thirty poles, more or less, according to the size of the cabin, it is planted, not upon the ground but upon the snow; then they throw upon these poles, which converge a little at the top, two or three rolls of bark sewed to-gether, beginning at the bottom, and behold, the house is made. The ground inside, as well as the wall of snow which extends all around the cabin, is covered with little branches of fir; and, as a finishing touch, a wretched skin is fastened to two poles to serve as a door, the doorposts being the snow itself. . . .

You cannot stand upright in this house, as much on account of its low roof as the suffocating smoke; and consequently you must always lie down, or sit flat upon the ground, the usual posture of the Savages. When you go out, the cold, the snow, and the danger of getting lost in these great woods drive you in again more quickly than the wind, and keep you a prisoner in a dungeon which has neither lock nor key.

This prison, in addition to the uncomfortable position that one must oc-cupy upon a bed of earth, has four other great discomforts, — cold, heat, smoke, and dogs. As to the cold, you have the snow at your head with only a pine branch between, often nothing but your hat, and the winds are free to enter in a thousand places. . . . When I lay down at night I could study through this opening both the Stars and the Moon as easily as if I had been in the open fields.

Nevertheless, the cold did not annoy me as much as the heat from the fire. A little place like their cabins is easily heated by a good fire, which sometimes roasted and broiled me on all sides, for the cabin was so narrow that I could not protect myself against the heat. You cannot move to right or left, for the Savages, your neighbors, are at your elbows; you cannot withdraw to the rear, for you encounter the wall of snow, or the bark of the cabin which shuts you in. I did not know what position to take. Had I stretched myself out, the place was so narrow that my legs would have been halfway in the fire; to roll myself up in a ball, and crouch down in their way, was a position I could not retain as long as they could; my clothes were all scorched and burned. You will ask me perhaps if the snow at our backs did not melt under so much heat. I answer, "no"; that if sometimes the heat softened it in the least, the cold immediately turned it into ice. I will say, however, that both the cold and the heat are endurable, and that some remedy may be found for these two evils.

But, as to the smoke, I confess to you that it is martyrdom. It almost killed me, and made me weep continually, although I had neither grief nor sadness in my heart. It sometimes grounded all of us who were in the cabin; that is, it caused us to place our mouths against the earth in order to breathe. For, although the Savages were accustomed to this torment, yet occasionally it became so dense that they, as well as I, were compelled to prostrate themselves, and as it were to eat the earth, so as not to drink the smoke. I have sometimes remained several hours in this position, especially during the most severe cold and when it snowed; for it was then the smoke assailed us with the greatest fury, seizing us by the throat, nose, and eyes. . . .

As to the dogs, which I have mentioned as one of the discomforts of the Savages' houses, I do not know that I ought to blame them, for they have sometimes rendered me good service. . . . These poor beasts, not being able to live outdoors, came and lay down sometimes upon my shoulders, sometimes upon my feet, and as I only had one blanket to serve both as covering and mattress, I was not sorry for this protection, willingly restoring to them a part of the heat which I drew from them. It is true that, as they were large and numerous, they occasionally crowded and annoyed me so much, that in giving me a little heat they robbed me of my sleep, so that I very often drove them away. . . .

7

Captured by Indians

Mary Jemison

Captivity narratives were popular during the entire period in which Native Americans were thought to constitute a danger to white settlers on the frontier. Mary Jemison's Narrative *is one of the most famous, having gone through dozens of printings since its initial publication in 1824. That she fell in love with an Indian man and remained a member of the Seneca tribe all her life obviously added spice to her life story.*

Although it is written in the first person, the Narrative *is not really an autobiography. Jemison was eighty years old and illiterate when James E. Seaver interviewed her and wrote it. By then she was long famous in western New York as the "white woman of the Genesee" who since her abduction, probably in 1758 at the age of fifteen, had lived among the Senecas. The* Narrative *is an important source description of Seneca life and culture as well as a fascinating account of a white Anglo-American woman's assimilation into that culture.*

BEFORE YOU READ

1. What was the Seneca custom of adoption as Jemison explained it?
2. How did Jemison explain the Indians' famous cruelty?
3. Why do you think captivity narratives were such popular reading?
4. What do you think Jemison meant when she said "Indians must and will be Indians, in spite of all the means that can be used to instruct them in the arts and sciences"?

CHAPTER III

The night was spent in gloomy forebodings. What the result of our captivity would be, it was out of our power to determine, or even imagine. At times, we could almost realize the approach of our masters to butcher and scalp us; again, we could nearly see the pile of wood kindled on which we were to be roasted; and then we could imagine ourselves at liberty, alone and defenseless in the forest, surrounded by wild beasts that were ready to devour us. The anxiety of our minds drove sleep from our eyelids; and it was with a dreadful hope and painful impatience that we waited for the morning to determine our fate.

The morning at length arrived, and our masters came early and let us out of the house, and gave the young man and boy to the French, who immediately

James E. Seaver, *A Narrative of the Life of Mary Jemison: Deh-He-Wä-Mis*, 4th ed. (New York: Miller, Orton, and Mulligan, 1856), pp. 52, 53–63, 67–70, 72–74.

took them away. Their fate I never learned, as I have not seen nor heard of them since.

I was now left alone in the fort, deprived of my former companions, and of every thing that was near or dear to me but life. But it was not long before I was in some measure relieved by the appearance of two pleasant-looking squaws, of the Seneca tribe, who came and examined me attentively for a short time, and then went out. After a few minutes' absence, they returned in company with my former masters, who gave me to the squaws to dispose of as they pleased.

The Indians by whom I was taken were a party of Shawnees, if I remember right, that lived, when at home, a long distance down the Ohio.

My former Indian masters and the two squaws were soon ready to leave the fort, and accordingly embarked—the Indians in a large canoe, and the two squaws and myself in a small one—and went down the Ohio. When we set off, an Indian in the forward canoe took the scalps of my former friends, strung them on a pole that he placed upon his shoulder, and in that manner carried them, standing in the stern of the canoe directly before us, as we sailed down the river, to the town where the two squaws resided.

On the way we passed a Shawnee town, where I saw a number of heads, arms, legs, and other fragments of the bodies of some white people who had just been burned. The parts that remained were hanging on a pole, which was supported at each end by a crotch stuck in the ground, and were roasted or burnt black as a coal. The fire was yet burning; and the whole appearance afforded a spectacle so shocking that even to this day the blood almost curdles in my veins when I think of them.

At night we arrived at a small Seneca Indian town, at the mouth of a small river that was called by the Indians, in the Seneca language, She-nan-jee, about eighty miles by water from the fort, where the two squaws to whom I belonged resided. There we landed, and the Indians went on; which was the last I ever saw of them.

Having made fast to the shore, the squaws left me in the canoe while they went to their wigwam or house in the town, and returned with a suit of Indian clothing, all new, and very clean and nice. My clothes, though whole and good when I was taken, were now torn in pieces, so that I was almost naked. They first undressed me, and threw my rags into the river; then washed me clean and dressed me in the new suit they had just brought, in complete Indian style; and then led me home and seated me in the center of their wigwam.

I had been in that situation but a few minutes before all the squaws in the town came in to see me. I was soon surrounded by them, and they immediately set up a most dismal howling, crying bitterly, and wringing their hands in all the agonies of grief for a deceased relative.

Their tears flowed freely, and they exhibited all the signs of real mourning. At the commencement of this scene, one of their number began, in a voice somewhat between speaking and singing, to recite some words to the following purport, and continued the recitation till the ceremony was ended; the company at the same time varying the appearance of their countenances, gestures, and tone of voice, so as to correspond with the sentiments expressed by their leader.

"Oh, our brother! alas! he is dead—he has gone; he will never return! Friendless he died on the field of the slain, where his bones are yet lying unburied! Oh! who will not mourn his sad fate? No tears dropped around him: oh, no! No tears of his sisters were there! He fell in his prime, when his arm was most needed to keep us from danger! Alas! he has gone, and left us in sorrow, his loss to bewail! Oh, where is his spirit? His spirit went naked, and hungry it wanders, and thirsty and wounded, it groans to return! Oh, helpless and wretched, our brother has gone! No blanket nor food to nourish and warm him; nor candles to light him, nor weapons of war! Oh, none of those comforts had he! But well we remember his deeds! The deer he could take on the chase! The panther shrunk back at the sight of his strength! His enemies fell at his feet! He was brave and courageous in war! As the fawn, he was harmless; his friendship was ardent; his temper was gentle; his pity was great! Oh! our friend, our companion, is dead! Our brother, our brother! alas, he is gone! But why do we grieve for his loss? In the strength of a warrior, undaunted he left us, to fight by the side of the chiefs! His warwhoop was shrill! His rifle well aimed laid his enemies low: his tomahawk drank of their blood: and his knife flayed their scalps while yet covered with gore! And why do we mourn? Though he fell on the field of the slain, with glory he fell; and his spirit went up to the land of his fathers in war! Then why do we mourn? With transports of joy, they received him, and fed him, and clothed him, and welcomed him there! Oh, friends, he is happy; then dry up your tears! His spirit has seen our distress, and sent us a helper whom with pleasure we greet. Deh-he-wä-mis has come: then let us receive her with joy!—she is handsome and pleasant! Oh! She is our sister, and gladly we welcome her here. In the place of our brother she stands in our tribe. With care we will guard her from trouble; and may she be happy till her spirit shall leave us."

In the course of that ceremony, from mourning they became serene,—joy sparkled in their countenances, and they seemed to rejoice over me as over a long-lost child. I was made welcome among them as a sister to the two squaws before mentioned, and was called Deh-hc-wä-mis; which, being interpreted, signifies a pretty girl, a handsome girl, or a pleasant, good thing. That is the name by which I have ever since been called by the Indians.

I afterward learned that the ceremony I at that time passed through was that of adoption. The two squaws had lost a brother in Washington's war, sometime in the year before, and in consequence of his death went up to Fort Du Quesne on the day on which I arrived there, in order to receive a prisoner, or an enemy's scalp, to supply their loss. It is a custom of the Indians, when one of their number is slain or taken prisoner in battle, to give to the nearest relative of the dead or absent a prisoner, if they have chanced to take one; and if not, to give him the scalp of an enemy. On the return of the Indians from the conquest, which is always announced by peculiar shoutings, demonstrations of joy, and the exhibition of some trophy of victory, the mourners come forward and make their claims. If they receive a prisoner, it is at their option either to satiate their vengeance by taking his life in the most cruel manner they can conceive of, or to receive and adopt him into the family, in the place of him whom they have lost. All the prisoners that are taken in battle and carried to the encampment or town by the Indians are given to the bereaved families, till their number is good. And unless the mourners have but just received the news of their bereavement, and are under the operation of a paroxysm of grief, anger, or revenge; or, unless the prisoner is very old, sickly, or homely, they generally save them, and treat them kindly. But if their mental wound is fresh, their loss so great that they deem it irreparable, or if their prisoner or prisoners do not meet their approbation, no torture, let it be ever so cruel, seems sufficient to make them satisfaction. It is family and not national sacrifices among the Indians, that has given them an indelible stamp as barbarians, and identified their character with the idea which is generally formed of unfeeling ferocity and the most barbarous cruelty.

It was my happy lot to be accepted for adoption. At the time of the ceremony I was received by the two squaws to supply the place of their brother in the family; and I was ever considered and treated by them as a real sister, the same as though I had been born of their mother.

During the ceremony of my adoption, I sat motionless, nearly terrified to death at the appearance and actions of the company, expecting every moment to feel their vengeance, and suffer death on the spot. I was, however, happily disappointed; when at the close of the ceremony the company retired, and my sisters commenced employing every means for my consolation and comfort.

Being now settled and provided with a home, I was employed in nursing the children, and doing light work about the house. Occasionally, I was sent out with the Indian hunters, when they went but a short distance, to help them carry their game. My situation was easy; I had no particular hardships to endure. But still, the recollection of my parents, my brothers and sisters, my home, and my own captivity, destroyed my happiness, and made me constantly solitary, lonesome, and gloomy.

My sisters would not allow me to speak English in their hearing; but remembering the charge that my dear mother gave me at the time I left her, whenever I chanced to be alone I made a business of repeating my prayer, catechism, or something I had learned, in order that I might not forget my own language. By practicing in that way, I retained it till I came to Genesee flats, where I soon became acquainted with English people, with whom I have been almost daily in the habit of conversing.

My sisters were very diligent in teaching me their language; and to their great satisfaction, I soon learned so that I could understand it readily, and speak it fluently. I was very fortunate in falling into their hands; for they were kind, good-natured women; peaceable and mild in their dispositions; temperate and decent in their habits, and very tender and gentle toward me. I have great reason to respect them, though they have been dead a great number of years.

In the second summer of my living at Wiishto, I had a child, at the time that the kernels of corn first appeared on the cob. When I was taken sick, Sheninjee was absent, and I was sent to a small shed on the bank of the river, which was made of boughs, where I was obliged to stay till my husband returned. My two sisters, who were my only companions, attended me; and on the second day of my confinement my child was born; but it lived only two days. It was a girl; and notwithstanding the shortness of the time that I possessed it, it was a great grief to me to lose it.

After the birth of my child I was very sick, but was not allowed to go into the house for two weeks; when, to my great joy, Sheninjee returned, and I was taken in, and as comfortably provided for as our situation would admit. My disease continued to increase for a number of days; and I became so far reduced that my recovery was despaired of by my friends, and I concluded that my troubles would soon be finished. At length, however, my complaint took a favorable turn, and by the time the corn was ripe I was able to get about. I continued to gain my health, and in the fall was able to go to our winter quarters, on the Saratoga, with the Indians.

From that time nothing remarkable occurred to me till the fourth winter of my captivity, when I had a son born, while I was at Sciota. I had a quick recovery, and my child was healthy. To commemorate the name of my much-lamented father, I called my son Thomas Jemison.

CHAPTER IV

In the spring, when Thomas was three or four moons (months) old, we returned from Sciota to Wiishto, and soon after set out to go to Fort Pitt, to dispose of our furs and our skins that we had taken in the winter, and procure some necessary articles for the use of our family.

I had then been with the Indians four summers and four winters, and had become so far accustomed to their mode of living, habits, and dispositions, that my anxiety to get away, to be set at liberty and leave them, had almost subsided. With them was my home; my family was there, and there I had many friends to whom I was warmly attached in consideration of the favors, affection, and friendship with which they had uniformly treated me from the time of my adoption. Our labor was not severe; and that of one year was exactly similar in almost every respect to that of the others, without that endless variety that is to be observed in the common labor of the white people. Notwithstanding the Indian women have all the fuel and bread to procure, and the cooking to perform, their task is probably not harder than that of white women, who have those articles provided for them; and their cares certainly are not half as numerous, nor as great. In the summer season, we planted, tended, and harvested our corn, and generally had all our children with us; but had no master to oversee or drive us, so that we could work as leisurely as we pleased. We had no plows on the Ohio, but performed the whole process of planting and hoeing with a small tool that resembled, in some respect, a hoe with a very short handle.

Our cooking consisted in pounding our corn into samp or hominy, boiling the hominy, making now and then a cake and baking it in the ashes, and in boiling or roasting our venison. As our cooking and eating utensils consisted of a hominy block and pestle, a small kettle, a knife or two, and a few vessels of bark or wood, it required but little time to keep them in order for use.

Spinning, weaving, sewing, stocking knitting, and the like, are arts which have never been practiced in the Indian tribes generally. After the revolutionary war, I learned to sew, so that I could make my own clothing after a poor fashion; but I have been wholly ignorant of the application of the other domestic arts since my captivity. In the season of hunting, it was our business, in addition to our cooking, to bring home the game that was taken by the Indians, dress it, and carefully preserve the eatable meat, and prepare or dress the skins. Our clothing was fastened together with strings of deerskin, and tied on with the same.

In that manner we lived, without any of those jealousies, quarrels, and revengeful battles between families and individuals, which have been common in the Indian tribes since the introduction of ardent spirits among them.

The use of ardent spirits among the Indians, and a majority of the attempts which have been made to civilize them by the white people, have constantly made them worse and worse; increased their vices, and robbed them of many of their virtues, and will ultimately produce their extermination. I have seen, in a number of instances, the effects of education upon some of our Indians, who were taken, when young, from their families, and placed at school before they had had an opportunity to contract many Indian habits, and there kept till they arrived to manhood; but I have never seen one of those but was an Indian in every respect after he returned. Indians must and will be Indians, in spite of all the means that can be used to instruct them in the arts and sciences.

One thing only marred my happiness while I lived with them on the Ohio, and that was the recollection that I once had tender parents, and a home that I loved. Aside from that recollection, which could not have existed had I been taken in my infancy, I should have been contented in my situation. Notwithstanding all that has been said against the Indians, in consequence of their cruelties to their enemies—cruelties that I have witnessed and had abundant proof of—it is a fact that they are naturally kind, tender, and peaceable toward their friends, and strictly honest; and that those cruelties have been practiced only upon their enemies, according to their idea of justice.

New World Contact

Native Americans did not consider themselves collectively as one group of people or as a single nation before their encounter with Europeans and had no common term for themselves. Upon discovering the need to adopt a common name to differentiate themselves from the new strangers in their midst, Native Americans may have had little choice but to choose one that the whites had applied to them. In the end both sides adopted the term *Indian*, based on Christopher Columbus's geographical error in supposing he had arrived in Asia rather than in a new world.

The next most common term to describe these people was much less attractive. Medieval legend had depicted wild club-swinging men of the forest as hairy, naked links between humans and animals. Named in Latin *silvaticus*, "men of the woods," they became *sauvage* in French and *salvage* in English, a word that finally turned into *savage*.

These and other names bestowed on Native Americans by whites, such as *wild-men* and *barbarians*, propagated a belief among Europeans that Indians were essentially their opposites. Defined as "the other," Indians were heathens; they performed human sacrifices and were cannibals; they were dirty, warlike, superstitious, sexually promiscuous, and brutal to their captives and to their women. Thus, evils observed anywhere among Indians (such as the Aztec practice of human sacrifice) and some not directly observed anywhere (like cannibalism) were generalized to all Indians.

At the same time Europeans, troubled by what they regarded as the decadence and overly elaborate character of their own society, recognized positive traits in the Indian that Europeans lacked. In a vision always more popular among those who stayed in Europe than with those who migrated to the New World, Indians seemed direct, innocent, hospitable, courteous, handsome, and especially courageous. Their independence, pride, stamina, and endurance suggested a nobility that Europeans, undergoing capitalist transformation, seemed to be losing. From this image came a composite ideal called the "Noble Savage."

Both images contrasted sharply with European and later American notions of "civilization." Particularly in the United States, white civilization was expected to spread over the entire continent, dooming the Indians, however noble or ignoble an image they were accorded.

Sye figur anzaigt vns das volck vnd insel die gefunden ist durch den christenlichen künig zů Portigal oder von seinen vnterthonen. Die leüt sind also nacket hübsch. braun wolgestalt von leib. ir heübter. hals. arm. scham. füß. frawen vnd mann ain wenig mit federn bedeckt. Auch haben die mann in iren angesichtern vnd brust vil edel gestain. Es hat auch nyemant nichts sünder sind alle ding gemain. Vnnd die mann habend weyber welche in gefallen. es sey müter. schwester oder freündtin. darinn haben sy kain vnderschayd. Sy streyten auch mit einander. Sy essen auch ainander selbs die erschlagen werden. vnd hencken das selbig fleisch in den rauch. Sy werden alt hundert vnd fünfzig iar. Vnd haben kain regiment.

Plate 1. Unknown artist, "First European Attempt to Depict the Domestic Life of
Native Americans," Germany, c. 1505

The first attempt by a European to depict the domestic lives of Native Americans can be seen in Plate 1 in an anonymous German woodcut published around 1505 and based on Amerigo Vespucci's account (see Selection 2). The inscription reads:

> This figure represents to us the people and island discovered by the Christian King of Portugal or his subjects. The people are thus naked, handsome, brown, well shaped in body; their head, necks, arms, private parts, feet of men and women are a little covered with feathers. The men also have many precious stones on their faces and breasts. No one has anything, but all things are in common. And the men have as wives those who please them, be they mothers, sisters or friends. . . . They also fight with each other; and they eat each other, even those who are slain, and hang the flesh of them in the smoke. They become a hundred and fifty years old and have no government.

What perception of the inhabitants of the New World does this image present? How accurate do you think it is? How might Europeans have reacted to it?

Plate 2 shows an engraving made from a drawing by John White, who from 1585 to 1586 lived in Roanoke, Virginia, part of the first English colony in North America. John White was commissioned to illustrate the first written account of that colony. Thomas Hariot's pamphlet, *A Brief and True Report of the New Found Land of Virginia*, published together with White's image in 1588, was "directed to

Plate 2. John White, "The Manner of Their Fishing," 1585

the investors, farmers, and well-wishers of the project of colonizing and planting there," and emphasized the economic possibilities of the region. The caption to White's engraving reads in part:

> It is a pleasing picture to see these people wading and sailing in their shallow rivers. They are untroubled by the desire to pile up riches for their children, and live in perfect contentment with their present state, in friendship with each other, sharing all those things with which God has so bountifully provided them. Yet they do not render Him the thanks which His providence deserves, for they are savage and have no knowledge [of Christianity].

Why do you think White and Hariot's image of the Indian is so different from that in Plate 1? In which readings can you find images of Indians most like that of the German woodcut? In which readings can you find images of Indians similar to White's engraving?

Plate 3. Unknown artist, "Huron Woman," 1664

Plate 3 is another domestic scene of Indian life, this time from a French source, François de Creux's *Historia Canadensis,* published in 1664. How does it differ from the way Plate 1 depicts the Indian? Note that both figures in this image are Indian women. How might the absence of men in this engraving change the European view of the character of Indians? Are Indian men described in different terms from Indian women in the various readings?

Plate 4 depicts a conference between Colonel Henry Bouquet and some of the Indians he defeated at the battle of Bushy Run in 1766. Many tribes in the Ohio Valley led by Pontiac, a chief of the Ottawas, rose up against the British in 1763, laying to waste many white settlements in the Ohio Valley. The central focus of the engraving is the return of white captives taken during these raids. The theme of whites, and especially white women, captured by Indians greatly fascinated the colonists and their European counterparts. What attitude toward the Indians and what view of Indian-white relations are suggested by this image?

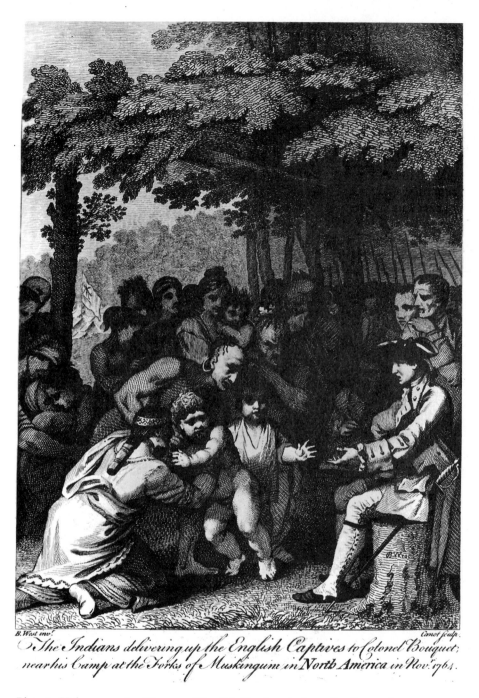

B. West inv.
Canot sculp.

The Indians delivering up the English Captives to Colonel Bouquet; near his Camp at the Forks of Muskingum in North America in Nov.ʳ 1764.

Plate 4. Unknown artist, "Return of English Captives during a Conference between Colonel Henry Bouquet and Indians on the Muskingum River," 1764

PART TWO

The Colonial Experience

A Rapidly Changing Society

The early seventeenth-century world of John and Margaret Winthrop of Massachussetts had a firmly fixed religious orientation that, for most settlers, faded as the century advanced. The Salem witchcraft trials of the 1690s demonstrated that early religious conviction certainly had been reduced to confusion. And the universe as envisioned by Benjamin Franklin a few generations later was yet further removed from Puritan roots. As adherence to orthodox Christianity declined so that it was no longer the encompassing view of the world, a number of colonists instead gradually embraced the Enlightenment confidence in science and human reason. And the physical, economic, and social circumstances of life in British America had undergone an equally great transformation. The entire white population of British America in 1660 would have fitted into Yankee Stadium; by 1750 the colonists numbered over one million. Conflict with Indian neighbors initially threatened virtually all the early colonies; by midcentury whites firmly controlled the eastern seaboard. As colonial political life had reflected the instability of seventeenth-century England's age of revolutions, so eighteenth-century colonial government mirrored a maturing if still clumsy empire that by 1763 dominated the world's diplomacy. And during the lengthy peace between the end of major European warfare in 1715 and the start of the French and Indian War in 1756, the depression of the late seventeenth century turned into a long economic boom.

African slaves, involuntary migrants to the New World, contributed enormously to the colonies' prosperity. Slaves imported through the trade in human beings that Olaudah Equiano graphically describes became the critical labor force for the sugar plantations of the West Indies. Supplying these islands with fish, grain, lumber, livestock, and other goods enriched the economies of the middle colonies and New England. After about 1680 African slavery became an important part of Southern plantation agriculture on the mainland. In South Carolina by 1720 slaves outnumbered whites by about two to one.

News of opportunity in the new land brought greater numbers of European immigrants throughout the eighteenth century. Many thousands of Germans came to the middle colonies. Like Gottlieb Mittelberger, most signed on as indentured servants to pay their passage. Harsh as their circumstances were, many eventually prospered in the New World. An even greater number of Scots-Irish—descendants of the Scottish Protestants who had settled in northern Ireland—followed to settle in the frontier valleys of Pennsylvania, Virginia, and the Carolinas.

Prosperity, security, and political stability enabled a new leadership to emerge in the British colonies. Men like Benjamin Franklin (women—Abigail Bailey, for example—rarely had even remotely similar opportunities) became outstanding citizens of the British empire, moving comfortably between the colonies and the mother country and contributing to the life and culture of both. At the same time, they were planting deep roots in their local environments. Franklin's Philadelphia was the second-largest city in the English-speaking world—only London exceeded it. From such a combination of imperial interests and colonial pride came the revolutionary generation.

POINTS OF VIEW

The Salem Witchcraft Trials (1692)

8

The Case against George Burroughs

Ann Putnam et al.

In 1692 the perception of many people was that the devil assaulted the seaport town of Salem, Massachusetts, north of Boston. Scores of warlocks and witches—men and women who had entered into a covenant with the devil to drive little children mad and to sicken and kill livestock and people—had seemingly invaded this village of a few hundred people. The jails bulged with over a hundred prisoners awaiting trial, including a four-year-old child bound for nine months in heavy iron chains. Twenty-seven people eventually came to trial; the court hanged nineteen—fourteen women and five men—as witches. One man, refusing to enter a plea, had heavy weights laid on his body until he was pressed to death.

Paul S. Boyer and Stephen Nissenbaum, eds., *Salem-Village Witchcraft: A Documentary Record* (Belmont, CA: Wadsworth Pub. Co., 1972), pp. 67–68, 69, 72, 74, 77–78, 80, 84–85, 86–87; Charles W. Upham, *Salem Witchcraft*, vol. 2 (New York: Ungar, 1969), pp. 300–01.

Only three New Englanders had ever been hanged as witches before 1692, when nine adolescent girls in Salem suddenly appeared bewitched. Under intense questioning, the shrieking and contorting girls accused some of their neighbors and even some from outside Salem of witchcraft. Cotton Mather and other leading Puritan ministers carefully advised Puritan leaders that the young women's testimony was insufficient to support a conviction for witchcraft in the absence of "other, and more human, and most convincing testimonies" since the devil could assume what shape he pleased, even that of a leading divine like Mather himself.

The leader of all the New England witches, the afflicted girls alleged, was the Reverend George Burroughs, Salem's former minister. Burroughs had left Salem village for Maine nearly twenty years earlier in the middle of controversies with several parishioners, chief among them John Putnam, whose twelve-year-old niece Ann was the first to identify Burroughs as the leader of all the witches and the murderer of at least three people by witchcraft. The magistrates issued a warrant, and he was seized and brought to Salem. His theology, local ministers discovered, had evolved in an unorthodox direction: he neither baptized infants nor celebrated communion. People remembered his boasting about his strength: though small and wiry, he was extraordinarily strong and agile and had been an outstanding athlete in his student days at Harvard. And some revived ancient gossip about mistreatment of his first two wives.

The court, well aware of its awesome responsibilities in trying a minister as a witch, nonetheless easily found Burroughs guilty. Faithful to the biblical injunction not to "suffer a witch to live," they sent him to Gallows Hill, where he protested his innocence, faultlessly recited the Lord's Prayer (which folklore said witches could not do), and stood to the snap of the rope.

BEFORE YOU READ

1. What evidence was presented to show that George Burroughs was a witch? Was it all "spectral evidence" (that is, evidence as to what his specter or shape had done to the adolescent girls)? What was the nonspectral evidence (evidence of what Burroughs himself rather than his specter had done)? Did it justify convicting Burroughs in a society that accepted unquestioningly the existence of witchcraft?

2. How do you explain the young women's accusations?

3. How do you explain the belief of the elders of the community in the accusations? What does your textbook say on this issue?

TESTIMONY OF ANN PUTNAM

The deposition of Ann Putnam, who testifies and says that on 20th of April, 1692, at evening, she saw the apparition of a minister, at which she was grievously affrighted and cried out, oh, dreadful, dreadful, here is a minister come. What, are ministers witches, too? Whence come you, and what is your name? For I will complain of you, though you be a minister, if you be a wizard. And immediately I was tortured by him, being racked and almost choked by him. And he tempted me to write in his book, which I refused with loud outcries, and said I would not write in his book though he tore me all to pieces, but told him that it was a dreadful thing that he, which was a minister that should teach children to fear God, should come to persuade poor creatures to give their souls to the devil. Oh, dreadful, dreadful. Tell me your name that I may know who you are. Then again he tortured me and urged me to write in his book, which I refused.

And then presently he told me that his name was George Burroughs, and that he had had three wives, and that he had bewitched the first two of them to death, and that he killed Mistress Lawson because she was so unwilling to go from the village, and also killed Mr. Lawson's child because he went to the eastward with Sir Edmond [Andros] and preached so to the soldiers, and that he had bewitched a great many soldiers to death at the eastward when Sir Edmond was there, and that he had made Abigail Hobbs a witch, and several witches more. And he has continued ever since, by times tempting me to write in his book and grievously torturing me by beating, pinching, and almost choking me several times a day. And he also told me that he was above a witch, he was a conjurer.

TESTIMONY OF THOMAS PUTNAM, PETER PRESCOTT, ROBERT MORRELL, AND EZEKIEL CHEEVER

We whose names are underwritten, being present with Ann Putnam at the time above mentioned, heard her declare what is abovewritten, what she said she saw and heard from the apparition of Mr. George Burroughs, and also beheld her tortures and perceived her hellish temptations by her loud outcries, I will not, I will not write though you torment me all [the] days of my life. And, being conversant with her ever since, have seen her tortured and complaining that Mr. Burroughs hurt her and tempts her to write in his book.

Thomas Putnam
Peter Prescott
Robert Morrell

COMPLAINT AGAINST GEORGE BURROUGHS

Salem, April the 30th, 1692

There being complaint this day made (before us) by Captain Jonathan Walcot and Sergeant Thomas Putnam of Salem Village, in behalf of their Majesties, for themselves, and also for several of their neighbors, against George Burroughs, minister in Wells in the province of Maine, Lydia Dasting in Reading, widow Susanah Martin of Amesbury, widow Dorcas Hoar of Beverly, widow Sarah Murrell of Beverly, and Phillip English of Salem, merchant, for high suspicion of sundry acts of witchcraft done or committed by them upon the bodies of Mary Walcot, Marcy Lewis, Abigail Williams, Ann Putnam, and Eliz Hubert, and Susanah Sheldon *(viz.)* upon some or all of them, of Salem Village or farms, whereby great hurt and damage been done to the bodies of said persons above named, therefore craved justice.

Signed by both the

Complainers $\left\{\begin{array}{l}\text{Jonathan Walcott} \\ \\ \text{Thomas Putnam}\end{array}\right.$

abovesaid

The abovesaid complaint was exhibited before us this 30th April, 1692.

John Hathorne
Jonathan Corwin $\Big\}$ Assistants

SUMMARY OF THE EXAMINATION OF GEORGE BURROUGHS

The examination of Geo. Burroughs, 9 May, 1692.

By the

Honoured $\left\{\begin{array}{l}\text{Wm. Stoughton} \\ \text{John Hathorne} \\ \text{Sam. Sewall} \\ \text{Jonath. Corwin}\end{array}\right\}$ Esq$^{s.}$

Being asked when he partook of the Lord's Supper, he being (as he said) in full communion at Roxbury, he answered it was so long since, he could not tell. Yet he owned he was at meeting one Sabbath at Boston part of the day, and the other at Charlestown part of a Sabbath, when that sacrament happened to be at both, yet did not partake of either. He denied that his house at Casco was haunted, yet he owned there were toads. He denied that he made his wife swear that she could not write to his father [-in-law] Ruck without his approbation of her letter to her father. He owned that none of his children but the eldest was baptized.

The above was in private, none of the bewitched being present. At his entry into the room, many, if not all, of the bewitched were grievously tortured.

1. Sus. Sheldon testified that Burroughs's two wives appeared in their winding sheets, and said that man killed them.
He was bid to look upon Sus. Sheldon.
He looked back and knocked down all (or most) of the afflicted who stood behind him. . . .
2. Mary Lewes deposition going to be read and he looked upon her, and she fell into a dreadful and tedious fit.

3. Mary Walcot

4. Eliz. Hubbard   } Testimony going to be read and they all fell into
    Susan Sheldon   fits.

5. Susan Sheldon   } Affirmed, each of them, that he brought the
    Ann Putnam jun.ʳ   book and would have them write.

Being asked what he thought of these things, he answered it was an amazing and humbling providence, but he understood nothing of it. And he said, some of you may observe that when they begin to name my name, they cannot name it. . . .

INDICTMENT OF GEORGE BURROUGHS

Essex Ss. The jurors for our Sovereign Lord and Lady, the King and Queen, presents that George Burroughs, late of Falmouth within the province of the Massachusetts Bay in New England, clerk, the ninth day of May, [1692] . . . and divers other days and times as well, before and after, certain detestable arts called witchcraft and sorceries, wickedly and feloniously hath used, practiced, and exercised at and within the Township of Salem in the County of Essex and aforesaid, in, upon, and against one Ann Putnam of Salem in the County of Essex, singlewoman, by which said wicked arts the said Ann Putnam . . . was, and is, tortured, afflicted, pined, consumed, wasted and tormented. Also for sundry other acts of witchcrafts by said George Burroughs committed and done against the peace of our Sovereign Lord and Lady, the King and Queen, their crown and dignity, and against the form of the statute in that case made and provided.

TESTIMONY OF SAMUEL WEBBER

Samuel Webber, aged about 36 years, testifies and says that about seven or eight years ago, I lived at Casco Bay and George Burroughs was then minister there. And having heard much of the great strength of him, said Burroughs, he coming to our house, we were in discourse about the same, and he then told me that he had put his fingers into the bung of a barrel of molasses and lifted it up and carried it round him and set it down again.

Salem, August 2d, 1692.

                                                                    Samuel Webber

TESTIMONY OF SIMON WILLARD

The deposition of Simon Willard, aged about forty two years, says, I being at the house of Mr. Robert Lawrence at Falmouth, in Casco Bay, in September 1689, said Mr. Lawrence was commenting [upon] Mr. George Borroughs's strength, saying that we, none of us, could do what he could do. For said Mr.

Borroughs can hold out this gun with one hand. Mr. Borroughs, being there, said, I held my hand here behind the lock and took it up and held it out.

I, said deponent, saw Mr. Borroughs put his hand on the gun to show us how he held it and where he held his hand, and saying there he held his hand when he held said gun out. But I saw him not hold it out then. Said gun was about seven-foot barrel, and very heavy. I then tried to hold out said gun with both hands, but could not do it long enough to take sight.

Simon Willard

Simon Willard owned to the Jury of Inquest that the abovewritten evidence is the truth,
August 3, 1692

Capt. Wm. Wormall sworn to the above, and that he saw him raise it from the ground himself.

TESTIMONY OF THOMAS GREENSLIT

The deposition of Thomas Greenslit, aged about forty years, testifies that about the breaking out of this last Indian war, being at the house of Capt. Scottow's, at Black Point, he saw Mr. George Burroughs lift and hold out a gun of six foot barrel or thereabouts, putting the forefinger of his right hand into the muzzle of said gun, and so held it out at arm's end, only with that finger. And further this deponent testifies that at the same time he saw the said Burroughs take up a full barrel of molasses with but two fingers of one of his hands in the bung, and carry it from the stage head to the door at the end of the stage, without letting it down, and that Lieut. Richard Hunniwell and John Greenslit and some other persons that are since dead were then present.

Salem, September 15, 1692. Thomas Greenslit appeared before their Majesties' Justices of Oyer and Terminer in open court and made oath that the above mentioned particulars, and every part of them, were true.

attest   Step. Sewall, Clerk

ROBERT CALEF'S ACCOUNT OF
GEORGE BURROUGHS'S EXECUTION

Mr. Burroughs was carried in a cart with the others, through the streets of Salem, to execution. When he was upon the ladder, he made a speech for the clearing of his innocency, with such solemn and serious expressions as were to the admiration of all present. His prayer (which he concluded by repeating the Lord's Prayer) was so well worded, and uttered with such composedness and such (at least seeming) fervency of spirit, as was very affecting, and drew tears from many, so that it seemed to some that the spectators would hinder the execution. The accusers said the black man stood and dictated to him. As soon as he was turned off, Mr. Cotton Mather, being mounted upon a horse, addressed himself to the people, partly to declare that he (Mr. Burroughs) was no ordained minister, and partly to possess the people of his guilt, saying that the Devil often had been transformed into an angel of light; and this somewhat appeased the people, and the executions went on. When he was cut down, he was dragged by a halter to a hole, or grave, between the rocks, about two feet deep; his shirt and breeches being pulled off, and an old pair of trousers of one executed put on his lower parts: he was so put in, together with Willard and Carrier, that one of his hands, and his chin, and a foot of one of them, was left uncovered.

9

Reconsidering the Verdict
Cotton Mather et al.

The witchcraft epidemic, so one interpretation has it, fed on local conflicts. In Salem, town and countryside were sharply diverging. Conservative back-country farmers struggled to cope with the demands of commerce. Sons coming of age—the potential marriage partners of the adolescent girls—needed land if they were to establish an independent family, but available reserves of land were shrinking. Puritan ministers lamented the "declension" from the piety of the colony's founders. Although ministers of every generation may be expected to denounce the decadence of their time, New England's preachers at the end of the seventeenth century had special reason to do so: the stern Puritanism of past generations was under real threat from a growth in luxury and secular manners. No wonder the people of Salem found it easy to believe the rantings of hysterical adolescents and think so ill of their neighbors.

Nor could the colony of which Salem was part provide the stability the beleaguered village needed. Massachusetts Bay as a whole was passing through a time of troubles. Its charter voided in 1684, Massachusetts had no stable legal base until it received a new and radically different charter from the king in 1691. People worried whether the old land claims would be valid under the new charter and whether voting would be restricted to church members. At the same time, the devil in the form of Roman Catholic France and heathen Indians was at their door. The Maine and New Hampshire frontiers had collapsed during King William's War (1689–1697), and the colony's counterattack had ended in disaster. Massachusetts Bay was bankrupt and increased taxes to unprecedented levels. The birthrate declined, and refugees from the war were suddenly everywhere. Some of the bewitched teenagers were orphans of the war. During this

George L. Burr, ed., *Narratives of the Witchcraft Cases, 1648–1706* (New York: Charles Scribner's Sons, 1914), pp. 215–22; Paul S. Boyer and Stephen Nissenbaum, eds., *Salem-Village Witchcraft: A Documentary Record* (Belmont, CA: Wadsworth Pub. Co., 1972), pp. 118–22; Charles W. Upham, *Salem Witchcraft*, vol. 2 (New York: Ungar, 1969), p. 510; Harvey Wish, ed., *The Diary of Samuel Sewall* (New York: G. P. Putnam's Sons, 1967), pp. 80–81.

time of political, religious, and social instability, how easy it must have been to believe that the devil had launched his greatest assault on New England. In fact, for a time the larger the net of accusations grew and the more people confessed to witchcraft, the easier it was to believe in the devil's conspiracy against the colony.

Then the accusations went too far, extending to prominent members of Puritan society, including the governor's wife. The ministers' cautions concerning spectral evidence became more persuasive, and the governor finally halted the trials. The public mood changed. To the regret of some but to the relief of many, the world of spirits again became invisible, and the witches fled New England, this time forever.

BEFORE YOU READ

1. Cotton Mather continued to defend the hanging of George Burroughs. What was his case against Burroughs? Does it depend on spectral evidence?

2. Why did Margaret Jacobs confess to being a witch? Do you consider her recantation sincere?

3. How did Governor Phips explain the witchcraft hysteria? Did he blame anyone for it?

4. Why did Samuel Sewall and Ann Putnam repent? What does it indicate about them?

COTTON MATHER EXPLAINS THE DIFFICULTY OF WITCHCRAFT TRIALS

Letter to John Foster, One of the Salem Witchcraft Judges (August 17, 1692)

Sir:

You would know whether I still retain my opinion about the horrible witchcrafts among us, and I acknowledge that I do.

I do still think that when there is no further evidence against a person but only this, that a specter in their shape does afflict a neighbor, that evidence is not enough to convict the [person] of witchcraft.

That the Devils have a natural power which makes them capable of exhibiting what shape they please I suppose nobody doubts, and I have no absolute promise of God that they shall not exhibit *mine*.

It is the opinion generally of all Protestant writers that the Devil may thus abuse the innocent; yea, 'tis the confession of some Popish ones. And our honorable judges are so eminent for their justice, wisdom, and goodness, that whatever their own particular sense may be, yet they will not proceed capitally against any upon a principle contested with great odds on the other side in the learned and Godly world.

Nevertheless, a very great use is to be made of the spectral impressions upon the sufferers. They justly introduce and determine an inquiry into the circumstances of the person accused, and they strengthen other presumptions.

When so much use is made of those things, I believe the use for which the great God intends them is made. And accordingly you see that the excellent judges have had such an encouraging presence of God with them as that scarce any, if at all any, have been tried before them against whom God has not strangely sent in other, and more human, and most convincing testimonies.

If any persons have been condemned about whom any of the judges are not easy in their minds that the evidence against them has been satisfactory, it would certainly be for the glory of the whole transaction to give that person a reprieve.

It would make all matters easier if at least bail were taken for people accused only by the invisible tormentors of the poor sufferers, and not blemished by any further grounds of suspicion against them.

The odd effects produced upon the sufferers by the look or touch of the accused are things wherein the Devils may as much impose upon some harmless people as by the representation of their shapes.

My notion of these matters is this. A suspected and unlawful communion with a familiar spirit is the thing inquired after. The communion on the Devil's part may be proved while, for aught I can say, the man may be innocent. The Devil may impudently impose his communion upon some that care not for his company. But if the communion on the man's part be proved, then the business is done.

I am suspicious lest the Devil may at some time or other serve us a trick by his constancy for a long while in one way of dealing. We may find the Devil using one constant course in nineteen several actions, and yet he be too hard for us at last, if we thence make a rule to form an infallible judgment of a twentieth. It is our singular happiness that we are blessed with judges who are aware of this danger. . . .

Our case is extraordinary. And so you and others will pardon the extraordinary liberty I take to address you on this occasion. But after all, I entreat you that whatever you do, you strengthen the hands of our honorable judges in the great work before them. They are persons for whom no man living has a greater veneration than

> Sir,
> Your servant
> C. Mather

COTTON MATHER DEFENDS
THE CONVICTION OF GEORGE BURROUGHS

This G. B. [George Burroughs] was indicted for witchcraft, and in the prosecution of the charge against him, he was accused by five or six of the bewitched, as the author of their miseries; he was accused by eight of the confessing witches as being a head actor at some of their hellish rendez-vouses and one who had the promise of being a king in Satan's kingdom, now going to be erected; he was accused by nine persons for extraordinary lifting, and such feats of strength, as could not be done without a diabolical assistance. And for other such things he was accused, until about thirty testimonies were brought in against him; nor were these judged the half of what might have been considered for his conviction: however, they were enough to fix the character of a witch upon him. . . .

And now upon his trial, one of the bewitched persons [Ann Putnam] testified that in her agonies a little black haired man came to her, saying his name was B. and bidding her set her hand unto a book which he showed her; and bragging that he was a conjurer, above the ordinary rank of witches. That he often persecuted her with the offer of that book, saying she should be well and need fear nobody if she would but sign it; but he inflicted cruel pains and hurts upon her because of her denying so to do. The testimonies of the other sufferers concurred with these, and it was remarkable, that whereas biting was one of the ways which the witches used for the vexing of the sufferers, when they cried out of G. B. biting them, the print of the teeth would be seen on the flesh of the complainers, and just such a set of teeth as G. B.'s would then appear upon them, which could be distinguished from those of some other men. . . .

It cost the court a wonderful deal of trouble to hear the testimonies of the sufferers, for when they were going to give in their depositions, they would for a long time be taken with fits that made them incapable of saying anything. The chief judge asked the prisoner who he thought hindered these witnesses from giving their testimonies and he answered, he supposed it was the Devil. That honorable person then replied, how comes the Devil, so loathe to have any testimony born against you? Which cast him into very great confusion.

It has been a frequent thing for the bewitched people to be entertained with apparitions of ghosts of murdered people, at the same time that the specters of the witches trouble them. Accordingly, several of the bewitched had given in their testimony that they had been troubled with the apparitions of two women, who said that they were G. B.'s two wives, and that he had been the death of them, and that the magistrates must be told of it before whom if B. upon his trial denied it, they did not know but that they should appear again in the Court. Now, G. B. had been infamous for the barbarous usage of his two successive wives, all the country over. . . .

[O]ne of the bewitched persons was cast into horror at the ghosts of B.'s two deceased wives then appearing before him, and crying for vengeance against him. Hereupon, several of the bewitched persons were successively called in, who all not knowing what the former had seen and said, concurred in their horror of the apparition, which they affirmed that he had before him. . . .

Judicious writers have assigned it a great place in the conviction of witches when persons are impeached by other notorious witches, to be as [evil] as themselves; especially if the persons have been much noted for neglecting the worship of God. Now, as there might have been testimonies enough of G. B.'s antipathy to prayer, and the other ordinances of God, though by his profession singularly obliged thereunto; so, there now came in against the prisoner the testimonies of several persons who confessed their own having been horrible witches, and ever since their confessions had been themselves terribly tortured by the devils and other witches, even like the other sufferers. . . .

These now testified that G. B. had been at witch meetings with them, and that he was the person who had seduced and compelled them into the snares of witchcraft. That he promised them fine clothes for doing it, that he brought dolls to them and thorns to stick into those dolls, for the afflicting of other people, and that he exhorted them with the rest of the crew to bewitch all Salem Village, but be sure to do it gradually, if they would prevail in what they did. . . .

A famous Divine recites this among the convictions of a witch, the testimony of the party bewitched, whether pining or dying, together with the joint oaths of sufficient persons that have seen certain prodigious pranks or feats wrought by the party accused. Now God had been pleased so to leave this G. B. that he had ensnared himself by several instances, which he had formerly given of a preternatural strength and which were now produced against him. He was a very puny man, yet he had often done things beyond the strength of a giant. A gun of about seven foot barrel and so heavy that strong men could not steadily hold it out with both hands, there were several testimonies given in by persons of credit and honor, that he made nothing of taking up such a gun behind the lock, with but one hand and holding it out like a pistol at arms' end. G. B. in his vindication was so foolish as to say, that an Indian was there, and held it out at the same time: whereas none of the spectators ever saw any such Indian, but they supposed the black man (as the witches call the devil, and they generally say he resembles an Indian) might give him that assistance. . . .

Faltering, faulty, inconsistent, and contrary answers upon judicial and deliberate examination are counted some unlucky symptoms of guilt in all crimes, especially in witchcraft. Now, there was never a prisoner more eminent for them then G. B. both at his examination and on his trial. His evasions, contradictions and falsehoods were very sensible, he had little to say, but that he had heard some things that he could not prove, reflecting upon the reputation of some of the witnesses. Only he gave in a paper to the jury, wherein although he had many times before granted not only that there are witches but also that the present sufferings of the country are the effect of horrible witchcrafts, yet he now goes to show that there neither are nor ever were witches that, having made a compact with the Devil, can send a devil to torment other people at a distance. . . .

The jury brought him in guilty. But when he came to die, he utterly denied the fact, whereof he had been thus convicted.

DECLARATION OF MARGARET JACOBS
TO THE SPECIAL WITCHCRAFT COURT
APPOINTED BY THE GOVERNOR

The humble declaration of Margaret Jacobs to the honoured court now sitting at Salem, shows:

That whereas your poor and humble declarant being closely confined here in Salem jail for the crime of witchcraft, which crime, thanks be to the Lord, I am altogether ignorant of, as will appear at the great day of judgment. May it please the honoured court, I was cried out upon by some of the possessed persons, as afflicting of them; whereupon I was brought to my examination, which persons at the sight of me fell down, which did very much startle and affright me. The Lord above knows I knew nothing, in the least measure, how or who afflicted them; they told me, without doubt I did, or else they would not fall down at me; they told me if I would not confess, I should be put down into the dungeon and would be hanged, but if I would confess I should have my life; the which did so affright me, with my own vile wicked heart, to save my life made me make the confession I did, which confession, may it please the honoured court, is altogether false and untrue. The very first night after I had made my confession, I was in such horror of conscience that I could not sleep, for fear the Devil should carry me away for telling such horrid lies. I was, may it please the honoured court, sworn to my confession, as I understand since, but then, at that time, was ignorant of it, not knowing what an oath did mean. The Lord, I hope, in whom I trust, out of the abundance of his mercy, will forgive me my false forswearing myself.

What I said was altogether false, against my grandfather, and Mr. Burroughs, which I did to save my life and to have my liberty; but the Lord, charging it to my conscience, made me in so much horror, that I could not contain myself before I had denied my confession, which I did, though I saw nothing but death before me, choosing rather death with a quiet conscience, than to live in such horror, which I could not suffer. . . .

GOVERNOR WILLIAM PHIPS ENDS THE TRIALS

Letter to the Earl of Nottingham
(February 21, 1693)

Boston in New England Febry 21st, 1692–93

May it please your Lordship,

At my arrival here I found the prisons full of people committed upon suspicion of witchcraft, and that continual complaints were made to me that many persons were grievously tormented by witches, and that they cried out upon several persons by name, as the cause of their torments. The number of these complaints increasing every day, by advice of the Lieutenant Governor and the Council I gave a Commission of Oyer and Terminer to try the suspected witches and at that time the generality of the people represented the matter to me as real witchcraft and gave very strange instances of the same. The first in Commission was the Lieutenant Governor and the rest persons of the best prudence and figure that could then be pitched upon, and I depended upon the Court for a right method of proceeding in cases of witchcraft.

At that time I went to command the army at the eastern part of the Province, for the French and Indians had made an attack upon some of our frontier towns. I continued there for some time but when I returned I found people much dissatisfied at the proceedings of the Court, for about twenty persons were condemned and executed of which number some were thought by many persons to be innocent. The Court still proceeded in the same method of trying them, which was by the evidence of the afflicted persons who, when they were brought into the Court—as soon as the suspected witches looked upon them, instantly fell to the ground in strange agonies and grievous torments, but when touched by them upon the arm or some other part of their flesh they immediately revived and came to themselves, upon [which] they made oath that the prisoner at the bar did afflict them and that they saw their shape or specter come from their bodies which put them to such pains and torments. When I inquired into the matter I was informed by the Judges that they began with this, but had human testimony against such as were condemned and undoubted proof of their being witches. But at length I found that the Devil did take upon him the shape of Innocent persons and some were accused of whose innocency I was well assured and many considerable persons of unblameable life and conversation were cried out upon as witches and wizards.

The Deputy Governor, notwithstanding, persisted vigorously in the same method, to the great dissatisfaction and disturbance of the people, until I put an end to the Court and stopped the proceedings, which I did because I saw many innocent persons might otherwise perish. . . . When I put an end to the Court there were at least fifty persons in prison in great misery by reason of the extreme cold and their poverty, most of them having only specter evidence against them, and their *mittimusses* [warrants] being defective, I caused some of them to be let out upon bail and put the Judges upon considering of a way to relieve others and prevent them from perishing in prison, upon which some of them were convinced and acknowledged that their former proceedings were too violent and not grounded upon a right foundation but that if they might sit again, they would proceed after another method, and whereas Mr. Increase Mathew [Mather] and several other Divines did give it as their Judgment that the Devil might afflict in the shape of an innocent person and that the look and the touch of the suspected persons was not sufficient proof against them, these things had not the same stress laid upon them as before. And upon this consideration I permitted a special Superior Court to be held at Salem in the County of Essex on the third day of January, the Lieutenant Governor being Chief Judge. Their method of proceeding being altered, all that were brought to trial, to the number of fifty two, were cleared saving [except] three, and I was informed by the King's Attorney General that some of the cleared and the condemned were under the same circumstances or that there was the same reason to clear the three condemned as the rest according to his Judgment. The Deputy Governor signed a Warrant for their speedy execution and also of five others who were condemned at the former Court of Oyer and Terminer, but considering how the matter had been managed I sent a reprieve whereby the execution was stopped until their Majesties' pleasure be signified and declared. The Lieutenant Governor upon this occasion was enraged and filled with passionate anger and refused to sit upon the bench in a Superior Court then held at Charlestown, and indeed has from the beginning hurried on these matters with great precipitancy and by his warrant has caused the estates, goods and chattels of the executed to be seized and disposed of without my knowledge or consent.

The stop put to the first method of proceedings has dissipated the black cloud that threatened this Province with destruction; for whereas this delusion of the Devil did spread and its dismal effects touched the lives and estates of many of their Majesties' subjects and the reputation of some of the principal persons here, and indeed unhappily clogged and interrupted their Majesties' affairs which has been a great vexation to me, I have no new complaints but people's minds before divided and distracted by differing opinions concerning this matter are now well composed.

> I am
> Your Lordship's most faithful
> humble Servant
> William Phips

SAMUEL SEWALL'S CONFESSION (1697)

[January 1] On the 22nd of May I buried my abortive son; . . . The Lord pardon all my sins of omission and commission: and by his almighty power make me meet to be partaker of the inheritance with the Saints in Light. Second-day January 11, 1697 God helped me to pray more than ordinarily, that He would make up our loss in the burial of our little daughter and other children, and that would give us a child to serve Him, pleading with Him as the institutor of marriage, and the author of every good work.

[January 15, 1697] Copy of the Bill I put up on the Fast day; giving it to Mr. Willard as he pass'd by, and standing up at the reading of it, and bowing when finished; in the Afternoon.

> Samuel Sewall, sensible of the reiterated strokes of God upon himself and family; and being sensible, that as to the Guilt contracted upon the opening of the late Commission of Oyer and Terminer at Salem [the special witchcraft court] (to which the order for this Day relates) he is, upon many accounts, more concerned than any that he knows of, desires to take the blame and shame of it, Asking pardon of men, And especially desiring prayers that God, who has an Unlimited Authority, would pardon that sin and all other his sins; personal and relative: And according to his infinite benignity, and sovereignty, not visit the sin of him, or of any other, upon himself or any of his, nor upon the land: But that He would powerfully defend him against all temptations to sin, for the future; and vouchsafe him the efficacious, saving conduct of his word and spirit.

ANN PUTNAM'S CONFESSION (1706)

I desire to be humbled before God for that sad and humbling providence that befell my father's family in the year about '92; that I, then being in my childhood, should, by such a providence of God, be made an instrument for the accusing of several persons of a grievous crime, whereby their lives were taken away from them, whom now I have just grounds and good reason to believe they were innocent persons; and that it was a great delusion of Satan that deceived me in that sad time, whereby I justly fear I have been instrumental, with others, though ignorantly and unwittingly, to bring upon myself and this land the guilt of innocent blood; though what was said or done by me against any person I can truly and uprightly say, before God and man, I did it not out of any anger, malice, or ill-will to any person, for I had no such thing against one of them; but what I did was ignorant, being deluded by Satan. And particularly, as I was a chief instrument of accusing of Goodwife Nurse and her two sisters, I desire to lie in the dust, and to be humbled for it, in that I was a cause, with others, of so sad a calamity to them and their families; for which cause I desire to lie in the dust, and earnestly beg forgiveness of God, and from all those unto whom I have given just cause of sorrow and offence, whose relations were taken away or accused.

[Signed]

This confession was read before the congregation, together with her relation, Aug. 25, 1706; and she acknowledged it.

J. GREEN, *Pastor*

FOR CRITICAL THINKING

1. Do you think trials are a good method for determining truth? In what ways did the Salem witchcraft trials obscure rather than clarify the truth about the witchcraft threat? In what other trials did the process of adjudication seem to have worked against revealing the truth? Can you think of trials where the public response of the time affected the ability of a court to arrive at justice?

2. Imagine Cotton Mather interviewing Margaret Jacobs. Would this interview have raised questions for him about George Burroughs's guilt? How might Mather have explained why Jacobs changed her story?

3. When Ann Putnam recanted her testimony, among her listeners were the sons and daughters of Rebecca Nurse, one of the people Ann Putnam had accused and who was subsequently hanged for witchcraft. If they had entered into conversation about it, what kind of dialogue might they have had regarding Putnam's confession?

10

Puritans in Love and Marriage
John and Margaret Winthrop

In the society that English settlers brought to the New World, English ministers told their congregations that "the woman is a weak creature not endued with like strength and constancy of mind" as the man. This lesson was taught throughout the American colonies. Women did not belong in public life. In church, their role was "not to teach, nor to hold authority over the man, but to be in silence." At home, their legal rights were obliterated by marriage. Women could not own property, enter legal contracts, or sue in a court of law. A woman's first obligation was obedience to her husband's will. "A true wife," wrote the Puritan leader John Winthrop (1588–1649), "accounts her subjection her honor and freedom, and would not think her condition safe and free, but in subjection to her husband's authority." In repeating this generally accepted view of the position of husband and wife, Winthrop could have been describing his own marriage to Margaret Tyndal Winthrop (1591–1647).

John and Margaret Winthrop were quintessential Puritans. Since most Americans believe that the Puritans were responsible for almost all repression of sexuality in American culture, the flourishing of love, even the flow of sexual currents, between husband and wife in these letters may be surprising. The Puritans do not deserve their reputation for prudery. They were actually a lusty bunch. They recognized the potential social disruption that sexual relations could create but believed that the safeguard against disruption was not abstinence (human beings, they thought, were not generally capable of that) but marriage. The well-ordered household was, Puritans believed, the social institution on which the stability of the church, the state, and the economy rested. The love of husband and wife was second only to the love of God in organizing and giving meaning to human existence. In the fortunate case of John and Margaret Winthrop, that Puritan ideal appears to have been lived to the fullest.

Most of the letters between the Winthrops were exchanged in the early years of the seventeenth century before their migration to New England. Both a London attorney and a leader in the wing of Puritanism that sought to escape the corruption of England by establishing a holy commonwealth in New England, John Winthrop was a major planner of the great migration of 1630 that brought thousands of Puritans to Massachusetts Bay. The letters reprinted here culminate in a series of exchanges as Winthrop prepared to leave England while Margaret stayed on to manage family affairs. The anticipated dangers of transatlantic travel fill these last several letters with the special urgency of two people deeply in love who fear they may never see each other again. John

Robert C. Winthrop, ed., *Life and Letters of John Winthrop* (Boston: Ticknor and Fields, 1864), pp. 166–67, 232–34, 300–01, 337–38, 356–57, 370–74, 376, 385, 388–91. The text has been modernized.

arrived safely in New England and became a major leader of the colony, serving many terms as governor, and Margaret followed him the following autumn, occasioning a public celebration with "fat hogs, kids, venison, poultry, geese, partridges, etc., so as the like joy and manifestation of love had never been seen in New England."

BEFORE YOU READ

1. Which details in the letters of John and Margaret Winthrop conform to conventional views of the Puritans?

2. Which details contradict most people's views of the Puritans?

3. What relationships do you find between the Winthrops' religion and their love for each other?

4. What feelings about their emigration to New England do the letters express?

John Winthrop to His Wife

My dear Wife,—I praise God, we are come safe to London, where we find all well. . . . We have often wished thee with us, but wishes are vain. I trust, God will give us to meet again shortly in peace and sweet comfort, in the fruition of our mutual love. In the mean time let this stay our hearts, that no distance of place or space of time can sever us, in respect of our true and fervent affections to each other; whereof every occasion shall give us more assurance. I am too much straightened in time to write to her whom I love so dearly (it being now eleven o'clock this Tuesday night); thy kind heart must gather a great deal of matter from a few scribbled lines. I will add no more, but beseech the Lord: to bless thee and all our young ones, and send us a joyful meeting. . . . Farewell my sweet wife, farewell.

Thy faithful loving husband

John Winthrop

Rederife, April 9, 1622

Margaret Winthrop to Her Husband

My dear Husband,—I received thy most kind letter and thank thee for it. I wish thy employments could suffer thee to come home, but I must wait the time till I may enjoy thee, though it cannot be without much want of thy beloved presence, which I desire always to have with me. I see it is the will of God that it should be so, which makes me bear it the more patiently, and not any want of love in my beloved husband. And now my dear I have nothing to write of to thee but my love which is all ready known to thee, and it would be needless for me to make relation of that which thou art so well assured. I will leave off this discourse for this time. . . . I being sleepy, as you may see by my writing, bid my good husband good night and commit him to the safe protection of almighty God and rest

Thy faithful and obedient wife

Margaret Winthrop

Margaret Winthrop to Her Husband

To my very loving Husband John Winthrop Esquire
at Mr. Downing's house in Fleet Street.

My most kind and loving Husband,—I did receive your most sweet letter by
my brother Gosling, and do praise God for the continuance of your health, and
the rest of our friends. I thank the Lord we are also in health, and think long for
your coming home. My good husband your love to me does daily give me cause
of comfort, and does much increase my love to you, for love lives by love. I
were worse then a brute beast if I should not love and be faithful to thee, who
hath deserved so well at my hands. I am ashamed and grieved with my self that I
have no thing within or without worthy of thee, and yet it pleases thee to accept
of both and to rest contented. I had need to amend my life and pray to God for
more grace that I may not deceive you of those good hopes which you have of
me,—a sinful woman, full of infirmities, continually failing of what I desire and
what I ought to perform to the Lord and thy self. I hope in God we shall now
shortly meet with comfort, for which I shall pray. . . . And thus with my love
and best affections even with a love increasing I take my leave and commit you
to the Lord, who is all sufficient and able to preserve you from all danger and
send you safe home.
   Your loving and obedient wife

Margaret Winthrop

John Winthrop to His Wife

To his very loving Wife, Mrs. Winthrop,
at her House in Groton.

My good Wife, . . .
   For news I have but one to write of, but that will be more welcome to thee
than a great deal of other. My office is gone, and my chamber, and I shall be a
saver in them both. So, as I hope, we shall now enjoy each other again, as we
desire. The Lord teach us to improve our time and society to more use for our
mutual comfort, and the good of our family, etc., than before. It is now bed
time; but I must lie alone; therefore I make less haste. Yet I must kiss my sweet
wife; and so, with my blessing to our children, and salutation to all our friends, I
commend thee to the grace and blessing of the Lord, and rest,
   Thy faithful husband,

John Winthrop

Margaret Winthrop to Her Husband

My dear Husband,—I received thy sweet and most welcome letter very late
this Monday night, and do bless God for thy health and welfare. I have heard
read the news from New England and much rejoice in it. The good Lord still
continues his mercy to that plantation, and blesses us in our intended purpose

that way. We see how the Lord gives us his warrant and daily encouragement
that way; we may I hope trust him for a blessing upon us and ours. . . . It is now
late and bed time and I must bid thee good night before I am willing, for I
could find in my heart to sit and talk with thee all night. Though I am a bad
watcher, I could well spare a night's sleep to do any thing for thee. . . . And so I
bid thee farewell: the Lord keep thee.

    Thy unworthy wife

                                           M. W.

Margaret Winthrop to Her Husband

My dear Husband, — I know not how to express my love to thee or my desires of
thy wished welfare, but my heart is well known to thee, which will make relation
of my affections though they be small in appearance. My thoughts are now on our
great change and alteration of our course here, which I beseech the Lord to bless
us in, and my good Husband cheer up thy heart in the expectation of God's goodness to us, and let nothing dismay or discourage thee. If the Lord be with us who
can be against us: my grief is the fear of staying behind thee, but I must leave all to
the good providence of God. I thank the Lord we are all here in reasonable good
health. I received a letter since you went from my son John, which brought good
news from New England. I pray thank him for it, I will write to him if I have time,
and thus with my best respect to thy self, . . . I commit you to God and rest.

    Your faithful wife

                                      Margaret Winthrop

John Winthrop to His Wife

My sweet Wife, — I received thy most kind letter, and blessed be our good God
that gives us still cause of rejoicing in the news of each other's welfare, and of
those who are dear to us. And blessed be God, who hath given me a wife, who is
such a help and encouragement to me in this great work, wherein so many
wives are so great an hindrance to theirs. I doubt not but the Lord will recom-
pence abundantly the faithfulness of thy love and obedience, and for my self, I
shall ever be mindful of thee, and careful to requite thee. . . .

    Thy faithful husband

                                      John Winthrop
                                      Nov. 12, 1629

John Winthrop to His Wife

My dear Wife, . . .

    I must now begin to prepare thee for our long parting, which grows very near.
I know not how to deal with thee by arguments; for if thou were as wise and patient as ever woman was, yet it must needs be a great trial to thee, and the greater,
because I am so dear to thee. That which I must chiefly look at in thee, for a
ground of contentment, is thy godliness. If now the Lord be thy God, thou must

show it by trusting in him, and resigning thyself quietly to his good pleasure. If now Christ be thy Husband, thou must show what sure and sweet intercourse is between him and thy soul, when it shall be no hard thing for thee to part with an earthly, mortal, infirm husband for his sake. The enlargement of thy comfort in the communion of the love and sweet familiarity of thy most holy, heavenly, and undefiled Lord and Husband, will abundantly recompense whatsoever want or inconvenience may come by the absence of the other. The best course is to turn all our reasons and discourse into prayers; for he only can help, who is Lord of sea and land, and has sole power of life and death.

It is now near eleven of the clock, and I shall write again ere long (if God will). The good Lord bless thee and all thy company. . . . So I kiss my sweet wife, and rest

Thy frail, yet faithful husband,

John Winthrop

January 31, 1629.

Margaret Winthrop to Her Husband

My most dear Husband,—I should not now omit any opportunity of writing to thee, considering I shall not long have thee to write to. But, by reason of my unfitness at this time, I must entreat thee to accept of a few lines from me, and not to impute it to any want of love, or neglect of my duty to thee, to whom I owe more than I shall ever be able to express. My request now shall be to the Lord to prosper thee in thy voyage, and enable thee and fit thee for it, and give all graces and gifts for such employments as he shall call thee to. I trust God will once more bring us together before you go, that we may see each other with gladness, and take solemn leave, till we, through the goodness of our God, shall meet in New England, which will be a joyful day to us. . . . And thus, with my best wishes to God for thy health and welfare, I take my leave, and rest

Thy faithful, and obedient wife,

Margaret Winthrop

January the last

John Winthrop to His Wife

To my very loving Wife Mrs. Winthrop the elder
at Groton, in Suffolk.

My sweet Wife,—Thy love is such to me, and so great is the bond between us, that I should neglect all others to hold correspondence of letters with thee. But I know thou art willing to dispense with somewhat of thine own right, to give me liberty to satisfy my other occasions for the present, which call me to much writing this evening. Otherwise I would have returned a larger answer to thy sweet letter. I praise God we are all in health, and we go on cheerfully in our business.

I purpose (if God will) to be with thee upon Thursday, . . . and then I must take my farewell of thee, for a summer's day and a winter's day. The Lord our good God will (I hope) send us a happy meeting again in his good time. Amen. . . . The Lord bless thee my sweet wife with all our children. My brother and sister salute you all. My sons remember their love and duty. Commend my love to all, farewell.
    Thy faithful husband,

John Winthrop

Feb. 5, 1629

    Being now ready to send away my letters, I received thine; the reading of it *has dissolved* my head into tears. I can write no more. If I live I *will see thee* ere I go. I shall part from thee with sorrow enough; be comfortable my most sweet wife, our God will be with thee. Farewell.

John Winthrop to His Wife

My sweet Wife, — The opportunity of so fit a messenger, and my deep engage-ment of affection to thee, makes me write at this time, though I hope to follow soon after. The Lord our God hath often brought us together with comfort, when we have been long absent; and, if it be good for us, he will do so still. When I was in Ireland, he brought us together again. When I was sick here at London, he re-stored us together again. How many dangers, near death, hast thou been in thy-self! and yet the Lord hath granted me to enjoy thee still. If he did not watch over us, we need not go over sea to seek death or misery: we should meet it at every step, in every journey. And is not he a God abroad as well as at home? Is not his power and providence the same in New England that it has been in Old England? If our ways please him, he can command deliverance and safety in all places, and can make the stones of the field and the beasts, yea, the raging seas, and our very enemies, to be in league with us. But, if we sin against him, he can raise up evil against us out of our own bowels, houses, estates, etc. My good wife, trust in the Lord, whom thou has found faithful. He will be better to thee than any husband, and will restore thee thy husband with advantage. But I must end, with all our salutations, with which I have laden this bearer, that he may be the more kindly welcome. So I kiss my sweet wife, and bless thee and all ours, and rest
    Thine ever,

John Winthrop

February 14, 1629

Thou must be my valentine, for none hath challenged me.

John Winthrop to His Wife

Mine only Best-beloved, —I now salute thee from South Hampton, where, by the Lord's mercy, we are all safe; but the winds have been such as our ships are not yet come. We wait upon God, hoping that he will dispose all for the best unto us. I supposed I should have found leisure to have written more fully to thee by this bearer; but here I meet with so much company and business, as I am forced to borrow of my sleep for this. I purpose to redeem this loss before I go hence, and to write to divers of my friends. I must entreat thee to supply this defect by remembering me in the kindest manner to them all. And now (my dear wife) what shall I say to thee? I am full of matter and affection toward thee, but want time to express it. I beseech the good Lord to take care of thee and thine; to seal up his loving kindness to thy soul; to fill thee with the sweet comfort of his presence, that may uphold thee in this time of trial; and grant us this mercy, that we may see the faces of each other again in the time expected. So, loving thee truly, and tender of thy welfare, studying to bestow thee safe, where I may have thee again, I leave thee in the arms of the Lord Jesus, our sweet Saviour, and, with many kisses and embracings, I rest

    Thine only, and ever thine,

                John Winthrop

                South Hampton, March 14, 1629

John Winthrop to His Wife

To Mrs. Marg. Winthrop, the elder,
at Groton.

My faithful and dear Wife, . . .

    And now (my sweet soul) I must once again take my last farewell of thee in Old England. It goeth very near to my heart to leave thee; but I know to whom I have committed thee, even to him who loves thee much better than any husband can, who hath taken account of the hairs of thy head, and puts all thy tears in his bottle, who can, and (if it be for his glory) will bring us together again with peace and comfort. Oh, how it refreshes my heart, to think, that I shall yet again see thy sweet face in the land of the living! — that lovely countenance, that I have so much delighted in, and beheld with so great content! I have hitherto been so taken up with business, as I could seldom look back to my former happiness; but now, when I shall be at some leisure, I shall not avoid the remembrance of thee, nor the grief for thy absence. Thou has thy share with me, but I hope the course we have agreed upon will be some ease to us both. Mondays and Fridays, at five o'clock at night, we shall meet in spirit till we meet in person. Yet, if all these hopes should fail, blessed be our God, that we are assured we shall meet one day, if not as husband and wife, yet in a better condition. Let that stay and comfort thy heart. Neither can the sea drown thy husband, nor enemies destroy, nor any adversity deprive thee of thy husband or children. Therefore I will only take thee now and my sweet children in mine arms, and kiss and embrace you all, and so leave you with my God. Farewell, farewell. I bless you all in the name of the Lord Jesus. . . .

    Thine wheresoever,

                John Winthrop

From aboard the Arbella, riding at the Cowes, March 28, 1630

John Winthrop to His Wife

To my very loving Wife, Mrs. Winthrop, the elder,
  at Groton, in Suffolk.

My Love, my Joy, my faithful One, . . .

    I am uncertain whether I shall have opportunity to send these to thee; for, if the wind turn, we shall soon be gone. Therefore I will not write much. I know it will be sufficient for thy present comfort, to hear of our welfare; and this is the third letter I have written to thee, since I came to Hampton, in requital of those two I received from thee, which I do often read with much delight, apprehending so much love and sweet affection in them, as I am never satisfied with reading, nor can read them without tears; but whether they proceed from joy, sorrow, or desire, or from that consent of affection, which I always hold with thee, I cannot conceive. Ah, my dear heart, I ever held thee in high esteem, as thy love and goodness hath well deserved; but (if it be possible) I shall yet prize thy virtue at a greater rate, and long more to enjoy thy sweet society than ever before. I am sure thou art not short of me in this desire. Let us pray hard, and pray in faith, and our God, in his good time, will accomplish our desire. Oh, how loath am I to bid thee farewell! but, since it must be, farewell, my sweet love, farewell. Farewell, my dear children and family. The Lord bless you all, and grant me to see your faces once again. Come, (my dear,) take him and let him rest in thine arms, who will ever remain,

    Thy faithful husband,

John Winthrop

From aboard the Arbella, riding before Yarmouth, in the Isle of Wight,
April 3, 1630

11

The African Slave Trade

Olaudah Equiano

The Life of Olaudah Equiano, or Gustavus Vassa, the African, Written by Himself *is one of the most important eyewitness accounts of the African slave trade. While scholars have long agreed on the horrors of the trade and the accuracy of Equiano's description, they have argued for more than a century over how many people were involved. Estimates range from about nine and a half million to nearly fifteen million Africans imported into the Western Hemisphere. And this does not include those who were killed while resisting capture or who died during passage.*

Equiano's book is also the pioneering African American narrative of the journey from slavery to freedom, setting many of the conventions for the more than six thousand subsequent interviews, essays, and books by which former slaves told their dramatic stories. And the book, a best seller that has gone through many editions since it was first published in London in 1789, is also a remarkable adventure story recounting Equiano's travels in Africa, Europe, and America as well as his part in expeditions to the Arctic and Turkey and his service in the Seven Years' War.

Equiano (c. 1750–1797), an Ibo prince kidnapped into slavery when he was eleven years old, was brought first to Barbados and then sent to Virginia. After service in the British navy, he was at last sold to a Quaker merchant who allowed Equiano to purchase his freedom in 1766. In later years he worked to advance the Church of England, his adopted religion, and to abolish the slave trade.

BEFORE YOU READ

1. Describe the treatment of slaves in the slave trade.
2. What were Equiano's greatest fears during passage?
3. Equiano asks, "Learned you this from your God, who says unto you, Do unto all men as you would men should do unto you?" How would a slave trader have answered his question?

The first object which saluted my eyes when I arrived on the [Western Africa] coast, was the sea, and a slave ship, which was then riding at anchor, and waiting for its cargo. These filled me with astonishment, which was soon converted

Olaudah Equiano, *The Life of Olaudah Equiano, or Gustavus Vassa, the African, Written by Himself* (New York: Isaac Knapp, 1837), pp. 41–52.

into terror, when I was carried on board. I was immediately handled, and tossed up to see if I were sound, by some of the crew; and I was now persuaded that I had gotten into a world of bad spirits, and that they were going to kill me. Their complexions, too, differing so much from ours, their long hair, and the language they spoke, (which was very different from any I had ever heard) united to confirm me in this belief. Indeed, such were the horrors of my views and fears at the moment, that, if ten thousand worlds had been my own, I would have freely parted with them all to have exchanged my condition with that of the meanest slave in my own country. When I looked round the ship too, and saw a large furnace of copper boiling, and a multitude of black people of every description chained together, every one of their countenances expressing dejection and sorrow, I no longer doubted of my fate; and, quite overpowered with horror and anguish, I fell motionless on the deck and fainted. When I recovered a little, I found some black people about me, who I believed were some of those who had brought me on board, and had been receiving their pay; they talked to me in order to cheer me, but all in vain. I asked them if we were not to be eaten by those white men with horrible looks, red faces, and long hair. They told me I was not: and one of the crew brought me a small portion of spirituous liquor in a wine glass, but, being afraid of him, I would not take it out of his hand. One of the blacks, therefore, took it from him and gave it to me, and I took a little down my palate, which, instead of reviving me, as they thought it would, threw me into the greatest consternation at the strange feeling it produced, having never tasted any such liquor before. Soon after this, the blacks who brought me on board went off, and left me abandoned to despair.

I now saw myself deprived of all chance of returning to my native country, or even the least glimpse of hope of gaining the shore, which I now considered as friendly; and I even wished for my former slavery in preference to my present situation, which was filled with horrors of every kind, still heightened by my ignorance of what I was to undergo. I was not long suffered to indulge my grief; I was soon put down under the decks, and there I received such a salutation in my nostrils as I had never experienced in my life: so that, with the loathsomeness of the stench, and crying together, I became so sick and low that I was not able to eat, nor had I the least desire to taste any thing. I now wished for the last friend, death, to relieve me; but soon, to my grief, two of the white men offered me eatables; and, on my refusing to eat, one of them held me fast by the hands, and laid me across, I think the windlass, and tied my feet, while the other flogged me severely. I had never experienced any thing of this kind before, and although not being used to the water, I naturally feared that element the first time I saw it, yet, nevertheless, could I have got over the nettings, I would have jumped over the side, but I could not; and besides, the crew used to watch us very closely who were not chained down to the decks, lest we should leap into the water; and I have seen some of these poor African prisoners most severely cut, for attempting to do so, and hourly whipped for not eating. This indeed was often the case with myself. In a little time after, amongst the poor chained men, I found some of my own nation, which in a small degree gave ease to my mind. I inquired of these what was to be done with us? they gave me to understand, we were to be carried to these white people's country to work for them. I then was a little revived, and thought, if it were no worse than working, my situation was not so desperate; but still I feared I should be put to death, the white people looked and acted, as I thought, in so savage a manner; for I had never seen among any people such instances of brutal cruelty; and this not only shown towards us blacks, but also to some of the whites themselves. One white man in particular I saw, when we were permitted to be on deck, flogged so unmercifully with a large rope near the foremast, that he died in consequence of it; and they tossed him over the side as they would have done a brute. This made me fear these people the more; and I expected nothing less than to be treated in the same manner. I could not help expressing my fears and apprehensions to some of my countrymen; I asked them if these people had no country, but lived in this hollow place? (the ship) they told me they did not, but came from a distant one. "Then," said I, "how comes it in all our country we never heard of them?" They told me because they lived so very far off. I then asked where were their women? Had they any like themselves? I was told they had. "And why," said I, "do we not see them?" They answered, because they were left behind. I asked how the vessel could go? They told me they could not tell; but that there was cloth put upon the masts by the help of the ropes I saw, and then the vessel went on; and the white men had some spell or magic they put in the water when they liked, in order to stop the vessel. I was exceedingly amazed at this account, and really thought they were spirits. I therefore wished much to be from amongst them, for I expected they would sacrifice me; but my wishes were vain — for we were so quartered that it was impossible for any of us to make our escape.

While we stayed on the coast I was mostly on deck; and one day, to my great astonishment, I saw one of these vessels coming in with the sails up. As soon as the whites saw it, they gave a great shout, at which we were amazed; and the more so, as the vessel appeared larger by approaching nearer. At last, she came to an anchor in my sight, and when the anchor was let go, I and my countrymen who saw it, were lost in astonishment to observe the vessel stop — and were now convinced it was done by magic. Soon after this the other ship got her boats out, and they came on board of us, and the people of both ships seemed very glad to see each other. — Several of the strangers also shook hands with us black people, and made motions with their hands, signifying I suppose, we were to go to their country, but we did not understand them.

At last, when the ship we were in, had got in all her cargo, they made ready with many fearful noises, and we were all put under deck, so that we could not see how they managed the vessel. But this disappointment was the least of my sorrow. The stench of the hold while we were on the coast was so intolerably loathsome, that it was dangerous to remain there for any time, and some of us had been permitted to stay on the deck for the fresh air; but now that the whole ship's cargo were confined together, it became absolutely pestilential. The closeness of the place, and the heat of the climate, added to the number in the ship, which was so crowded that each had scarcely room to turn himself, almost suffocated us. This produced copious perspirations, so that the air soon became unfit for respiration, from a variety of loathsome smells, and brought on a sickness among the slaves, of which many died — thus falling victims to the improvident avarice, as I may call it, of their purchasers. This wretched situation was again aggravated by the galling of the chains, now became insupportable; and the filth of the necessary tubs, into which the children often fell, and were almost suffocated. The shrieks of the women, and the groans of the dying, rendered the whole a scene of horror almost inconceivable. Happily perhaps, for myself, I was soon reduced so low here that it was thought necessary to keep me almost always on deck; and from my extreme youth I was not put in fetters. In this situation I expected every hour to share the fate of my companions, some of whom were almost daily brought upon deck at the point of death, which I began to hope would soon put an end to my miseries. Often did I think many of the inhabitants of the deep much more happy than myself. I envied them the freedom they enjoyed, and as often wished I could change my condition for theirs. Every circumstance I met with, served only to render my state more painful, and heightened my apprehensions, and my opinion of the cruelty of the whites.

One day they had taken a number of fishes; and when they had killed and satisfied themselves with as many as they thought fit, to our astonishment who were on deck, rather than give any of them to us to eat, as we expected, they tossed the remaining fish into the sea again, although we begged and prayed for some as well as we could, but in vain; and some of my countrymen, being pressed by hunger, took an opportunity, when they thought no one saw them, of trying to get a little privately; but they were discovered, and the attempt procured them some very severe floggings. One day, when we had a smooth sea and moderate wind, two of my wearied countrymen who were chained together, (I was near them at the time,) preferring death to such a life of misery, somehow made through the nettings and jumped into the sea: immediately, another quite dejected fellow, who, on account of his illness, was suffered to be out of irons, also followed their example; and I believe many more would very soon have done the same, if they had not been prevented by the ship's crew, who were instantly alarmed. Those of us that were the most active, were in a moment put down under the deck, and there was such a noise and confusion amongst the people of the ship as I never heard before, to stop her, and get the boat out to go after the slaves. However, two of the wretches were drowned, but they got the other, and afterward flogged him unmercifully, for thus attempting to prefer death to slavery. In this manner we continued to undergo more hardships than I can now relate, hardships which are inseparable from this accursed trade. Many a time we were near suffocation from the want of fresh air, which we were often without for whole days together. This, and the stench of the necessary tubs, carried off many.

During our passage, I first saw flying fishes, which surprised me very much; they used frequently to fly across the ship, and many of them fell on the deck. I also now first saw the use of the quadrant; I had often with astonishment seen the mariners make observations with it, and I could not think what it meant. They at last took notice of my surprise; and one of them, willing to increase it, as well as to gratify my curiosity, made me one day look through it. The clouds appeared to me to be land, which disappeared as they passed along. This heightened my wonder; and I was now more persuaded than ever, that I was in another world, and that every thing about me was magic. At last, we came in sight of the island of Barbados, at which the whites on board gave a great shout, and made many signs of joy to us. We did not know what to think of this; but as the vessel drew nearer, we plainly saw the harbor, and other ships of different kinds and sizes, and we soon anchored amongst them, off Bridgetown. Many merchants and planters now came on board, though it was in the evening. They put us in separate parcels, and examined us attentively. They also made us jump, and pointed to the land, signifying we were to go there. We thought by this, we should be eaten by these ugly men, as they appeared to us; and, when soon after we were all put down under the deck again, there was much dread and trembling among us, and nothing but bitter cries to be heard all the night from these apprehensions, insomuch, that at last the white people got some old slaves from the land to pacify us. They told us we were not to be eaten, but to work, and were soon to go on land, where we should see many of our country people. This report eased us much. And sure enough, soon after we were landed, there came to us Africans of all languages.

We were conducted immediately to the merchant's yard, where we were all pent up together, like so many sheep in a fold, without regard to sex or age. As every object was new to me, every thing I saw filled me with surprise. What struck me first, was, that the houses were built with bricks and stories, and in every other respect different from those I had seen in Africa; but I was still more astonished on seeing people on horseback. I did not know what this could mean; and, indeed, I thought these people were full of nothing but magical arts. While I was in this astonishment, one of my fellow-prisoners spoke to a countryman of his, about the horses, who said they were the same kind they had in their country. I understood them, though they were from a distant part of Africa; and I thought it odd I had not seen any horses there; but afterwards, when I came to converse with different Africans, I found they had many horses amongst them, and much larger than those I then saw.

We were not many days in the merchant's custody before we were sold after their usual manner, which is this:—On a signal given, (as the beat of a drum,) the buyers rush at once into the yard where the slaves are confined, and make choice of that parcel they like best. The noise and clamor with which this is attended, and the eagerness visible in the countenances of the buyers, serve not a little to increase the apprehension of terrified Africans, who may well be supposed to consider them as the ministers of that destruction to which they think themselves devoted. In this manner, without scruple, are relations and friends separated, most of them never to see each other again. I remember, in the vessel in which I was brought over, in the men's apartment, there were several brothers, who, in the sale, were sold in different lots; and it was very moving on this occasion, to see and hear their cries at parting. O, ye nominal Christians! might not an African ask you—Learned you this from your God, who says unto you, Do unto all men as you would men should do unto you? Is it not enough that we are torn from our country and friends, to toil for your luxury and lust of gain? Must every tender feeling be likewise sacrificed to your avarice? Are the dearest friends and relations, now rendered more dear by their separation from their kindred, still to be parted from each other, and thus prevented from cheering the gloom of slavery, with the small comfort of being together, and mingling their sufferings and sorrows? Why are parents to lose their children, brothers their sisters, or husbands their wives? Surely, this is a new refinement in cruelty, which, while it has no advantage to atone for it, thus aggravates distress, and adds fresh horrors even to the wretchedness of slavery.

12

On the Misfortune
of Indentured Servants

Gottlieb Mittelberger

Indentured, or bonded, servants were an important source of labor in seventeenth- and eighteenth-century America. The term generally refers to immigrants who, in return for passage from Europe to America, bound themselves to work in America for a number of years, after which time they would become completely free. The practice was closely related to the tradition of apprenticeship, in which a youth was assigned to work for a master in a trade for a certain number of years and in return was taught the skills of that trade. Convicts were another important source of colonial labor; thousands of English criminals were sentenced to labor in the colonies for a specified period, after which they were freed.

Many indentured servants had valuable skills that they hoped to make better use of in the New World than they had been able to do at home. Some in fact did just that, while others, as Gottlieb Mittelberger describes, did not fare well. Mittelberger came to Pennsylvania from Germany in 1750. His own fortunes were not so bleak as those of his shipmates. He served as a schoolmaster and organist in Philadelphia for three years and then returned to Germany in 1754.

BEFORE YOU READ

1. Why do you think immigrants chose to endure the miseries of a transatlantic passage to come to the New World?

2. How did the treatment of indentured servants described by Mittelberger compare to the treatment of slaves in the slave trade described in the previous reading?

3. What happened to children whose parents died during the journey?

4. Why do you think Mittelberger returned to Germany?

Both in Rotterdam and in Amsterdam the people are packed densely, like herrings so to say, in the large sea-vessels. One person receives a place of scarcely 2 feet width and 6 feet length in the bedstead, while many a ship carries four to six hundred souls; not to mention the innumerable implements, tools, provisions, water-barrels and other things which likewise occupy much space.

Gottlieb Mittelberger, *Journey to Pennsylvania in the Year 1750 and Return to Germany in the Year 1754*, trans. Carl Theo (Philadelphia: John Joseph McVey, 1898), pp. 19–29.

On account of contrary winds it takes the ships sometimes 2, 3 and 4 weeks to make the trip from Holland to . . . England. But when the wind is good, they get there in 8 days or even sooner. Everything is examined there and the custom-duties paid, whence it comes that the ships ride there 8, 10 to 14 days and even longer at anchor, till they have taken in their full cargoes. During that time every one is compelled to spend his last remaining money and to consume his little stock of provisions which had been reserved for the sea; so that most passengers, finding themselves on the ocean where they would be in greater need of them, must greatly suffer from hunger and want. Many suffer want already on the water between Holland and Old England.

When the ships have for the last time weighed their anchors near the city of Kaupp [Cowes] in Old England, the real misery begins with the long voyage. For from there the ships, unless they have good wind, must often sail 8, 9, 10 to 12 weeks before they reach Philadelphia. But even with the best wind the voyage lasts 7 weeks.

But during the voyage there is on board these ships terrible misery, stench, fumes, horror, vomiting, many kinds of sea-sickness, fever, dysentery, headache, heat, constipation, boils, scurvy, cancer, mouth-rot, and the like, all of which come from old and sharply salted food and meat, also from very bad and foul water, so that many die miserably.

Add to this want of provisions, hunger, thirst, frost, heat, dampness, anxiety, want, afflictions and lamentations, together with other trouble, as . . . the lice abound so frightfully, especially on sick people, that they can be scraped off the body. The misery reaches the climax when a gale rages for 2 or 3 nights and days, so that every one believes that the ship will go to the bottom with all human beings on board. In such a visitation the people cry and pray most piteously.

When in such a gale the sea rages and surges, so that the waves rise often like high mountains one above the other, and often tumble over the ship, so that one fears to go down with the ship; when the ship is constantly tossed from side to side by the storm and waves, so that no one can either walk, or sit, or lie, and the closely packed people in the berths are thereby tumbled over each other, both the sick and the well—it will be readily understood that many of these people, none of whom had been prepared for hardships, suffer so terribly from them that they do not survive it.

I myself had to pass through a severe illness at sea, and I best know how I felt at the time. These poor people often long for consolation, and I often entertained and comforted them with singing, praying and exhorting; and whenever it was possible and the winds and waves permitted it, I kept daily prayer-meetings with them on deck. Besides, I baptized five children in distress, because we had no ordained minister on board. I also held divine service every Sunday by reading sermons to the people; and when the dead were sunk in the water, I commended them and our souls to the mercy of God.

Among the healthy, impatience sometimes grows so great and cruel that one curses the other, or himself and the day of his birth, and sometimes come near killing each other. Misery and malice join each other, so that they cheat and rob one another. One always reproaches the other with having persuaded him to undertake the journey. Frequently children cry out against their parents, husbands against their wives and wives against their husbands, brothers and sisters, friends and acquaintances against each other. But most against the soul-traffickers.

Many sigh and cry: "Oh, that I were at home again, and if I had to lie in my pig-sty!" Or they say: "O God, if I only had a piece of good bread, or a good fresh drop of water." Many people whimper, sigh and cry piteously for their homes; most of them get home-sick. Many hundred people necessarily die and perish in such misery, and must be cast into the sea, which drives their relatives, or those who persuaded them to undertake the journey, to such despair that it is almost impossible to pacify and console them. . . .

No one can have an idea of the sufferings which women in confinement have to bear with their innocent children on board these ships. Few of this class escape with their lives; many a mother is cast into the water with her child as soon as she is dead. One day, just as we had a heavy gale, a woman in our ship, who was to give birth and could not give birth under the circumstances, was pushed through a loop-hole [port-hole] in the ship and dropped into the sea, because she was far in the rear of the ship and could not be brought forward.

Children from 1 to 7 years rarely survive the voyage. I witnessed . . . misery in no less than 32 children in our ship, all of whom were thrown into the sea. The parents grieve all the more since their children find no resting-place in the earth, but are devoured by the monsters of the sea.

That most of the people get sick is not surprising, because, in addition to all other trials and hardships, warm food is served only three times a week, the rations being very poor and very little. Such meals can hardly be eaten, on account of being so unclean. The water which is served out on the ships is often very black, thick and full of worms, so that one cannot drink it without loathing, even with the greatest thirst. Toward the end we were compelled to eat the ship's biscuit which had been spoiled long ago; though in a whole biscuit there was scarcely a piece the size of a dollar that had not been full of red worms and spiders' nests. . . .

At length, when, after a long and tedious voyage, the ships come in sight of land, so that the promontories can be seen, which the people were so eager and anxious to see, all creep from below on deck to see the land from afar, and they weep for joy, and pray and sing, thanking and praising God. The sight of the land makes the people on board the ship, especially the sick and the half dead, alive again, so that their hearts leap within them; they shout and rejoice, and are content to bear their misery in patience, in the hope that they may soon reach the land in safety. But alas!

When the ships have landed at Philadelphia after their long voyage, no one is permitted to leave them except those who pay for their passage or can give good security; the others, who cannot pay, must remain on board the ships till they are purchased, and are released from the ships by their purchasers. The sick always fare the worst, for the healthy are naturally preferred and purchased first; and so the sick and wretched must often remain on board in front of the city for 2 or 3 weeks, and frequently die, whereas many a one, if he could pay his debt and were permitted to leave the ship immediately, might recover and remain alive.

The sale of human beings in the market on board the ship is carried on thus: Every day Englishmen, Dutchmen, and High-German people come from the city of Philadelphia and other places, in part from a great distance, say 20, 30, or 40 hours away, and go on board the newly arrived ship that has brought and offers for sale passengers from Europe, and select among the healthy persons such as they deem suitable for their business, and bargain with them how long they will serve for their passage money, which most of them are still in debt for. When they have come to an agreement, it happens that adult persons bind themselves in writing to serve 3, 4, 5, or 6 years for the amount due by them, according to their age and strength. But very young people, from 10 to 15 years, must serve till they are 21 years old.

Many parents must sell and trade away their children like so many head of cattle; for if their children take the debt upon themselves, the parents can leave the ship free and unrestrained; but as the parents often do not know where and to what people their children are going, it often happens that such parents and children, after leaving the ship, do not see each other again for many years, perhaps no more in all their lives.

It often happens that whole families, husband, wife, and children, are separated by being sold to different purchasers, especially when they have not paid any part of their passage money.

When a husband or wife has died at sea, when the ship has made more than half of her trip, the survivor must pay or serve not only for himself or herself, but also for the deceased.

When both parents have died over half-way at sea, their children, especially when they are young and have nothing to pawn or to pay, must stand for their own and their parents' passage, and serve till they are 21 years old. When one has served his or her term, he or she is entitled to a new suit of clothes at parting; and if it has been so stipulated, a man gets in addition a horse, a woman, a cow.

When a serf has an opportunity to marry in this country, he or she must pay for each year which he or she would have yet to serve, 5 to 6 pounds. But many a one who has thus purchased and paid for his bride, has subsequently repented his bargain, so that he would gladly have returned his exorbitantly dear ware, and lost the money besides.

If some one in this country runs away from his master, who has treated him harshly, he cannot get far. Good provision has been made for such cases, so that a runaway is soon recovered. He who detains or returns a deserter receives a good reward.

If such a runaway has been away from his master one day, he must serve for it as a punishment a week, for a week a month, and for a month half a year.

13

A Man of the American Enlightenment
Benjamin Franklin

The new science of the Enlightenment, epitomized by Isaac Newton's Philosophiae Naturalis Principia Mathematica *(1687), profoundly influenced the outlook of educated people in eighteenth-century Europe and North America alike, including the leaders of the patriot cause in colonial America. Fundamental to the world view of people like Benjamin Franklin (1725–1802) was a belief in the power of human reason to understand the laws of nature, to improve human life, and to establish rational governments and a code of moral conduct.*

Franklin exemplified Enlightenment thinking in America. He was a scientist studying the natural laws of electricity; an inventor improving human life through such inventions as the lightning rod, the Franklin stove, and bifocals; a philanthropist organizing libraries and scientific societies to spread secular scientific knowledge; a journalist advancing popular learning; a reformer improving fire prevention and other civic needs; and the author of an autobiography unlike anything that had preceded it in its didactic yet thoroughly secular account of his own remarkable moral development.

BEFORE YOU READ

1. Why is Benjamin Franklin considered the supreme representative of the American Enlightenment?

2. Why did Franklin perform so many public services? What view of the world was the basis of his activities?

3. Why did Franklin decide not to answer the criticisms of Abbé Nollet? What does this decision indicate about his understanding of the scientific method?

I should have mentioned before, that in the Autumn of the preeceding Year [1727] I had formed most of my ingenious Acquaintance into a Club of mutual Improvement, which we called the Junto. We met on Friday Evenings. The Rules I drew up required that every member in his Turn should produce one or more Queries on any Point of Morals, Politics or Natural Philosophy, to be discussed by the Company, and once in three Months produce and read an Essay of his own Writing on any Subject he pleased. Our Debates were to be under

Benjamin Franklin, "Autobiography," in Frank Luther Mott and Chester E. Jorgenson, eds., *Benjamin Franklin: Representative Selections* (New York: American Book Company, 1936), pp. 58, 68–70, 84–89, 92–95.

the Direction of a President and to be conducted in the sincere Spirit of Enquiry after Truth, without Fondness for Dispute, or Desire of Victory; and to
prevent Warmth all Expressions of Positiveness in Opinions or direct
Contradiction, were after some time made contraband and prohibited under
small pecuniary Penalties. . . .

And now I sent on foot my first Project of a public Nature, [th]at for a Subscription Library. [I] drew up the Proposals, got them put into Form by our
great Scrivener Brockden, and by the help of my Friends in the Junto, procur'd
Fifty Subscribers . . . for 50 Years, the Term our Company was to continue. We
afterwards obtain'd a Charter, the Company being increas'd to 100. This was
the Mother of all the N American Subscription Libraries now so numerous, is
become a great thing itself, and continually increasing.—These Libraries have
improv'd the general Conversation of the Americans, made the common
Tradesmen and Farmers as intelligent as most Gentlemen from other Countries, and perhaps have contributed in some degree to the Stand so generally
made throughout the Colonies in Defence of their Privileges. . . .

I had been religiously educated as a Presbyterian; and tho' some of the dog-
mas of that persuasion, such as *the eternal decrees of God, election, reprobation, etc.*,
appeared to me unintelligible, others doubtful, and I early absented myself from
the public assemblies of the sect, Sunday being my studying day, I never was
without some religious principles. I never doubted, for instance, the existence
of the Deity; that he made the world, and govern'd it by his Providence; that
the most acceptable service of God was the doing good to man; that our souls
are immortal; and that all crime will be punished, and virtue rewarded, either
here or hereafter. These I esteem'd the essentials of every religion; and, being
to be found in all the religions we had in our country, I respected them all, tho'
with different degrees of respect, as I found them more or less mix'd with other
articles, which, without any tendency to inspire, promote, or confirm morality,
serv'd principally to divide us, and make us unfriendly to one another. . . .

In 1732 I first publish'd my Almanack, under the name of *Richard Saunders;* it
was continu'd by me about twenty-five years, commonly call'd *Poor Richard's Almanack.* I endeavour'd to make it both entertaining and useful, and it accordingly
came to be in such demand, that I reap'd considerable profit from it, vending annually near ten thousand. And observing that it was generally read, scarce any
neighborhood in the province being without it, I consider'd it as a proper vehicle
for conveying instruction among the common people, who bought scarcely any
other books; I therefore filled all the little spaces that occurr'd between the remarkable days in the calendar with proverbial sentences, chiefly such as inculcated industry and frugality, as the means of procuring wealth, and thereby
securing virtue; it being more difficult for a man in want, to act always honestly,
as, to use here one of those proverbs, *it is hard for an empty sack to stand upright.*

These proverbs, which contained the wisdom of many ages and nations, I assembled and form'd into a connected discourse prefix'd to the Almanack of 1757,
as the harangue of a wise old man to the people attending an auction. The bringing all these scatter'd counsels thus into a focus enabled them to make greater

impression. The piece, being universally approved, was copied in all the newspapers of the Continent; reprinted in Britain on a broad side, to be stuck up in houses; two translations were made of it in French, and great numbers bought by the clergy and gentry, to distribute gratis among their poor parishioners and tenants. In Pennsylvania, as it discouraged useless expense in foreign superfluities, some thought it had its share of influence in producing that growing plenty of money which was observable for several years after its publication.

I considered my newspaper, also, as another means of communicating instruction, and in that view frequently reprinted in it extracts from the Spectator, and other moral writers; and sometimes publish'd little pieces of my own, which had been first compos'd for reading in our Junto. . . .

In the conduct of my newspaper, I carefully excluded all libelling and personal abuse, which is of late years become so disgraceful to our country. Whenever I was solicited to insert any thing of that kind, and the writers pleaded, as they generally did, the liberty of the press, and that a newspaper was like a stage-coach, in which any one who would pay had a right to a place, my answer was, that I would print the piece separately if desired, and the author might have as many copies as he pleased to distribute himself, but that I would not take upon me to spread his detraction; and that, having contracted with my subscribers to furnish them with what might be either useful or entertaining, I could not fill their papers with private altercation, in which they had no concern, without doing them manifest injustice. Now, many of our printers make no scruple of gratifying the malice of individuals by false accusations of the fairest characters among ourselves, augmenting animosity even to the producing of duels; and are, moreover, so indiscreet as to print scurrilous reflections on the government of neighboring states, and even on the conduct of our best national allies, which may be attended with the most pernicious consequences. These things I mention as a caution to young printers, and that they may be encouraged not to pollute their presses and disgrace their profession by such infamous practices, but refuse steadily, as they may see by my example that such a course of conduct will not, on the whole, be injurious to their interests. . . .

Our club, the Junto, was found so useful, and afforded such satisfaction to the members, that several were desirous of introducing their friends, which could not well be done without exceeding what we had settled as a convenient number, viz., twelve. We had from the beginning made it a rule to keep our institution a secret, which was pretty well observ'd; the intention was to avoid applications of improper persons for admittance, some of whom, perhaps, we might find it difficult to refuse. I was one of those who were against any addition to our number, but, instead of it, made in writing a proposal, that every member separately should endeavour to form a subordinate club, with the same rules respecting queries, etc., and without informing them of the connection with the Junto. The advantages proposed were, the improvement of so many more young citizens by the use of our institutions; our better acquaintance with the general sentiments of the inhabitants on any occasion, as the Junto member might propose what queries we should desire, and was to report to the Junto what pass'd in his separate club; the promotion of our particular interests in business by more extensive recommendation, and the increase of our influence in public affairs, and our power of doing good by spreading thro' the several clubs the sentiments of the Junto.

The project was approv'd, and every member undertook to form his club, but they did not all succeed. Five or six only were compleated, which were called by different names, as the Vine, the Union, the Band, etc. They were useful to themselves, and afforded us a good deal of amusement, information, and instruction, besides answering, in some considerable degree, our views of influencing the public opinion on particular occasions, of which I shall give some instances in course of time as they happened.

I began now to turn my thoughts a little to public affairs, beginning, however, with small matters. . . .

About this time I wrote a paper (first to be read in Junto, but it was afterward publish'd) on the different accidents and carelessnesses by which houses were set on fire, with cautions against them, and means proposed of avoiding them. This was much spoken of as a useful piece, and gave rise to a project, which soon followed it, of forming a company for the more ready extinguishing of fires, and mutual assistance in removing and securing of goods when in danger. Associates in this scheme were presently found, amounting to thirty. Our articles of agreement oblig'd every member to keep always in good order, and fit for use, a certain number of leather buckets, with strong bags and baskets (for packing and transporting of goods), which were to be brought to every fire; and we agreed to meet once a month and spend a social evening together, in discoursing and communicating such ideas as occurred to us upon the subject of fires, as might be useful in our conduct on such occasions.

The utility of this institution soon appeared, and many more desiring to be admitted than we thought convenient for one company, they were advised to form another, which was accordingly done; and this went on, one new company being formed after another, till they became so numerous as to include most of the inhabitants who were men of property; and now, at the time of my writing this, tho' upward of fifty years since its establishment, that which I first formed, called the Union Fire Company, still subsists and flourishes, tho' the first members are all deceas'd but myself and one, who is older by a year than I am. The small fines that have been paid by members for absence at the monthly meetings have been apply'd to the purchase of fire-engines, ladders, fire-hooks, and other useful implements for each company, so that I question whether there is a city in the world better provided with the means of putting a stop to beginning conflagrations; and, in fact, since these institutions, the city has never lost by fire more than one or two houses at a time, and the flames have often been extinguished before the house in which they began has been half consumed. . . .

I had, on the whole, abundant reason to be satisfied with my being established in Pennsylvania. There were, however, two things that I regretted, there being no provision for defense, nor for a compleat education of youth; no militia, nor any college. . . .

The first step [toward establishing a college] I took was to associate in the design a number of active friends, of whom the Junto furnished a good part; the next was to write and publish a pamphlet, entitled *Proposals Relating to the Education of Youth in Pennsylvania*. This I distributed among the principal inhabitants gratis, and as soon as I could suppose their minds a little prepared by the perusal of it, I set on foot a subscription for opening and supporting an academy; it was to be paid in quotas yearly for five years; by so dividing it, I judg'd the subscription might be larger, and I believe it was so, amounting to no less, if I remember right, than five thousand pounds.

In the introduction to these proposals, I stated their publication, not as an act of mine, but of some *publick-spirited gentlemen,* avoiding as much as I could, according to my usual rule, the presenting myself to the publick as the author of any scheme for their benefit.

The subscribers, to carry the project into immediate execution, chose out of their number twenty-four trustees, and appointed Mr. Francis, then attorney-general, and myself to draw up constitutions for the government of the academy; which being done and signed, a house was hired, masters engag'd, and the schools opened, I think, in the same year, 1749.

In 1746, being at Boston, I met there with a Dr. Spence, who was lately arrived from Scotland, and show'd me some electric experiments. They were imperfectly perform'd, as he was not very expert; but, being on a subject quite new to me, they equally surpris'd and pleased me. Soon after my return to Philadelphia, our library company receiv'd from Mr. P. Collinson, Fellow of the Royal Society of London, a present of a glass tube, with some account of the use of it in making such experiments. I eagerly seized the opportunity of repeating what I had seen at Boston; and, by much practice, acquir'd great readiness in performing those, also, which we had an account of from England, adding a number of new ones. I say much practice, for my house was continually full, for some time, with people who came to see these new wonders.

To divide a little this incumbrance among my friends, I caused a number of similar tubes to be blown at our glass-house, with which they furnish'd themselves, so that we had at length several performers. Among these, the principal was Mr. Kinnersley, an ingenious neighbor, who, being out of business, I encouraged to undertake showing the experiments for money, and drew up for him two lectures, in which the experiments were rang'd in such order, and accompanied with such explanations in such method, as that the foregoing should assist in comprehending the following. He procur'd an elegant apparatus for the purpose, in which all the little machines that I had roughly made for myself were nicely form'd by instrument-makers. His lectures were well attended, and gave great satisfaction; and after some time he went thro' the colonies, exhibiting them in every capital town, and pick'd up some money. In the West India

Islands, indeed, it was with difficulty the experiments could be made, from the general moisture of the air.

Oblig'd as we were to Mr. Collinson for his present of the tube, etc., I thought it right he should be inform'd of our success in using it, and wrote him several letters containing accounts of our experiments. He got them read in the Royal Society, where they were not at first thought worth so much notice as to be printed in their Transactions. . . .

It was, however, some time before those papers were much taken notice of in England. A copy of them happening to fall into the hands of the Count de Buffon, a philosopher deservedly of great reputation in France, and, indeed, all over Europe, he prevailed with M. Dalibard to translate them into French, and they were printed at Paris. The publication offended the Abbé Nollet, preceptor in Natural Philosophy to the royal family, and an able experimenter, who had form'd and publish'd a theory of electricity, which then had the general vogue. He could not at first believe that such a work came from America, and said it must have been fabricated by his enemies at Paris, to decry his system. Afterwards, having been assur'd that there really existed such a person as Franklin at Philadelphia, which he had doubted, he wrote and published a volume of Letters, chiefly address'd to me, defending his theory, and denying the verity of my experiments, and of the positions deduc'd from them.

I once purpos'd answering the abbé, and actually began the answer; but, on consideration that my writings contain'd a description of experiments which any one might repeat and verify, and if not to be verifi'd, could not be defended; or of observations offer'd as conjectures, and not delivered dogmatically, therefore not laying me under any obligation to defend them; and reflecting that a dispute between two persons, writing in different languages, might be lengthened greatly by mistranslations, and thence misconceptions of one another's meaning, much of one of the abbé's letters being founded on an error in the translation, I concluded to let my papers shift for themselves, believing it was better to spend what time I could spare from public business in making new experiments, than in disputing about those already made. I therefore never answered M. Nollet, and the event gave me no cause to repent my silence; for my friend M. le Roy, of the Royal Academy of Sciences, took up my cause and refuted him; my book was translated into the Italian, German, and Latin languages; and the doctrine it contain'd was by degrees universally adopted by the philosophers of Europe, in preference to that of the abbé.

14

Leaving an Abusive Husband
Abigail Abbot Bailey

Memoirs of Mrs. Abigail Bailey, *originally published in 1815, is the first American autobiography detailing family violence and abuse. Abigail Abbot Bailey (1746–1815), a profoundly religious woman after her conversion to Christianity at the age of eighteen, claimed that "God gave me a heart to resolve never to be obstinate, or disobedient to my husband; but to be always kind, obedient, and obliging in all things not contrary to the word of God." However, her marriage to Asa Bailey, which lasted twenty-six years and included the birth of seventeen children, continuously and severely tested this belief. Within a month of the wedding, Asa began physically abusing Abigail so that at times she feared "that he wanted to kill" her. Then within three years he had committed adultery with a servant. A few yeas later he attempted to rape another servant girl but was repulsed and brought into court, only to be released for lack of evidence. After Asa committed incest with their sixteen-year-old daughter, Abigail finally began a painful effort to end the marriage. Seeking to avoid the attendant division of property, Asa persuaded Abigail to accompany him to upstate New York, where he abandoned her far from her family, church friends, and their children. She made a torturous journey back to their home in New Hampshire alone. Then her brothers accompanied her to a justice of the peace, enabling her to have Asa arrested and forcing him into a property settlement and an uncontested "bill of divorcement."*

Bailey based her Memoirs *in part on the diaries she kept throughout much of her marriage, writings largely given over to religious devotions and musings. The minister who edited the manuscript recommended it to "the intelligent reader" who would find "strikingly exhibited" there "the dreadful depravity of fallen man; the abomination of intrigue and deceit; the horrid cruelty, of which man is capable; the hardness of the way of transgressors; . . . and the wisdom of God in turning headlong the devices of the crafty." The modern reader will note as well how difficult it was for a woman of the late eighteenth century to achieve any control over a dreadful situation. As Ann Taves, a modern scholar of the* Memoirs, *writes: "Given the difficulty of obtaining a divorce in practice, if not in theory, in late-eighteenth-century New Hampshire, it is perhaps more surprising that Abigail extricated herself from her marriage at all than that it took her four and a half years to do so."*

BEFORE YOU READ

1. Given the laws and customs of the era, do you think that Abigail Abbot Bailey acted as assertively as she could in dealing with her husband's transgressions?

Ann Taves, ed., *Religion and Domestic Violence in Early New England: The Memoirs of Abigail Abbot Bailey* (Bloomington: Indiana University Press, 1989), pp. 56–58, 68–72, 75–83.

2. What role did religion play in Bailey's life, and how did it influence the way she responded to her domestic situation?

3. What similarities or differences do you see between the situation of the Bailey family and current examples of domestic violence and abuse?

I Abigail Bailey (daughter of Deacon James Abbot of Newbury, Coos, who moved thither from Concord, N.H. A.D. 1763) do now undertake to record some of the dealings of the allwise God with me, in events, which I am sure I ought solemnly to remember, as long as I live.

I shall first, in few words, record the merciful dealings of my heavenly Father, in casting my lot, not only under the gospel, but in a family, where I was ever treated with the greatest kindness by my tender parents; and particularly with the most religious attention from my very pious mother; and where I was ever treated with the greatest tenderness by my brothers and sisters. I can truly say, it was seldom that an angry word was ever spoken in my father's family— by parents, brothers, or sisters—against me, from my infancy, and during my continuance in my father's house. So that I passed the morning of my days in peace and contentment.

April 15, 1767. I was married to Asa Bailey, just after having entered the 22nd year of my age. I now left my dear parents;—hoping to find in my husband a true hearted and constant friend. My desires and hopes were, that we might live together in peace and friendship; seeking each other's true happiness till death. I did earnestly look to God for his blessing upon this solemn undertaking;—sensible, that "Except the Lord build the house, they labor in vain that build it." As, while I lived with my parents, I esteemed it my happiness to be in subjection to them; so now I thought it must be a still greater benefit to be under the aid of a judicious companion, who would rule well his own house. . . .

Relative to my new companion, though I had found no evidence that he was a subject of true religion; yet I did hope and expect, from my acquaintance with him, that he would wish for good regulations in his family, and would have its external order accord with the word of God. But I met with sore disappointment,—I soon found that my new friend was naturally of a hard, uneven, rash temper; and was capable of being very unreasonable. My conviction of this was indeed grievous, and caused me many a sorrowful hour. For such were my feelings and habits, that I knew not how to endure a hard word, or a frowning look from any one; much less from a companion. I now began to learn, with trembling, that it was the sovereign pleasure of the allwise God to try me with afflictions in that relation, from which I had hoped to receive the greatest of my earthly comforts. I had placed my highest worldly happiness in the love, tenderness, and peace of relatives and friends. But before one month, from my marriage day, had passed, I learned that I must expect hard and cruel treatment in my new habitation, and from my new friend. . . .

I think God gave me a heart to resolve never to be obstinate, or disobedient to my husband; but to be always kind, obedient, and obliging in all things not contrary to the word of God. I thought if Mr. B. were sometimes unreasonable, I would be reasonable, and would rather suffer wrong than do wrong. And as I hoped Mr. B. would kindly overlook my infirmities and failings, with which I was conscious I should abound; so I felt a forgiving spirit towards him. Many times his treatment would grieve my heart. But I never was suffered to my knowledge, to return any wickedness in my conduct towards him; nor ever to indulge a revengeful feeling or ill will. For some years I thought his repeated instances of hard treatment of me arose, — not from any settled ill will, or real want of kind affection toward me; — but from the usual depravity of the human heart; and from a want of self-government. I still confided in him, as my real friend, and loved him with increasing affection. . . .

[Her husband is on two occasions unfaithful with servants. He repents both times, but her confidence in him has been eroded.]

Now, alas! I must begin the sad detail of events, the most distressing; and which awfully verified my most fearful apprehensions; and convinced me, that all my trials of life hitherto, were as nothing. . . .

[Her husband concocts a pretext to go away for a lengthy period with a teenage daughter.]

But alas! words fail to set forth the things which followed! All this pretended *plan* was but a specious cover to infernal designs. . . .

I have already related that Mr. B. said he would take one of our sons, and one daughter, to wait on him in his distant tour, before he would take all the family. After he had talked of this for a few days, he said he had altered his plan; he would leave his son, and take only his daughter: he would hire what men's help he needed: his daughter must go and cook for him. He now commenced a new series of conduct in relation to this daughter, whom he selected to go with him, in order (as he pretended) to render himself pleasing and familiar to her; so that she might be willing to go with him, and feel happy: for though, as a father, he had a right to command her to go, yet (he said) he would so conduct toward her, as to make her cheerful and well pleased to go with him. A great part of the time he now spent in the room where she was spinning; and seemed shy of me, and of the rest of the family. He seemed to have forgotten his age, his honor, and all decency, as well as all virtue. He would spend his time with this daughter, in telling idle stories, and foolish riddles, and singing songs to her, and sometimes before the small children, when they were in that room. He thus pursued a course of conduct, which had the most direct tendency to corrupt young and tender minds, and lead them the greatest distance from every serious subject. He would try to make his daughter tell stories with him; wishing to make her free and sociable, and to erase from her mind all that fear and reserve, which he had ever taught his children to feel toward him. He had ever been sovereign, severe and hard with his children, and they stood in the greatest fear of him. His whole conduct, toward this daughter especially, was now changed, and became most disagreeable.

For a considerable time I was wholly at a loss what to think of his conduct, or what his wish or intentions could be. Had such conduct appeared toward any young woman beside his own young daughter, I should have had no question what he intended: but as it now was, I was loth to indulge the least suspicion of base design. His daily conduct forced a conviction upon my alarmed and tortured mind, that his designs were the most vile. All his tender affections were withdrawn from the wife of his youth, the mother of his children. My room was deserted, and left lonely. His care for the rest of his family seemed abandoned, as well as all his attention to his large circle of worldly business. Every thing must lie neglected, while this one daughter engrossed all his attention.

Though all the conduct of Mr. B. from day to day, seemed to demonstrate to my apprehension, that he was determined, and was continually plotting, to ruin this poor young daughter, yet it was so intolerably crossing to every feeling of my soul to admit such a thought, that I strove with all my might to banish it from my mind, and to disbelieve the possibility of such a thing. . . . And such were my infirmities, weakness and fears, (my circumstances being very difficult) that I did not dare to hint any thing of my fears to him, or to any creature. This may to some appear strange; but with me it was then a reality. I labored to divert his mind from his follies, and to turn his attention to things of the greatest importance. But I had the mortification to find that my endeavors were unsuccessful.

I soon perceived that his strange conduct toward this daughter was to her very disagreeable. And she shewed as much unwillingness to be in the room with him, as she dared. I often saw her cheeks bedewed with tears, on account of his new and astonishing behaviour. But as his will had ever been the law of the family, she saw no way to deliver herself from her cruel father. Such were her fears of him, that she did not dare to talk with me, or any other person, upon her situation: for he was exceedingly jealous of my conversing with her, and cautioning her. If I ever dropped words, which I hoped would put her upon her guard, or inquired the cause of her troubles, or what business her father had so much with her? if I was ever so cautious, he would find it out, and be very angry. He watched her and me most narrowly; and by his subtle questions with her, he would find out what I had said, during his absence. He would make her think I had informed him what I had said, and then would be very angry with me: so that at times I feared for my life. I queried with myself which way I could turn. How could I caution a young daughter in such a case? My thoughts flew to God for relief, that the Father of mercies would protect a poor helpless creature marked out for a prey; and turn the heart of a cruel father from every wicked purpose. . . .

The black cloud, rising like a storm of hail, had rolled on, and had gathered over my head. I clearly saw that Mr. B. entertained the most vile intentions relative to his own daughter. Whatever difficulty attended the obtaining of legal proof, yet no remaining doubt existed in my mind, relative to the existence of his wickedness: and I had no doubt remaining of the violence, which he had used; and that hence arose his rage against her. It must have drawn tears of anguish from the eyes of the hardest mortals, to see the barbarous corrections, which he, from time to time, inflicted on this poor young creature; and for no just cause. Sometimes he corrected her with a rod; and sometimes with a beach

stick, large enough for the driving of a team; and with such sternness and anger
sparkling in his eyes, that his visage seemed to resemble an infernal; declaring,
that if she attempted to run from him again, she should never want but one cor-
rection more; for he would whip her to death! This his conduct could be for no
common disobedience; for she had ever been most obedient to him in all lawful
commands. It seemed as though the poor girl must now be destroyed under his
furious hand. She was abashed, and could look no one in the face. . . .

None can describe the anguish of my heart on the beholding of such
scenes. How pitiful must be the case of a poor young female, to be subjected to
such barbarous treatment by her own father; so that she knew of no way of
redress!

It may appear surprising that such wickedness was not checked by legal re-
straints. But great difficulties attend in such a case. While I was fully convinced
of the wickedness, yet I knew not that I could make legal proof. I could not prevail upon this daughter to make known to me her troubles; or to testify against
the author of them. Fear, shame, youthful inexperience, and the terrible peculiarities of her case, all conspired to close her mouth against affording me, or
any one, proper information. My soul was moved with pity for her wretched
case: and yet I cannot say I did not feel a degree of resentment, that she would
not, as she ought, expose the wickedness of her father, that she might be relieved from him, and he brought to due punishment. But no doubt his intrigues,
insinuations, commands, threats, and parental influence, led her to feel that it
was in vain for her to seek redress.

My circumstances, and peculiar bodily infirmities [pregnancy], at that time,
were such as to entitle a woman to the tenderest affection and sympathies of a
companion. On this account, and as Mr. B. was exceeding stern, and angry with
me for entertaining hard thoughts of him, I felt unable to do any thing more for
the relief of my poor daughter. My hope in God was my only support. And I did
abundantly and earnestly commit my cause to him. I felt confident that he would,
in his own time, and as his infinite wisdom should determine, grant relief. . . .

. . . I took an opportunity with Mr. B. alone to have solemn conversation.
My health being now restored, I thought it high time, and had determined, to
adopt a new mode of treatment with Mr. B. I calmly introduced the subject, and
told him, plainly and solemnly, all my views of his wicked conduct, in which he
had long lived with his daughter. He flew into a passion, was high, and seemed
to imagine, he could at once frighten me out of my object. But I was carried
equally above fear, and above temper. Of this I soon convinced him, I let him
know, that the business I now had taken in hand was of too serious a nature, and
too interesting, to be thus disposed of, or dismissed with a few angry words. I
told him I should no longer be turned off in this manner; but should pursue my
object with firmness, and with whatever wisdom and ability God might give me;
and that God would plead my cause, and prosper my present undertaking, as he
should see best. I reminded Mr. B. of my long and unusually distressing illness;
how he had treated me in it; how wicked and cruel he had been to the wife of
his youth; how unable I had been to check him in that awful wickedness, which

I knew he had pursued; that all my inexpressible griefs and solemn entreaties had been by him trampled under foot.

I therefore had not known what to do better than to wait on God as I had done, to afford me strength and opportunity to introduce the means of his effectual control. This time I told him had arrived. And now, if God spared my life, (I told Mr. B.) he should find a new leaf turned over;—and that I would not suffer him to go on any longer as he had done. I would now soon adopt measures to put a stop to his abominable wickedness and cruelties. For this could and ought to be done. And if I did it not, I should be a partaker of his sins, and should aid in bringing down the curse of God upon our family.

By this time Mr. B. had become silent. He appeared struck with some degree of fear. He, by and by, asked me what I intended or expected to do, to bring about such a revolution as I had intimated? whether I knew what an awful crime I had laid to his charge? which he said could not be proved. He wished to know whether I had considered how difficult it would be for me to do any such thing against him? as I was under his legal control; and he could overrule all my plans as he pleased. I told him, I well knew I had been placed under his lawful government and authority, and likewise under his care and protection. And most delightful would it have been to me, to have been able quietly and safely to remain there as long as I lived. Gladly would I have remained a kind faithful, obedient wife to him, as I had ever been. But I told Mr. B. he *knew* he had violated his marriage covenant; and hence had forfeited all legal and just right and authority over me; and I should convince him that I well knew it. I told him I was not in any passion. I acted on principle, and from long and mature consideration. And though it had ever been my greatest care and pleasure (among my earthly comforts) to obey and please him; yet by his most wicked and cruel conduct, he had compelled me to undertake this most undesirable business—of stopping him in his mad career; and that I now felt strength, courage and zeal to pursue my resolution. And if my life was spared, he would find that I should bring something to pass, and probably more than he now apprehended.

As to what I could prove against him I told Mr. B. he knew not how much evidence I had of his unnatural crimes, of which I had accused him, and of which *he knew he was guilty*. I asked him why he should not expect that I should institute a process against him, for that most horrid conduct, which he had long allowed himself to pursue, and with the most indecent and astonishing boldness?

I told him I well knew that he was naturally a man of sense; and that his conscience now fully approved of my conduct.

Mr. B. seeing me thus bold and determinate, soon changed his countenance and conduct. He appeared panic-struck; and he soon became mild, sociable and pleasant. He now made an attempt, with all his usual subtlety, and flatteries to induce me to relinquish my design. He pretended to deny the charge of incest. But I told him I had no confidence in his denial of it; it was therefore in vain! Upon this he said, he really did not blame, or think hard of me, for believing him guilty of this sin. He said, he knew he had behaved foolishly; and had given me full reason to be jealous of him; and he repeated that he did not at all think hard of me for entertaining the views which I had of him. He then took the Bible, and said, he would lay his hand on it, and swear that he was not guilty of the crime laid to his charge. Knowing what I did, I was surprised and disgusted at this impious attempt. I stepped towards him, and in a resolute and solemn manner begged of him to forbear! assuring him, that such an oath could not undo or alter real facts, of which he was conscious. And this proceeding, I assured him, would be so far from giving me any satisfaction, that it would greatly increase the distress of my soul for him in his wickedness. Upon this he forbore, and laid his Bible aside.

Mr. B. now said, he was very sorry he had given me so much reason to think such things of him; and that he had so far destroyed my confidence in him as a man of truth. He then begged of me to forgive all that was past; and he promised that he would ever be kind and faithful to me in future, and never more give me reason to complain of him for any such conduct. I told him, if I had but evidence of his real reformation, I could readily forgive him as a fellow creature, and could plead with God to forgive him. But as to my living with him in the most endearing relation any longer, after such horrid crimes, I did not see that I *could,* or *ought* to do it! He then anxiously made some remarks upon the consequences of my refusing to remain his wife, and seeking a separation from him. These he seemed unable to endure. I remarked, that I well knew it was no small thing for a husband and wife to part, and their family of children to be broken up; that such a separation could not be rendered expedient or lawful, without great sin indeed: and that I would not be the cause of it, and of breaking up our family, for *all the world.* But, said I, you have done all in your power to bring about such a separation, and to ruin and destroy our family. And I meet it as my duty now to do all in my power to save them from further destruction. . . .

But God, in his infinite wisdom, did not see fit that my peculiar trials should end thus. A long and most insupportable series of afflictions still awaited me, to be occasioned by this most perfidious of men.

I again clearly perceived that the same wicked passions, as before, were in operation in Mr. B.'s heart. Alas, "Can the Ethiopian change his skin?" Upon a certain sabbath, I went to meeting. Mr. B. did not go. Before I reached home at night, I met with evidence, which convinced me, that the same horrid conduct had on this holy day been repeated in my family! I rode up to the door. Mr. B. stood waiting for me. He seemed very kind, and was coming to take me tenderly from my horse. I leaped from my saddle, before he had opportunity to reach me. My heart was disgusted at the proffer of his deceitful help. I said nothing upon the dreadful subject this day. Some broken stories of the children corroborated the information I had received. But Mr. B. probably pleased himself with the idea that all was concealed, and he was safe.

The next day, I took him alone, and told him of what he had again been guilty, even after all his vows, and fair promises of fidelity. He started, and seemed very angry, that I should think such a thing [of] him. I told him I charged him only with facts; and hence I was not worthy of his censure! He asked how I knew any such thing? I replied, that the thing was true; and he knew it! And I felt myself under no obligations to inform him how I came by the knowledge of it. If that God, who protects the innocent, and upon whom with his angels he (Mr. B.) had lately so solemnly called to witness his vows of fidelity, had sent an angel to inform me of this renewed perfidy, he had no right to object. But the truth of the thing he knew; and a holy Providence had unfolded it to me. I added, that as he was now renewing my most grievous afflictions, by his unnatural wickedness; and violating his most solemn appeals to God; so he had reason to expect that God (who regards the cry of the afflicted, and relieves those who trust in him) would bring to light his abominable deeds, and deliver an injured wife from such cruel hands. I added, your right hand, which so lately renewed the covenant, is a right hand of falsehood. And, though you did wish and hope to hide from me, and from every eye, that conduct, of which you now know not how to endure the mention; yet God, who seeth in secret, was determined to bring your deeds to light, after all your vain dreams of secrecy. . . .

Mr. B. said he believed there never before was any man, who was so great a fool as he had been! that after I had so kindly settled with him for his past offences, and upon such low and reasonable terms, that he should again move me to jealousy, and thus destroy all my confidence in him. He said he wished he could be set back on the ground he had left, or had remained on so favorable a footing, as that on which I had placed him, in our settlement. I replied, that I really thought too, that he was one of the most foolish of men; that I had long been constrained to view him not only extremely *wicked*, but extremely *foolish!*

I told him he had truly been a wonder to me[;] I had looked upon him with astonishment. He was naturally, I added, a man of sense; he was a man of much knowledge;—had acquired property; and had been a man of considerable note. And that he should thus degrade and ruin himself, soul and body, and destroy a large promising family, as he had done, it was indeed most astonishing! I reminded him that he had been much in good company; and many gentlemen had honored him with their friendly attention. I asked, if any sum of money would induce him to be willing that those gentlemen should know that of him, which I knew? And, that though he seemed to be too willing to throw himself away, as though he were of no worth, I assured him, I did yet set something more by myself, than to be viewed as capable of conniving at such detestable conduct.

Mr. B. replied, that if I had made up my mind no longer to live with him, I need not be at any trouble to obtain a legal separation. For he would depart to some distant country, where I should be troubled with him no more. I remarked, that when Abraham's wife was dead, he wished, however well he had loved her, to have her now buried out of his sight. And, though I could by no means compare him to the pious Sarah; yet, if true virtue and friendship in my husband were dead, I did truly wish him to be removed from my sight. And that true virtue and friendship were indeed dead in him, I thought I had the most melancholy and incontestable evidence.

Our unhappy daughter now became eighteen years of age, and thus legally free from her father. She immediately left us, and returned no more. As she was going, I had solemn conversation with her relative to her father's conduct. She gave me to understand that it had been most abominable. But I could not induce her to consent to become an evidence against him. I plead with her the honor and safety of our family; the safety of her young sisters; and her own duty; but she appeared overwhelmed with shame and grief; and nothing effectual could yet be done.

I hence saw, that in relation to commencing a legal process, God's time seemed not yet to have arrived. I must still wait and look to him to open the path of my duty.

PART THREE

Resistance and Revolution

Struggling for Liberty

The generation that guided the colonies through the revolutionary era was welded together, despite remarkable differences among the colonies and their peoples, by a common commitment to American nationality. That nationality was defined partly by placement in the new continent but also partly by a long-standing British political heritage, which was a major ideological reason for the rupture with Great Britain.

When, after 1763, the English developed restrictive colonial policies to raise revenues for the administration of an enlarged empire that now included India and Canada, the colonists quickly perceived threats to their traditional liberties. Newspapers like the *Boston Gazette and Country Journal* and political leaders and pamphleteers like John Adams directly challenged Great Britain's right to legislate for the colonies. So did many English critics of the mother country's governance of her North American colonies, as is evidenced by the brisk market in England for Paul Revere's engraving of the Boston Massacre. Leaders such as Captain Thomas Preston discovered how the rules of order had changed. Plain people like shoemaker George R. T. Hewes, who took part in both the Boston Massacre and the Boston Tea Party, and Joseph Plumb Martin, who fought throughout the long war, developed new visions of their position in society.

To other colonists, commitment to the British tradition meant adherence to Britain. At least one in six white Americans remained loyal to the king, often at great personal cost, as Philip and Catherine Van Cortlandt's experience illustrated.

For many African and Native Americans, patriot success portended crushed expectations or even disaster. Slaves took desperate risks seeking freedom and suffered when their gamble failed or at best secured freedom at the price of expatriation. Most Native American nations found their strength undermined by the long war and its freeing of the colonists from British restrictions.

The American Revolution challenged long-held convictions that denied the capacity of human beings to use their reason in creating a new form of government. Women like Abigail Adams and Eliza Pinckney reflected this new spirit as vividly as any founding father. Such were the high stakes in the argument raging throughout the colonies over Shays's Rebellion (1786), which offered a prelude to the debates over ratification of the Constitution of the United States. At issue in both was a vision of the American Revolution as one of the climactic events of human history—a demonstration that people of virtue and reason can deliberately establish order and justice.

POINTS OF VIEW

The Boston Massacre (1770)

15

A British Officer's Description

Thomas Preston

Some historians in recent years have stressed the role of the "crowd" in the coming of the American Revolution. Anonymous colonists taking to the streets in the years after 1763 were an important part of the dynamic of revolution.

Firsthand accounts of an event do not necessarily make it easy to determine precisely what occurred. In early 1770 British troops were quartered in Boston. Many townspeople resented their presence, and on March 5 a mob of about sixty attacked a small group of soldiers. In the ensuing disturbance, some soldiers, without orders, fired on the mob, killing five people and wounding eight. The incident was taken up by anti-British radicals—the "patriots"—in Boston, who called it the "Boston Massacre." This selection is the account of the British officer who was tried for murder along with several of his men. John Adams and Josiah Quincy Jr., convinced that anyone accused of a crime should have legal counsel, defended the men. Two of the soldiers were convicted of manslaughter, and the others, including Preston, were acquitted, but the "Massacre" served to inflame anti-British sentiment throughout the colonies.

BEFORE YOU READ

1. What was Captain Preston's view of the Boston crowd?
2. Do you think his soldiers were justified in using violence?
3. Do you think the outcome of the trial was fair?

Merrill Jensen, ed., *English Historical Documents*, vol. 9 (London: Eyre and Spottiswoode, 1955), pp. 750–53.

CAPTAIN THOMAS PRESTON'S ACCOUNT
OF THE BOSTON MASSACRE (MARCH 13, 1770)

It is [a] matter of too great notoriety to need any proofs that the arrival of his Majesty's troops in Boston was extremely obnoxious to its inhabitants. They have ever used all means in their power to weaken the regiments, and to bring them into contempt by promoting and aiding desertions, and with impunity, even where there has been the clearest evidence of the fact, and by grossly and falsely propagating untruths concerning them. On the arrival of the 64th and 65th their ardour seemingly began to abate; it being too expensive to buy off so many, and attempts of that kind rendered too dangerous from the numbers.

And [conflict in the streets of Boston] has ever since their departure been breaking out with greater violence after their embarkation. One of their justices, most thoroughly acquainted with the people and their intentions, on the trial of a man of the 14th Regiment, openly and publicly in the hearing of great numbers of people and from the seat of justice, declared "that the soldiers must now take care of themselves, *nor trust too much to their arms,* for they were but a handful; that the inhabitants carried weapons concealed under their clothes, and would destroy them in a moment, *if they pleased."* This, considering the malicious temper of the people, was an alarming circumstance to the soldiery. Since which several disputes have happened between the townspeople and the soldiers of both regiments, the former being encouraged thereto by the countenance of even some of the magistrates, and by the protection of all the party against government. In general such disputes have been kept too secret from the officers. On the 2d instant two of the 29th going through one Gray's ropewalk, the rope-makers insultingly asked them if they would empty a vault. This unfortunately had the desired effect by provoking the soldiers, and from words they went to blows. Both parties suffered in this affray, and finally the soldiers retired to their quarters. The officers, on the first knowledge of this transaction, took every precaution in their power to prevent any ill consequence. Notwithstanding which, single quarrels could not be prevented, the inhabitants constantly provoking and abusing the soldiery. The insolence as well as utter hatred of the inhabitants to the troops increased daily, insomuch that Monday and Tuesday, the 5th and 6th instant, were privately agreed on for a general engagement, in consequence of which several of the militia came from the country armed to join their friends, menacing to destroy any who should oppose them. This plan has since been discovered.

On Monday night about 8 o'clock two soldiers were attacked and beat. But the party of the townspeople in order to carry matters to the utmost length, broke into two meeting houses and rang the alarm bells, which I supposed was for fire as usual, but was soon undeceived. About 9 some of the guard came to and informed me the town inhabitants were assembling to attack the troops, and that the bells were ringing as the signal for that purpose and not for fire, and the beacon intended to be fired to bring in the distant people of the country. This, as I was captain of the day, occasioned my repairing immediately to the main guard. On my way there I saw the people in great commotion, and heard them use the most cruel and horrid threats against the troops. In a few minutes after I reached the guard, about 100 people passed it and went towards the custom house where the king's money is lodged. They immediately surrounded the sentry posted there, and with clubs and other weapons threatened to execute their vengeance on him. I was soon informed by a townsman their intention was to carry off the soldier from his post and probably murder him. On which I desired him to return for further intelligence, and he soon came back and assured me he heard the mob declare they would murder him. This I feared might be a prelude to their plundering the king's chest. I immediately sent a non-commissioned officer and 12 men to protect both the sentry and the king's money, and very soon followed myself to prevent, if possible, all disorder, fearing lest the officer and soldiers, by the insults and provocations of the rioters, should be thrown off their guard and commit some rash act. They soon rushed through the people, and by charging their bayonets in half-circles, kept them at a little distance. Nay, so far was I from intending the death of any person that I suffered the troops to go to the spot where the unhappy affair took place without any loading in their pieces; nor did I ever give orders for loading them. This remiss conduct in me perhaps merits censure; yet it is evidence, resulting from the nature of things, which is the best and surest that can be offered, that my intention was not to act offensively, but the contrary part, and that not without compulsion. The mob still increased and were more outrageous, striking their clubs or bludgeons one against another, and calling out, come on you rascals, you bloody backs, you lobster scoundrels, fire if you dare, G—d damn you, fire and be damned, we know you dare not, and much more such language was used. At this time I was between the soldiers and the mob, parleying with, and endeavouring all in my power to persuade them to retire peaceably, but to no purpose. They advanced to the points of the bayonets, struck some of them and even the muzzles of the pieces, and seemed to be endeavoring to close with the soldiers. On which some well behaved persons asked me if the guns were charged. I replied yes. They then asked me if I intended to order the men to fire. I answered no, by no means, observing to them that I was advanced before the muzzles of the men's pieces, and must fall a sacrifice if they fired; that the soldiers were upon the half cock and charged bayonets, and my giving the word fire under those circumstances would prove me to be no officer. While I was thus speaking, one of the soldiers having received a severe blow with a stick, stepped a little on one side and instantly fired, on which turning to and asking him why he fired without orders, I was struck with a club on my arm, which for some time deprived me of the use of it, which blow had it been placed on my head, most probably would have destroyed me. On this a general attack was made on the men by a great number of heavy clubs and snowballs being thrown at them, by which all our lives were in imminent danger, some persons at the same time from behind calling out, damn your bloods—why don't you fire. Instantly three or four of the soldiers fired, one after another, and directly after three more in the same confusion and hurry. The mob then ran away, except three unhappy men who instantly expired, in which number was Mr. Gray at whose rope-walk the prior quarrels took place; one more is since dead, three others are dangerously, and four slightly wounded. The whole of this melancholy affair was transacted in almost 20 minutes. On my asking the soldiers why they fired without orders, they said they heard the word fire and supposed it came from me. This might be the case as many of the mob called out fire, fire, but I assured the men that I gave no such order; that my words were, don't fire, stop your firing. In short, it was scarcely possible for the soldiers to know who said fire, or don't fire, or stop your firing. On the people's assembling again to take away the dead bodies, the soldiers supposing them coming to attack them, were making ready to fire again, which I prevented by striking up their firelocks with my hand. Immediately after a townsman came and told me that 4 or 5,000 people were assembled in the next street, and had sworn to take my life with every man's with me. On which I judged it unsafe to remain there any longer, and therefore sent the party and sentry to the main guard, where the street is narrow and short, there telling them off into street firings, divided and planted them at each end of the street to secure their rear, momently expecting an attack, as there was a constant cry of the inhabitants to arms, to arms, turn out with your guns; and the town drums beating to arms, I ordered my drums to beat to arms, and being soon after joined by the different companies of the 29th regiment, I formed them as the guard into street firings. The 14th regiment also got under arms but remained at their barracks. I immediately sent a sergeant with a party to Colonel Dalrymple, the commanding officer, to acquaint him with every particular. Several officers going to join their regiment were knocked down by the mob, one very much wounded and his sword taken from him. The lieutenant-governor and Colonel Carr soon after met at the head of the 29th regiment and agreed that the regiment should retire to their barracks, and the people to their houses, but I kept the picket to strengthen the guard. It was with great difficulty that the lieutenant-governor prevailed on the people to be quiet and retire. At last they all went off, excepting about a hundred.

A Council was immediately called, on the breaking up of which three justices met and issued a warrant to apprehend me and eight soldiers. On hearing of this procedure I instantly went to the sheriff and surrendered myself, though for the space of 4 hours I had it in my power to have made my escape, which I most undoubtedly should have attempted and could have easily executed, had I been the least conscious of any guilt. On the examination before the justices, two witnesses swore that I gave the men orders to fire. The one testified he was within two feet of me; the other that I swore at the men for not firing at the first word. Others swore they heard me use the word "fire," but whether do or do not fire, they could not say; others that they heard the word fire, but could not say if it came from me. The next day they got 5 or 6 more to swear I gave the word to fire. So bitter and inveterate are many of the malcontents here that they are industriously using every method to fish out evidence to prove it was a concerted scheme to murder the inhabitants. Others are infusing the utmost malice and revenge into the minds of the people who are to be my jurors by false publications, votes of towns, and all other artifices. That so from a settled rancour against the officers and troops in general, the suddenness of my trial after the affair while the people's minds are all greatly inflamed, I am, though perfectly innocent, under most unhappy circumstances, having nothing in reason to expect but the loss of life in a very ignominious manner, without the interposition of his Majesty's royal goodness.

16

Colonial Accounts

George Robert Twelves Hewes
and the *Boston Gazette*
and Country Journal

George Robert Twelves Hewes (1742–1840) was in his nineties in 1833 when he told James Hawkes the story of his experiences in revolutionary Boston. Hewes claimed not to have read any published account of the happenings there and could "therefore only give the information which I derived from the event[s] of the day." Careful checking by the distinguished labor historian Alfred F. Young has authenticated much of Hewes's account. His story provides a rare opportunity to see an ordinary citizen taking a direct part in a great historical event. Hewes also participated in the Boston Tea Party of December 16, 1773, as one of the "Indians" pitching casks of tea into the harbor. These experiences had a profound personal effect on Hewes. In the 1760s he had been an awkward young cobbler nervously deferring to his aristocratic customers. A decade later, with these experiences behind him, he would risk his employment and perhaps even a beating for his refusal to take off his hat "for any man." For Hewes, the American Revolution meant that the poor and the ordinary no longer owed the rich and powerful what in the eighteenth century was called "deference."

The Boston Gazette and Country Journal *was one of several struggling journals published in Boston. Ever since being threatened with taxation under the Stamp Act of 1763, colonial newspapers, particularly those in Boston, had tended to support the patriot perspective. Journalism was not yet a profession, as most newspapers were produced by printers or postmasters, and the tradition of impartial reporting was still far in the future.*

BEFORE YOU READ

1. According to Hewes, what sparked the Boston Massacre?
2. What role did he play in the event and subsequent trial?

James Hawkes [supposed author], *A Retrospect of the Boston Tea-Party, with a Memoir of George R. T. Hewes, a Survivor of the Little Band of Patriots who Drowned the Tea in Boston Harbour in 1773, by a Citizen of New York* (New York, 1834), pp. 27–33, 36–41; *Boston Gazette and Country Journal*, March 12, 1770, reprinted in Merrill Jensen, ed., *English Historical Documents*, vol. 9 (London: Eyre and Spottiswoode, 1955), pp. 745–49.

3. How does the account of the riot as reported in the *Boston Gazette and Country Journal* differ from Hewes's account?

4. What political points does the *Boston Gazette and Country Journal* make about the Boston Massacre?

ACCOUNT OF GEORGE ROBERT TWELVES HEWES

[W]hen I was at the age of twenty-six, I married the daughter of Benjamin Sumner, of Boston. At the time of our intermarriage, the age of my wife was seventeen. We lived together very happily seventy years. She died at the age of eighty-seven.

At the time when the British troops were first stationed at Boston, we had several children, the exact number I do not recollect. By our industry and mutual efforts we were improving our condition.

An account of the massacre of the citizens of Boston, in the year 1770, on the 5th of March, by some of the British troops, has been committed to the record of our history, as one of those interesting events which lead to the revolutionary contest that resulted in our independence.... We have been informed by the historians of the revolution, that a series of provocations had excited strong prejudices, and inflamed the passion of the British soldiery against our citizens, previous to the commencement of open hostilities; and prepared their minds to burst out into acts of violence on the application of a single spark of additional excitement, and which finally resulted in the unfortunate massacre of a number of our citizens.

On my inquiring of Hewes what knowledge he had of that event, he replied, that he knew nothing from history, as he had never read any thing relating to it from any publication whatever, and can therefore only give the information which I derived from the event of the day upon which the catastrophe happened. On that day, one of the British officers applied to a barber, to be shaved and dressed; the master of the shop, whose name was Pemont, told his apprentice boy he might serve him, and receive the pay to himself, while Pemont left the shop. The boy accordingly served him, but the officer, for some reason unknown to me, went away from the shop without paying him for his service. After the officer had been gone some time, the boy went to the house where he was, with his account, to demand payment of his bill, but the sentinel, who was before the door, would not give him admittance, nor permit him to see the officer; and as some angry words were interchanged between the sentinel and the boy, a considerable number of the people from the vicinity, soon gathered at the place where they were, which was in King street, and I was soon on the ground among them. The violent agitation of the citizens, not only on account of the abuse offered to the boy, but other causes of excitement, then fresh in the recollection, was such that the sentinel began to be apprehensive of danger, and knocked at the door of the house, where the officers were, and told the servant who came to the door, that he was afraid of his life, and would quit his post unless he was protected. The officers in the house then sent a messenger to the guard-house, to require Captain Preston to come with a sufficient number of his soldiers to defend them from the threatened violence of the people. On receiving the message, he came immediately with a small guard of grenadiers, and paraded them before the custom-house, where the British officers were shut up. Captain Preston then ordered the people to disperse, but they said they would not, they were in the king's highway, and had as good a right to be there as he had. The captain of the guard then said to them, if you do not disperse, I will fire upon you, and then gave orders to his men to make ready, and immediately after gave them orders to fire. Three of our citizens fell dead on the spot, and two, who were wounded, died the next day; and nine others were also wounded. The persons who were killed I well recollect, said Hewes; they were, Gray, a rope maker, Marverick, a young man, Colwell, who was the mate of Captain Colton, Attuck, a mulatto, and Carr, who was an Irishman. Captain Preston then immediately fled with his grenadiers back to the guard-house. The people who were assembled on that occasion, then immediately chose a committee to report to the governor the result of Captain Preston's conduct, and to demand of him satisfaction. The governor told the committee, that if the people would be quiet that night he would give them satisfaction, so far as was in his power; the next morning Captain Preston, and those of his guard who were concerned in the massacre, were, accordingly, by order of the governor, given up, and taken into custody the next morning, and committed to prison.

It is not recollected that the offence given to the barber's boy is mentioned by the historians of the revolution; yet there can be no doubt of its correctness. The account of this single one of the exciting causes of the massacre, related by Hewes, at this time, was in answer to the question of his personal knowledge of that event.

A knowledge of the spirit of those times will easily lead us to conceive, that the manner of the British officers application to the barber, was a little too strongly tinctured with the dictatorial hauteur, to conciliate the views of equality, which at that period were supremely predominant in the minds of those of the whig party, even in his humble occupation; and that the disrespectful notice of his loyal customer, in consigning him to the attention of his apprentice boy, and abruptly leaving his shop, was intended to be treated by the officer with contempt, by so underrating the services of his apprentice, as to deem any reward for them beneath his attention. The boy too, may be supposed to have imbibed so much of the spirit which distinguished that period of our history, that he was willing to improve any occasion to contribute his share to the public excitement; to add an additional spark to the fire of political dissention which was enkindling.

When Hewes arrived at the spot where the massacre happened, it appears his attention was principally engaged by the clamours of those who were disposed to aid the boy in avenging the insult offered to him by the British officer, and probably heard nothing, at that time, of any other of the many exciting causes which lead to that disastrous event, though it appeared from his general conversation, his knowledge of them was extensive and accurate.

But to pursue the destiny of Captain Preston, and the guard who fired on the citizens; in about a fortnight after, said Hewes, they were brought to trial and indicted for the crime of murder.

The soldiers were tried first, and acquitted, on the ground, that in firing upon the citizens of Boston, they only acted in proper obedience to the captain's orders. When Preston, their captain, was tried, I was called as one of the witnesses, on the part of the government, and testified, that I believed it was the same man, Captain Preston, that ordered his soldiers to make ready, who also ordered them to fire. Mr. John Adams, former president of the United States, was advocate for the prisoners, and denied the fact, that Captain Preston gave orders to his men to fire; and on his cross examination of me asked whether my position was such, that I could see the captain's lips in motion when the order to fire was given; to which I answered, that I could not. Although the evidence of Preston's having given orders to the soldiers to fire, was thought by the jury sufficient to acquit them, it was not thought to be of weight enough to convict him of a capital offence; he also was acquitted.

Although the excitement which had been occasioned by the wanton massacre of our citizens, had in some measure abated, it was never extinguished until open hostilities commenced, and we had declared our independence. The citizens of Boston continued inflexible in their demand, that every British soldier should be withdrawn from the town, and within four days after the massacre, the whole army decamped. But the measures of the British parliament, which led the American colonies to a separation from that government, were not abandoned.

ACCOUNT IN THE *BOSTON GAZETTE AND COUNTRY JOURNAL*

March 12, 1770

The town of Boston affords a recent and melancholy demonstration of the destructive consequences of quartering troops among citizens in a time of peace, under a pretence of supporting the laws and aiding civil authority; every considerate and unprejudiced person among us was deeply impressed with the apprehension of these consequences when it was known that a number of regiments were ordered to this town under such a pretext, but in reality to enforce oppressive measures; to awe and control the legislative as well as executive power of the province, and to quell a spirit of liberty, which however it may have been basely opposed and even ridiculed by some, would do honour to any age or country. A few persons amongst us had determined to use all their influence to procure so destructive a measure with a view to their securely enjoying the profits of an American revenue, and unhappily both for Britain and this country they found means to effect it.

It is to Governor Bernard, the commissioners, their confidants and coadjutors, that we are indebted as the procuring cause of a military power in this capital. The Boston Journal of Occurrences, as printed in Mr. Holt's *New York Gazette*, from time to time, afforded many striking instances of the distresses brought upon the inhabitants by this measure; and since those Journals have been discontinued, our troubles from that quarter have been growing upon us. We have known a party of soldiers in the face of day fire off a loaden musket upon the inhabitants, others have been pricked with bayonets, and even our magistrates assaulted and put in danger of their lives, when offenders brought before them have been rescued; and why those and other bold and base criminals have as yet escaped the punishment due to their crimes may be soon matter of enquiry by the representative body of this people. It is natural to suppose that when the inhabitants of this town saw those laws which had been enacted for their security, and which they were ambitious of holding up to the soldiery, eluded, they should more commonly resent for themselves; and accordingly it has so happened. Many have been the squabbles between them and the soldiery; but it seems their being often worsted by our youth in those rencounters, has only served to irritate the former. What passed at Mr. Gray's rope-walk has already been given the public and may be said to have led the way to the late catastrophe. That the rope-walk lads, when attacked by superior numbers, should defend themselves with so much spirit and success in the club-way, was too mortifying, and perhaps it may hereafter appear that even some of their officers were unhappily affected with this circumstance. Divers stories were propagated among the soldiery that served to agitate their spirits; particularly on the Sabbath that one Chambers, a sergeant, represented as a sober man, had been missing the preceding day and must therefore have been murdered by the townsmen. An officer of distinction so far credited this report that he entered Mr. Gray's rope-walk that Sabbath; and when required of by that gentleman as soon as he could meet him, the occasion of his so doing, the officer replied that it was to look if the sergeant said to be murdered had not been hid there. This sober sergeant was found on the Monday unhurt in a house of pleasure. The evidences already collected show that many threatenings had been thrown out by the soldiery, but we do not pretend to say that there was any preconcerted plan. When the evidences are published, the world will judge. We may, however, venture to declare that it appears too probable from their conduct that some of the soldiery aimed to draw and provoke the townsmen into squabbles, and that they then intended to make use of other weapons than canes, clubs, or bludgeons.

On the evening of Monday, being the fifth current, several soldiers of the 29th Regiment were seen parading the streets with their drawn cutlasses and bayonets, abusing and wounding numbers of the inhabitants.

A few minutes after nine o'clock four youths, named Edward Archbald, William Merchant, Francis Archbald, and John Leech, jun., came down Cornhill together, and separating at Doctor Loring's corner, the two former were passing the narrow alley leading to Murray's barrack in which was a soldier brandishing a broad sword of an uncommon size against the walls, out of which he struck fire plentifully. A person of mean countenance armed with a large cudgel bore him company. Edward Archbald admonished Mr. Merchant to take care of the sword, on which the soldier turned round and struck Archbald on the arm, then pushed at Merchant and pierced through his clothes inside the arm close to the armpit and grazed the skin. Merchant then struck the soldier with a short stick he had; and the other person ran to the barrack and brought with him two soldiers, one armed with a pair of tongs, the other with a shovel. He with the tongs pursued Archbald back through the alley, collared and laid him over the head with the tongs. The noise brought people together; and John Hicks, a young lad, coming up, knocked the soldier down but let him get up again; and more lads gathering, drove them back to the barrack where the boys stood some time as it were to keep them in. In less than a minute ten or twelve of them came out with drawn cutlasses, clubs, and bayonets and set upon the unarmed boys and young folk who stood them a little while but, finding the inequality of their equipment, dispersed. On hearing the noise, one Samuel Atwood came up to see what was the matter; and entering the alley from dock square, heard the latter part of the combat; and when the boys had dispersed he met the ten or twelve soldiers aforesaid rushing down the alley towards the square and asked them if they intended to murder people? They answered Yes, by G—d, root and branch! With that one of them struck Mr. Atwood with a club which was repeated by another; and being unarmed, he turned to go off and received a wound on the left shoulder which reached the bone and gave him much pain. Retreating a few steps, Mr. Atwood met two officers and said, gentlemen, what is the matter? They answered, you'll see by and by. Immediately after, those heroes appeared in the square, asking where were the boogers? where were the cowards? But notwithstanding their fierceness to naked men, one of them advanced towards a youth who had a split of a raw stave in his hand and said, damn them, here is one of them. But the young man seeing a person near him with a drawn sword and good cane ready to support him, held up his stave in defiance; and they quietly passed by him up the little alley by Mr. Silsby's to King Street where they attacked single and unarmed persons till they raised much clamour, and then turned down Cornhill Street, insulting all they met in like manner and pursuing some to their very doors. Thirty or forty persons, mostly lads, being by this means gathered in King Street, Capt. Preston with a party of men with charged bayonets, came from the main guard to the commissioner's house, the soldiers pushing their bayonets, crying, make way! They took place by the custom house and, continuing to push to drive the people off, pricked some in several places, on which they were clamorous and, it is said, threw snow balls. On this, the Captain commanded them to fire; and more snow balls coming, he again said, damn you, fire, be the consequence what it will! One soldier then fired, and a townsman with a cudgel struck him over the hands with such force that he dropped his firelock; and, rushing forward, aimed a blow at the Captain's head which grazed his hat and fell pretty heavy upon his arm. However, the soldiers continued the fire successively till seven or eight or, as some say, eleven guns were discharged.

By this fatal maneuver three men were laid dead on the spot and two more struggling for life; but what showed a degree of cruelty unknown to British troops, at least since the house of Hanover has directed their operations, was an attempt to fire upon or push with their bayonets the persons who undertook to remove the slain and wounded!

Mr. Benjamin Leigh, now undertaker in the Delph manufactory, came up; and after some conversation with Capt. Preston relative to his conduct in this affair, advised him to draw off his men, with which he complied.

The dead are Mr. Samuel Gray, killed on the spot, the ball entering his head and beating off a large portion of his skull.

A mulatto man named Crispus Attucks, who was born in Framingham, but lately belonged to New-Providence and was here in order to go for North Carolina, also killed instantly, two balls entering his breast, one of them in special goring the right lobe of the lungs and a great part of the liver most horribly.

Mr. James Caldwell, mate of Capt. Morton's vessel, in like manner killed by two balls entering his back.

Mr. Samuel Maverick, a promising youth of seventeen years of age, son of the widow Maverick, and an apprentice to Mr. Greenwood, ivory-turner, mortally wounded; a ball went through his belly and was cut out at his back. He died the next morning.

A lad named Christopher Monk, about seventeen years of age, an apprentice to Mr. Walker, shipwright, wounded; a ball entered his back about four inches above the left kidney near the spine and was cut out of the breast on the same side. Apprehended he will die.

A lad named John Clark, about seventeen years of age, whose parents live at Medford, and an apprentice to Capt. Samuel Howard of this town, wounded; a ball entered just above his groin and came out at his hip on the opposite side. Apprehended he will die.

Mr. Edward Payne of this town, merchant, standing at his entry door received a ball in his arm which shattered some of the bones.

Mr. John Green, tailor, coming up Leverett's Lane, received a ball just under his hip and lodged in the under part of his thigh, which was extracted.

Mr. Robert Patterson, a seafaring man, who was the person that had his trousers shot through in Richardson's affair, wounded; a ball went through his right arm, and he suffered a great loss of blood.

Mr. Patrick Carr, about thirty years of age, who worked with Mr. Field, leather breeches-maker in Queen Street, wounded; a ball entered near his hip and went out at his side.

A lad named David Parker, an apprentice to Mr. Eddy, the wheelwright, wounded; a ball entered in his thigh.

The people were immediately alarmed with the report of this horrid massacre, the bells were set a-ringing, and great numbers soon assembled at the place where this tragical scene had been acted. Their feelings may be better conceived than expressed; and while some were taking care of the dead and wounded, the rest were in consultation what to do in those dreadful circumstances. But so little intimidated were they, notwithstanding their being within a few yards of the main guard and seeing the 29th Regiment under arms and drawn up in King Street, that they kept their station and appeared, as an officer of rank expressed it, ready to run upon the very muzzles of their muskets. The lieutenant-governor soon came into the town house and there met some of his Majesty's Council and a number of civil magistrates. A considerable body of the people immediately entered the council chamber and expressed themselves to his honour with a freedom and warmth becoming the occasion. He used his utmost endeavours to pacify them, requesting that they would let the matter sub-side for the night and promising to do all in his power that justice should be done and the law have its course. Men of influence and weight with the people were not wanting on their part to procure their compliance with his Honour's request by representing the horrible consequences of a promiscuous and rash engagement in the night, and assuring them that such measures should be en-tered upon in the morning as would be agreeable to their dignity and a more likely way of obtaining the best satisfaction for the blood of their fellow towns-men. The inhabitants attended to these suggestions; and the regiment under arms being ordered to their barracks, which was insisted upon by the people, they then separated and returned to their dwellings by one o'clock. At three o'clock Capt. Preston was committed, as were the soldiers who fired, a few hours after him.

Tuesday morning presented a most shocking scene, the blood of our fellow citizens running like water through King Street and the Merchants' Exchange, the principal spot of the military parade for about eighteen months past. Our blood might also be tracked up to the head of Long Lane, and through divers other streets and passages.

At eleven o'clock the inhabitants met at Faneuil Hall; and after some ani-mated speeches becoming the occasion, they chose a committee of fifteen re-spectable gentlemen to wait upon the lieutenant-governor in Council to request of him to issue his orders for the immediate removal of the troops.

For Critical Thinking

1. If you were John Adams, determined to prove that British officers and soldiers could receive a fair trial in Boston, how would you defend Captain Preston?

2. Compare the Boston Massacre with later urban riots in American history de-scribed in your textbook. What similarities and differences do you find?

A Soldier's View of the Revolutionary War
Joseph Plumb Martin

Joseph Plumb Martin was born in western Massachusetts in 1760 and became a soldier in the Revolution before his sixteenth birthday. After serving with Connecticut troops in 1776, he enlisted as a regular in the Continental Army in April 1777 and persevered until the army was demobilized in 1783. During this period he fought with the Light Infantry as well as in the Corps of Sappers and Miners, who built fortifications and dug trenches. One of the few soldiers to serve for virtually the entire war, he repeatedly risked health and life: in the defense of New York City in 1776, at the Battle of Germantown in Pennsylvania in 1777, at Valley Forge in the winter of 1777–78, at the Battle of Monmouth in New Jersey in 1778, and at the climactic siege of Yorktown in 1781.

Published in Maine in 1830, Martin's A Narrative of Some of the Adventures, Dangers, and Sufferings of a Revolutionary Soldier *is a usually good-humored, unvarnished picture of an ordinary soldier whose major concern is often his next meal or keeping warm through a cold night. Yet he expresses sharply the widely shared resentment among common soldiers toward civilian patriots "sitting still and expecting the army to do notable things while fainting from sheer starvation." And he fundamentally objects to the way his generation remembered the history of the war: "great men get great praise, little men, nothing. But it always was so and always will be." In fact, historians in the present age have at last devoted energy to recapturing the contributions of men like Joseph Plumb Martin, whose narrative offers the only detailed account historians have discovered of the wartime experience of a common Revolutionary War soldier.*

Before You Read

1. Why do you think Martin begins with an apology for writing his memoirs?
2. What does the account of the sergeant who was almost executed suggest about the discipline of the Continental Army and the relations between officers and soldiers?
3. According to Martin, how well did the people support the soldiers of the Continental Army?

PREFACE

I have somewhere read of a limner, who, when he had daubed a representation of some animal, was always compelled, for the information of the observer, to write under it what he intended it to represent: As, "this is a goose, this is a

James Kirby Martin, ed., *Ordinary Courage: The Revolutionary War Adventures of Joseph Plumb Martin*, rev. ed. (St. James, NY: Brandywine Press, 1999), pp. 1–2, 15–17, 29, 34–35, 61–64.

dog," &c. So, many books, and mine in particular among the rest, would perhaps be quite unintelligible as to the drift of them, unless the reader was informed beforehand what the author intended.

I shall, therefore, by way of preface, inform the reader that my intention is to give a succinct account of some of my adventures, dangers, and sufferings during my several campaigns in the Revolutionary army. My readers (who, by the by, will, I hope, none of them be beyond the pale of my own neighborhood) must not expect any great transactions to be exhibited to their notice. "No alpine wonders thunder through my tale," but they are here, once for all, requested to bear it in mind, that they are not the achievements of an officer of high grade which they are perusing, but the common transactions of one of the lowest in station in an army, a private soldier.

Should the reader chance to ask himself this question (and I think it very natural for him to do so) how could any man of common sense ever spend his precious time in writing such a rhapsody of nonsense? To satisfy his inquiring mind, I would inform him, that, as the adage says, "every crow thinks her own young the whitest," so every private soldier in an army thinks his particular services as essential to carry on the war he is engaged in, as the services of the most influential general: And why not? What could officers do without such men? Nothing at all. Alexander never could have conquered the world without private soldiers.

But, says the reader, this is low; the author gives us nothing but everyday occurrences; I could tell as good a story myself. Very true, Mr. Reader, everyone can tell what he has done in his lifetime, but everyone has not been a soldier, and consequently can know but little or nothing of the sufferings and fatigues incident to an army. All know everyday occurrences, but few know the hardships of the "tented field." I wish to have a better opinion of my readers, whoever they may be, than even to think that any of them would wish me to stretch the truth to furnish them with wonders that I never saw, or acts or deeds I never performed. I can give them no more than I have to give, and if they are dissatisfied after all, I must say I am sorry for them and myself too; for them, that they expect more than I can do, and myself, that I am so unlucky as not to have it in my power to please them. . . .

The critical grammarian may find enough to feed his spleen upon if he peruses the following pages; but I can inform him beforehand, I do not regard his sneers; if I cannot write grammatically, I can think, talk, and feel like other men. Besides, if the common readers can understand it, it is all I desire; and to give them an idea, though but a faint one, of what the army suffered that gained and secured our independence, is all I wish. I never studied grammar an hour in my life. When I ought to have been doing that, I was forced to be studying the rules and articles of war. . . .

A note of interrogation: Why we were made to suffer so much in so good and just a cause; and a note of admiration to all the world, that an army voluntarily engaged to serve their country, when starved, and naked, and suffering everything short of death (and thousands even that), should be able to persevere through an eight years war, and come off conquerors at last!

But lest I should make my preface longer than my story, I will here bring it to a close.

CAMPAIGN OF 1776

I remained in New York two or three months, in which time several things occurred, but so trifling that I shall not mention them; when, sometime in the latter part of the month of August, I was ordered upon a fatigue party. We had scarcely reached the grand parade when I saw our sergeant major directing his course up Broadway toward us in rather an unusual step for him. He soon arrived and informed us, and then the commanding officer of the party, that he had orders to take off all belonging to our regiment and march us to our quarters, as the regiment was ordered to Long Island, the British having landed in force there. Although this was not unexpected to me, yet it gave me rather a disagreeable feeling, as I was pretty well assured I should have to sniff a little gunpowder. However, I kept my cogitations to myself, went to my quarters, packed up my clothes, and got myself in readiness for the expedition as soon as possible. I then went to the top of the house where I had a full view of that part of the Island; I distinctly saw the smoke of the field artillery, but the distance and the unfavorableness of the wind prevented my hearing their report, at least but faintly. The horrors of battle then presented themselves to my mind in all their hideousness; I must come to it now, thought I. Well, I will endeavor to do my duty as well as I am able and leave the event with Providence.

We were soon ordered to our regimental parade, from which, as soon as the regiment was formed, we were marched off for the ferry. At the lower end of the street were placed several casks of sea bread, . . . nearly hard enough for musket flints; the casks were unheaded and each man was allowed to take as many as he could as he marched by. As my good luck would have it, there was a momentary halt made; I improved the opportunity thus offered me, as every good soldier should upon all important occasions, to get as many of the biscuits as I possibly could; no one said anything to me, and I filled my bosom and took as many as I could hold in my hand, a dozen or more in all, and when we arrived at the ferry stairs I stowed them away in my knapsack. We quickly embarked on board the boats. As each boat started, three cheers were given by those on board, which was returned by the numerous spectators who thronged the wharves; they all wished us good luck, apparently, although it was with most of them perhaps nothing more than ceremony.

We soon landed at Brooklyn, upon the Island, marched up the ascent from the ferry to the plain. We now began to meet the wounded men, another sight I was unacquainted with, some with broken arms, some with broken legs, and some with broken heads. The sight of these a little daunted me, and made me think of home, but the sight and thought vanished together. We marched a short distance, when we halted to refresh ourselves. Whether we had any other victuals besides the hard bread I do not remember, but I remember my gnawing at them; they were hard enough to break the teeth of a rat. One of the soldiers complaining of thirst to his officer, "Look at that man," said he, pointing to me, "he is not thirsty, I will warrant it." I felt a little elevated to be styled a man.

While resting here, which was not more than 20 minutes or half an hour, the Americans and British were warmly engaged within sight of us. What were the feelings of most or all the young soldiers at this time, I know not, but I know what were mine. But let mine or theirs be what they might, I saw a lieutenant who appeared to have feelings not very enviable; whether he was actuated by fear or the canteen I cannot determine now. I thought it fear at the time, for he ran round among the men of his company, sniveling and blubbering, praying each one if he had aught against him, or if *he* had injured anyone that they would forgive him, declaring at the same time that he, from his heart, forgave them if they had offended him, and I gave him full credit for his assertion; for had he been at the gallows with a halter about his neck, he could not have shown more fear or penitence. A fine soldier you are, I thought, a fine officer, an exemplary man for young soldiers! I would have then suffered anything short of death rather than have made such an exhibition of myself. . . .

Another affair . . . deserves to be recorded by me, as no one else has to my knowledge ever mentioned it. A sergeant belonging to the Connecticut forces, being sent by his officers in the heat of the action to procure ammunition, was met by a superior officer, an aide-de-camp to some general officer (I believe), who accused him of deserting his post in time of action. He remonstrated with the officer and informed him of the absolute necessity there was of his obeying the orders of his own officers; that the failure of his procuring a supply of ammunition might endanger the success of the day, but all to no purpose. The officer would not allow himself to believe him, but drew his sword and threatened to take his life on the spot if he did not immediately return to his corps. The sergeant, fired with just indignation at hearing and seeing his life threatened, cocked his musket, and stood in his own defense. He was, however, taken, confined and tried for mutiny, and condemned to be shot.

The sentence of the court martial was approved by the Commander in Chief, and the day for his execution set. When it arrived, an embankment was thrown up to prevent the shot fired at him from doing other damage, and all things requisite on such occasions were in readiness. The Connecticut troops were then drawn out and formed in a square, and the prisoner brought forth; after being blindfolded and pinioned, he knelt upon the ground. The corporal with his six executioners were then brought up before him, ready at the fatal word of command to send a brave soldier into the eternal world because he persisted in doing his duty and obeying the lawful and urgent orders of his superior officers, the failure of which might, for aught the officer who stopped him knew, have caused the loss of hundreds of lives. But the sergeant was reprieved, and I believe it was well that he was, for his blood would not have been the only blood that would have been spilt.[1]

1. Colonel Joseph Reed of Pennsylvania, Washington's talented but quirky adjutant general and the officer in question, demanded the court martial of the sergeant, Ebenezer Leffingwell of Colonel John Durkee's 20th Continental regiment, originally organized in Connecticut. On September 22 a hearing board condemned Leffingwell to die, but he won this dramatic reprieve because Reed, having mused about the incident, implored Washington to pardon the sergeant. [Editor's note.]

The troops were greatly exasperated, and they showed what their feelings were by their lively and repeated cheerings after the reprieve, but more so by their secret and open threats before it. The reprieve was read by one of the chaplains of the army after a long harangue to the soldiers setting forth the enormity of the crime charged upon the prisoner, repeatedly using this sentence, "crimes for which men ought to die," which did much to further the resentment of the troops already raised to a high pitch. But, as I said before, it was well that it ended as it did, both on account of the honor of the soldiers and the safety of some others. . . .

. . . A number of our sick were sent off to Norwalk in Connecticut to recruit [rest]. I was sent with them as a nurse. We were billeted among the inhabitants. I had in my ward seven or eight *sick soldiers*, who were (at least soon after their arrival there) as well in health as I was. All they wanted was a cook and something for a cook to exercise his functions upon. The inhabitants here were almost entirely what were in those days termed tories. An old lady, of whom I often procured milk, used always when I went to her house to give me a lecture on my opposition to our good King George. She had always said (she told me) that the regulars would make us fly like pigeons. . . .

The man of the house where I was quartered had a smart-looking Negro man, a great politician. I chanced one day to go into the barn where he was threshing. He quickly began to upbraid me with my opposition to the British. The king of England was a very powerful prince, he said—a very powerful prince; and it was a pity that the colonists had fallen out with him; but as we had, we must abide by the consequences. I had no inclination to waste the shafts of my rhetoric upon a Negro slave. I concluded he had heard his betters say so. As the old cock crows, so crows the young one; and I thought, as the white cock crows, so crows the black one. He ran away from his master before I left there, and went to Long Island to assist King George; but it seems the King of Terrors was more potent than King George, for his master had certain intelligence that poor Cuff was laid flat on his back.

This man had likewise a Negress who (as he was a widower) kept his house. She was as great a doctress as Cuff was a politician, and she wished to be a surgeon. There was an annual thanksgiving while we were here. The *sick* men of my ward had procured a fine roasting pig, and the old Negro woman having seen the syringe that I picked up in the retreat from Kip's Bay, fell violently in love with it and offered me a number of pies of one sort or other for it. Of the pig and the pies we made an excellent thanksgiving dinner, the best meal I had eaten since I left my grandsire's table.

Our surgeon came among us soon after this and packed us all off to camp, save two or three who were discharged. I arrived at camp with the rest, where we remained, moving from place to place as occasion required, undergoing hunger, cold, and fatigue until the 25th day of December, 1776, when I was discharged (my term of service having expired) at Philipse Manor, in the state of New York near Hudson's River.

Here ends my first campaign. I had learned something of a soldier's life, enough I thought to keep me at home for the future. Indeed, I was then fully determined to rest easy with the knowledge I had acquired in the affairs of the army. But the reader will find . . . that the ease of a winter spent at home caused me to alter my mind. I had several *kind* invitations to enlist into the standing army then about to be raised, especially a very pressing one to engage in a regiment of horse, but I concluded to try a short journey on foot first. Accordingly, I set off for my good old grandsire's, where I arrived, I think, on the 27th, two days after my discharge, and found my friends all alive and well. They appeared to be glad to see me, and I am sure I was *really* glad to see them.

CAMPAIGN OF 1777

Next morning we joined the grand army near Philadelphia, and the heavy baggage being sent back to the rear of the army, we were obliged to put us up huts by laying up poles and covering them with leaves, a capital shelter from winter storms. Here we continued to fast; indeed we kept a continual Lent as faithfully as ever any of the most rigorous of the Roman Catholics did. But there was this exception; we had no fish or eggs or any other substitute for our commons. Ours was a real fast and, depend upon it, we were sufficiently mortified.

About this time the whole British army left the city, came out, and encamped, or rather lay, on Chestnut Hill in our immediate neighborhood. We hourly expected an attack from them; we had a commanding position and were very sensible of it. We were kept constantly on the alert, and wished nothing more than to have them engage us, for we were sure of giving them a drubbing, being in excellent fighting trim, as we were starved and as cross and ill-natured as curs. The British, however, thought better of the matter, and, after several days maneuvering on the hill, very civilly walked off into Philadelphia again.

Starvation seemed to be entailed upon the army and every animal connected with it. The oxen, brought from New England for draught, all died, and the southern horses fared no better; even the wild animals that had any concern with us suffered. A poor little squirrel, who had the ill luck to get cut off from the woods and fixing himself on a tree standing alone and surrounded by several of the soldier's huts, sat upon the tree till he starved to death and fell off the tree. He, however, got rid of his misery soon. He did not live to starve by piecemeal six or seven years. . . .

Soon after the British had quit their position on Chestnut Hill, we left this place, and after marching and countermarching back and forward some days, we crossed the Schuylkill on a cold, rainy, and snowy night upon a bridge of wagons set end to end and joined together by boards and planks. And after a few days more maneuvering we at last settled down at a place called "the Gulf" (so named on account of a remarkable chasm in the hills); and here we encamped some time, and here we had liked to have encamped forever—for starvation here *rioted* in its glory. . . .

While we lay here, there was a Continental thanksgiving ordered by Congress; and as the army had all the cause in the world to be particularly thankful, if not for being well off, at least that it was no worse, we were ordered to participate in it. We had nothing to eat for two or three days previous, except what the trees of the fields and forests afforded us. But we must now have what Congress said—a sumptuous thanksgiving to close the year of high living we had now nearly seen brought to a close. Well, to add something extraordinary to our present stock of provisions, our country, ever mindful of its suffering army, opened her sympathizing heart so wide upon this occasion as to give us something to make the world stare. And what do you think it was, reader? Guess. You cannot guess, be you as much of a Yankee as you will. I will tell you: It gave each and every man *half* a *gill* of rice and a *tablespoonful* of vinegar!!

After we had made sure of this extraordinary superabundant donation, we were ordered out to attend a meeting and hear a sermon delivered upon the happy occasion. We accordingly went, for we could not help it. . . . I remember the text, like an attentive lad at church. I can *still* remember that it was this, "And the soldiers said unto him, And what shall we do? And he said unto them, Do violence to no man, nor accuse anyone falsely." The preacher ought to have added the remainder of the sentence to have made it complete: "And be content with your wages." But that would not do, it would be too apropos; however, he heard it as soon as the service was over, it was shouted from a hundred tongues. . . .

The army was now not only starved but naked. The greatest part were not only shirtless and barefoot but destitute of all other clothing, especially blankets. I procured a small piece of raw cowhide and made myself a pair of moccasins, which kept my feet (while they lasted) from the frozen ground, although as I well remember the hard edges so galled my ankles while on a march that it was with much difficulty and pain that I could wear them afterwards; but the only alternative I had was to endure this inconvenience or to go barefoot, as hundreds of my companions had to, till they might be tracked by their blood upon the rough frozen ground. But hunger, nakedness, and sore shins were not the only difficulties we had at that time to encounter; we had hard duty to perform and little or no strength to perform it with.

The army continued at and near the Gulf for some days, after which we marched for the Valley Forge in order to take up our winter quarters. We were now in a truly forlorn condition—no clothing, no provisions, and as disheartened as need be. We arrived, however, at our destination a few days before Christmas. Our prospect was indeed dreary. In our miserable condition, to go into the wild woods and build us habitations to *stay* (not to *live*) in, in such a weak, starved, and naked condition, was appalling in the highest degree, especially to New Englanders, unaccustomed to such kind of hardships at home. However, there was no remedy, no alternative but this or dispersion; but dispersion, I believe, was not thought of—at least I did not think of it. We had engaged in the defense of our injured country and were willing, nay, we were determined to persevere as long as such hardships were not altogether intolerable. I had experienced what I thought sufficient of the hardships of a military life the year before (although nothing in comparison to what I had suffered the present campaign) . . . ; but we were now absolutely in danger of perishing, and that too in the midst of a plentiful country. We then had but little and often nothing to eat for days together; but now we had nothing and saw no likelihood of any betterment of our condition. Had there fallen deep snows (and it was the time of year to expect them) or even heavy and long rainstorms, the whole army must inevitably have perished. Or had the enemy, strong and well provided as he then was, thought fit to pursue us, our poor emaciated carcasses must have "strewed the plain." But a kind and holy Providence took more notice and better care of us than did the country in whose service we were wearing away our lives by piecemeal.

We arrived at the Valley Forge in the evening. It was dark; there was no water to be found, and I was perishing with thirst. I searched for water till I was weary and came to my tent without finding any; fatigue and thirst, joined with hunger, almost made me desperate. I felt at that instant as if I would have taken victuals or drink from the best friend I had on earth by force. I am not writing fiction, all are sober realities. Just after I arrived at my tent, two soldiers whom I did not know passed by; they had some water in their canteens which they told me they had found a good distance off, but could not direct me to the place as it was very dark. I tried to beg a draught of water from them, but they were as rigid as Arabs. At length I persuaded them to sell me a drink for three pence, Pennsylvania currency, which was every cent of property I could then call my own, so great was the necessity I was then reduced to.

I lay here two nights and one day and had not a morsel of anything to eat all the time, save half of a small pumpkin, which I cooked by placing it upon a rock, the skin side uppermost, and making a fire upon it. By the time it was heat[ed] through I devoured it with as keen an appetite as I should a pie made of it at some other time.

The second evening after our arrival here I was warned to be ready for a two days command. I never heard a summons to duty with so much disgust before or since as I did that; how I could endure two days more fatigue without nourishment of some sort I could not tell. . . . However, in the morning . . . I went to the parade where I found a considerable number ordered upon the same business, whatever it was. We were ordered to go to the quartermaster general and receive from him our final orders. We accordingly repaired to his quarters, which was about three miles from camp; here we understood that our destiny was to go into the country on a foraging expedition, which was nothing more nor less than to procure provisions from the inhabitants for the men in the army and forage for the poor perishing cattle belonging to it, at the point of the bayonet. We stayed at the quartermaster general's quarters till sometime in the afternoon, during which time a beef creature was butchered for us. I well remember what fine stuff it was; it was quite transparent. I thought at that time what an excellent lantern it would make. I was, notwithstanding, very glad to get some of it, bad as it looked. We got, I think, two days allowance of it and some sort of bread kind, I suppose. . . .

We were then divided into several parties and sent off upon our expedition. Our party consisted of a lieutenant, a sergeant, a corporal, and 18 privates. We marched till night when we halted, and . . . this day we arrived at Milltown, or Downingstown, a small village halfway between Philadelphia and Lancaster, which was to be our quarters for the winter. It was dark when we had finished our day's march. There was a commissary and a wagonmaster general stationed here, the commissary to take into custody the provisions and forage that we collected, and the wagonmaster general to regulate the conduct of the wagoners and direct their motions. The next day after our arrival at this place we were put into a small house in which was only one room, in the center of the village. We were immediately furnished with rations of good and wholesome beef and flour, built us up some berths to sleep in, and filled them with straw, and felt as happy as any other pigs that were no better off than ourselves. And now having got into winter quarters and ready to commence our foraging business, I shall here end my account of my second campaign.

Secret Correspondence of a Loyalist Wife
Catherine Van Cortlandt

The Revolution was also a civil war. While most white Americans favored the patriot cause, loyalists were strong in many areas and among many groups. The areas surrounding New York City and along the Hudson River were predominately Tory, as were the eastern shore of Maryland and much of what was then the western frontier, particularly the Carolinas and Georgia. Old loyalties died hard. While Eliza Pinckney stood with her sons in the patriot cause, Benjamin Franklin's son William, as governor of New Jersey, was a prominent loyalist. George Washington, already commanding the Continental Army, still drank to the king's health daily until January 1776, when Thomas Paine's Common Sense *convinced him that the day of monarchy had passed.*

Philip Van Cortlandt of Hanover, New Jersey, retained his allegiance to the king. He escaped arrest by a patriot party in December 1776 and entered military service on the British side, receiving his commission from William Franklin. In letters sent to him by secret messenger from the patriot stronghold in which they were living, his wife, Catherine Van Cortlandt, described the family's plight. Finally, George Washington took pity on the family and gave them a pass to join Van Cortlandt in New York. The Van Cortlandts never returned to New Jersey. Like many loyalists, they migrated first to Nova Scotia and then to England.

BEFORE YOU READ

1. Do you think that Revolutionary soldiers had the right to seize Catherine Van Cortlandt's provisions and destroy her property?

2. Why do you think George Washington gave the family a pass to rejoin Van Cortlandt in New York?

December 15, 1776, Hanover, New Jersey

My dearest love,

You had not left us ten minutes last Sunday when a party of Light Horsemen, headed by Joseph Morris, came to our once peaceful mansion all armed, who said they had positive orders to take you, my dear Philly, prisoner to Easton, and your favourite horse Sampson to be carried to Morristown for the use of General Lee from whom these cruel mandates were issued. What were my emotions on seeing these wretches alight and without ceremony enter the

H. O. H. Vernon-Jackson, ed., "A Loyalist's Wife: Letters of Mrs. Philip Van Cortlandt, December 1776–February 1777," *History Today* 14 (1964): 574–80.

doors you can only conceive, you who know their base characters and how their present errand must be received by your beloved family. When these bloody-minded men came into the dining room our little flock gathered around me and with anxious eyes watched my looks, whilst I was answering questions. . . . One of them (flourishing his sword) swore bitterly that, if you was to be found alive on earth, he would take you or have your heart's blood. This was too much. They fled into their nursery, bursting into tears; screams out, "Oh my dear Pappa, they will kill him, they will kill him." One of the inhuman men seemed touched and endeavoured an excuse by saying they were sent by their General and therefore were obliged to do their duty, even though against a person they formerly much esteemed, but had been represented to General Lee as one too dangerous to be permitted to stay in the country. Finding you was certainly gone . . . they went off and left me in a situation . . . scarce to be described. My first care was the nursery to comfort those innocent pledges of our mutual love. . . . Their sobbing and crying had almost overcome them; and they would not be persuaded from a belief that the wretches were gone to murder their dear Pappa. . . .

. . . The house is surrounded by eighteen or twenty armed men every night in expectation of intercepting you, as they observed that you was too much at-tached to your family to be long absent. Our dear children are again taken from school in consequence of the cruel insults they daily receive for the principles of their parents.

I now write in fear and trembling and venture this by an honest Dutch farmer who says he will deliver it into your hands.

January 20, 1777, Hanover, New Jersey

My beloved Philly,

. . . The arrival of the Rebel Troops in this neighbourhood has been se-verely felt by us. Parties continually passing this way were always directed by officious people to stop at our house to breakfast, dine, or stay the night; the horses from the teams were put into our barns to feed, without even the cere-mony of asking liberty. During the stay of the officers of the hospital we had some protection. But immediately on their removal, several field officers from the New England line and a company of privates took possession. . . . They were the most disorderly of their species and their officers were from the dregs of the people. Indeed, two lieutenants messed and slept in the kitchen alto-gether, and would not be prevailed upon to leave their quarters. . . . A French general has also come on the hill at Dashwood, and daily draws his supply for his numerous cavalry from our granary and barrack.

Many of our female neighbours have been here, but I find their visits are only to gratify curiosity and to add insult to our unremitted distress. One of them who lives across the river, whose family we took so much pleasure in re-lieving when friendless . . . said that formerly she always respected you and loved the ground over which you walked, but now could with pleasure see your blood run down the road. . . . The pious, devout and Reverend Mr. Green is very industrious in promoting your ruin by declaring you an enemy to their cause. The farmers are forbid to sell me provisions, and the millers to grind our grain. Our woods are cut down for the use of their army, and that which you bought and left corded near the river my servants are forbid to touch, though we are in the greatest distress for the want of it. . . . Our dear children have been six weeks without any other covering to their tender feet but woollen rags sewed round them to keep them from freezing.

A few days ago, the colonel and other officers quartered here told me they expected some of their brother officers to dine and spend the evening with them. This I understood as a hint to provide accordingly, which I was determined to do to the utmost of my powers, *though from necessity*. . . . After removal of the cloth, I took the earliest opportunity . . . to absent myself; and then they set in for a drinking match, every few minutes calling aloud upon the *landlady* to replenish the decanters which were kept continually going. . . . At length, one of them [the children] observed that the Gentlemen who used to dine with Papa never did so; and if these were not his friends, why did Mamma treat them so well. . . .

A Servant came down and said the Gentlemen desired my company, as they were going to dance. This confounded me. . . . Though I was much distressed, my resolution supported me whilst I told him that the present situation of myself and children would sufficiently apologize for my refusing to partake of any scenes of mirth where my husband could not attend me. . . . Near ten o'clock . . . he returned and entreated me to honour the Company for a few minutes as a Spectator. . . . The Officers were dancing Reels with some tawdry dressed females I had never seen. . . .

February 12, 1777, Hanover, New Jersey

. . . The narrow escape of your last was something remarkable. I was sitting about the dusk of evening in my room, very disconsolate with our dear children around me, reflecting on our deplorable situation and the gloomy prospects before me, when I heard a sudden rap at the street door. . . . I went myself to see who it was, and lucky I did. A tall, thin man presented himself, and on my stooping to unbolt the door whispered, he had a letter for me. My heart fluttered. The sentry was walking before the door, and two of the Officers were coming towards me. I recollected myself and *"desired the good man to walk into my room until I could give him a little wine for the sick woman."* He took the hint, and as soon as he came to my fireside gave me a letter, the outside of which I just looked at and threw it under the head of my bed and immediately set about getting him some wine for his wife to prevent suspicion. . . . The honest man after taking a dram went away, being followed out of doors and questioned by the Officers, who had been venting, cursing, and swearing against the sentry for permitting anyone to approach the house or speak to me without their first being acquainted with it. . . . The frequent frolics of the Officers in the house, the Soldiers in the Nursery, and Cattle constantly fed here has reduced our late Stock of plenty to a miserable pittance. The other day was almost too much for me. We had been several days without bread and were subsisting upon a half bushel of Indian meal which had been given me by a Dutch farmer I did not know, who said he had heard of our situation and would take no pay. . . . Our stock of meal had been expended five days and the Soldiers not being about, our little Sally immediately went into the Nursery, and picking up a piece of dirty bread which had been trod under their feet came running up to me, wiping it with her frock, and with joy sparkling in her eyes presented it to me crying out, "Do eat it, Mamma. 'Tis good. 'Tis charming good bread. Indeed it is. I have tasted it." This was too much.

The next day Doctor Bond . . . came to the house, and passing me suddenly went into the back room and taking from under his coat a loaf of bread he gave it to the children and before I could thank him he ran past me with his handkerchief and hat before his face. . . .

A few days after, Doctor Bond came here and with a faltering voice told me he was sent by General Washington to inform me that it was his positive orders that our house should be taken as an Hospital to innoculate his Army with the smallpox, and if I chose he would innoculate my family at the same time. . . . He . . . promised to use his influence with the General to obtain the only favour I had now to ask of him; which was, to go to my husband with my children, servants, and such effects as I could take with me. . . .

February 19, 1777, Hoboken Ferry

My beloved husband,

Doctor Bond succeeded and with orders for my removal brought me General Washington's pass which I now enclose.

To describe the scene at parting with our few though sincere friends, the destruction of our property, the insulting looks and behaviour of those who had been accessory to our ruin . . . is more than I dare attempt. At four in the afternoon, a cold, disagreeable day, we bid adieu to our home to make room for the sick of General Washington's Army and, after an unpleasant and fatiguing journey, arrived at twelve o'clock at night at the Fork of the Rivers Rockaway, Pompton and Haakinsack. A Young Woman, whose father and brother were both in the Rebel service, was much affected with my situation and endeavoured to remove me into another room. The next evening, after a most distressing ride through snow and rain . . . we arrived at Campbell's Tavern at Haakinsack, the mistress of which refused me admittance when she was informed whose family it was, alleging as an excuse that she expected a number of Officers. . . .

The town was filled with Soldiers and the night advancing . . . a person came up to me, looked me in the face, and asked me to accompany him to his Uncle's house with my whole family. On entering a room with a large fire, it had an effect on the children, whose stomachs had been empty the greatest part of the day, that caused instant puking, and was near proving fatal to them.

The next morning early, we again set off in a most uncomfortable sleet and snow. . . . Our youngest children could not pass a farm yard where they were milking cows without wishing for some. My little Willing was almost in agonies, springing in my Arms and calling for milk. I therefore rode up and requested the good man to let me have some from one of his pails. . . . The man stopped, asked who we were, and . . . swore bitterly he would not give a drop to any Tory Bitch. I offered him money, my children screamed; and, as I could not prevail, I drove on.

. . . the servants . . . had been obliged to leave me soon after setting off from Haakinsack, on account of the baggage and the badness of the roads. About two hours ago, they came in and inform me that, crossing the river on the ice at the ferry, they were stopped and fired upon by a party of armed Rebels, nearly killing several of them. . . . Upon being shewn a copy of General Washington's pass, . . . they damned the General "for giving the mistress a pass" and said they were sorry they had not come a little sooner as they would have stopped the whole . . . and immediately fell to plundering chests, trunks, boxes, etc., throwing the heavy Articles into a hole in the ice, and breaking a barrel of old fashioned China into a thousand pieces. . . .

. . . be not surprised, my dear Pappa, if you see your Kitty altered. Indeed, I am much altered. But I know your heart, you will not love me less, but heal with redoubled affection and tenderness the wounds received in your behalf for those principles of loyalty which alone induced you to leave to the mercy of Rebels nine innocent children and your fond and ever affectionate Wife,

C.V.C.

19

Republican Motherhood
Eliza Pinckney and Abigail Adams

When George Washington insisted on serving as a pallbearer at Eliza Pinckney's funeral in 1793, he was recognizing a new ideal that both Pinckney and Abigail Adams exemplified, that of the "Republican mother." These women took an active role in affairs within the narrow bounds allowed by eighteenth-century marriage while inculcating the love of virtue and country in their children.

Eliza Pinckney, born Eliza Lucas in the West Indies in 1722, moved to South Carolina in 1737. Two years later, when her father returned to the Caribbean island of Antigua to become governor, seventeen-year-old Eliza remained in South Carolina to take charge of the family's three plantations. A remarkable agriculturalist, she pioneered the cultivation of several new crops, most notably indigo, a source for dye that became a staple exported from the Carolinas for decades. In 1744, she married Charles Pinckney, a prominent lawyer, political leader, and planter and had three children by him. After her husband died in 1758, Eliza again managed extensive properties. She constantly impressed on her children the family tradition of opposition to "wrong, oppression, or tyranny of any sort, public or private"—an injunction that in the eighteenth century did not prohibit slaveholding. Her two sons, Charles Cotesworth Pinckney and Thomas Pinckney, both rose to the rank of general in the Revolutionary War, were signers of the Constitution, and held major offices in the new federal government.

Abigail Adams (1744–1818) was born Abigail Smith in Weymouth, Massachusetts. Like most young women of the era, she was educated at home by her parents and relatives. John Adams, a serious young lawyer, began courting her in 1761, and three years later they wed. The couple had five children, four of whom survived into adulthood.

Abigail Adams's letters to her husband and her son John Quincy Adams illustrate the power of her personality and the sense of authority—different from the authority accorded eighteenth-century men—that she created from the role of wife and mother. Never forgetting the sharp distinction that society made between men's responsibilities and women's, she nonetheless took clear stands on the moral and political issues of her day and molded her son into a man of virtue and patriotism according to her definitions of those traits.

Harriott Horry Ravenel, *Eliza Pinckney* (New York: Charles Scribner's Sons, 1896), pp. 264–65, 275–76, 307–10; Charles Francis Adams, ed., *Letters of Mrs. Adams, the Wife of John Adams* (Boston: Wilkins, Carter, 1848), pp. 94–96, 152–55; Charles Francis Adams, ed., *Familiar Letters of John Adams and His Wife Abigail Adams, during the Revolution* (Boston: Houghton, Mifflin, 1875), pp. 148–50.

BEFORE YOU READ

1. What standards did Eliza Pinckney and Abigail Adams set for their sons?

2. What lessons did Eliza Pinckney and Abigail Adams expect their sons to learn from the American Revolution?

3. Compare the tone of Abigail Adams's letter to her son with that of the letter to her husband.

4. What does this famous letter ask of John Adams?

ELIZA PINCKNEY

August 1775

I see by these preparations of tents etc, that our soldiers are making ready for the field. I hope there will be little occasion for them. Heaven interests itself in favor of those who have Virtue to assert the birthright of mankind, Divine Liberty! and Britain surely will be shortly taught by our successes and continued unanimity, in spite of all their base arts to disunite us, that America determines to be free, and that it is beyond their force of arms to enslave so vast a Continent.

What shall we think of those few base souls among us, who, leaving penury and want in their own country have lived luxuriously in our land, and raised themselves a name; who now spurn at their benefactors, and betray the place that has been their asylum. From the misrepresentation of such wretches, do we doubtless owe much of our present calamity.

Tell Mr. Horry his friend G. threatened the Committee with an assault the other day, for which pretty performance . . . could they have caught him, [patriots] intended him a genteel souse in the River or perhaps a fashionable suit [of tar and feathers].

Hampton, Santee, May 1779

My Dear Tomm, — I have just received your letter with the account of my losses, and your almost ruined fortunes by the enemy. A severe blow! but I feel not for myself, but for you; 't is for your losses my greatly beloved child that I grieve; the loss of fortune could affect me little, but that it will deprive my dear Children of my assistance when they may stand most in need of it. . . . Your Brother's timely generous offer, to divide what little remains to him among us, is worthy of him. I am greatly affected, but not surprised at his Liberality.

I know his disinterestedness, his sensibility and affection. You say, I must be sensible you can't agree to this offer; indeed my dear Tomm I am very sensible of it, nor can I take a penny from his young helpless family. Independence is all I want and a little will make us that. Don't grieve for my child as I assure you I do not for myself. While I have such children dare I think my lot hard? God forbid! I pray the Almighty disposer of events to preserve them and my grandchildren to me, and for all the rest I hope I shall be able to say not only contentedly but cheerfully, God's Sacred will be done!

Undated [after 1783]

[To her grandson, Daniel Horry]

With the most resigned acquiescence in the Divine Will, I submit to the loss of Fortune, when I see my dear children, after being exposed to a variety of suffering, danger and Death, alive and well around me. And when I contemplate with what philosophick firmness and calmness they both of them supported pain, sickness and evils of various sorts, and withstood the utmost efforts of the ennemies' malice, and see with what greatness of mind they now generously conduct themselves to all; my heart overflows with gratitude to their great Preserver for continuing to me such children. Be assured, my dear Daniel, no pleasure can equal that which a mother feels when she knows her children have acted their part well through life, and when she sees them happy in the consciousness of having done so. May the Almighty in his infinite goodness and condescencion accept my prayer when I earnestly entreat that your dear and greatly beloved mother may enjoy the same comfort in seeing you and your sister answer her most sanguine hopes: for though I hope your Country will never want your aid in a Millitary capacity you may be guided by the same principles of true honour and real virtue that have always actuated them, and though not called exactly to the same exertion, your conduct in publick and private life may Emulate the Example they have set you, and give your mother a comfort which nothing else can. . . .

When I take a retrospective view of our past sufferings, so recent too, and compare them with our present prospects, the change is so great and sudden it appears like a dream, and I can hardly believe the pleasing reality, that peace, with all its train of blessings is returned, and that everyone may find Shelter under his own Vine and his own Fig-tree, and be happy. Blessed be God! the effusion of human blood is stopped. Truth may now also appear in its full force and native Lustre, without dread of the oppressive hand of power as heretofore, when the injured were not heard, or heard only to be treated with contempt and insult; when in justice to themselves they would disprove those horrid falsehoods and misrepresentations which natural malevolence or party rage inspired. How much has this unhappy land felt the insolence of power and wanton cruelty; there are but few here but can feelingly tell a tale of woe. Were I to enumerate the distresses that have come to my own knowledge I should distress you and myself beyond measure, for their sorrows were greater than mine, and I experienced a large share of the bitter portion dealt out at those evil times. Both my Sons, their wives and Infants were exiled. Wounded sick and emaciated with a very pittance to support them in a strange Land [Philadelphia] they imbarked. Their estates had been long before sequestrated and mine was shattered and ruined, which left me little power to assist them; nor had I in Country or Town a place to lay my head, all was taken out of my possession; my house I lived in, that in Colleton Square, and at Belmont, all was taken from me, nor was I able to hire a lodging. But let me forget as soon as I can their cruelties, I wish to forgive and will say no more on this subject, and hope our joy and gratitude for our great deliverance may equal our former anguish, and our contentment in mediocrity, and moderation in prosperity, equal the fortitude with which the greatest number even of our sex sustained the great reverse of fortune they experienced.

ABIGAIL ADAMS

Letters to John Quincy Adams

June, 1778

My Dear Son,

'Tis almost four months since you left your native land, and embarked upon the mighty waters, in quest of a foreign country. Although I have not particularly written to you since, yet you may be assured you have constantly been upon my heart and mind.

It is a very difficult task, my dear son, for a tender parent to bring her mind to part with a child of your years going to a distant land; nor could I have acquiesced in such a separation under any other care than that of the most excellent parent and guardian who accompanied you. You have arrived at years capable of improving under the advantages you will be likely to have, if you do but properly attend to them. They are talents put into your hands, of which an account will be required of you hereafter; and being possessed of one, two, or four, see to it that you double your numbers.

The most amiable and most useful disposition in a young mind is diffidence of itself; and this should lead you to seek advice and instruction from him, who is your natural guardian, and will always counsel and direct you in the best manner, both for your present and future happiness. You are in possession of a natural good understanding, and of spirits unbroken by adversity and untamed with care. Improve your understanding by acquiring useful knowledge and virtue, such as will render you an ornament to society, an honor to your country, and a blessing to your parents. Great learning and superior abilities, should you ever possess them, will be of little value and small estimation, unless virtue, honor, truth, and integrity are added to them. Adhere to those religious sentiments and principles which were early instilled into your mind, and remember that you are accountable to your Maker for all your words and actions.

You have entered early in life upon the great theatre of the world, which is full of temptations and vice of every kind. You are not wholly unacquainted with history, in which you have read of crimes which your inexperienced mind could scarcely believe credible. You have been taught to think of them with horror, and to view vice as

> a monster of so frightful mien,
> That, to be hated, needs but to be seen.

Yet you must keep a strict guard upon yourself, or the odious monster will soon lose its terror by becoming familiar to you. The modern history of our own times, furnishes as black a list of crimes, as can be paralleled in ancient times, even if we go back to Nero, Caligula, or Cæsar Borgia. Young as you are, the cruel war, into which we have been compelled by the haughty tyrant of Britain and the bloody emissaries of his vengeance, may stamp upon your mind this certain truth, that the welfare and prosperity of all countries, communities, and, I may add, individuals, depend upon their morals. That nation to which we were once united, as it has departed from justice, eluded and subverted the wise laws which formerly governed it, and suffered the worst of crimes to go unpunished, has lost its valor, wisdom and humanity, and, from being the dread and terror of Europe, has sunk into derision and infamy.

Be assured I am most affectionately yours,

—————— .

12 January, 1780

My Dear Son,

... These are times in which a genius would wish to live. It is not in the still calm of life, or the repose of a pacific station, that great characters are formed. Would Cicero have shone so distinguished an orator if he had not been roused, kindled, and inflamed by the tyranny of Catiline, Verres, and Mark Anthony? The habits of a vigorous mind are formed in contending with difficulties. All history will convince you of this, and that wisdom and penetration are the fruit of experience, not the lessons of retirement and leisure. Great necessities call out great virtues. When a mind is raised and animated by scenes that engage the heart, then those qualities, which would otherwise lie dormant, wake into life and form the character of the hero and the statesman. War, tyranny, and desolation are the scourges of the Almighty, and ought no doubt to be deprecated. Yet it is your lot, my son, to be an eyewitness of these calamities in your own native land, and, at the same time, to owe your existence among a people who have made a glorious defence of their invaded liberties, and who, aided by a generous and powerful ally, with the blessing of Heaven, will transmit this inheritance to ages yet unborn.

Nor ought it to be one of the least of your incitements towards exerting every power and faculty of your mind, that you have a parent who has taken so large and active a share in this contest, and discharged the trust reposed in him with so much satisfaction as to be honored with the important embassy which at present calls him abroad.

The strict and inviolable regard you have ever paid to truth, gives me pleasing hopes that you will not swerve from her dictates, but add justice, fortitude, and every manly virtue which can adorn a good citizen, do honor to your country, and render your parents supremely happy, particularly your ever affectionate mother,

A. A.

Braintree, 26 December, 1783

My Dear Son,

The early age at which you went abroad gave you not an opportunity of becoming acquainted with your own country. Yet the revolution, in which we were engaged, held it up in so striking and important a light, that you could not avoid being in some measure irradiated with the view. The characters with which you were connected, and the conversation you continually heard, must have impressed your mind with a sense of the laws, the liberties, and the glorious privileges, which distinguish the free, sovereign, independent States of America.

Let your observations and comparisons produce in your mind an abhorrence of domination and power, the parent of slavery, ignorance, and barbarism, which places man upon a level with his fellow tenants of the woods;

> A day, an hour, of virtuous liberty
> Is worth a whole eternity of bondage.

You have seen power in its various forms, — a benign deity, when exercised in the suppression of fraud, injustice, and tyranny, but a demon, when united with unbounded ambition, — a wide-wasting fury, who has destroyed her thousands. Not an age of the world but has produced characters, to which whole human hecatombs have been sacrificed.

What is the history of mighty kingdoms and nations, but a detail of the ravages and cruelties of the powerful over the weak? Yet it is instructive to trace the various causes, which produced the strength of one nation, and the decline and weakness of another; to learn by what arts one man has been able to subjugate millions of his fellow creatures, the motives which have put him upon action, and the causes of his success; — sometimes driven by ambition and a lust of power; at other times, swallowed up by religious enthusiasm, blind bigotry, and ignorant zeal; sometimes enervated with luxury and debauched by pleasure, until the most powerful nations have become a prey and been subdued by these Sirens, when neither the number of their enemies, nor the prowess of their arms, could conquer them. . . .

The history of your own country and the late revolution are striking and recent instances of the mighty things achieved by a brave, enlightened, and hardy people, determined to be free; the very yeomanry of which, in many instances, have shown themselves superior to corruption, as Britain well knows, on more occasions than the loss of her André. Glory, my son, in a country which has given birth to characters, both in the civil and military departments, which may vie with the wisdom and valor of antiquity. As an immediate descendant of one of those characters, may you be led to an imitation of that disinterested patriotism and that noble love of your country, which will teach you to despise wealth, titles, pomp, and equipage, as mere external advantages, which cannot add to the internal excellence of your mind, or compensate for the want of integrity and virtue.

May your mind be thoroughly impressed with the absolute necessity of universal virtue and goodness, as the only sure road to happiness, and may you walk therein with undeviating steps, — is the sincere and most affectionate wish of

Your mother,
A. Adams

Letter to John Adams

Braintree, 31 March, 1776

I wish you would ever write me a letter half as long as I write you, and tell me, if you may, where your fleet are gone; what sort of defense Virginia can make against our common enemy; whether it is so situated as to make an able defense. Are not the gentry lords, and the common people vassals? Are they not like the uncivilized vassals Britain represents us to be? I hope their riflemen, who have shown themselves very savage and even blood-thirsty, are not a specimen of the generality of the people. I am willing to allow the colony great merit for having produced a Washington; but they have been shamefully duped by a Dunmore [British commander].

I have sometimes been ready to think that the passion for liberty cannot be equally strong in the breasts of those who have been accustomed to deprive their fellow-creatures of theirs. Of this I am certain, that it is not founded upon that generous and Christian principle of doing to others as we would that others should do unto us.

I long to hear that you have declared an independency. And, by the way, in the new code of laws which I suppose it will be necessary for you to make, I desire you would remember the ladies and be more generous and favorable to them than your ancestors. Do not put such unlimited power into the hands of the husbands. Remember, all men would be tyrants if they could. If particular care and attention is not paid to the ladies, we are determined to foment a rebellion, and will not hold ourselves bound by any laws in which we have no voice or representation.

That your sex are naturally tyrannical is a truth so thoroughly established as to admit of no dispute; but such of you as wish to be happy willingly give up the harsh title of master for the more tender and endearing one of friend. Why, then, not put it out of the power of the vicious and the lawless to use us with cruelty and indignity with impunity? Men of sense in all ages abhor those customs which treat us only as the vassals of your sex; regard us then as beings placed by Providence under your protection, and in imitation of the Supreme Being make use of that power only for our happiness.

20

Shays's Rebellion: Prelude to the Constitution
George Richards Minot

During the 1780s, political conflict splintered much of the country. For relief from the economic hardships that followed the war, farmers looked to local and state government to pass and enforce laws that favored debtors over creditors. Their more cosmopolitan neighbors wanted strong government that would ensure sound money, promote trade, pay the public debt, and keep order.

Nowhere was this battle waged more fiercely than in Massachusetts. Poor harvests made it difficult for farmers to pay their debts to merchants and to meet the high taxes levied by the state to discharge its Revolutionary War obligations. Soon creditors and the state were dispossessing farmers of their land and stock, and some were even thrown into jail for nonpayment of debt. Farmers began demanding legislation to improve their situation. They called for lower taxes, the issuance of paper money to make debt repayment easier, and "stay laws" to postpone payment to creditors. When these efforts failed, the farmers took more dramatic action. Adopting as their symbol the "sprig of green" on the soldiers' caps worn during the Revolutionary War, these men, many of them veterans of that conflict themselves, formed paramilitary units. Their main target was the courts to which creditors and tax collectors repaired to exact what they were owed. In a careful, orderly, but plainly illegal manner they surrounded courthouses and stopped proceedings. Informally organized, they had few recognized leaders, but the former Revolutionary War officers among them, like Daniel Shays of Pelham, drilled the men and became at least nominal leaders of the movement.

Merchants, professionals, and government leaders were horrified by the court closings, describing the Shaysites as "the most idle, vicious and disorderly set of men" who would "plunge the community into anarchy." Boston lawyer George Richards Minot (1758–1802) shouted for "Daniel Shays's decapitation," although a year later, when he wrote the account excerpted here, he had moderated his opinion so that historians have praised the fairness of his judgments. Governor James Bowdoin called for "the most vigorous measures . . . to enforce obedience to the law," and the legislature responded as Massachusetts organized an army under Revolutionary War general Benjamin Lincoln.

The Shaysite armies harassed merchants and tried to capture the federal arsenal at Springfield. In the end, though, General Lincoln's army of militiamen easily defeated them; the rebellion dissipated, and its leaders fled the state. By the following year the

George Richards Minot, *The History of the Insurrections in Massachusetts, in the Year Seventeen Hundred and Eighty Six, and the Rebellion Consequent Thereon*, 2nd ed. (Boston: Books for Libraries Press, 1810), pp. 108–25.

economy had swung upward, and the Massachusetts government, though firmly set against the Shaysites, eased the credit squeeze by a limited issuance of paper money.

The crisis was over, but its political effect was not. The rebellion had alarmed political leaders throughout the colonies and greatly strengthened the position of those who advocated a stronger central government to control such uprisings. Shays's Rebellion was extensively debated as the Constitution was drafted and approved. The arguments over ratification in Massachusetts followed quite closely the political divisions expressed in the insurrection. Only their superior organization enabled the Federalists to achieve victory in this pivotal state by the close vote of 187 to 168.

BEFORE YOU READ

1. What position on Shays's Rebellion does George Richards Minot take in his account?

2. What strategy did the Shaysites pursue? How aggressive do they seem? How determined were they to bring the issue to actual combat?

3. What strategy did General Benjamin Lincoln, who led the state's army, pursue? How aggressive does he seem? How determined was he to bring the issue to actual combat?

4. Why do you think Shays's Rebellion became an important issue throughout the colonies?

The insurgents having collected these forces, which were respectable from their numbers, and from the large proportion of old continental soldiers which they contained, Shays, on the 24th of the month, sent a message to Day, informing him that he proposed to attack the post at Springfield the next day, on the east side; and desiring that Day's forces might co-operate with him on the other. . . . His reply to Shays's letter was, that he could not assist in the attack on the day proposed, but would do it on the 26th. This answer however, was luckily intercepted by General Shephard, and Shays took it for granted, that Day would co-operate with him, at the time he had mentioned. But instead of this, Day only sent in an insolent summons to General Shepard, acquainting him, that the body of the people assembled in arms, adhering to the first principles in nature, self preservation, did in the most peremptory manner, demand

> 1st. That the troops in Springfield should lay down their arms.
>
> 2d. That their arms should be deposited in the publick stores, under the care of the proper officers, to be returned to the owners at the termination of the contest.
>
> 3d. That the troops should return to their several homes upon parole.

On the same day, Shays sent a petition, as it was termed, from Wilbraham, to General Lincoln, in which he observed, that from his unwillingness to be accessary to the shedding of blood, and from his desire of promoting peace, he was led to propose, that all the insurgents should be indemnified, until the next sitting of the General Court, and until an opportunity could be had for a hearing of their complaints; that the persons who had been taken by the government should be released, without punishment; that these conditions should be made sure by proclamation of the Governour: On which the insurgents should return to their homes, and wait for constitutional relief from the insupportable burdens under which they laboured. When this petition was written, General Lincoln was two days march from Springfield; and if the object of it had been really pacifick, some time would have been allowed for an answer.

The situation of General Shephard and his party, whom no one doubted the insurgents intended to attack with all their force, was truly alarming. His troops were decidedly inferiour in numbers to those of the enemy; and though he was possessed of artillery, yet he could derive little advantage from works thrown up on such a sudden emergency. So doubtful was the issue of an attack upon him, in the mind of General Lincoln, and so great was the chance of Shays's gaining importance and numbers from success, that on the 25th, General Brooks was called upon to march with the Middlesex militia to Springfield, as early as possible.

While affairs were in this critical state, General Shepard, about 4 o'clock in the afternoon of the 25th, perceived Shays advancing on the Boston road, towards the arsenal where the militia were posted, with his troops in open column. Possessed of the importance of that moment, in which the first blood should be drawn in the contest, the General sent one of his aids with two other gentlemen, several times, to know the intention of the enemy, and to warn them of their danger. The purport of their answer was, that they would have possession of the barracks; and they immediately marched onwards to within 250 yards of the arsenal. A message was again sent to inform them, that the militia were posted there by order of the Governour, and of Congress, and that if they approached nearer, they would be fired upon. To this, one of their leaders replied, that *that* was all they wanted; and they advanced one hundred yards further. Necessity now compelled General Shepard to fire, but his humanity did not desert him. He ordered the two first shot to be directed over their heads; this however, instead of retarding, quickened their approach; and the artillery was at last pointed at the centre of their column. This measures was not without its effect. A cry of murder arose from the rear of the insurgents, and their whole body was thrown into the utmost confusion. Shays attempted to display his column, but it was in vain. His troops retreated with precipitation to Ludlow, about ten miles from the place of action, leaving three of their men dead, and one wounded on the field.

The advantages which the militia had in their power, both from the disorder of this retreat, which was as injudicious as the mode of attack, and from the nature of the ground, would have enabled them to have killed the greater part of the insurgents, had a pursuit taken place. But, the object of the commander was rather to terrify, than to destroy the deluded fugitives. . . .

Notwithstanding the fatigue of a march, performed in an uncommonly severe winter, the army were ordered under arms at half past three o'clock, the same day on which they arrived. Four regiments, with four pieces of artillery, and the horse, crossed the river upon the ice, while the Hampshire troops, under the command of General Shepard, moved up the river, as well to prevent a junction of the party under Shays, who were on the east side, with those under Day, on the west, as to cut off the retreat of the latter. It was also a great object by this manœuvre, to encircle Day, with a force so evidently superior, as to prevent his people from firing, and thereby to avoid the shedding of blood. Upon the appearance of the army on the river, the guard at the ferry house turned out, but forsook the pass; and after a small shew of opposition, near the meeting house, retired in the utmost confusion. This was attended with the flight of all Day's party, who escaped to Northampton, with the loss of a very small number, that were overtaken by the light horse. The insurgent forces under Shays, made no greater opposition, on the day following. When the army approached him, he immediately began a retreat, through South-Hadley to Amherst, supplying the hunger of his men by plunder. . . .

The appearance of things was exceedingly changed by the flight of the insurgents from Springfield. . . . The apprehensions of the inhabitants had been . . . greatly raised, from the various reports of the numbers and objects of the insurgents; and more than all, from the aid which they affected to rely on, from secret, but influential characters within the state, and the discontented of neighbouring governments. From such ideas, the meeting of the two armies in full force, at Springfield was dreaded by all, in whose minds the tranquillity of the country was the primary object. But these fears wholly vanished, by the dispersing of the insurgent forces, and a security naturally arose from the flattering view of their broken and forlorn condition. . . .

The pursuit of Shays and his party, which commenced at two o'clock in the morning, was continued till the army reached Amherst, through which place, however, he passed before their arrival, on his way to Pelham, with the main body of his men. General Lincoln, finding the enemy out of his reach, directed his march to Hadley, the nearest place which could be found to afford a cover for his troops. Upon an examination of the houses at Amherst, it was discovered, that most of the male inhabitants had quitted them to follow the insurgents; and that ten sleigh loads of provisions had gone forward from the county of Berkshire for their use. Under such appearances, a strict prohibition was laid upon the remaining inhabitants, against affording any supplies to their deluded neighbours.

The morning after the arrival of the army at Hadley, information was received that a small number of General Shepard's men had been captured at Southampton, and that the enemy's party still continued there. The Brookfield volunteers, consisting of fifty men, and commanded by Colonel Baldwin, were sent in sleighs, with 100 horse, under the command of Colonel Crafts, to pursue them. They were soon found to consist of eighty men with ten sleighs, and at twelve o'clock the same night were overtaken at Middlefield. They had quartered themselves in separate places; and about one half of them, with one Luddington their captain, being lodged in a house together, were first surrounded. It was a singular circumstance, that among the government's volunteers, happened to be General Tupper, who had lately commanded a continental regiment, in which Luddington had served as a Corporal. The General, ignorant of the character of his enemy, summoned the party to surrender. How astonished was the Corporal at receiving the summons, in a voice to which he had never dared to refuse obedience! A momentary explanation took place, which but heightened the General's commands. Resistance was no longer made, the doors were opened, and a surrender was agreed to. By this time, the rest of the party had paraded under arms, at the distance of 200 yards, where they were met by a number of men prepared for their reception. Both sides were on the point of firing, but, upon an artful representation of the strength of the government's troops, the insurgents laid down their arms, and fifty-nine prisoners, with nine sleigh loads of provisions, fell into the hands of the conquerors, who returned to the army on the day following.

The whole force of the insurgents having taken post on two high hills in Pelham, called east and west hills, which were rendered difficult of access by the depth of the snow around them, General Lincoln, on the 30th of January, sent a letter directed to Captain Shays, and the officers commanding the men in arms against the government of the Commonwealth, as follows:

> Whether you are convinced or not of your error in flying to arms, I am fully persuaded that before this hour, you must have the fullest conviction upon your own minds, that you are not able to execute your original purposes.
>
> Your resources are few, your force is inconsiderable, and hourly decreasing from the disaffection of your men; you are in a post where you have neither cover nor supplies, and in a situation in which you can neither give aid to your friends, nor discomfort to the supporters of good order and government. — Under these circumstances, you cannot hesitate a moment to disband your deluded followers. If you should not, I must approach, and apprehend the most influential characters among you. Should you attempt to fire upon the troops of government, the consequences must be fatal to many of your men, the least guilty. To prevent bloodshed, you will communicate to your privates, that if they will instantly lay down their arms, surrender themselves to government, and take and subscribe the oath of allegiance to this Commonwealth, they shall be recommended to the General Court for mercy. If you should either withhold this information from them, or suffer your people to fire upon our approach, you must be answerable for all the ills which may exist in consequence thereof.

To this letter the following Answer was received.

Pelham, January 30th, 1787

To General Lincoln, commanding the government troops at Hadley.

Sir,

> The people assembled in arms from the counties of Middlesex, Worcester, Hampshire and Berkshire, taking into serious consideration the purport of the flag just received, return for answer, that however unjustifiable the measures may be which the people have adopted, in having recourse to arms, various circumstances have induced them thereto. We are sensible of the embarrassments the people are under; but that virtue which truly characterizes the citizens of a republican government, hath hitherto marked our paths with a degree of innocence; and we wish and trust it will still be the case. At the same time, the people are willing to lay down their arms, on the condition of a general pardon, and return to their respective homes, as they are unwilling to stain the land, which we in the late war purchased at so dear a rate, with the blood of our brethren and neighbours. Therefore, we pray that hostilities may cease, on

your part, until our united prayers may be presented to the General Court, and we receive an answer, as a person is gone for that purpose. If this request may be complied with, government shall meet with no interruption from the people, but let each army occupy the post where they now are.

DANIEL SHAYS, *Captain*

On the next day, three of the insurgent leaders came to Head Quarters with the following letter.

The Honourable General Lincoln.
Sir,

As the officers of the people, now convened in defence of their rights and privileges, have sent a petition to the General Court, for the sole purpose of accommodating our present unhappy affairs, we justly expect that hostilities may cease on both sides, until we have a return from our legislature.

Your Honour will therefore be pleased to give us an answer.
Per order of the committee for reconciliation.

FRANCIS STONE, *Chairman*
DANIEL SHAYS, *Captain*
ADAM WHEELER

Pelham, January 31, 1787

To this the following Answer was sent.

Hadley, January 31*st*, 1787

Gentlemen,

Your request is totally inadmissible, as no powers are delegated to me which would justify a delay of my operations. Hostilities I have not commenced.

I have again to warn the people in arms against government, immediately to disband, as they would avoid the ill consequences which may ensue, should they be inattentive to this caution.

B. LINCOLN

To FRANCIS STONE,
DANIEL SHAYS,
ADAM WHEELER

During these negotiations between the army and the insurgents, the time arrived for the assembling of the legislature. . . . The Court then acquainted the Governour, that they were prepared to receive his communications, and he addressed them by a speech from the chair, which contained a retrospective account of the malcontents, as to their views and proceedings, and of the measures which the government had adopted to oppose them. Vigour and energy were strongly recommended, as the proper means of crushing so unprovoked an insurrection, while a want of them might draw on the evils of a civil war. . . .

Affairs had been brought to such a crisis, that there was no room left for the legislature to waver in their opinions, or to delay their measures. The whole community were in an alarm, and the appeal to the sword was actually made. One army or the other was to be supported, and there could be no hesitation in the mind of any reasonable man, which it ought to be. On the next day, therefore, a declaration of Rebellion was unanimously passed in the Senate, and concurred by the lower House. This however was accompanied by a resolve, approving of General Lincoln's offer of clemency to the privates among the insurgents, and empowering the Governour in the name of the General Court to promise a pardon, under such disqualifications, as should afterwards be provided, to all privates and noncommissioned officers, that were in arms against the Commonwealth, unless excepted by the general officer commanding the troops, upon condition of their surrendering their arms, and taking and subscribing the oath of allegiance, within a time to be prescribed by the Governour.

On the same day, an answer was also sent to the Governour's speech. In this the Court informed his Excellency of their entire satisfaction, in the measures which he had been pleased to take for subduing a turbulent spirit, that had too long insulted the Government of the Commonwealth; and congratulated him on the success which had attended them. They earnestly intreated him still to continue them, with such further constitutional measures, as he might think necessary, to extirpate the spirit of rebellion; for the better enabling of him to do which, they thought it necessary to declare that a rebellion existed. . . . They subjoined that they would vigorously pursue every measure, which would be calculated to support the constitution, and would continue to redress any real grievances, if such should be found to exist.

PART FOUR

The Young Republic

People in Motion

Thomas Jefferson presided over a new kind of society and polity that historian Robert H. Wiebe has described as "the society of white men." In this world the "self-government" of individual white men replaced the power of the state, which "did little and intruded less." Jefferson's governance of his own private world of Monticello with its many slaves—including the enigmatic Sally Hemings—has recently become an issue of significance to students of Jefferson's life, raising questions about how this "society of white men" affected the lives of women and people of color.

Within one generation, Jefferson's world of gentlemanly governance had been replaced by a noisier, more raucous set of contests among white men that we call Jacksonian democracy. The new society is caught at the very start of Andrew Jackson's tenure in the White House, when his adoring fans mobbed the presidential reception. The issue of extending democracy beyond that world of white men arose when the Cherokee Indians sought to blur the borders between white and Indian cultures. And the movement westward that engaged the deepest interests of the entire society finally forced to the center of American life the issue of slavery that both defined and divided that society of white men.

For almost two hundred years American society had been confined to the corridor between the Atlantic Ocean and the Appalachian mountain range. Mountains, Indians, and conflict among European powers discouraged Americans from pushing west. Then, after about 1795, with the Indian tribes defeated during the Revolution and the price of good eastern land mounting, a white migration began. Thomas Jefferson's purchase of the vast Louisiana Territory and his sponsorship of the Lewis and Clark expedition quickened this movement as did rising prices worldwide for agricultural products. A revolution in transportation further encouraged the migration: turnpikes began to replace stump-filled rutted paths; steamboats overtook sailing ships and river rafts; canals offered the first economical means of moving eastward the bulky products of western farms; and finally railroads spread westward in the 1840s and 1850s, overshadowing all other forms of long-distance transportation. The land seemed to have tilted permanently, shaking its human burden westward in a long, rough tumble toward the Pacific.

The life people sought in the West engaged more than economic ambition: evangelical preachers such as James B. Finley and Peter Cartwright crisscrossed the Western territories, and believers like Priscilla Merriman Evans and her husband trekked heroically to reach their Mormon Zion in the wilderness.

These new Westerners were not entering empty territory. Early explorers such as Meriwether Lewis and William Clark became diplomats among the Indians who were thinly spread across these lands. Forced westward, Native Americans such as the Cherokee, represented here by John Ross, faced competition from other tribes already living in the West. And the Spanish and then their heirs, the Mexicans, owned much of these Western territories. Conflicts with Mexico determined the future of nearly a million square miles of what is now Texas, New Mexico, Arizona, Nevada, California, Utah, and parts of Colorado, Wyoming, Kansas, and Oklahoma. The discovery of gold in California in 1848 and the rush of miners, guided by books like that of Edward Gould Buffum, accelerated the evolution of the West, forcing decisions about its future that soon led to the Civil War.

POINTS OF VIEW

Two Families: Hemings and Jefferson (1858–1873)

21

Hemings Family Accounts

Madison Hemings and Israel Jefferson

In 1802, the Richmond Recorder, *a newspaper published by Thomas Jefferson's political opponents, the Federalists, contained sensational stories accusing the president of having fathered several children by one of his slaves, Sally Hemings. The author of these articles, James Callender, was a scoundrel, a blackmailer, and a bigot whose attacks on*

Annette Gordon-Reed, *Thomas Jefferson and Sally Hemings: An American Controversy* (Charlottesville: University Press of Virginia, 1997), pp. 245–60; "Life among the Lowly, No. 1," *Pike County (Ohio) Republican*, March 13, 1873; "Life among the Lowly, No. 3," *Pike County (Ohio) Republican*, December 25, 1873.

Jefferson paled in comparison with his characterization of the alleged presidential mistress. "This wench Sally," as he referred to her, was a "slut as common as the pavement," her milieu "the kitchen or perhaps the pigstye," her children by Jefferson "a litter." With this vicious prose was born the story of "dusky Sally," often affirmed by Federalists, denied by Republicans, and rejected by historians for most of the two hundred years since.

Some of the story is not in dispute. Born in 1773, Sally Hemings was the daughter of Jefferson's father-in-law, John Wayles, by one of his slaves, Elizabeth Hemings, making her the half-sister of Jefferson's wife, Martha Wayles Jefferson, who died in 1782. Five years later Sally accompanied Jefferson's youngest daughter to France where Jefferson was serving as American minister to the French court. In accordance with French law, by virtue of living in France, Sally became free. Nonetheless, she returned with Jefferson to Virginia in 1789, and rumors soon spread among Jefferson's neighbors that the two were lovers. Sally bore either six or seven children. Four of Hemings's children, three sons and one daughter, lived to become adults. Although Jefferson freed few of his many slaves, all four Hemings children lived their adult lives free of bondage. Two were runaways, of which one, Sally's daughter Harriet, was spirited away with Jefferson's knowledge, and the two youngest boys Jefferson freed in his will. Soon after his death, Sally Hemings was freed as well and settled with her two younger sons. The census taker in 1830 listed all three as white.

Beyond these facts we have conflicting family traditions. This section presents only the Hemings family's version of the story. For the Jefferson family's version, see the accounts in Selection 22.

Madison Hemings (1805–1878), who left Virginia after his mother died and spent most of his adult life in Ohio, told a journalist in 1873 that his mother had told him that he and his siblings were children of Jefferson. Sally Hemings, he claimed, was induced to return to the United States from France by Jefferson's promise to free all her children when they reached the age of twenty-one. Israel Jefferson, another former slave at Monticello who had settled near Madison Hemings in Ohio, confirmed Madison's account later that year.

All of Jefferson's early biographers rejected this story, as did almost all historians throughout the twentieth century. Then in 1997 the University of Virginia Press published Annette Gordon-Reed's Thomas Jefferson and Sally Hemings: An American Controversy. *A professor of law rather than of history, Gordon-Reed was ultimately agnostic on whether Jefferson fathered Hemings's children, but she vigorously and effectively challenged the way historians had used—or, mostly, failed to use—evidence in considering the question. In a prophetic passage in her preface, she wrote:*

> This book is a critique of the defense that has been mounted to counter the notion of a Jefferson-Hemings liaison. It is not my goal to prove that the story is true or that it is false. I suspect that if that is ever done, it will be the result of the miracles of modern science and all the wonders of DNA research, and not because of any interpretation of documents and statements.

In November 1998, the prestigious British scientific journal Nature *published an article based on just such DNA research. The technique compared the Y or male chromosome of a descendant of Sally Hemings's youngest son, Eston, with that of a descendant of Thomas Jefferson's paternal grandfather. (Comparison with Jefferson's direct descendants was not possible because the test requires an unbroken male line and he had no son who lived to bear children.) This genetic comparison demonstrated with a probability of more than ninety-nine percent that Eston Hemings was a descendant of a male Jefferson. Combined with the long-available circumstantial evidence (which includes several reports of contemporaries noting a physical resemblance between Eston Hemings and Thomas Jefferson), this finding—though not conclusive—shifts the burden of proof in establishing the paternity of Hemings's children. The likelihood that Thomas Jefferson fathered children with Sally Hemings is greater than many historians had previously thought. Yet the issue is not settled, and even if it were, we would still be left with fascinating historical questions that will never be resolved to everyone's satisfaction: What was the relationship between Hemings and Jefferson? Were they deeply in love? What was Jefferson's true character?*

BEFORE YOU READ

1. How plausible is Madison Hemings's account of his mother's life and her relationship to Thomas Jefferson?

2. Why do you think Madison Hemings refers to his sister Harriet's children as "never suspected of being tainted with African blood"? Is this comment in character? Why or why not?

3. How much does Israel Jefferson's account add to Madison Hemings's in establishing the likelihood of the Jefferson-Hemings relationship?

THE MEMOIRS OF MADISON HEMINGS

I never knew of but one white man who bore the name of Hemings; he was an Englishman and my great grandfather. He was captain of an English tracking vessel which sailed between England and Williamsburg, Va., then quite a port. My great-grandmother was a fullblooded African, and possibly a native of that country. She was the property of John Wales, a Welchman. Capt. Hemings happened to be in the port of Williamsburg at the time my grandmother was born, and acknowledging her fatherhood he tried to purchase her of Mr. Wales, who would not part with the child, though he was offered an extraordinarily large price for her. She was named Elizabeth Hemings. Being thwarted in the purchase, and determined to own his own flesh and blood he resolved to take the child by force or stealth, but the knowledge of his intention coming to John Wales' ears, through leaky fellow servants of the mother, she and the child were taken into the "great house" under their master's immediate care. I have been informed that it was not the extra value of that child over other slave children that induced Mr. Wales to refuse to sell it, for slave masters then, as in later days, had no compunctions of conscience which restrained them from parting mother and child of however tender age, but he was restrained by the fact that just about that time amalgamation[1] began, and the child was so great a curiosity that its owner desired to raise it him-

---

1. **amalgamation:** intermarriage between races.

self that he might see its outcome. Capt. Hemings soon afterwards sailed from Williamsburg, never to return. Such is the story that comes down to me.

Elizabeth Hemings grew to womanhood in the family of John Wales, whose wife dying she (Elizabeth) was taken by the widower Wales as his concubine, by whom she had six children—three sons and three daughters, viz: Robert, James, Peter, Critty, Sally and Thena. These children went by the name of Hemings.

Williamsburg was the capital of Virginia, and of course it was an aristocratic place, where the "bloods" of the Colony and the new State most did congregate. Thomas Jefferson, the author of the Declaration of Independence, was educated at William and Mary College, which had its seat at Williamsburg. He afterwards studied law with Geo. Wythe, and practiced law at the bar of the general court of the Colony. He was afterwards elected a member of the provincial legislature from Albemarle county. Thos. Jefferson was a visitor at the "great house" of John Wales, who had children about his own age. He formed the acquaintance of his daughter Martha (I believe that was her name, though I am not positively sure,) and intimacy sprang up between them which ripened into love, and they were married. They afterwards went to live at his country seat Monticello, and in course of time had born to them a daughter whom they named Martha. About the time she was born my mother, the second daughter of John Wales and Elizabeth Hemings was born. On the death of John Wales, my grandmother, his concubine, and her children by him fell to Martha, Thomas Jefferson's wife, and consequently became the property of Thomas Jefferson.... About the time of the appointment [as minister to France] and before he was ready to leave the country his wife died, and ... soon after ... he left for France, taking his eldest daughter with him. He had sons born to him, but they died in early infancy, so he then had but two children—Martha and Maria. The latter was left home, but afterwards was ordered to follow him to France. She was three years or so younger than Martha. My mother accompanied her as a body servant. When Mr. Jefferson went to France Martha was just budding into womanhood. Their stay (my mother's and Maria's) was about eighteen months. But during that time my mother became Mr. Jefferson's concubine, and when he was called back home she was *enciente*[2] by him. He desired to bring my mother back to Virginia with him but she demurred. She was just beginning to understand the French language well, and in France she was free, while if she returned to Virginia she would be re-enslaved. So she refused to return with him. To induce her to do so he promised her extraordinary privileges, and made a solemn pledge that her children should be freed at the age of twenty-one years. In consequence of his promise, on which she implicitly relied, she returned with him to Virginia. Soon after their arrival, she gave birth to a child, of whom Thomas Jefferson was the father. It lived but a short time. She gave birth to four others, and Jefferson was the father of all of them. Their names were Beverly, Harriet,

2. *enciente:* pregnant (Fr.).

Madison (myself), and Eston—three sons and one daughter. We all became free agreeably to the treaty entered into by our parents before we were born. We all married and have raised families.

Beverly left Monticello and went to Washington as a white man. He married a white woman in Maryland, and their only child, a daughter, was not known by the white folks to have any colored blood coursing in her veins. Beverly's wife's family were people in good circumstances.

Harriet married a white man in good standing in Washington City, whose name I could give, but will not, for prudential reasons. She raised a family of children, and so far as I know they were never suspected of being tainted with African blood in the community where she lived or lives. I have not heard from her for ten years, and do not know whether she is dead or alive. She thought it to her interest, on going to Washington, to assume the role of a white woman, and by her dress and conduct as such I am not aware that her identity as Harriet Hemings of Monticello has ever been discovered.

Eston married a colored woman in Virginia, and moved from there to Ohio, and lived in Chillicothe several years. In the fall of 1852 he removed to Wisconsin, where he died a year or two afterwards. He left three children.

As to myself, I was named Madison by the wife of James Madison, who was afterwards President of the United States. Mrs. Madison happened to be at Monticello at the time of my birth, and begged the privilege of naming me, promising my mother a fine present for the honor. She consented, and Mrs. Madison dubbed me by the name I now acknowledge, but like many promises of white folks to the slaves she never gave my mother anything. I was born at my father's seat of Monticello, in Albemarle county, Va., near Charlottesville, on the 19th day of January, 1805. My very earliest recollections are of my grandmother Elizabeth Hemings. That was when I was about three years old. She was sick and upon her death bed. I was eating a piece of bread and asked if she would have some. She replied: "No, granny don't want bread any more." She shortly afterwards breathed her last. I have only a faint recollection of her.

Of my father, Thomas Jefferson, I knew more of his domestic than his public life during his life time. It is only since his death that I have learned much of the latter, except that he was considered as a foremost man in the land, and held many important trusts, including that of President. I learned to read by inducing the white children to teach me the letters and something more; what else I know of books I have picked up here and there till now I can read and write. I was almost 21½ years of age when my father died on the 4th of July, 1826.

About his own home he was the quietest of men. He was hardly ever known to get angry, though sometimes he was irritated when matters went wrong, but even then he hardly ever allowed himself to be made unhappy any great length of time. Unlike Washington he had but little taste or care for agricultural pursuits. He left matters pertaining to his plantations mostly with his stewards and overseers. He always had mechanics at work for him, such as carpenters, blacksmiths, shoemakers, coopers, &c. It was his mechanics he seemed mostly to direct, and in their operations he took great interest. Almost every day of his later years he might have been seen among them. He occupied much of the time in his office engaged in correspondence and reading and writing. His general temperament was smooth and even; he was very undemonstrative. He was uniformly kind to all about him. He was not in the habit of showing partiality or fatherly affection to us children. We were the only children of his by a slave woman. He was affectionate toward his white grandchildren, of whom he had fourteen, twelve of whom lived to manhood and womanhood. . . .

My father generally enjoyed excellent health. I never knew him to have but one spell of sickness, and that was caused by a visit to the Warm Springs in 1818. Till within three weeks of his death he was hale and hearty, and at the age of 83 years walked erect and with a stately tread. I am now 68, and I well remember that he was a much smarter man physically, even at that age, than I am.

When I was fourteen years old I was put to the carpenter trade under the charge of John Hemings, the youngest son of my grandmother. . . . My brothers, sister Harriet and myself, were used alike. We were permitted to stay about the "great house," and only required to do such light work as going on errands. Harriet learned to spin and to weave in a little factory on the home plantation. We were free from the dread of having to be slaves all our lives long, and were measurably happy. We were always permitted to be with our mother, who was well used. It was her duty, all her life which I can remember, up to the time of father's death, to take care of his chamber and wardrobe, look after us children and do such light work as sewing, &c. Provision was made in the will of our father that we should be free when we arrived at the age of 21 years. We had all passed that period when he died but Eston, and he was given the remainder of his time shortly after. He and I rented a house and took mother to live with us, till her death, which event occurred in 1835.

In 1834 I married Mary McCoy. . . . We lived and labored together in Virginia till 1836, when we voluntarily left and came to Ohio. . . . I worked at my trade. . . . I did the carpenter work for the brick building now owned by John J. Kellison in which the *Pike County Republican* is printed. . . . I also reconstructed the building on the corner of Market and Water Streets from a store to a hotel. . . .

When we came from Virginia we brought one daughter (Sarah) with us, leaving the dust of a son in the soil near Monticello. We have born to us in this State nine children. Two are dead. The names of the living, besides Sarah, are Harriet, Mary Ann, Catharine, Jane, William Beverly, James Madison, Ellen Wales. Thomas Eston died in the Andersonville prison pen, and Julia died at home. William, James and Ellen are unmarried and live at home in Huntington township, Ross County. All the others are married and raising families. My post office address is Pee Pee, Pike County Ohio.

THE MEMOIRS OF ISRAEL JEFFERSON

I was born at Monticello, the seat of Thos. Jefferson, third President of the United States, December 25 — Christmas day in the morning. The year, I suppose was 1797. . . .

My mother's name was Jane. She was a slave of Thomas Jefferson's and was born and always resided at Monticello till about five years after the death of Mr. Jefferson. She was sold, after his death, by the administrator, to a Mr. Joel Brown, and was taken to Charlottesville, where she died in 1837. . . .

[He recounts his life story and how he came to be free and settled in Ohio.]

Since I have been in Ohio I have learned to read and write, but my duties as a laborer would not permit me to acquire much of an education. But such as I possess I am truly thankful, and consider what education I have as a legitimate fruit of freedom.

The private life of Thomas Jefferson, from my earliest remembrances, in 1804, till the day of his death, was very familiar to me. For fourteen years I made the fire in his bedroom and private chamber, cleaned his office, dusted his books, run of errands and attended him about home. . . .

I know that it was a general statement among the older servants at Monticello, that Mr. Jefferson promised his wife, on her death bed, that he would not again marry. I also know that his servant, Sally Hemmings, (mother to my old friend and former companion at Monticello, Madison Hemmings,) was employed as his chamber-maid, and that Mr. Jefferson was on the most intimate terms with her; that, in fact, she was his concubine. This I know from my intimacy with both parties, and when Madison Hemmings declares that he is a natural son of Thomas Jefferson, the author of the Declaration of Independence, and that his brothers Beverly and Eston and sister Harriet are of the same parentage, I can as conscientiously confirm his statement as any other fact which I believe from circumstances but do not positively know.

22

Jefferson Family Accounts

Henry S. Randall, Ellen Randolph Coolidge, and Edmund Bacon

The 1790s were a period of intense political passions. Two parties, the Federalists and the Democratic-Republicans, arose to contest some of the major policies of President George Washington's administration, particularly the financial program of Alexander Hamilton. Paralleling the grand debates among highly educated and cultured leaders, a partisan press arose that, by today's standards, was astonishingly crude and vicious. As the leader of the opposition party, Thomas Jefferson became the subject of a barrage of

The Papers of James Parton, bMS Am 1248.1 (240), by permission by Houghton Library, Harvard University; Coolidge Family Papers, acc. no. 9090, Special Collections Department, University of Virginia Library; James A. Bear Jr., ed., *Jefferson at Monticello* (Charlottesville: University Press of Virginia, 1967), pp. 99–102.

personal attacks, the most famous of which is James Callender's allegation of a liaison with his slave, Sally Hemings. Jefferson sensibly refused to respond to all attacks: "I had laid it down as a law to myself," he wrote to a friend in 1809, "to take no notice of the thousand calumnies issued against me, but to trust my character to my own conduct and the good sense and candor of my fellow citizens."

Jefferson's family, friends, and loyal supporters largely followed the same rule. In particular, the Jefferson family made no public statements about it, and the few private ones, reprinted here, were — like the Hemings family accounts — made long after the fact. Ellen Randolph Coolidge (1797–1887), a granddaughter of Jefferson, and Henry Randall (1811–1876), an early Jefferson biographer, cite information from Jefferson's oldest grandchild, Thomas Jefferson Randolph, that held that Sally Hemings's children had been fathered by either Samuel Carr or his brother Peter, both nephews of Jefferson. Edmund Bacon, a loyal Jefferson retainer and for many years overseer at Monticello, asserted in his recollections that Jefferson definitely had not fathered Sally Hemings's children, but he or his interviewer discreetly omitted the name of the man Bacon had seen "come out of [Sally Hemings's] room many a morning when I went up to Monticello very early." In addition, family tradition claimed a fifteen-month period before the birth of one of Sally Hemings's children when Jefferson was absent from Monticello.

Historians until the 1970s unanimously believed the Jefferson family story and rejected that of the Hemingses. Few scholars before Annette Gordon-Reed in 1997 (see the previous headnote) expressed any doubts about this consensus. Yet the main points in the Jefferson family's refutation of the "dusky Sally" story now seem highly suspect. The new evidence from the DNA research published in 1998 virtually eliminates Jefferson's nephews, Samuel and Peter Carr, as possible fathers. Moreover, children of Jefferson's sister, Martha Carr, could not have supplied Y chromosomes derived from their grandfather's line. The recollections of Edmund Bacon, told to a local clergyman, Hamilton Wilcox Pierson, are inconclusive: Bacon arrived at Monticello after all but one of Sally Hemings's children had been born, and we do not know when he saw another man exiting Hemings's room. And the family belief that one of the Hemings children was born after Jefferson had been away from Monticello for fifteen months is definitely incorrect. Although he rejects the "dusky Sally" story as a violation of Jefferson's character, Dumas Malone, the great twentieth-century Jefferson biographer, traced Jefferson's movements through all of Sally Hemings's childbearing years and established that Jefferson was present at Monticello nine months before the birth of each of Sally Hemings's children.

Still, although the DNA evidence does shift the burden of proof, it does not answer the question of the Hemings children's paternity with finality. Since Jefferson had no sons who lived to start families, comparing the DNA of a descendant of Hemings's youngest son with that of descendants of Jefferson's grandfather through a paternal uncle establishes only an indirect linkage to Jefferson himself. Strictly in terms of DNA evidence, the father could have been any of a handful of males of the Jefferson family of that generation — many of whom lived close to Monticello. Some have pointed to Jefferson's younger brother Randolph as possibly the father. Or the whole scandal could have begun because Sally Hemings returned from France pregnant by someone of unknown identity, offering Jefferson's enemies the chance to allege that the child was his. Even though Jefferson's comings and goings coincided with the conception dates of the

Hemings children, some uncertainty remains: male relatives whose DNA would match that found by the scientists might have typically visited Monticello only when their famous relative, Thomas Jefferson, was in residence there. They would be far less noticed in dalliance with a slave woman than he, and most were younger than he was. Eston Hemings, whose paternity by a Jefferson has been established by the DNA research, was conceived when Thomas Jefferson was in his mid-sixties, although still quite active and healthy. Scholars and students must now put all the evidence—family traditions, documentary evidence, perceptions of Jefferson and of Hemings, and the DNA studies—together into a single picture. Richard Ellis, a contemporary Jeffersonian scholar, has referred to the writer of the Declaration of Independence as an "American Sphinx." And, as legend promises, the riddle of the Sphinx is not easily solved.

BEFORE YOU READ

1. Given that DNA testing has demonstrated that Jefferson's nephews, Peter and Samuel Carr, could not have sired the one son of Sally Hemings whose descendants could be tested, why might the Jefferson family point to the Carr brothers as being responsible for the rumors about Jefferson's paternity of Hemings's children?

2. Why did the Jefferson family allow no public statements to be made in Thomas Jefferson's defense to counter the "dusky Sally" story?

HENRY S. RANDALL TO JAMES PARTON

Courtland Village, N.Y.
June 1, 1868

Dear Sir—

The "Dusky Sally Story"—the story that Mr. Jefferson kept one of his slaves, (Sally Hemings) as his mistress and had children by her, was once extensively believed by respectable men, and I believe both John Quincy Adams and our Bryant sounded poetical lyres on this very poetical subject!

Walking about mouldering Monticello one day with Col. T. J. Randolph (Mr. Jefferson's oldest grandson) he showed me a smoke blackened and sooty room in one of the collonades, and informed me it was Sally Hemings' room. He asked me if I knew how the story of Mr. Jefferson's connexion with her originated. I told him I did not. "There was a better excuse for it, said he, than you might think: she had children which resembled Mr. Jefferson so closely that it was plain that they had his blood in their veins." He said in one case that the resemblance was so close, that at some distance or in the dusk the slave, dressed in the same way, might be mistaken for Mr. Jefferson.—He said in one instance, a gentleman dining with Mr. Jefferson, looked so startled as he raised his eyes from the latter to the servant behind him, that his discovery of the resemblance was perfectly obvious to all. Sally Hemings was a house servant and her children were brought up house servants—so that the likeness between master and slave was blazoned to all the multitudes who visited this political Mecca.

Mr. Jefferson had two nephews, Peter Carr and Samuel Carr whom he brought up in his house. There were the sons of Mr. Jefferson's sister and her husband Dabney Carr that young and brilliant orator, described by Wirt, who shone so conspicuously in the dawn of the Revolution, but died in 17—. Peter was peculiarly gifted and amiable. Of Samuel I know less. But he became a man of repute and sat in the State Senate of Virginia. Col. Randolph informed me that Sally Hemings was the mistress of Peter, and her sister Betsey the mistress of Samuel—and from these connections sprang the progeny which resembled Mr. Jefferson. Both the Hemings girls were light colored and decidedly good-looking. The Colonel said their connexion with the Carrs was perfectly notorious at Monticello, and scarcely disguised by the latter—never disavowed by them. Samuel's proceedings were particularly open.

Col. Randolph informed me that there was not the shadow of suspicion that Mr. Jefferson in this or any other instance ever had commerce with his female slaves. At the periods when these Carr children were born, he, Col. Randolph, had charge of Monticello. He gave all the general directions, gave out their clothes to the slaves, etc., etc. He said Sally Hemings was treated, dressed, etc., exactly like the rest. He said Mr. Jefferson never locked the door of his room by day: and that he (Col. R.) slept within sound of his breathing at night. He said he had never seen a motion, or a look, or a circumstance which led him to suspect for an instant that there was a particle more of familiarity between Mr. Jefferson and Sally Hemings than between him and the most repulsive servant in the establishment—and that no person ever living at Monticello dreamed of such a thing. With Betsy Hemings, whose children also resembled him, his habitual meeting, was less frequent, and the chance for suspicion still less, and his connexion with her was never indeed alleged by any of our northern politicians, or *poets.*

Col. Randolph said that he had spent a good share of his life closely about Mr. Jefferson—at home and on journeys—in all sorts of circumstances and he fully believed him chaste and pure—as "immaculate a man as God ever created."

Mr. Jefferson's oldest daughter, Mrs. Gov. Randolph, took the Dusky Sally stories much to heart. But she never spoke to her sons but once on the subject. Not long before her death she called two of them—the Colonel and George Wythe Randolph—to her. She asked the Colonel if he remembered when "——Hemings (the slave who most resembled Mr. Jefferson) was born." He said he could answer by referring to the book containing the list of slaves. He turned to the book and found that the slave was born at the time supposed by Mrs. Randolph. She then directed her sons attention to the fact that Mr. Jefferson and Sally Hemings could not have met—were far distant from each other—for fifteen months prior to such birth. She bade her sons remember this fact, and always to defend the character of their grandfather. It so happened when I was afterwards examining an old account book of the Jeffersons I came *pop* on the original entry of this slaves birth: and I was then able from well known circumstances to prove the fifteen months separation—but those circumstances had faded from my memory. I have no doubt I could recover them however did Mr. Jefferson's vindication in the least depend upon them.

Colonel Randolph said that a visitor at Monticello dropped a newspaper from his pocket or accidentally left it. After he was gone, he (Colonel R.) opened the paper and found some very insulting remarks about Mr. Jefferson's Mulatto Children. The Col. said he felt provoked. Peter and Sam Carr were lying not far off under a shade tree. He took the paper and put it in Peters hands, pointing out the article. Peter read it, tears coursing down his cheeks, and then handed it to Sam. Sam also shed tears. Peter exclaimed, "arnt you and I a couple of——pretty fellows to bring this disgrace on poor old uncle who has always fed us! We ought to be——by——!"

I could give fifty more facts were there time, and were there any need of it, to show Mr. Jefferson's innocence of this and all similar offenses against propriety.

I asked Col. R. why on earth Mr. Jefferson did put these slaves who looked like him out of the public sight by sending them to his Bedford estate or elsewhere—He said Mr. Jefferson never betrayed the least consciousness of the resemblance—and although he (Col. R.) had no doubt his mother, would have been very glad to have them removed, that both and all venerated Mr. Jefferson too deeply to broach such a topic to him. What suited him, satisfied them. Mr. Jefferson was deeply attached to the Carrs—especially to Peter. He was extremely indulgent to them and the idea of watching them for faults or vices probably never occurred to him.

Do you ask why I did not state, or at least hint the above facts in my Life of Jefferson? I wanted to do so, but Colonel Randolph, in this solitary case alone, prohibited me from using at my discretion the information he had furnished me with. When I rather pressed him on the point he said, pointing to the family graveyard, "You are not bound to prove a negation. If I should allow you to take Peter Carr's corpse into Court and plead guilty over it to shelter Mr. Jefferson, I should not dare again to walk by his grave; he would rise and spurn me." I am exceedingly glad Col. Randolph *did* overrule me in this particular. I should have made a *shameful* mistake. If I had *unnecessarily* defended him (and it was purely unnecessary to offer any defense) at the expense of a dear nephew— and a noble man—hating a single folly.—

I write this currente calamo,[1] and you will not understand that in telling what Col. R. and others said, I claim to give the precise language. I give it as I *now* recall it. I believe I hit at least the essential purport and spirit of it in every case.

Do you wonder that the above explanations were not made by Mr. Jeffersons friends when the old Federal Party were hurling their missiles at him for keeping a Congo Harem! Nobody could have furnished a hint of explanation outside of the family. The secrets of an old Virginia manor house were like the secrets of an Old Norman Castle. Dr. Dungleson, and Professor Tucker had lived years near Mr. Jefferson, in the University, and were often at Monti-

---

1. **currente calamo:** offhand.

cello. They saw what others saw. But Dr. D. told me that neither he nor Professor T. ever heard the subject *named* in Virginia. An awe and veneration was felt for Mr. Jefferson among his neighbors which in their view rendered it shameful to even talk about his name in such a connexion. Dr. D. told me that he never heard of Col. Randolph talking with anyone on the subject but me. But he said in his own secret mind he had always believed the matter stood just as Col. Randolph explained it to me. . . .

Very truly yours,
Henry S. Randall

James Parton, Esq.

ELLEN RANDOLPH COOLIDGE
TO JOSEPH COOLIDGE

Edgehill
24 October 1858 . . .

I have been talking freely with my brother Jefferson on the subject of the "yellow children" and will give you the substance of our conversation, with my subsequent reflections.

It is difficult to prove a negative. It is impossible to prove that Mr. Jefferson never had a coloured mistress or coloured children and that these children were never sold as slaves. The latter part of the charge however is disproved by its atrocity, and its utter disagreement with the general character and conduct of Mr. Jefferson, acknowledged to be a humane man and eminently a kind master. Would he who was always most considerate of the feelings and the well-being of his slaves, treat them barbarously only when they happened to be his own children, and leave them to be sold in a distant market when he might have left them free — as you know he did several of his slaves, directing his executor to petition the Legislature of Virginia for leave for them to remain in the State after they were free. Some of them are here to this day.

It was his principle (I know that of my own knowledge) to allow such of his slaves as were sufficiently white to pass for white men, to withdraw quietly from the plantation; it was called running away, but they were never reclaimed, I remember four instances of this, three young men and one girl, who walked away and staid away. Their whereabouts was perfectly known but they were left to themselves — for they were white enough to pass for white. Some of the children currently reported to be Mr. Jefferson's were about the age of his own grandchildren. Of course he must have been carrying on his intrigues in the midst of his daughters family and insulting the sanctity of the home by his profligacy. But he had a large family of grandchildren of all ages, older & younger. Young men and young girls. He lived, whenever he was at Monticello, and entirely for the last seventeen years of his life, in the midst of these young people, surrounded by them, his intercourse with them of the freest and most affectionate kind. How comes it that his immoralities were never suspected by his own family—that his daughter and her children rejected with horror and contempt the charges brought against him. That my brother, then a young man certain to know all that was going on behind the scenes, positively declares his indignant belief in the imputations and solemnly affirms that he never saw or heard the smallest thing which could lead him to suspect that his grandfather's life was other than perfectly pure. His apartments had no private entrance not perfectly accessible and visible to all the household. No female domestic ever entered his chambers except at hours when he was known not to be in the public gaze. But again I put it to any fair mind to decide if a man so admirable to his domestic character as Mr. Jefferson, so devoted to his daughters and their children, so fond of their society, so tender, considerate, refined in his intercourse with them, so watchful over them in all respects, would be likely to rear a race of half-breeds under their eyes and carry on his low amours in the circle of his family.

Now many causes existed which might have given rise to suspicions, setting aside the inveterate rage and malice of Mr. Jefferson's traducers.

The house at Monticello was a long time in building and was principally built by Irish workmen. These men were known to have had children of whom the mothers were black women. But these women were much better pleased to have it supposed that such children were their master's. . . . There were dissipated young men in the neighborhood who sought the society of the mulatresses and they in like manner were not anxious to establish any claim of paternity in the results of such associations.

One woman known to Mr. J. Q. Adams and others as "dusky Sally" was pretty notoriously the mistress of a married man, a near relation of Mr. Jefferson's, and there can be small question that her children were his. They were all fair and all set free at my grandfather's death, or had been suffered to absent themselves permanently before he died. The mother, Sally Hemmings, had accompanied Mr. Jefferson's younger daughter to Paris and was lady's maid to both sisters. Again I ask is it likely that so fond, so anxious a father, whose letters to his daughters are replete with tenderness and with good counsels for their conduct, should (when there were so many other objects upon whom to fix his illicit attentions) have selected the female attendant of his own pure children to become his paramour? The thing will not bear telling. There are such things, after, as moral impossibilities.

The habit that the Southern slaves have of adopting their master's names is another cause of misrepresentation and misapprehension. There is no doubt that such of Mr. Jefferson's slaves as were sold after his death would call themselves by his name. One very notorious villain who never had been the property of Mr. Jefferson, took his name and proclaimed himself his son. He was as black as a crow, and born either during Mr. Jefferson's absence abroad, or under some other circumstances which rendered the truth of his assertion simply impossible.

I have written thus far thinking you might chuse to communicate my letter to Mr. Bulfinch. Now I will tell you in confidence what Jefferson told me under the like condition. Mr. Southall and himself young men together, heard Mr.

Peter Carr say with a laugh, that "the old gentleman had to bear the blame of his and Sam's (Col. Carr) misdeeds."

There is a general impression that the four children of Sally Hemmings were *all* the children of Col. Carr, the most notorious good-natured Turk that ever was master of a black seraglio kept at other men's expense. His deeds are as well known as his name.

EDMUND BACON

The house servants were Betty Brown, Sally, Critta, and Betty Hemings, Nance, and Ursula. They were old family servants and great favorites. They were in the room when Mrs. Jefferson died. She died before I went to live with him, and left four little children. He never married again. They have often told my wife that when Mrs. Jefferson died they stood around the bed. Mr. Jefferson sat by her, and she gave him directions about a good many things that she wanted done. When she came to the children, she wept and could not speak for some time. Finally she held up her hand, and spreading out her four fingers, she told him she could not die happy if she thought her four children were ever to have a stepmother brought in over them. Holding her other hand in his, Mr. Jefferson promised her solemnly that he would never marry again. And he never did. He was then quite a young man and very handsome, and I suppose he could have married well; but he always kept that promise.

These women remained at Monticello while he was President. I was instructed to take no control of them. . . .

Sally Hemings went to France with Maria Jefferson when she was a little girl. Mr. Jefferson was Minister to France, and he wanted to put her in school there. They crossed the ocean alone. I have often heard her tell about it. When they got to London, they stayed with Mr. Adams, who was Minister there, until Mr. Jefferson came or sent for them. . . .

Mr. Jefferson freed a number of his servants in his will. I think he would have freed all of them if his affairs had not been so much involved that he could not do it. He freed one girl some years before he died, and there was a great deal of talk about it. She was nearly as white as anybody and very beautiful. People said he freed her because she was his own daughter. She was not his daughter; she was——'s daughter. I know that. I have seen him come out of her mother's room many a morning when I went up to Monticello very early. When she was nearly grown, by Mr. Jefferson's direction I paid her stage fare to Philadelphia and gave her fifty dollars. I have never seen her since and don't know what became of her. From the time she was large enough, she always worked in the cotton factory. She never did any hard work.

FOR CRITICAL THINKING

1. Which position is more plausible on the Jefferson-Hemings relationship—that of the Hemings family or the Jefferson family? What are the strengths and weaknesses of each? Are the Hemings accounts suspect because they are interviews of obscure people

conducted by a journalist? Are the Jefferson family accounts suspect because they insist on specific points that have been disproved?

2. The Jefferson Foundation, which supervises Monticello, early in 2000 acknowledged that at least one of Sally Hemings's children was sired by Thomas Jefferson, and the Foundation has begun planning exhibits at the manor to reflect this. How would you suggest they organize such a display? What should they show? What should they emphasize? Does the evidence bear out the acknowledgment?

3. What was the probable relationship between Thomas Jefferson and Sally Hemings, and how should we think of either of them as a result of what we know? While this question does not admit of any single answer, how would you address it? What does it say about race relations in that era, about love, lust, or romance between the races, or about the third president of the United States?

23

Crossing the Great Divide
Meriwether Lewis and William Clark

The most famous expedition in American history was the brainchild of Thomas Jefferson. For years Jefferson had dreamed that a party of explorers could search out a passage to the Pacific, win the allegiance of the Indians to the new republic, and study the geography, plants, and minerals of a vast and unknown territory.

Meriwether Lewis (1774–1809) and William Clark (1770–1838) were two young men willing to follow Jefferson's dream. Their expedition from St. Louis to the mouth of the Columbia River and back is one of the great adventure stories of our history. The journals and notebooks that members of the party kept have been invaluable to historians, geographers, anthropologists, botanists, and zoologists.

The selections here present the expedition crossing the Great Divide—the peak of the Rocky Mountains where the rivers flow either to the east or the west—in one of the most difficult parts of their journey. The reader can see their careful search for information about the best way west and their close observation of Native American ways. Here also is the most famous single dramatic episode of the expedition: the extraordinary moment when Sacajawea, wife of one of their interpreters, meets a party of Shoshone, her native nation, headed by a chief who is the brother she has not seen since she was a small child. The first excerpt was written by Nicholas Biddle, who was later head of the Bank of the United States. Biddle's descriptions are taken from the notes of various participants in the expedition. They have sometimes been published—incorrectly—as part of the actual journals of Lewis and Clark.

BEFORE YOU READ

1. How did Lewis characterize the Indians and Indian life? What about them did he find fascinating, hard to understand, or admirable?
2. What did he offer Chief Cameahwait in return for his help and horses?
3. Why was crossing the Rocky Mountains so difficult?

NICHOLAS BIDDLE

Saturday, August 17th 1805.

Captain Lewis rose very early and despatched Drewyer and the Indian down the river in quest of the boats. Sheilds was sent out at the same time to hunt, while

Bernard DeVoto, *The Journals of Lewis and Clark* (Boston: Houghton Mifflin Co., 1953), pp. 202–06, 207–11, 213–14.

M'Neal prepared a breakfast out of the remainder of the meat. Drewyer had been gone about two hours, and the Indians were all anxiously waiting for some news, when an Indian who had straggled a short distance down the river, returned with a report that he had seen the white men, who were only a short distance below, and were coming on. The Indians were all transported with joy, and the chief in the warmth of his satisfaction renewed his embrace to Capt. Lewis. . . .

On setting out at seven o'clock, Captain Clarke with Chaboneau and his wife walked on shore, but they had not gone more than a mile before Clarke saw Sacajawea, who was with her husband 100 yards ahead, began to dance and show every mark of the most extravagant joy, turning round him and pointing to several Indians, whom he now saw advancing on horseback, sucking her fingers at the same time to indicate that they were of her native tribe. As they advanced, Captain Clarke discovered among them Drewyer dressed like an Indian, from whom he learnt the situation of the party. While the boats were performing the circuit, he went towards the forks with the Indians, who as they went along, sang aloud with the greatest appearance of delight.

We soon drew near to the camp, and just as we approached it a woman made her way through the crowd towards Sacajawea, and recognising each other, they embraced with the most tender affection. The meeting of these two young women had in it something peculiarly touching, not only in the ardent manner in which their feelings were expressed, but from the real interest of their situation. They had been companions in childhood, in the war with the Minetarees they had both been taken prisoners in the same battle, they had shared and softened the rigours of their captivity, till one of them had cscapcd from the Minnetarees, with scarce a hope of ever seeing her friend relieved from the hands of her enemies. While Sacajawea was renewing among the women the friendships of former days, Captain Clarke went on, and was received by Captain Lewis and the chief, who after the first embraces and salutations were over, conducted him to a sort of circular tent or shade of willows. Here he was seated on a white robe; and the chief immediately tied in his hair six small shells resembling pearls, an ornament highly valued by these people, who procure them in the course of trade from the sea-coast. The moccasins of the whole party were then taken off, and after much ceremony the smoking began. After this the conference was to be opened, and glad of an opportunity of being able to converse more intelligibly, Sacajawea was sent for; she came into the tent, sat down, and was beginning to interpret, when in the person of Cameahwait she recognised her brother: She instantly jumped up, and ran and embraced him, throwing over him her blanket and weeping profusely: The chief was himself moved, though not in the same degree. After some conversation between them she resumed her seat, and attempted to interpret for us, but her new situation seemed to overpower her, and she was frequently interrupted by her tears. After the council was finished the unfortunate woman learnt that all her family were dead except two brothers, one of whom was absent, and a son of her eldest sister, a small boy, who was immediately adopted by her.

MERIWETHER LEWIS

Saturday August 17th 1805.

we made them [the Indians] sensible of their dependance on the will of our government for every species of merchandize as well for their defence & comfort; and apprized them of the strength of our government and it's friendly dispositions towards them. we also gave them as a reason why we wished to pe[ne]trate the country as far as the ocean to the west of them was to examine and find out a more direct way to bring merchandize to them. that as no trade could by carryed on with them before our return to our homes that it was mutually advantageous to them as well as to ourselves that they should render us such aids as they had in their power to furnish in order to haisten our voyage and of course our return home. that such were their horses to transport our baggage without which we could not subsist, and that a pilot to conduct us through the mountains was also necessary if we could not decend the river by water. but that we did not ask either their horses or their services without giving a satisfactory compensation in return. that at present we wished them to collect as many horses as were necessary to transport our baggage to their village on the Columbia where we would then trade with them at our leasure for such horses as they could spare us.

the chief thanked us for friendship towards himself and nation & declared his wish to serve us in every rispect. that he was sorry to find that it must yet be some time before they could be furnished with firearms but said they could live as they had done heretofore until we brought them as we had promised. he said they had not horses enough with them at present to remove our baggage to their village over the mountain, but that he would return tomorrow and encourage his people to come over with their horses and that he would bring his own and assist us. this was complying with all we wished at present.

we next enquired who were chiefs among them. Cameahwait pointed out two others whom he said were Chiefs. we gave him a medal of the small size with the likeness of Mr. Jefferson the President of the U' States in releif on one side and clasp hands with a pipe and tomahawk in the other, to the other Chiefs we gave each a small medal which were struck in the Presidency of George Washing[ton] Esqr. we also gave small medals of the last discription two young men whom the 1st Chief informed us were good young men and much rispected among them. we gave the 1st Chief an uniform coat shirt a pair of scarlet legings a carrot of tobacco and some small articles to each of the others we gave a shi[r]t leging[s] handkerchief a knife some tobacco and a few small articles we also distributed a good quantity paint mockerson awles knives beads looking-glasses &c among the other Indians and gave them a plentifull meal of lyed corn which was the first they had ever eaten in their lives. they were much pleased with it. every article about us appeared to excite astonishment in there minds; the appearance of the men, their arms, the canoes, our manner of working them, the b[l]ack man york and the sagacity of my dog were equally objects of admiration. I also shot my air-gun which was so perfectly incomprehensible that they immediately denominated it the great medicine.

Capt. Clark and myself now concerted measures for our future operations, and it was mutually agreed that he should set out tomorrow morning with eleven men furnished with axes and other necessary tools for making canoes, their arms accoutrements and as much of their baggage as they could carry. also to take the indians, C[h]arbono and the indian woman with him; that on his arrival at the Shoshone camp he was to leave Charbono and the Indian woman to haisten the return of the Indians with their horses to this place, and to proceede himself with the eleven men down the Columbia in order to examine the river and if he found it navigable and could obtain timber to set about making canoes immediately. In the mean time I was to bring the party and baggage to the Shoshone Camp, calculating that by the time I should reach that place that he would have sufficiently informed himself with rispect to the state of the river &c. as to determine us whether to prosicute our journey from thence by land or water. in the former case we should want all the horses which we could perchase, and in the latter only to hire the Indians to transport our baggage to the place at which we made the canoes.

Sunday August 18th 1805.

This morning while Capt. Clark was busily engaged in preparing for his rout, I exposed some articles to barter with the Indians for horses as I wished a few at this moment to releive the men who were going with Capt Clark from the labour of carrying their baggage, and also one to keep here in order to pack the meat to camp which the hunters might kill. I soon obtained three very good horses. for which I gave an uniform coat, a pair of legings, a few handkerchiefs, three knives and some other small articles the whole of which did not cost more than about 20$ in the U' States. the Indians seemed quite as well pleased with their bargin as I was. the men also purchased one for an old checked shirt a pair of old legings and a knife. two of those I purchased Capt. C. took on with him. at 10 A.M. Capt. Clark departed with his detachment and all the Indians except 2 men and 2 women who remained with us.

after there departure this morning I had all the stores and baggage of every discription opened and aired. and began the operation of forming the packages in proper parsels for the purpose of transporting them on horseback. the rain in the evening compelled me to desist from my operations. I had the raw hides put in the water in order to cut them in throngs proper for lashing the packages and forming the necessary geer for pack horses, a business which I fortunately had not to learn on this occasion. I had the net arranged and set this evening to catch some trout which we could see in great abundance at the bottom of the river.

Monday August 19th 1805.

The Shoshonees may be estimated at about 100 warriors, and about three times that number of women and children[1] they have more children among them than I expected to have seen among a people who procure subsistence with such difficulty. there are but few very old persons, nor did they appear to treat those with much tenderness or rispect. The man is the sole propryetor of his wives

1. Lewis's figures refer to this band only.

and daughters, and can barter or dispose of either as he thinks proper. a plurality of wives is common among them, but these are not generally sisters as with the Minnitares & Mandans but are purchased of different fathers. The father frequently disposes of his infant daughters in marriage to men who are grown or to men who have sons for whom they think proper to provide wives. the compensation given in such cases usually consists of horses or mules which the father receives at the time of contract and converts to his own uce. the girl remains with her parents untill she is conceived to have obtained the age of puberty which with them is considered to be about the age of 13 or 14 years. the female at this age is surrendered to her soveriegn lord and husband agreeably to contract, and with her is frequently restored by the father quite as much as he received in the first instance in payment for his daughter; but this is discretionary with the father. Sah-car-gar-we-ah had been thus disposed of before she was taken by the Minnetares, or had arrived to the years of puberty. the husband was yet living with this band. he was more than double her age and had two other wives. he claimed her as his wife but said that as she had had a child by another man, who was Charbono, that he did not want her.

They seldom correct their children particularly the boys who soon become masters of their own acts. they give as a reason that it cows and breaks the sperit of the boy to whip him, and that he never recovers his independence of mind after he is grown. They treat their women but with little rispect, and compel them to perform every species of drudgery. they collect the wild fruits and roots, attend to the horses or assist in that duty, cook, dress the skins and make all their apparel, collect wood and make their fires, arrange and form their lodges, and when they travel pack the horses and take charge of all the baggage; in short the man dose little else except attend his horses hunt and fish. the man considers himself degraded if he is compelled to walk any distance; and if he is so unfortunately poor as only to possess two horses he rides the best himself and leavs the woman or women if he has more than one, to transport their baggage and children on the other, and to walk if the horse is unable to carry the additional weight of their persons. the chastity of their women is not held in high estimation, and the husband will for a trifle barter the companion of his bead for a night or longer if he conceives the reward adiquate; tho' they are not so importunate that we should caress their women as the siouxs were. and some of their women appear to be held more sacred than in any nation we have seen. I have requested the men to give them no cause of jealousy by having connection with their women without their knowledge, which with them, strange as it may seem is considered as disgracefull to the husband as clandestine connections of a similar kind are among civilized nations. to prevent this mutual exchange of good offices altogether I know it impossible to effect, particularly on the part of our young men whom some months abstanence have made very polite to those tawney damsels. no evil has yet resulted and I hope will not from these connections.

notwithstanding the late loss of horses which this people sustained by the Minnetares the stock of the band may be very safely estimated at seven hundred of which they are perhaps about 40 coalts and half that number of mules. their arms offensive and defensive consist in the bow and arrows shield, some, lances, and a weapon called by the Cippeways who formerly used it, the pog-gar´-

mag-gon´ [war club]. in fishing they employ wairs, gigs, and fishing hooks. the salmon is the principal object of their pursuit. they snair wolves and foxes.

I was anxious to learn whether these people had the venerial, and made the enquiry through the interpreter and his wife; the information was that they sometimes had it but I could not learn their remedy; they most usually die with it's effects. this seems a strong proof that these disorders bothe ganaraehah and Louis Venerae[2] are native disorders of America. tho' these people have suffered much by the small pox which is known to be imported and perhaps those other disorders might have been contracted from other indian tribes who by a round of communications might have obtained from the Europeans since it was introduced into that quarter of the globe. but so much detached on the other ha[n]d from all communication with the whites that I think it most probable that those disorders are original with them.

from the middle of May to the first of September these people reside on the waters of the Columbia where they consider themselves in perfect security from their enimies as they have not as yet ever found their way to this retreat; during this season the salmon furnish the principal part of their subsistence and as this fish either perishes or returns about the 1st of September they are compelled at this season in surch of subsistence to resort to the Missouri, in the vallies of which, there is more game even [than] within the mountains. here they move slowly down the river in order to collect and join other bands either of their own nation or the Flatheads, and having become sufficiently strong as they conceive venture on the Eastern side of the Rocky mountains into the plains, where the buffaloe abound. but they never leave the interior of the mountains while they can obtain a scanty subsistence, and always return as soon as they have acquired a good stock of dryed meat in the plains; when this stock is consumed they venture again into the plains; thus alternately obtaining their food at the risk of their lives and retiring to the mountains, while they consume it. These people are now on the eve of their departure for the Missouri, and inform us that they expect to be joined at or about the three forks by several bands of their own nation, and a band of the Flatheads.

Tuesday August 20th 1805.

I walked down the river about 3/4 of a mile and selected a place near the river bank unperceived by the Indians for a cash [cache], which I set three men to make, and directed the centinel to discharge his gun if he perceived any of the Indians going down in that direction which was to be the signal for the men at work on the cash to desist and seperate, least these people should discover our deposit and rob us of the baggage we intend leaving here. by evening the cash was completed unperceived by the Indians, and all our packages made up. the Pack-saddles and harness is not yet complete. in this operation we find ourselves at a loss for nails and boards; for the first we substitute throngs of raw hide which answer verry well, and for the last [had] to cut off the blades of our oars and use the plank of some boxes which have heretofore held other articles

---

2. **ganaraehah and Louis Venerae:** gonorrhea and syphilis.

and put those articles into sacks of raw hide which I have had made for the purpose. by this means I have obtained as many boards as will make 20 saddles which I suppose will be sufficient for our present exegencies. I made up a small assortment of medicines, together with the specemines of plants, minerals, seeds &c, which, I have collected between this place and the falls of the Missouri which I shall deposit here.

I now prevailed on the Chief to instruct me with rispect to the geography of his country. this he undertook very cheerfully, by delineating the rivers on the ground. but I soon found that his information fell far short of my expectation or wishes. he drew the river on which we now are [the Lemhi] to which he placed two branches just above us, which he shewed me from the openings of the mountains were in view; he next made it discharge itself into a large river which flowed from the S.W. about ten miles below us [the Salmon], then continued this joint stream in the same direction of this valley or N.W. for one days march and then enclined it to the West for 2 more days march. here we placed a number of heaps of sand on each side which he informed me represented the vast mountains of rock eternally covered with snow through which the river passed. that the perpendicular and even juting rocks so closely hemned in the river that there was no possibil[it]y of passing along the shore; that the bed of the river was obstructed by sharp pointed rocks and the rapidity of the stream such that the whole surface of the river was beat into perfect foam as far as the eye could reach. that the mountains were also inaccessible to man or horse. he said that this being the state of the country in that direction that himself nor none of his nation had ever been further down the river than these mountains.

in this manner I spend the day smoking with them and acquiring what information I could with respect to their country. they informed me that they could pass to the Spaniards by the way of the yellowstone river in 10 days. I can discover that these people are by no means friendly to the Spaniards. their complaint is, that the Spaniards will not let them have fire arms and ammunition, that they put them off by telling them that if they suffer them to have guns they will kill each other, thus leaving them defenceless and an easy prey to their bloodthirsty neighbours to the East of them, who being in possession of fire arms hunt them up and murder them without rispect to sex or age and plunder them of their horses on all occasions. they told me that to avoid their enemies who were eternally harrassing them that they were obliged to remain in the interior of these mountains at least two thirds of the year where the[y] suffered as we then saw great heardships for the want of food sometimes living for weeks without meat and only a little fish roots and berries. but this added Câmeahwait, with his ferce eyes and lank jaws grown meager for the want of food, would not be the case if we had guns, we could then live in the country of buffaloe and eat as our enimies do and not be compelled to hide ourselves in these mountains and live on roots and berries as the bear do. we do not fear our enimies when placed on an equal footing with them. I told them that the Minnetares Mandans . . . had promised us to desist from making war on them & that we would indevour to find the means of making the Minnetares of fort d[e] Prarie or as they call them Pahkees desist from waging war against them also. that after our finally returning to our homes towards the rising sun whitemen would come to them with an abundance of guns and every other article necessary to their defence and comfort, and that they would be enabled to supply themselves with these articles on reasonable terms in exchange for the skins of the beaver Otter and Ermin so abundant in their country. they expressed great pleasure at this information and said they had been long anxious to see the whitemen that traded guns; and that we might rest assured of their friendship and that they would do whatever we wished them.

24

The Great Revival of 1800
James B. Finley and Peter Cartwright

Evangelicalism, the highly emotional proselytizing religion so characteristic of American Protestantism, began in the 1730s and 1740s with the visits to the colonies of the English preacher, George Whitefield. The meetings Whitefield held triggered what became known as the Great Awakening. Thousands responded to the dynamic preaching of Whitefield and the ministers he inspired with dramatic experiences of religious conversion. The Revolutionary War and the rise of the Enlightenment greatly weakened enthusiastic religion, but at the turn of the nineteenth century revivalism once again burst forth, giving rise to a religious movement still vibrant in America today. To the surprise of religious leaders, who had worried about the religious state of the rude, unchurched Western frontier, the new inspiration came from the settlements that were farthest west — in Kentucky.

Ministers in Kentucky's Presbyterian and Methodist churches revolted against the "formality and deadness" of their churches and, encouraging direct displays of religious fervor, provoked emotional scenes in which, according to one observer, the floors of churches were "covered with the slain; their screams for mercy pierced the heavens." Word spread, and large crowds of people traveled from considerable distances to gather at these services. With churches too small to hold them and distant travelers not wishing to return home after only a few hours of worship, services were held out of doors, and many camped out for several days. In this way the camp meeting was born. In 1801, a meeting was announced for August 6 at Cane Ridge, Kentucky. Word flew about the hollows and cabins, and a crowd estimated at over twenty thousand people (nearly ten percent of the state's population) gathered for the largest religious service ever experienced up to that time in the United States.

Western evangelists traveled endlessly across sparsely settled territory preaching their highly emotional and individualistic religion during the first decades of the nineteenth century. Their creeds emphasized the importance of personal morality, civic virtue, and education. Their contribution to the characteristic culture of the American Middle West soon provided a model for much of American life. In these readings you will see the great revivals through the eyes of James B. Finley (1781–1856), one of the preachers who conducted the early revivals, as well as share the experience of Peter Cartwright (1785–1872), whose conversion during one of these revivals led to a life spent as an itinerant preacher for the Methodist Church, riding across vast circuits of congregations in Kentucky, Indiana, Ohio, and Illinois.

Rev. James B. Finley, *Autobiography or, Pioneer Life in the West*, ed. W. P. Strickland (Cincinnati: Methodist Book Concern, 1853), pp. 362–69; Peter Cartwright, *Autobiography of Peter Cartwright, the Backwoods Preacher*, ed. W. P. Strickland (New York: Carlton & Porter, 1857), pp. 34–38.

BEFORE YOU READ

1. Why is James B. Finley writing this account of the revivals? Who is his audience, and what is he attempting to persuade them to do?

2. How do you explain the various physical states accompanying conversion, such as people going into trances or experiencing the jerks? How does Finley analyze and explain them?

3. What spurred Peter Cartwright's conversion?

JAMES B. FINLEY

Great Revival in the West

In the spring of 1800 one of the most astonishing and powerful revivals occurred that has ever been known in the western country. This was also the most extensive revival that perhaps ever was witnessed in this country. It was marked by some peculiarities which had not been known to characterize any revival in former times. The nearest approximation to it, of which I can form any conception, was the revival on the day of pentecost, when thousands were awakened and converted to God under the most exciting circumstances.

The commencement of the revival is traceable to the joint labors of two brothers in Cumberland county, Kentucky, one of whom was a Presbyterian and the other a Methodist preacher. They commenced laboring together, every Sabbath preaching, exhorting, and praying alternately. This union was regarded as quite singular, and excited the curiosity of vast multitudes, who came to the places of meeting to hear two men preach who held views in theology supposed to be entirely antagonistic. Nothing was discoverable in their preaching of a doctrinal character, except the doctrine of man's total depravity and ruin by sin, and his recovery therefrom by faith in Christ. All were exhorted to flee the wrath to come, and be saved from their sins. The word which they preached was attended with the power of God to the hearts of listening thousands. The multitudes who flocked from all parts of the country to hear them, became so vast that no church would hold them, and they were obliged to resort to the fields and woods. Every vehicle was put in requisition; carriages, wagons, carts and sleds. Many came on horseback, and larger crowds still came on foot.

As the excitement increased, and the work of conviction and conversion continued, several brought tents, which they pitched on the ground, and remained day and night for many days. The reader will here find the origin of camp meetings.

In the spring of 1801 Bishop M'Kendree was appointed presiding elder of the Kentucky district; and being thus brought in contact with this wonderful work, he was prepared to form a correct judgment of its character. That there were extravagances that constituted no part of religion, he was prepared to admit, but that it was all a wild, fanatical delusion, he was very far from conceding. Nay, he believed that it was the work of God's Spirit on the hearts of the people, and that thousands were genuinely converted to God.

These meetings began to follow one another in quick succession, and the numbers which attended were almost incredible. While the meetings lasted, crowds were to be seen in all directions, passing and repassing the roads and paths, while the woods seemed to be alive with people. Whole settlements appeared to be vacated, and only here and there could be found a house having an inhabitant. All ages, sexes, and conditions, pressed their way to the camp meeting. At these meetings the Presbyterians and Methodists united. They were held at different places. On the 22d of May, 1801, one was held at Cabin creek; the next was held at Concord, in one of my father's old congregations; the next was at Point Pleasant, and the succeeding one at Indian creek, in Harrison county. At these meetings thousands fell under the power of God, and cried for mercy. The scenes which successively occurred at these meetings were awfully sublime, and a general terror seemed to have pervaded the minds of all people within the reach of their influences.

The great general camp meeting was held at Cane Ridge meeting-house. This house was built for my father, and here was my old home. I have elsewhere described this meeting, or, rather, attempted to do so. Language is utterly impuissant to convey any thing like an adequate idea of the sublimity and grandeur of the scene. Twenty thousand persons tossed to and fro, like the tumultuous waves of the sea in a storm, or swept down like the trees of the forest under the blast of the wild tornado, was a sight which mine own eyes witnessed, but which neither my pen nor tongue can describe.

During the religious exercises within the encampment, all manner of wickedness was going on without. So deep and awful is man's depravity, that he will sport while the very fires of perdition are kindling around him. Men, furious with the effects of the maddening bowl, would outrage all decency by their conduct; and some, mounted on horses, would ride at full speed among the people. I saw one, who seemed to be a leader and champion of the party, on a large, white horse, ride furiously into the praying circle, uttering the most horrid imprecations. Suddenly, as if smitten by lightning, he fell from his horse. At this a shout went up from the religious multitude, as if Lucifer himself had fallen. I trembled, for I feared God had killed the bold and daring blasphemer. He exhibited no signs whatever of life; his limbs were rigid, his wrists pulseless, and his breath gone. Several of his comrades came to see him, but they did not gaze long till the power of God came upon them, and they fell like men slain in battle. I was much alarmed, but I had a great desire to see the issue. I watched him closely, while for thirty hours he lay, to all human appearance, dead. During this time the people kept up singing and praying. At last he exhibited signs of life, but they were fearful spasms, which seemed as if he were in a convulsive fit, attended by frightful groans, as if he were passing through the intensest agony. It was not long, however, till his convulsions ceased, and springing to his feet, his groans were converted into loud and joyous shouts of praise. The dark, fiend-like scowl which overspread his features, gave way to a happy smile, which lighted up his countenance.

A certain Dr. P., accompanied by a lady from Lexington, was induced, out of mere curiosity, to attend the meeting. As they had heard much about the involuntary jerkings and falling which attended the exercises, they entered into an agreement between themselves that, should either of them be thus strangely attacked or fall, the other was to stand by to the last. It was not long till the lady was brought down in all her pride, a poor sinner in the dust, before her God. The Doctor, agitated, came up and felt for her pulse; but, alas! her pulse was gone. At this he turned pale, and, staggering a few paces, he fell beneath the power of the same invisible hand. After remaining for some time in this state, they both obtained pardon and peace and went rejoicing home. They both lived and died happy Christians. Thousands were affected in the same way.

These camp meetings continued for some time, the Presbyterians and Methodists uniting together as one in the army of the Lord. Some ministers had serious doubts concerning the character of the work; but its genuineness was demonstrated by the fruits. Men of the most depraved hearts and vicious habits were made new creatures, and a whole life of virtue subsequently confirmed the conversion. To all but Methodists the work was entirely strange. Some of the peculiarities had been witnessed before by the preachers, and they were enabled to carry it on.

These meetings exhibited nothing to the spectator unacquainted with them but a scene of confusion, such as scarcely could be put into human language. They were generally opened with a sermon or exhortation, at the close of which there would be a universal cry for mercy, some bursting forth in loud ejaculations of prayer or thanksgiving for the truth; some breaking forth in strong and powerful exhortations, others flying to their careless friends with tears of compassion, entreating them to fly to Christ for mercy; some, struck with terror and conviction, hastening through the crowd to escape, or pulling away from their relations, others trembling, weeping, crying for mercy; some falling and swooning away, till every appearance of life was gone and the extremities of the body assumed the coldness of death. These were surrounded with a company of the pious, singing melodious songs adapted to the time, and praying for their conversion. But there were others collected in circles round this variegated scene, contending for and against the work.

Many circumstances transpired that are worthy of note in reference to this work. Children were often made the instruments through which the Lord wrought. At one of these powerful displays of Divine power, a boy about ten years old broke from the stand in time of preaching under very strong impressions, and having mounted a log at some distance, and raising his voice in a most affecting manner, cried out, "On the last day of the feast Jesus stood and cried, If any man thirst, let him come unto me and drink." He attracted the main body of the congregation, and, with streaming eyes, he warned the sinners of their danger, denouncing their doom, if they persevered in sin, and strongly expressed his love for the salvation of their souls, and the desire that they would turn to God and live. By this time the press was so great that he was taken up by two men and held above the crowd. He spoke for near an hour with that convincing eloquence that could be inspired only from heaven; and when exhausted, and language failed to describe the feelings of his soul, he raised his handkerchief, and dropping it, cried, "Thus, O sinner, will you drop into hell unless you forsake your sins and turn to God." At this moment the power of God fell upon the assembly, and sinners fell as men slain in mighty battle, and the cries for mercy seemed as though they would rend the heavens, and the work spread in a manner which human language can not describe.

We will now try to give something in reference to the manner and the exercise of mind of those who were the subjects of this work. Immediately before they became totally powerless, they were sometimes seized with a general tremor, and often uttered several piercing shrieks in the moment of falling. Men and women never fell when under this jerking exercise till they became exhausted. Some were unable to stand, and yet had the use of their hands and could converse with companions. Others were unable to speak. The pulse became weak, and they drew a difficult breath about once a minute. In many instances they became cold. Breathing, pulsation, and all signs of life forsook them for hours; yet I never heard of one who died in this condition, and I have conversed with persons who have laid in this situation for many hours, and they have uniformly testified that they had no bodily pain, and that they had the entire use of their reason and powers of mind. From this it appears that their falling was neither common fainting nor a nervous affection. Indeed, this strange work appears to have taken every possible turn to baffle the conjectures and philosophizing of those who were unwilling to acknowledge it was the work of God. Persons have fallen on their way home from meeting, some after they had arrived at home, others pursuing their common business on their farms, and others when they were attending to family or secret devotions. Numbers of thoughtless, careless sinners have fallen as suddenly as if struck by lightning. Professed infidels, and other vicious characters, have been arrested, and sometimes at the very moment when they were uttering their blasphemies against God and the work, and have, like Saul, declared that to be God's work which they so vehemently persecuted.

I trust I have said enough on this subject to enable my readers to judge how far the charge of enthusiasm and delusion is applicable to this work, unequaled for power and for the entire change of the hearts and lives of so many thousands of men and women. Lord Lyttleton, in his letter on the conversion of St. Paul, observes, and I think justly, that enthusiasm is a vain, self-righteous spirit, swelled with self-sufficiency and disposed to glory in its religious attainments. If this be a good definition, there was as little enthusiasm in this work as any other. Never were there more genuine marks of that humility which disclaims the merits of its own works, and looks to the Lord Jesus Christ as the only way of acceptance with God. Christ was all and in all in their exercises and religion, and their Gospel, and all believers in their highest attainments seemed most sensible of their entire dependence upon Divine grace; and it was truly affecting to hear with what anxiety awakened sinners inquired for Christ as the only Physician who could give them help. Those who call this enthusiasm ought to tell us what they understand by the spirit of Christianity. Upon the whole, this revival in the west was the most extraordinary that ever visited the Church of Christ, and was peculiarly adapted to the circumstances of the country. Infidelity was triumphant, and religion at the point of expiring. Something of an extraordinary nature was necessary to arrest the attention of a wicked and skeptical people, who were ready to conclude that Christianity was a fable and futurity a dream. This great work of God did do it. It confounded infidelity and vice into silence, and brought numbers beyond calculation under the influence of experimental religion and practical piety.

PETER CARTWRIGHT

Chapter IV. Conversion

In 1801, when I was in my sixteenth year, my father, my eldest half brother, and myself, attended a wedding about five miles from home, where there was a great deal of drinking and dancing, which was very common at marriages in those days. I drank little or nothing; my delight was in dancing. After a late hour in the night, we mounted our horses and started for home. I was riding my race-horse.

A few minutes after we had put up the horses, and were sitting by the fire, I began to reflect on the manner in which I had spent the day and evening. I felt guilty and condemned. I rose and walked the floor. My mother was in bed. It seemed to me, all of a sudden, my blood rushed to my head, my heart palpi-tated, in a few minutes I turned blind; an awful impression rested on my mind that death had come and I was unprepared to die. I fell on my knees and began to ask God to have mercy on me.

My mother sprang from her bed, and was soon on her knees by my side, praying for me, and exhorting me to look to Christ for mercy, and then and there I promised the Lord that if he would spare me, I would seek and serve him; and I never fully broke that promise. My mother prayed for me a long time. At length we lay down, but there was little sleep for me. Next morning I rose, feeling wretched beyond expression. I tried to read in the Testament, and retired many times to secret prayer through the day, but found no relief. I gave up my race-horse to my father, and requested him to sell him. I went and brought my pack of cards, and gave them to mother, who threw them into the fire, and they were consumed. I fasted, watched, and prayed, and engaged in regular reading of the Testament. I was so distressed and miserable, that I was incapable of any regular business.

My father was greatly distressed on my account, thinking I must die, and he would lose his only son. He bade me retire altogether from business, and take care of myself. . . .

In the spring of this year, Mr. M'Grady, a minister of the Presbyterian Church, who had a congregation and meeting-house, as we then called them, about three miles north of my father's house, appointed a sacramental meeting in this congregation, and invited the Methodist preachers to attend with them, and especially John Page, who was a powerful Gospel minister, and was very popular among the Presbyterians. Accordingly he came, and preached with great power and success.

There were no camp-meetings in regular form at this time, but as there was a great waking up among the Churches, from the revival that had broken out at Cane Ridge, before mentioned, many flocked to those sacramental meetings.

The church would not hold the tenth part of the congregation. Accordingly, the officers of the Church erected a stand in a contiguous shady grove, and prepared seats for a large congregation.

The people crowded to this meeting from far and near. They came in their large wagons, with victuals mostly prepared. The women slept in the wagons, and the men under them. Many stayed on the ground night and day for a number of nights and days together. Others were provided for among the neighbors around. The power of God was wonderfully displayed; scores of sinners fell under the preaching, like men slain in mighty battle; Christians shouted aloud for joy.

To this meeting I repaired, a guilty, wretched sinner. On the Saturday evening of said meeting, I went, with weeping multitudes, and bowed before the stand, and earnestly prayed for mercy. In the midst of a solemn struggle of soul, an impression was made on my mind, as though a voice said to me, "Thy sins are all forgiven thee." Divine light flashed all round me, unspeakable joy sprung up in my soul. I rose to my feet, opened my eyes, and it really seemed as if I was in heaven; the trees, the leaves on them, and everything seemed, and I really thought were, praising God. My mother raised the shout, my Christian friends crowded around me and joined me in praising God; and though I have been since then, in many instances, unfaithful, yet I have never, for one moment, doubted that the Lord did, then and there, forgive my sins and give me religion.

Our meeting lasted without intermission all night, and it was believed by those who had a very good right to know, that over eighty souls were converted to God during its continuance. I went on my way rejoicing for many days. This meeting was in the month of May. In June our preacher, John Page, attended at our little church, *Ebenezer,* and there in June, 1801, I joined the Methodist Episcopal Church, which I have never for one moment regretted. I have never for a moment been tempted to leave the Methodist Episcopal Church, and if they were to turn me out, I would knock at the door till taken in again.

A Disorderly Democracy
Benjamin Perley Poore and James Parton

For over a century history books portrayed Andrew Jackson as the champion of frontier democracy. It was said that during Jackson's presidency the common man won the right to vote and took politics out of the hands of the elite. Socially and economically, too, the Jacksonian era was believed to have brought greater equality, even, as the nineteenth-century historian George Bancroft put it, "a new day . . . in American history."

Historians no longer believe this. Jackson, they have found, sided with the wealthy in the politics of his home state of Tennessee. The political power of the common man increased steadily after the revolutionary era so that in most states all adult white males could vote and the number of elected public offices was growing. Jackson's candidacy for president in 1828 did not create mass-based political parties but was instead the beneficiary of this development. The most notable political innovation of the period was the national convention. Initially a democratic way of capturing public sentiment, it was invented not by Jacksonians, although they quickly adopted it, but by the short-lived Anti-Masonic Party in 1831. And during the Jacksonian era an inegalitarian society developed: urban elites grew in wealth while industrialism created new lower classes. For many—including slaves, free blacks, most women, and many immigrants—social and economic equality was unattainable.

Yet people at the time chose to believe that Jackson's eminence was linked to the "rise of the common man," and the readings here by his contemporaries suggest why. Millions of Americans—for diverse and often conflicting reasons—readily identified with the crusty old warrior and saw him as emblematic of the egalitarian style of the nation: a child of the frontier, self-made, independent, heroic, and democratic. Their antics at his inaugural celebration horrified conservative anti-Jacksonians like the author and journalist Benjamin Perley Poore (1820–1887), known to his readers as "Ben: Perley Poore." And even a staunch supporter of Jackson like James Parton (1822–1891), author of a laudatory multivolume biography of the old general, found the popular enthusiasm demonstrated by his followers too vulgar and disorderly to be acceptable by those of more genteel breeding. While they would have agreed on little else, Perley and Parton both viewed the havoc of Jackson's inauguration as indicative of a new style of politics in which common people perhaps too easily identified with their political hero.

Benjamin Perley Poore, *Perley's Reminiscences of Sixty Years in the National Metropolis*, vol. 1 (Philadelphia: Hubbard, 1886), pp. 88–97; James Parton, *Life of Andrew Jackson*, vol. 3 (New York: Mason, 1861), pp. 169–71.

BEFORE YOU READ

1. How does Benjamin Perley Poore account for Andrew Jackson's electoral victory?

2. What does Poore claim were the consequences of Jackson's victory?

3. Why did the inauguration celebration shock both Poore and pro-Jackson James Parton?

4. What do you understand from the phrase "Jacksonian democracy"?

BEN: PERLEY POORE

The Political Machine

As the time for another Presidential election approached, the friends of General Jackson commenced active operations in his behalf. The prime mover in the campaign was General John Henry Eaton, then a Senator from Tennessee. He had published in 1818 a brief life of the hero of New Orleans, which he enlarged in 1824 and published with the title, "The Life of Andrew Jackson, Major-General in the Service of the United States, comprising a History of the War in the South from the Commencement of the Creek Campaign to the Termination of Hostilities Before New Orleans." The facts in it were obtained from General Jackson and his wife, but every incident of his life calculated to injure him in the public estimation was carefully suppressed. It was, however, the recognized text-book for Democratic editors and stump speakers, and although entirely unreliable, it has formed the basis for the lives of General Jackson since published.

President Adams enjoined neutrality upon his friends, but some of them, acting with Democrats who were opposed to the election of General Jackson, had published and circulated, as an offset to General Eaton's book, a thick pamphlet entitled, "Reminiscences; or, an Extract from the Catalogue of General Jackson's Youthful Indiscretions, between the Age of Twenty-three and Sixty," which contained an account of Jackson's fights, brawls, affrays, and duels, numbered from one to fourteen. Broadsides, bordered with wood-cuts of coffins, and known as "coffin hand-bills," narrated the summary and unjust execution as deserters of a number of militiamen in the Florida campaign whose legal term of service had expired. Another handbill gave the account of General Jackson's marriage to Mrs. Robards before she had been legally divorced from her husband. . . .

After a political campaign of unprecedented bitterness, General Jackson was elected, receiving one hundred and seventy-eight electoral votes against eighty-three cast for John Quincy Adams, and so a new chapter was commenced in the social as well as the political chronicles of the National Capital. Those who had known the Presidential successors of Washington as educated and cultivated gentlemen, well versed in the courtesies of private life and of ceremonious statesmanship, saw them succeeded by a military chieftain, whose life had been "a battle and a march," thickly studded with personal difficulties and duels; who had given repeated evidences of his disregard of the laws when they stood in the way of his imperious will; and who, when a United States Senator, had displayed no ability as a legislator. His election was notoriously the work of Martin Van Buren, inspired by Aaron Burr, and with his inauguration was initiated a sordidly selfish political system entirely at variance with the broad views of Washington and of Hamilton. It was assumed that every citizen had his price; that neither virtue nor genius was proof against clever although selfish corruption; that political honesty was a farce; and that the only way of governing those knaves who elbowed their way up through the masses was to rule them by cunning more acute than their own and by knavery more subtle and calculating than theirs.

Before leaving his rural home in Tennessee, General Jackson had been afflicted by the sudden death of his wife. . . . After her funeral her sorrow-stricken husband came to Washington with a stern determination to punish those who had maligned her during the preceding campaign. Having been told that President Adams had sanctioned the publication of the slanders, he did not call at the White House, in accordance with usage, but paid daily visits to his old friends in the War Department. Mr. Adams, stung by this neglect, determined not to play the part of the conquered leader of the inauguration, and quietly removed to the house of Commodore Porter, in the suburbs, on the morning of the 3d of March.

The weather on the 4th of March, 1829, was serene and mild, and at an early hour Pennsylvania Avenue, then unpaved, with a double row of poplar trees along its centre, was filled with crowds of people, many of whom had journeyed immense distances on foot. The officials at Washington, who were friends of Mr. Adams, had agreed not to participate in the inaugural ceremonies, and the only uniformed company of light infantry, commanded by Colonel Seaton, of the *National Intelligencer*, had declined to offer its services as an escort. A number of old Revolutionary officers, however, had hastily organized themselves, and waited on General Jackson to solicit the honor of forming his escort to the Capitol, an offer which was cordially accepted. The General rode in an open carriage which had been placed at his disposal, and was surrounded by these gallant veterans. The assembled thousands cheered lustily as their favorite passed along, every face radiant with defiant joy, and every voice shouting "Hurrah for Jackson!"

After the installation of John C. Calhoun as Vice-President in the Senate Chamber, the assembled dignitaries moved in procession through the rotunda to the east front of the Capitol. As the tall figure of the President-elect came out upon the portico and ascended the platform, uplifted hats and handkerchiefs waved a welcome, and shouts of "Hurrah for Jackson!" rent the air. Looking around for a moment into ten thousand upturned and exultant human faces, the President-elect removed his hat, took the manuscript of his address from his pocket, and read it with great dignity. When he had finished, Chief Justice Marshall administered the oath, and as the President, bending over the sacred Book, touched it with his lips, there arose such a shout as was never before heard in Washington, followed by the thunder of cannons, from two light batteries near by, echoed by the cannon at the Navy Yard and at the Arsenal. The crowd surged toward the platform, and had it not been that a ship's cable had been stretched across the portico steps would have captured their beloved leader. As it was, he shook hands with hundreds, and it was with some difficulty that he could be escorted back to his carriage and along Pennsylvania Avenue to the White House. . . .

The broad sidewalks of Pennsylvania Avenue were again packed as the procession returned from the Capitol. "I never saw such a crowd," wrote Daniel Webster to a friend. "Persons have come five hundred miles to see General Jackson, and they really seem to think that the country is rescued from some dreadful danger." Hunters of Kentucky and Indian fighters of Tennessee, with sturdy frontiersmen from the Northwest, were mingled in the throng with the more cultured dwellers on the Atlantic slope.

On their arrival at the White House, the motley crowd clamored for refreshments and soon drained the barrels of punch, which had been prepared, in drinking to the health of the new Chief Magistrate. A great deal of china and glassware was broken, and the East Room was filled with a noisy mob. At one time General Jackson, who had retreated until he stood with his back against the wall, was protected by a number of his friends, who formed a living barrier about him. Such a scene had never before been witnessed at the White House, and the aristocratic old Federalists saw, to their disgust, men whose boots were covered with the red mud of the unpaved streets standing on the damask satin-covered chairs to get a sight at the President of their choice.

Late in the afternoon President Jackson sat down to dinner with Vice-President Calhoun and a party of his personal friends, the central dish on the table being a sirloin from a prize ox, sent to him by John Merkle, a butcher of Franklin Market, New York. Before retiring that night, the President wrote to the donor: "Permit me, sir, to assure you of the gratification which I felt in being enabled to place on my table so fine a specimen from your market, and to offer you my sincere thanks for so acceptable a token of your regard for my character."

This was naturally the commencement of a series of presents which poured in on President Jackson during the eight years of his administration. So palpable a bid for other tokens of regard for the President's character could hardly fail to evoke responses. From the days of Solomon it has been true that "a man's gift maketh room for him," and though many of Jackson's gift-senders failed to find the room made, yet it was true nevertheless that room was seldom made where the gifts were not forthcoming, so come the gifts did in abundance.

The Democratic journalists from all parts of the country were also well represented at the inauguration, attracted, doubtless, by this luring, semi-official declaration in the *Telegraph:* "We know not what line of policy General Jackson will adopt. We take it for granted, however, that he will reward his friends and punish his enemies."

The leader of this editorial phalanx was Amos Kendall, a native of Dunstable, Massachusetts, who had by pluck and industry acquired an education and migrated westward in search of fame and fortune. Accident made him an inmate of Henry Clay's house and the tutor of his children; but many months had not elapsed before the two became political foes, and Kendall, who had become the conductor of a Democratic newspaper, triumphed, bringing to Washington the official vote of Kentucky for Andrew Jackson. He found at the National metropolis other Democratic editors, who, like himself, had labored to bring about the political revolution, and they used to meet daily at the house of a preacher-politician, Rev. Obadiah B. Brown, who had strongly advocated Jackson's election. Mr. Brown, who was a stout, robust man, with a great fund of anecdotes, was a clerk in the Post Office Department during the week, while on Sundays he performed his ministerial duties in the Baptist Church.

Organizing under the lead of Amos Kendall . . . the allied editors claimed their rewards. They were not to be appeased by sops of Government advertising, or by the appointment of publisher of the laws of the United States in the respective States, but they demanded some of the most lucrative public offices as their share of the spoils. No sooner did General Jackson reach Washington then they made a systematic attack upon him, introducing and praising one another, and reciprocally magnifying their faithful services during the canvass so successfully ended. The result was that soon after the inauguration nearly fifty of those editors who had advocated his election were appointed to official Federal positions as rewards for political services rendered.

Up to that time the national elections in the United States had not been mere contests for the possession of Federal offices—there was victory and there was defeat; but the quadrennial encounters affected only the heads of departments, and the results were matters of comparative indifference to the subordinate official drudges whose families depended on their pay for meat and bread. A few of these department clerks were Revolutionary worthies; others had followed the Federal Government from New York or Philadelphia; all had expected to hold their positions for life. Some of these desk-slaves had originally been Federalists, others Democrats; and while there was always an Alexander Hamilton in every family of the one set, there was as invariably a Thomas Jefferson in every family of the other set. But no subordinate clerk had ever been troubled on account of his political faith by a change of the Administration, and the sons generally succeeded their fathers when they died or resigned. Ordinarily, these clerks were good penmen and skillful accountants, toiling industriously eight hours every week day without dreaming of demanding a month's vacation in the summer, or insisting upon their right to go to their homes to vote in the fall. National politics was to them a matter of profound indifference until, after the inauguration of General Jackson, hundreds of them found themselves decapitated by the Democratic guillotine, without qualifications for any other employment had the limited trade of Washington afforded any. Many of them were left in a pitiable condition, but when the *Telegraph* was asked what these men could do to ward off starvation, the insolent reply was, "Root, hog, or die!"

JAMES PARTON

The day of the inauguration was one of the brightest and balmiest of the spring. An eye-witness shall describe to us the memorable scene:

> No one who was at Washington at the time of General Jackson's inauguration is likely to forget that period to the day of his death. To us, who had witnessed the quiet and orderly period of the Adams' administration, it seemed as if half the nation had rushed at once into the Capital. It was like the inundation of the northern barbarians into Rome, save that the tumultuous tide came in

from a different point of the compass. The West and the South seemed to have precipitated themselves upon the North and overwhelmed it. On that memorable occasion you might tell a "Jackson man" almost as far as you could see him. Their every motion seemed to cry out "victory"! Strange faces filled every public place, and every face seemed to bear defiance on its brow. It appeared to me that every Jackson editor in the country was on the spot. They swarmed, especially in the lobbies of the House, an expectant host, a sort of Prætorian band, which, having borne in upon their shields their idolized leader, claimed the reward of the hard-fought contest. His quarters were assailed, surrounded, hemmed in, so that it was an achievement to get into his presence. On the morning of the inauguration, the vicinity of the Capitol was like a great agitated sea; every avenue to the fateful spot was blocked up with people, in so much that the legitimate procession which accompanied the President-elect could scarce make its way to the eastern portico, where the ceremony was to be performed. To repress the crowd in front, a ship's cable was stretched across about two-thirds of the way up the long flight of steps by which the Capitol is approached on that side, but it seemed, at times, as if even this would scarce prove sufficient to restrain the eagerness of the multitude, every man of whom seemed bent on the glory of shaking the President's hand. Never can I forget the spectacle which presented itself on every side, nor the electrifying moment when the eager, expectant eyes of that vast and motley multitude caught sight of the tall and imposing form of their adored leader, as he came forth between the columns of the portico, the color of the whole mass changed, as if by miracle; all hats were off at once, and the dark tint which usually pervades a mixed map of men was turned, as by a magic wand, into the bright hue of ten thousand upturned and exultant human faces, radiant with sudden joy. The peal of shouting that arose rent the air, and seemed to shake the very ground. But when the Chief Justice took his place and commenced the brief ceremony of administering the oath of office, it quickly sank into comparative silence; and as the new President proceeded to read his inaugural address, the stillness gradually increased; but all efforts to hear him, beyond a brief space immediately around, were utterly vain.[1]

. . . The ceremony over, the President drove from the Capitol to the White House, followed soon by a great part of the crowd who had witnessed the inauguration. Judge Story, a strenuous Adams man, did not enjoy the scene which the apartments of the "palace," as he styles it, presented on this occasion. "After the ceremony was over," he wrote, "the President went to the palace to receive company, and there he was visited by immense crowds of all sorts of people, from the highest and most polished, down to the most vulgar and gross in the nation. I never saw such a mixture. The reign of King MOB seemed triumphant. I was glad to escape from the scene as soon as possible." A letter writer said: "A profusion of refreshments had been provided. Orange punch by barrels full was made, but as the waiters opened the door to bring it out, a rush would be made, the glasses broken, the pails of liquor upset, and the most painful confusion

---

1. Arthur J. Stansbury, in *Arthur's Home Gazette*, May, 1851. [Poore's note.]

prevailed. To such a painful degree was this carried, that wine and ice-creams could not be brought out to the ladies, and tubs of punch were taken from the lower story into the garden, to lead off the crowd from the rooms. On such an occasion it was certainly difficult to keep any thing like order, but it was mortifying to see men, with boots heavy with mud, standing on the damask satin covered chairs, from their eagerness to get a sight of the President."

26

The Trail of Tears

John Ross

*John Ross (1790–1866), of mixed Cherokee and white ancestry, was exactly the phe-
nomenon that led Georgians and their great ally, Andrew Jackson, to insist on the removal of the so-called civilized tribes. Ross epitomized the "civilized," literate,
prosperous, politically astute Native American who successfully competed with whites.
He had fought as an officer under Jackson against the Creek Indians at Horseshoe
Bend. In the years after the War of 1812, he became a leader of the Cherokee as well as
the successful owner of a three-hundred-acre plantation run with the labor of more
than twenty slaves. As leader of the fight against the removal, Ross was the chief author
of the Cherokee nation's* Memorial and Petition *against Jackson's policy and took the
bitter responsibility for managing his people's journey west (in which his wife, Quatie,
was one of the many casualties) after all his efforts to prevent it had failed.*

*Ross never ceased his service to the Cherokee, remaining as principal chief of the
nation in Indian Territory until his death. He also developed a new cotton plantation in
the West, again using numerous slaves.*

BEFORE YOU READ

1. How did John Ross argue the case against the removal of the Cherokees in the
Memorial and Petition submitted to the Senate and House of Representatives? What are
the chief points he made? How persuasive do you think his argument is?

2. What were the main problems facing Ross in carrying out the removal of his
people to the West?

TO THE SENATE AND
HOUSE OF REPRESENTATIVES

Washington City February 22ed 1837

The memorial and petition of the undersigned, a delegation appointed by the
Cherokee nation in full council respectfully showeth:

That the Cherokee Nation deeply sensible of the evils under which they
are now laboring and the still more frightful miseries which they have too much
reason to apprehend, have in the most formal and solemn manner known to

Gary E. Moulton, ed., *The Papers of Chief John Ross: Volume I, 1807–1839* (Tulsa: University of Oklahoma Press, 1985).

them, assembled in General Council to deliberate upon their existing relations with the Government of the United States, and to lay their case with respectful deference before your honorable bodies.

Invested with full powers to conclude an arrangement upon all the matters which interest them we have arrived at the seat of Government, and, in accordance with our usual forms of proceeding have notified the Honorable the Secretary of War [Benjamin F. Butler] that we had reached this place and, through him, solicited an interview with the Executive [Andrew Jackson]. This request has not yet been granted, nor has it to this day received an official answer, but we have reason to apprehend from circumstances which have reached us that we shall be denied this application, and are thus compelled in the discharge of our duty to our constituents, to submit to your Honorable bodies the memorial of which we are the bearers.

On former occasions we have in much detail laid before you the prominent facts of our case. We have reminded you of our long and intimate connexion with the United States, of the scenes of peril and difficulty which we have shared in common; of the friendship which had so long been generously proffered and affectionately and gratefully accepted; of the aids which were supplied us in promoting our advancement in the arts of civilized life, of the political principles which we had imbibed, of the religious faith we have been taught.

We have called your attention to the progress which under your auspices we have made, of the improvements which have marked our social and individual states; our lands brought into cultivation, our natural resources developed, our farms, workshops and factories, approximating in character and value to those of our brethren whose example we had diligently imitated.

A smooth and beautiful prospect of future advancement was opened before us. Our people had abandoned the pursuits, the habits and the tastes of the savage, and had put on the vestments of civilization, of intelligence and of a pure religion. The progress we had made furnished us with the most assured hopes of continued improvement, and we indulged in the anticipation that the time was not far distant when we should be recognised, on the footing of equality by the brethren from whom we had received all which we were now taught to prize.

This promise of golden sunshine is now overspread. Clouds and darkness have obscured its brilliancy. The winds are beginning to mutter their awful forebodings, the tempest is gathering thick and heavy over our heads, and threatens to burst upon us with terrific energy and overwhelming ruin.

In this season of calamity, where can we turn with hope or confidence? On all former occasions of peril or of doubt the Government of the United States spread over us its broad and paternal shield. It invited us to seek an asylum and a protection under its mighty arm. It assisted us with its encouragement and advice, it soothed us with its consoling assurances, it inspired us with hope and gave us a feeling of confidence and security.

But alas! this our long-cherished friend seems now to be alienated from us: this our father has raised his arm to inflict the hostile blow; this strength so long our protection is now exerted against us, and on the wide scene of existence no human aid is left us. Unless you avert your arm we are destroyed. Unless your feelings of affection and compassion are once more awakened towards your destitute and despairing children our annihilation is complete.

It is a natural inquiry among all who commiserate our situation what are the causes which have led to this disastrous revolution, to this entire change of relations? By what agency have such results been accomplished?

We have asked, and we reiterate the question how have we offended? Show us in what manner we have, however unwittingly, inflicted upon you a wrong, you shall yourselves be the judges of the extent and manner of compensation. Show us the offence which has awakened your feelings of justice against us and we will submit to that measure of punishment which you shall tell us we have merited. We cannot bring to our recollections anything we have done or anything we have omitted calculated to awaken your resentment against us.

But we are told a treaty has been made and all that is required at our hands is to comply with its stipulations. Will the faithful historian, who shall hereafter record our lamentable fate, say—the Cherokee Nation executed a treaty by which they freely and absolutely ceded the country in which they were born and educated, the property they had been industriously accumulating and improving, and, abandoning the high road to which they had been advancing from savagism had precipitated themselves into worse than their pristine degradation, will not the reader of such a narrative require the most ample proof before he will credit such a story? Will he not inquire where was the kind and parental guardian who had heretofore aided the weak, assisted the forlorn, instructed the ignorant and elevated the depressed? Where was the Government of the United States with its vigilant care over the Indian when such a bargain was made? How will he be surprised at hearing that the United States was a party to the transaction—that the authority of that Government, and the representatives of that people, which had for years been employed in leading the Cherokees from ignorance to light, from barbarism to civilization, from paganism to christianity, who had taught them new habits and new hopes was the very party which was about to appropriate to itself the fruits of the Indian's industry, the birth places of his children and the graves of his ancestors.

If such a recital could command credence must it not be on the ground that experience had shown the utter failure of all the efforts and the disappointment of all the hopes of the philanthropist and the Christian? That the natives of this favored spot of God's creation were incapable of improvement and unsusceptible of education and that they in wilful blindness, spurning the blessings which had been proffered and urged upon them would pertinaciously prefer the degradation from which it had been attempted to lead them and the barbarism from which it had been sought to elevate them?

How will his astonishment be augmented when he learns that the Cherokee people almost to a man denied the existence and the obligation of the alleged compact—that they proclaimed it to have been based in fraud and concocted in perfidy—that no authority was ever given to those who undertook in their names and on their behalf to negotiate it; that it was repudiated with unexampled unanimity when it was brought to their knowledge; that they denied that it conferred any rights or imposed any obligations.

Yet such must be the story which the faithful historian must record. In the name of the whole Cherokee people we protest against this unhallowed and unauthorized and unacknowledged compact. We deny its binding force. We recognise none of its stipulations. If contrary to every principle of justice it is to be enforced upon us, we shall at least be free from the disgrace of self humiliation. We hold the solemn disavowal of its provisions by eighteen thousand of our people.

We, the regularly commissioned delegation of the Cherokee Nation in the face of Heaven and appealing to the Searcher of all hearts for the truth of our statements ask you to listen to our remonstrances. We implore you to examine into the truth of our allegations. We refer you to your own records, to your own agents, to men deservedly enjoying your esteem and confidence as our witnesses, and we proffer ourselves ready if you will direct the inquiry to establish the truth of what we aver. If we fail to substantiate our statements overwhelm us with ignominy and disgrace. Cast us off from you forever. If however on the other hand every allegation we make shall be sustained by the most convincing and abundant proof, need we make further or stronger appeals than the simple facts of the case will themselves furnish, to secure your friendship, your sympathy and your justice.

We will not and we cannot believe after the long connexion that has subsisted between us, after all that has been done and all that has been promised that our whole nation will be forcibly ejected from their native land and from their social hearths without the pretence of crime, without charge, without evidence, without trial: that we shall be exiled from all that we hold dear and venerable and sacred, and driven into a remote, a strange and a sterile region, without even the imputation of guilt. We will not believe that this will be done by our ancient allies, our friends, our brethren. Yet between this and the abrogation to the pretended treaty there is no medium. Such an instrument so obtained, so contaminated cannot cover the real nature of the acts which it is invoked to sanction. If power is to be exerted let it come unveiled. We shall but submit and die.

Jno Ross

TO WINFIELD SCOTT[1]

Cherokee Agency East October 6th 1838

Sir

I had the honor to receive your communication of the 3rd inst. on the subject of my requisition of the 2ed and the state of the emigration generally. In reply, I beg leave to say, that although those detachments, only, which are in the greatest state of forwardness, are formally announced in my estimates and requisition; it ought to be borne in mind that, our efforts are directed, to carrying on the emigration with so much dispatch that, simultaneous preparations

1. **Winfield Scott:** Major General Scott was in overall charge of the Cherokee removal.

must be going on for the whole number of detachments by land, and even for the final clearing out of the sick, the infirm, the aged &c by water, who are unable to bear the fatigues of the journey by land. And that these preparations, may be made, with the least possible delay, I deemed it indispensable to have the necessary funds in readiness.

With regard to the number in some of the detachments, I would respectfully observe that the number one thousand, was understood by the Cherokees to be merely a common measure, assumed as the basis of the pecuniary calculations; and not as a precise, stipulated number which must absolutely be filled by each detachment; yet, their intention was, that each detachment should approximate that number as nearly as might be convenient. And it was expected that some would exceed and some come short of it.

In regard to Capt. [Hair] Conrad's detachment, I am sorry to say that it has been greatly diminished by causes beyond human control. That detachment was not, at first, expected to be large, and the amount of sickness with which it has been visited has greatly reduced its numbers, and even deprived it of the original conductor. I am happy to find, however, that a considerable number who have recovered are now on their way to join their friends in that detachment.

Mr. [George] Hick's detachment was expected to number one thousand or more, but the same afflictive causes have operated extensively among them also, and a considerable number were unavoidably left behind. In addition to this it may not be improper to say that Mr. Hicks and some of the other conductors have had to contend with extraneous, counteracting influences which were used to frustrate their arrangements in particular, and to embarrass and retard the progress of the general arrangements, between yourself and the authorities of the nation. And here, Sir, permit me to say, that having secured your confidence in our good faith and integrity, on which we place the highest estimate; we should be extremely sorry that you should find the authority or the moral influence of the Nation inadequate to the prompt and faithful, discharge of its duties. I trust there does exist, in the Nation, a sufficient amount of energy, moral and official, for the performance of all its engagements. And here it may be proper to call your attention to the fact that certain individual Cherokees namely [John A.] Bell, [William] Boling & their associates under the assumed protection of the United States prompted and sustained, as I am assured, by individuals in official stations, of whose conduct I have more than once verbally complained; have been practising a course of interference, tending to retard the progress and disturb the arrangements of the detachments preparing for the road. We have refrained from exercising, the National Authority over those persons, from the feeling of uncertainty, whether, they were to be considered under the jurisdiction of the United States or that of the Cherokee Nation. If they are under the control of the Nation it would be desirable to have the fact known; but if they are under the control of the U. States we would respectfully call upon you to apply the corrective. In this connexion, it may not be out of place to add, that the continuing to issue rations, by the Govt. Agents at places from which the detachments have removed or after the regular organization of the detachments preparatory to their journey, as well as issuing, at the Agency,

to little secluded parties, some of them many miles distant; is calculated to produce delay, in their being embodied with the detachments to which they properly belong, and more especially so, when this practice is connected with a
systematic propagation of falsehoods and misrepresentations by the individuals
alluded to and their emissaries.

The counteracting of these malign influences by prudent and gentle means,
has, it is true, occasioned a little undesirable delay; but I have the pleasure to
say, that our movements are now in a state of activity, which I trust will pre-
clude all cause of complaint, with the assurance that our best efforts will be exerted to carry out our arrangements, with all reasonable dispatch. I remain with
high respect, Sir, your obt. Servt.

Jno Ross

TO MATTHEW ARBUCKLE[2]

Illinois [Cherokee Nation] Apl 23rd 1839

Sir

From the many complaints which are daily made to me by Cherokees who
have been recently removed into this country, of their sufferings, from the want
of being properly subsisted with provisions, I am constrained to address you
this hasty letter. It is reported that, apart from the scantiness of the ration allowed under the contract made on the part of the United States Government
with [James] Glasgow & [James] Harrison, many inconveniences have been experienced by the Cherokee people, from the irregularity of proceedings on the
part of those employed for carrying out the contract.

It has also been stated that the contractors were only required to furnish "one
pound of fresh beef, three half pints of corn & four qts. of salt to every 100 lbs. of
beef—or, if they (the contractors) choose they might furnish in lieu of the beef,
3/4 lb. salt pork or bacon provided the Indians will receive it." The beef being
poor & not considered wholesome this season of the year, the Cherokees have
generally objected to and refused receiving it and have insisted on being furnished
with Salt Pork or Bacon in lieu of the beef, but it seems that the contractors do not
choose and have refused to comply with the demand; saying that they were only
bound to furnish Beef rations. Yet they would commute the ration by paying in
money one dollar pr. month for the same. Thus the Cherokees are placed in a situation by compulsion to accept of either the beef or the money offered or to go
unsupplied altogether. Here I must beg leave to remark, that previous to the removal of the Cherokees from the East to the West, the subject of providing subsistence for them after their arrival in this country was fully discussed with Major
Genl. [Winfield] Scott who communicated with the War Deptmt. in reference to
it. And we were afterwards informed by that distinguished officer that the Hon.
Secry. of War [Joel R. Poinsett] had decided that the Cherokees should at least for

2. **Matthew Arbuckle:** Brigadier General Arbuckle was area commander in the Indian
Territory.

a time be subsisted with provisions in kind, until they could provide for themselves, and then such an arrangement as would be most satisfactory to them should be made with them through Capt. Collins. Now Sir, it is evident from the exorbitant prices of meat and bread stuffs in this country that the Cherokees who have thus been forced to receive commutation in money from the contractors at the rate stated will soon be found in a starving condition—instead of being provided with subsistence as was anticipated and promised them. If the articles of agreement entered into with the contractors are to be construed so as to leave it wholly optional with them whether to furnish Salt Pork or Bacon in lieu of Beef, then it is obvious that there were no practical advantage for the interest of the Cherokees to have inserted any clause in that instrument in regard to Salt Pork or Bacon—for its effect has only been and will continue to be to mislead the mind of the people. And how it can be reconciled with the obligations imposed by the contract for the contractors to adopt the mode of commuting the subsistence rations they have engaged to furnish the Cherokees with and that too by a rate fixed by themselves, is a mystery which the Cherokees cannot understand—for it is not pretended that such a right or discretion has ever been given to them by the contract with the agents or the U.S. Govt. for subsisting the Cherokees. Nor can the sacred principle of justice sanction such a course under existing circumstances. Confiding however in the fair intentions of the Government towards them on this subject, the Cherokees still believe that the Hon. Secry. of War will when deemed expedient commute their rations at a rate at least equal to any sum fully ample to purchase provisions with for their comfortable subsistence—and that no sum less will be offered than what others would engage to supply the same for. I beg leave herewith to lay before you copies of sundry letters which I have just received from several leading men on behalf of the Cherokees on this very unpleasant subject. And in conclusion will further remark, that the health and existence of the whole Cherokee people who have recently been removed to this distant country demands a speedy remedy for the inconveniences and evils complained of, & unless a change of the quantity and the kind of rations as well as of the mode of issuing the same, be made from that which has heretofore been granted and observed, the Cherokees must inevitably suffer. Therefore to avoid hunger & starvation they are reduced to the necessity of calling upon you and other officers as the proper representatives of the U.S. Govt. in this matter, to take immediate steps as will ensure the immediate subsistence of the Cherokees who have recently been removed here, with ample and wholesome provisions, until such other arrangements, as may be most satisfactory to them, can be made for subsisting themselves &c. When every thing in reference to the late removal of the Cherokee nation from the East to the West is considered, and seen that it has been consummated through the military authority of the U.S. Govt. I trust you will pardon me for addressing this communication to you, especially when you are assured that the Cherokee people have been taught to expect that justice and protection would be extended to them through the Commanding General in this Hemisphere.

Jno Ross

27

Six Months in the Gold Mines

Edward Gould Buffum

On January 24, 1848, while erecting a sawmill on a branch of the American River in the lower Sacramento Valley, about forty miles from present-day Sacramento, workers found tiny nuggets of gold in the riverbed. Although the story at first was greeted with skepticism, word spread quickly once President James K. Polk confirmed the discovery in his annual message to Congress that December. Then, lured by dreams of the fortunes to be made there, adventurers from all over the world flocked to California by the thousands.

When news of the gold strikes first spread, Edward Gould Buffum (1820–1867) was an army lieutenant in California. As soon as he mustered out in September 1848, Buffum headed for the gold fields. His Six Months in the Gold Mines, *hurriedly published in 1850 "in consequence of the public interest in all that pertains to California," is one of the most important accounts of the California gold rush. Many ambitious Easterners, relying on his detailed accounts of mining procedures, used the book as a combined atlas and instruction manual as they headed west in search of riches. Buffum's vivid and exciting account of life on the mining frontier still attracts students of the American West.*

BEFORE YOU READ

1. California has long been seen as the land of the American dream. Does Buffum's account contribute to that image? If so, how?
2. What social and economic effects of the gold rush did Buffum depict?
3. What kinds of books published today are like Buffum's?

Next morning early, in better spirits than we had enjoyed for a week previously, we started for Yuba River [north of Sacramento]. About a mile from the camping-place we struck into the mountains, the same range at whose base we had been before travelling, and which are a portion of the Sierra Nevada. The hills here were steep and rugged, but covered with a magnificent growth of oak and red-wood. As we reached the summit of a lofty hill, the Yuba River broke upon our view, winding like a silver thread beneath us, its banks dotted with white tents, and fringed with trees and shrubbery.

Edward Gould Buffum, *Six Months in the Gold Mines* (Ann Arbor: University Microfilms, 1966), pp. 50–58, 60–65, 110–11.

We had at last reached the "mines," although a very different portion of them than that for which we started. We turned out our tired horses, and immediately set forth on an exploring expedition. As my clothing was all dirty and wet, I concluded to indulge in the luxury of a new shirt, and going down to the river found a shrewd Yankee in a tent surrounded by a party of naked Indians, and exposing for sale jerked beef at a dollar a pound, flour at a dollar and a half do., and for a coarse striped shirt which I picked up with the intention of purchasing, he coolly asked me the moderate price of sixteen dollars! I looked at my dirty shirt, then at the clean new one I held in my hand, and finally at my little gold bag, not yet replenished by digging, and concluded to postpone my purchase until I had struck my pick and crowbar into the bowels of the earth, and extracted therefrom at least a sufficiency to purchase a shirt. The diggings on Yuba River had at that time been discovered only about three months, and were confined entirely to the "bars," as they are called, extending nearly a mile each way from where the road strikes the river, on both its banks. The principal diggings were then called the "upper" and the "lower diggings," each about half a mile above and below the road. We started for the upper diggings to "see the elephant," and winding through the hills, for it was impossible to travel all the way on the river's bank, struck the principal bar then wrought on the river. This has since been called Foster's Bar, after an American who was then keeping a store there, and who had a claim on a large portion of the bar.

Upon reaching the bar, a curious scene presented itself. About one hundred men, in miner's costume, were at work, performing the various portions of the labour necessary in digging the earth and working a rocking machine. The apparatus then used upon the Yuba River, and which has always been the favourite assistant of the gold-digger, was the common rocker or cradle, constructed in the simplest manner. It consists of nothing more than wooden box or hollowed log, two sides and one end of which are closed, while the other end is left open. At the end which is closed and called the "mouth" of the machine, a sieve, usually made of a plate of sheet iron, or a piece of raw hide, perforated with holes about half an inch in diameter, is rested upon the sides. A number of "bars" or "rifflers," which are little pieces of board from one to two inches in height, are nailed to the bottom, and extend laterally across it. Of these, there are three or four in the machine, and one at the "tail," as it is called, i.e. the end where the dirt is washed out. This, with a pair of rockers like those of a child's cradle, and a handle to rock it with, complete the description of the machine, which being placed with the rockers upon two logs, and the "mouth" elevated at a slight angle above the tail, is ready for operation. Modified and improved as this may be, and as in fact it already has been, so long as manual labour is employed for washing gold, the "cradle" is the best agent to use for that purpose.

The manner of procuring and washing the golden earth was this. The loose stones and surface earth being removed from any portion of the bar, a hole from four to six feet square was opened, and the dirt extracted therefrom was thrown upon a raw hide placed at the side of the machine. One man shovelled the dirt into the sieve, another dipped up water and threw it on, and a third rocked the "cradle." The earth, thrown upon the sieve, is washed through with the water, while the stones and gravel are retained and thrown off. The continued motion of the machine, and the constant stream of water pouring through it, washes the earth over the various bars or rifflers to the "tail," where it runs out, while the gold, being of greater specific gravity, sinks to the bottom, and is prevented from escaping by the rifflers. When a certain amount of earth has been thus washed (usually about sixty pans full are called "a washing"), the gold, mixed with a heavy black sand, which is always found mingled with gold in California, is taken out and washed in a tin pan, until nearly all the sand is washed away. It is then put into a cup or pan, and when the day's labour is over is dried before the fire, and the sand remaining carefully blown out. This is a simple explanation of the process of gold-washing in the placers of California. At present, however, instead of dipping and pouring on water by hand, it is usually led on by a hose or forced by a pump, thereby giving a better and more constant stream, and saving the labour of one man. The excavation is continued until the solid rock is struck, or the water rushing in renders it impossible to obtain any more earth, when a new place is opened. We found the gold on the Yuba in exceedingly fine particles, and it has always been considered of a very superior quality. We inquired of the washers as to their success, and they, seeing we were "green horns," and thinking we might possibly interfere with them, gave us either evasive answers, or in some cases told us direct lies. We understood from them that they were making about twenty dollars per day, while I afterwards learned, from the most positive testimony of two men who were at work there at the time, that one hundred dollars a man was not below the average estimate of a day's labour.

On this visit to Foster's Bar I made my first essay in gold-digging. I scraped up with my hand my tin cup full of earth, and washed it in the river. How eagerly I strained my eyes as the earth was washing out, and the bottom of the cup was coming in view! and how delighted, when, on reaching the bottom, I discerned about twenty little golden particles sparkling in the sun's rays, and worth probably about fifty cents. I wrapped them carefully in a piece of paper, and preserved them for a long time, — but, like much more gold in larger quantities, which it has since been my lot to possess, it has escaped my grasp, and where it now is Heaven only knows.

The labour on Yuba River appeared very severe, the excavations being sometimes made to a depth of twelve feet before the soil containing the gold, which was a gravelly clay, was reached. We had not brought our tools with us, intending, if our expedition in the mountains had succeeded, that one of our party should return for our remaining stock of provisions and tools. We had no facilities for constructing a machine, and no money to buy one (two hundred dollars being the price for which a mere hollowed pine log was offered us), and besides, all the bars upon which men were then engaged in labour were "claimed," a claim at that time being considered good when the claimant had cleared off the top soil from any portion of the bar. We returned to our camp, and talked over our prospects, in a quandary what to do. Little did we then dream that, in less than six months, the Yuba River, then only explored some three miles above where we were, would be successfully wrought for forty miles above us, and that thousands would find their fortunes upon it.

We concluded to return to the *Embarcadero*, and take a new start. Accordingly, next morning we packed up and set off, leaving at work upon the river about two hundred men. Having retraced our steps, we arrived at Sutter's Fort in safety on the evening of November 30th, just in time to find the member of our party whom we had left behind, packing all our remaining provisions and tools into a cart, ready to start for the "dry diggings" on the following morning.

The history of John A. Sutter, and his remarkable settlement on the banks of the Sacramento, has been one of interest since California first began to attract attention. Captain Sutter is by birth a Swiss, and was formerly an officer in the French army. He emigrated to the United States, became a naturalized citizen, and resided in Missouri several years. In the year 1839 he emigrated to the then wilderness of California, where he obtained a large grant of land, to the extent of about eleven leagues, bordering on the Sacramento River, and made a settlement directly in the heart of an Indian country, among tribes of hostile savages. For a long time he suffered continual attacks and depredations from the Indians, but finally succeeded, by kind treatment and good offices, in reducing them to subjection, and persuading them to come into his settlement, which he called New Helvetia. With their labour he built a large fort of *adobes* or sunburnt bricks, brought a party of his Indians under military discipline, and established a regular garrison. His wheat-fields were very extensive, and his cattle soon numbered five thousand, the whole labour being performed by Indians. These he paid with a species of money made of tin, which was stamped with dots, indicating the number of days' labour for which each one was given; and they were returned to him in exchange for cotton cloth, at a dollar a yard, and trinkets and sweetmeats at corresponding prices. The discovery of the gold mines of California has, however, added more to Sutter's fame than did his bold settlement in the wilderness. This has introduced him to the world almost as a man of gold, and connected his name for ever with the most prized metal upon earth. He is quite "a gentleman of the old school," his manners being very cordial and prepossessing. . . .

With all our worldly gear packed in an ox-wagon, we left Sutter's Fort on the morning of the 1st of December, and travelling about seven miles on the road, encamped in a beautiful grove of evergreen oak, to give the cattle an opportunity to lay in a sufficient supply of grass and acorns, preparatory to a long march. As we were to remain here during the day, we improved the opportunity by taking our dirty clothing, of which by that time we had accumulated a considerable quantity, down to the banks of the American Fork, distant about one mile from camp, for the purpose of washing. While we were employed in this laborious but useful occupation, Higgins called my attention to the salmon which were working up the river over a little rapid opposite us. Some sport suggested itself; and more anxious for this than labour, we dropped our half-washed shirts, and started back to camp for our rifles, which we soon procured, and brought down to the river. In making their way over the bar, the backs of the salmon were exposed some two inches above water; and the instant one appeared, a well-directed rifle-ball perforated his spine. The result was, that before dark Higgins and myself carried into camp thirty-five splendid salmon, procured by this novel mode of sport. We luxuriated on them, and gave what we could not eat for supper and breakfast to some lazy Indians, who had been

employed the whole day in spearing some half dozen each. There is every probability that the salmon fishery will yet prove a highly lucrative business in
California.

Next morning we packed up and made a fresh start. That night we encamped at the "Green Springs," about twenty-five miles distant from Sutter's
Fort. These springs are directly upon the road, and bubble up from a muddy
black loam, while around them is the greenest verdure,—the surrounding plain
being dotted with beautiful groves and magnificent flowers. Their waters are
delicious.

As the ox-team was a slow traveller, and quarters were to be looked for in
our new winter home, on the next morning Higgins and myself were appointed
a deputation to mount two horses we had brought with us and proceed post-
haste to the "dry diggings." We started at 10 A.M., and travelled through some
beautiful valleys and over lofty hills. As we reached the summit of a high ridge,
we paused by common consent to gaze upon the landscape and breathe the delicious air. The broad and fertile valleys of the Sacramento and San Joaquin lay
stretched at our feet like a highly coloured map. The noble rivers which lend
their names to these rich valleys were plainly visible, winding like silver threads
through dark lines of timber fringing their banks; now plunging amid dense
forests, and now coming in view sparkling and bright as the riches they contain;
the intermediate plains, here parched and browned with the sun's fierce rays;
there brilliant with all the hues of the rainbow, and dotted with the autumnal
flowers and open groves of evergreen oak. Herds of elk, black-tailed deer, and
antelope browsed near the mountain sides, on the summit of which the eagle
builds his eyry. The surrounding atmosphere, fragrant with delightful odours,
was so pure and transparent as to render objects visible at a great distance, and
so elastic and bracing as to create a perceptible effect on our feelings. Far in the
distance the massive peak of Shaste reared its snow-capped head, from amid a
dense forest, fourteen thousand feet into the sky. We arrived at what was then
called Weaver's Creek, about dusk. . . .

The "dry diggings" of Weaver's Creek being a fair specimen of dry diggings
in all parts of the mining region, a description of them will give the reader a general idea of the various diggings of the same kind in California. They are called
"dry" in contradistinction to the "wet" diggings, or those lying directly on the
banks of streams, and where all the gold is procured by washing. As I before said,
the stream coursed between lofty tree-clad hills, broken on both sides of the river
into little ravines or gorges. In these ravines most of the gold was found. The loose
stones and top earth being thrown off, the gravelly clay that followed it was usually laid aside for washing, and the digging continued until the bottom rock of the
ravine was reached, commonly at a depth of from one to six feet. The surface of
this rock was carefully cleared off, and usually found to contain little crevices and
holes, the latter in miner's parlance called "pockets," and in which the gold was
found concealed, sparkling like the treasures in the cave of Monte Cristo. A careful examination of the rock being made, and every little crevice and pocket being
searched with a sharp pointed-knife, gold in greater or less quantities invariably
made its appearance. I shall never forget the delight with which I first struck and

worked out a crevice. It was the second day after our installation in our little log hut; the first having been employed in what is called "prospecting," or searching for the most favourable place at which to commence operations. I had slung pick, shovel, and bar upon my shoulder, and trudged merrily away to a ravine about a mile from our house. Pick, shovel, and bar did their duty, and I soon had a large rock in view. Getting down into the excavation I had made, and seating myself upon the rock, I commenced a careful search for a crevice, and at last found one extending longitudinally along the rock. It appeared to be filled with a hard, bluish clay and gravel, which I took out with my knife, and there at the bottom, strewn along the whole length of the rock, was bright, yellow gold, in little pieces about the size and shape of a grain of barley. Eureka! Oh how my heart beat! I sat still and looked at it some minutes before I touched it, greedily drinking in the pleasure of gazing upon gold that was in my very grasp, and feeling a sort of independent bravado in allowing it to remain there. When my eyes were sufficiently feasted, I scooped it out with the point of my knife and an iron spoon, and placing it in my pan, ran home with it very much delighted. I weighed it, and found that my first day's labour in the mines had made me thirty-one dollars richer than I was in the morning.

The gold, which, by some great volcanic eruption, has been scattered upon the soil over an extensive territory, by the continual rains of the winter season has been sunk into the hills, until it has reached either a hard clay which it cannot penetrate, or a rock on which it rests. The gold in the hills, by the continual rains, has been washing lower and lower, until it has reached the ravines. It has washed down the ravines until it has there reached the rock, and thence, it has washed along the bed of the ravines until it has found some little crevice in which it rests, where the water can carry it no farther. Here it gathers, and thus are formed the "pockets" and "nests" of gold, one of which presents such a glowing golden sight to the eye of the miner, and such a field for his imagination to revel in. How often, when I have struck one of these, have I fondly wished that it might reach to the centre of the earth, and be filled as it was at its mouth with pure, bright, yellow gold.

Our party's first day's labour produced one hundred and fifty dollars, I having been the most successful of all. But we were satisfied, although our experience had not fulfilled the golden stories we had heard previous to our reaching the *placers*. Finding the average amount of gold dug on Weaver's Creek at that time to be about an ounce per day to a man, we were content so long as we could keep pace with our neighbours. There is a spirit of emulation among miners which prevents them from being ever satisfied with success whilst others around them are more successful. We continued our labours for a week, and found, at the end of that time, our whole party had dug out more than a thousand dollars; and after paying for our house, and settling between ourselves our little private expenses, we were again on a clear track, unencumbered by debt, and in the heart of a region where treasures of unknown wealth were lying hidden in the earth on which we daily trod.

About this time, the most extravagant reports reached us from the Middle Fork, distant in a northerly direction about thirty miles from Weaver's Creek.

Parties who had been there described the river as being lined with gold of the finest quality. One and two hundred dollars was not considered a great day's labour, and now was the time to take advantage of it, while in its pristine richness. The news was too blooming for me to withstand. I threw down my pick-axe, and leaving a half-wrought crevice for some other digger to work out, I packed up and held myself in readiness to proceed by the earliest opportunity, and with the first party ready to go for the Middle Fork. . . .

Passing to the northward of the Dry Diggings, we encamped at dusk in a little oak grove about three miles from Sutter's Mill, killed a deer, ate a hearty supper, spread our blankets on the ground, and slept quietly and peacefully beneath a star-studded and cloudless heaven. Next morning we went into Culoma, the Indian name for the territory around Sutter's Mill, and here we were to purchase our provisions previous to going to the river. Three stores only, at that time, disputed the trade at what is now the great centre of the northern mining region; and where now are busy streets, and long rows of tents and houses, was a beautiful hollow, which, in our romantic version, we named as we were entering it, "The Devil's Punch-Bowl." Surrounded on all sides by lofty mountains, its ingress and egress guarded by an ascent and descent through narrow passes, it seemed like a huge bowl which some lofty spirit might seize, and placing it to his lips, quaff the waters of the golden stream that circled through it. Here it was that gold was first discovered in California; this was the locality where was commenced a new era, and where a new page was opened in the history of mankind.

The city of Sacramento had assumed a very different aspect at the time I reached it on my return from the northern mines, from that which it exhibited when I previously left it. Where the old store-ship used to be, on the banks of the Sacramento, tall-masted ships were moored, and the extensive plain on which I pitched my tent was dotted with houses. Around the fort itself, which is nearly two miles from the bank of the river, houses had begun to spring up. Building-lots which, four months previously, had sold at from fifty to two hundred dollars, were now held by their owners at from one to three thousand. I looked on with astonishment at the remarkable progress, and then little thought that the ensuing six months would develope a growth, both in size and prices, which would entirely outstrip what I then witnessed.

Getting on board a launch, I spent a weary five days in sailing down the Sacramento, and arrived at San Francisco in the early part of May. What a change had occurred in six months! San Francisco, when I saw it before, was almost entirely deserted, everybody having gone to the mines. Now it was being daily recruited by the arrival of travellers across the plains, by vessels around Cape Horn, by Sandwich Islanders, Chinese, French, English, and Mexicans. The age of speculation had commenced. The building-lots which, when I landed in San Francisco, were granted by the alcaldes for the sum of fifteen dollars, and in the autumn before were worth but five hundred, had now risen in value to from three to five thousand. Hundreds and thousands of men with capital were arriving, who readily seized upon the opportunities for speculating.

Houses were going up on the vacant lots, and the town beginning to assume an air of business. Goods of all kinds had fallen in price, owing to the arrival of fleets of loaded ships from all parts of the world, and in some cases from wilful neglect on the part of consignees. Large hotels had been erected, and life began to be rendered comfortable. Gambling in all its forms was carried on to an enormous extent, and money, as before, was almost as plentiful as the sea-sands.

28

Pulling a Handcart to the Mormon Zion
Priscilla Merriman Evans

Many of the men and women who settled the Far West often endured extraordinary physical hardships and dangers to reach their destinations. The Mormon pioneers who walked from Iowa City, Iowa, to Salt Lake City, Utah, pulling handcarts made of hickory, were driven by both economic and religious motives. The handcart immigrants were poor: if they could have afforded to migrate any other way, they would have. They spoke one or more of several languages — German, Welsh, Danish, Swedish — as well as English. And they did not all have so successful a journey as the pregnant Mrs. Thomas D. Evans. With her one-legged husband, Priscilla Merriman Evans walked the one thousand miles in five months, arriving in Salt Lake City in October 1856, comfortably ahead of the winter weather. In two parties later that year, hundreds died in winter blizzards.

Nine more handcart companies reached the Mormon Zion in the five years after the Evanses' journey. All received rich welcomes with prayers and hymns. Priscilla Merriman Evans concluded her narrative by saying that she always "thanked the Lord for a contented mind, a home and something to eat."

BEFORE YOU READ

1. Why do you think Priscilla Merriman Evans became a Mormon and chose to emigrate?
2. What were the principal difficulties of the trip to Utah?
3. What rewards did Evans find in "Zion"?

I, Priscilla Merriman Evans, born May 4, 1835 at Mounton New Marbeth, Pembrokeshire, Wales, am the daughter of Joseph and Ann James Merriman. About 1839, father moved his family from Mounton up to Tenby, about ten miles distant. Our family consisted of father, mother, Sarah, aged six, and myself, aged four. Tenby was a beautiful place, as are all those Celtic Islands, with remains of old castles, vine- and moss-covered walls, gone to ruin since the time of the Conqueror. . . .

Besides reading, writing, spelling, and arithmetic, we were taught sewing and sampler making. The sampler work was done in cross stitch, worked in

Kate B. Carter, comp., *Heart Throbs of the West*, vol. 9 (Salt Lake City: International Society Daughters of Utah Pioneers), pp. 8–13.

192

bright colors, on canvas made for that purpose. . . . We were also taught the Bible. I was greatly interested in school, but was taken out at eleven years of age, owing to the illness in our family. I was a natural student, and greatly desired to continue my studies, but mother's health was very poor, so I was taken out to help with the work. My sister, Sarah, continued school, as she did not like housework and wished to learn a trade. She went to Mrs. Hentin and learned the millinery trade. Mother's health continued [to be] poor, and she died at the birth of her eighth child, Emma, when I was sixteen. I had many duties for a girl so young, caring for my sisters and brothers. While Sarah was learning millinery, she would sometimes wake me in the night to try on a hat— one she was practicing on. She learned the millinery business and then went up to London, opened a shop of her own and was very successful. She married a gentleman . . . who was devoted to her, and followed her to London. She died at the birth of her fourth child.

[When] Mother died on the eighth of November 1851 . . . the responsibility of the family rested on my young shoulders. . . . After the death of my mother we were very lonely, and one evening I accompanied my father to the house of a friend. When we reached there, we learned that they were holding a cottage meeting. Two Mormon Elders were the speakers, and I was very much interested in the principles they advocated. I could see that my father was very worried, and would have taken me away, had he known how. When he became aware that I believed in the Gospel as taught by the Elders, I asked him if he had ever heard of the restored Gospel. He replied, "Oh, yes, I have heard of Old Joe Smith, and his Golden Bible." When my father argued against the principles taught by the Elders, I said, "If the Bible is true, then Mormonism is true."

My father was very much opposed to my joining the Church . . . as he thought the Saints were too slow to associate with. . . . But I had found the truth and was baptized into the Church of Jesus Christ of Latter-day Saints in Tenby, February 26, 1852. My sister Sarah took turns with me going out every Sunday. She would go where she pleased on Sunday, while I would walk seven miles to Stepaside and attend the Mormon meeting. My father was very much displeased with me going out every Sunday. He forbade me to read the Church literature, and threatened to burn all I brought home. At the time I had a Book of Mormon borrowed from a friend, and when Father found out I had it, he began looking for it. It was in plain sight, among other books in the book case. I saw him handling it with the other books, and I sent up a silent prayer that he might not notice it, which he did not, although it was before him in plain sight. I do not think my father was as bitter against the principles of the Gospel as he seemed to be, for many times when the Elders were persecuted, he defended them, and gave them food and shelter. But he could not bear the idea of my joining them and leaving home.

About this time, Thomas D. Evans, a young Mormon Elder, was sent up from Merthyr Tydfil, Wales, as a missionary to Pembrokeshire. He was a fine speaker, and had a fine tenor voice, and I used to like to go around with the missionaries and help with the singing. Elder Evans and I seemed to be congenial from our first meeting, and we were soon engaged. He was traveling and preaching the restored Gospel without purse or script. Perhaps his mission will be better understood if I give a little account: [his father had died] and left his mother a widow with eight children, Thomas D. being four years old and the youngest. He was placed in a large forge of two-thousand men at the age of seven years to learn the profession of Iron Roller. At nine years of age, he had the misfortune to lose his left leg at the knee. He went through the courses and graduated as an Iron Roller. When I think of [when they met in 1852] it seems that we had put the world aside, and were not thinking of our worldly pleasures, and what our next dress would be. We had no dancing in those days, but we were happy in the enjoyment of the spirit of the Gospel. . . .

I was familiar with the Bible doctrine, and when I heard the Elders explain it, it seemed as though I had always known it, and it sounded like music in my ears. We had the spirit of gathering and were busy making preparations to emigrate.

About that time the Principle of Plurality of Wives was preached to the world, and it caused quite a commotion in our branch. One of the girls came to me with tears in her eyes and said, "Is it true that Brigham Young has nine wives? I can't stand that, Oh, I can't stand it!" I asked her how long it had been since I had heard her testify that she knew the Church was true, and I said if it was then, it is true now. I told her I did not see anything for her to cry about. After I talked to her awhile, she dried her eyes and completed her arrangements to get married and emigrate. She came with us. My promised husband and I went to Merthyr to visit his Mother, brothers, sisters, and friends, preparatory to emigrating. His family did all in their power to persuade him to remain with them. They were all well off, and his brothers said they would send him to school, support his wife, and pay all of his expenses but all to no avail. He bade them all goodbye, and returned to Tenby.

I think I would have had a harder time getting away, had it not been that my father was going to be married again, and I do not suppose the lady cared to have in the home, the grown daughter who had taken the place of the mother for so many years.

Elder Thomas D. Evans, my promised husband, and I walked the ten miles from Tenby to Pembroke, where we got our license and were married, and walked back to Tenby. We were married on the third of April, 1856. On our return from Pembroke we found a few of our friends awaiting us with supper ready. We visited our friends and relatives and made our preparations to emigrate to Zion. We took a tug from Pembroke to Liverpool, where we set sail on the 17th of April, 1856, on the sailing vessel S.S. Curling. Captain Curling said he would prefer to take a load of Saints than others, as he always felt safe with Saints on board. We learned that the next trip across the water that he was loaded with gentiles and his vessel sank with all on board. We were on the sea five weeks; we lived on the ship's rations. I was sick all the way. [Priscilla was then pregnant with their first child.]

We landed in Boston on May 23rd, then travelled in cattle cars . . . to Iowa City. We remained in Iowa City three weeks, waiting for our carts to be made. We were offered many inducements to stay there. My husband was offered ten dollars a day to work at his trade of Iron Roller, but money was no inducement to us, for we were anxious to get to Zion. We learned afterwards that many who stayed there apostatized or died of cholera.

When the carts were ready we started on a three-hundred-mile walk to Winterquarters on the Missouri River. There were a great many who made fun of us as we walked, pulling our carts, but the weather was fine and the roads were excellent and although I was sick and we were tired out at night, we still thought, "This is a glorious way to come to Zion."

We began our journey of one thousand miles on foot with a handcart for each family, some families consisting of man and wife, and some had quite large families. There were five mule teams to haul the tents and surplus flour. Each handcart had one hundred pounds of flour, that was to be divided and [more got] from the wagons as required. At first we had a little coffee and bacon, but that was soon gone and we had no use for any cooking utensils but a frying pan. The flour was self-raising and we took water and baked a little cake; that was all we had to eat.

After months of travelling we were put on half rations and at one time, before help came, we were out of flour for two days. We washed out the flour sacks to make a little gravy.

There were in our tent my husband with one leg, two blind men . . . a man with one arm, and a widow with five children. The widow, her children, and myself were the only ones who could not talk Welsh. My husband was commissary for our tent, and he cut his own rations short many times to help little children who had to walk and did not have enough to eat to keep up their strength.

The tent was our covering, and the overcoat spread on the bare ground with the shawl over us was our bed. My feather bed, and bedding, pillows, all our good clothing, my husband's church books, which he had collected through six years of missionary work, with some genealogy he had collected, all had to be left in a storehouse. We were promised that they would come to us with the next emigration in the spring, but we never did receive them. It was reported that the storehouse burned down, so that was a dreadful loss to us.

Edward Bunker was the Captain of our Company. His orders of the day were, "If any are sick among you, and are not able to walk, you must help them along, or pull them on your carts." No one rode in the wagons. Strong men would help the weaker ones, until they themselves were worn out, and some died from the struggle and want of food, and were buried along the wayside. It was heart rending for parents to move on and leave their loved ones to such a fate, as they were so helpless, and had no material for coffins. Children and young folks, too, had to move on and leave father or mother or both.

Sometimes a bunch of buffaloes would come and the carts would stop until they passed. Had we been prepared with guns and ammunition, like people who came in wagons, we might have had meat, and would not have come to near starving. President Young ordered extra cattle sent along to be killed to help the sick and weak, but they were never used for that purpose. One incident happened which came near being serious. Some Indians came to our camp and my husband told an Indian who admired me that he could have me for a pony. He was always getting off jokes. He thought no more about it, but in a day or two, here came the Indian with the pony, and wanted his pretty little squaw. It was no joke with him. I never was so frightened in all my life. There was no place to hide, and we did not know what to do. The Captain was called, and they had some difficulty in settling with the Indian without trouble.

In crossing rivers, the weak women and the children were carried over the deep places, and they waded the others. We were much more fortunate than those who came later, as they had snow and freezing weather. Many lost limbs, and many froze to death. President Young advised them to start earlier, but they got started too late. My husband, in walking from twenty to twenty-five miles per day [had pain] where the knee rested on the pad: the friction caused it to gather and break and was most painful. But he had to endure it, or remain behind, as he was never asked to ride in a wagon.

We reached Salt Lake City on October 2, 1856, tired, weary, with bleeding feet, our clothing worn out and so weak we were nearly starved, but thankful to our Heavenly Father for bringing us to Zion. William R. Jones met us on the Public Square in Salt Lake City and brought us to his home in Spanish Fork. I think we were over three days coming from Salt Lake City to Spanish Fork by ox team, but what a change to ride in a wagon after walking 1330 miles from Iowa City to Salt Lake City!

We stayed in the home of an ex-bishop, Stephen Markham. His home was a dugout. It was a very large room built half underground. His family consisted of three wives, and seven children. . . . There was a large fireplace in one end with bars, hooks, frying pans, and bake ovens, where they did the cooking for the large family, and boiled, fried, baked, and heated their water for washing.

There was a long table in one corner, and pole bedsteads fastened to the walls in the three other corners. They were laced back and forth with rawhide cut in strips, and made a nice springy bed. There were three trundle beds, made like shallow boxes, with wooden wheels, which rolled under the mother's bed in the daytime to utilize space. There was a dirt roof, and the dirt floor was kept hard and smooth by sprinkling and sweeping. The bed ticks were filled with straw. . . .

Aunt Mary [Markham] put her two children . . . in the foot of her bed and gave us the trundle bed. . . . How delightful to sleep on a bed again, after sleeping on the ground for so many months with our clothes on. We had not slept in a bed since we left the ship *Sam Curling*.

On the 31st of December, 1856, our first daughter was born. . . . My baby's wardrobe was rather meager: I made one night gown from her father's white shirt, another out of a factory lining of an oilcloth sack. Mrs. Markham gave me a square of homemade linsey for a shoulder blanket, and a neighbor gave me some old underwear, that I worked up into little things. They told me I could have an old pair of jean pants left at the adobe yard. I washed them and made them into petticoats. I walked down to the Indian farm and traded a gold pen for four yards of calico that made her two dresses.

One day my husband went down in the field to cut some willows to burn. The ax slipped and cut his good knee cap. It was with difficulty that he crawled to the house. He was very weak from the loss of blood. My baby was but a few days old, and the three of us had to occupy the trundle bed for awhile.

Wood and timber were about thirty miles up in the canyon, and when the men went after timber to burn, they went in crowds, armed, for they never knew when they would be attacked by Indians. Adobe houses were cheaper than log or frame, as timber was so far away. Many of the people who had lived in the dugouts after coming from Palmyra got into houses before the next winter. They exchanged work with each other, and in that way got along fine. Mr. Markham had an upright saw, run by water. The next spring they got timber from the canyon, and my husband helped Mr. Markham put up a three-roomed house and worked at farming.

He worked for William Markham a year, for which he received two acres of land. I helped in the house, for which, besides the land, we got our board and keep. The next Spring we went to work for ourselves. We saved our two acres of wheat, and made adobes for a two-roomed house, and paid a man in adobes for laying it up. It had a dirt roof. He got timber from Mr. Markham to finish the doors, windows, floors, shelves, and to make furniture. My husband made me a good big bedstead and laced it with rawhides. There were benches and the frames of chairs with the rawhide seat, with the hair left on; a table, shelves in the wall on either side of the fireplace, which was fitted with iron bars and hooks to hang kettles on to boil, frying pans and bake oven. A tick for a bed had to be pieced out of all kinds of scraps, as there were no stores, and everything was on a trade basis.

If one neighbor had something they could get along without, they would exchange it for something they could use. We were lucky to get factory, or sheeting to put up to the windows instead of glass. We raised a good crop of wheat that fall, for which we traded one bushel for two bushels of potatoes. We also exchanged for molasses and vegetables. We had no tea, coffee, meat, or grease of any kind for seasoning. No sugar, milk, or butter. In 1855–1856 the grasshoppers and crickets took the crops and the cattle nearly all died. They were dragged down in the field west [and left to die].

We bought a lot on Main Street, and my husband gave his parents our first little home with five acres of land. They had a good ox team, two cows, a new wagon, and they soon got pigs, chickens and a few sheep. It wasn't long before they were well off. . . .

It was indeed comfortable to be in a good house with a shingled roof and good floors. He set out an orchard of all kinds of fruit; also currents and goose-berries, planted lucern . . . in a patch by itself for cows and pigs. We had a nice garden spot, and we soon had butter, milk, eggs, and meat. We raised our bread, potatoes, and vegetables. While our fruit trees were growing is when the saleratus[1] helped. When I had the babies all about the same size, I could not get

---

1. **saleratus:** a form of baking soda.

out to gather saleratus as others did; so we went with team and wagon, pans, buckets, old brooms, and sacks down on the alkali land, between Spanish Fork and Springville. The smallest children were put under the wagon on a quilt, and the rest of us swept and filled the sacks, and the happiest time was when we were headed for home. The canyon wind seemed always to blow and our faces, hands and eyes were sore for some time after. We took our saleratus over to Provo, where they had some kind of refining machinery where it was made into soda for bread. It was also used extensively in soap making. We got our pay in merchandise.

Most people who had land kept a few sheep which furnished them meat, light and clothing. We had no sheep, but I, and my oldest daughter, learned to spin and we did spinning on shares to get our yarn for stockings and socks, which we knitted for the family. Before this time my sister, Sarah, had sent me a black silk dress pattern, with other things, which I sold [and] I bought a cow and a pair of blankets. Before the building of the Provo factory, the people had wool-picking bees. The wool was greased and the trash picked out of it; then it was carded into rolls. We made our own cloth, which was mostly gray in color, for dresses, by mixing the black and white wool. If a light gray was wanted, more white than black was put in, and dark was added if a darker gray was wanted. The dresses for grown people were three widths, and for younger women two widths, one yard wide. There was a row of bright colors—red, blue, green—about half way up the skirt, which was hemmed and pleated onto a plain waist with coat sleeves. When our dresses wore thin in front, they could be turned back to front and upside down, and have a new lease on life. With madder, Indigo, logwood, copperas, and other roots, I have colored beautiful fast colors. We were kept busy in those days carding, spinning, knitting, and doing all of our own sewing by hand.

After getting settled in our new home, my husband went over to Camp Floyd, where he worked quite a bit. He found a friend who was selling out prior to leaving for California. He bought quite a number of articles, which greatly helped us. One thing was a door knob and lock. He also bought me a stepstove. Stoves were very scarce at that time in Spanish Fork. I had never cooked on a stove in my life, and I burned my first batch of bread. Where I came from people mixed their dough and had it baked in the public oven, and at home we had a gate with an oven at the side. When the soldier camp broke up, they left many useful things which helped the people.

. . . My husband had poor luck farming. His farm was in the low land, near the river where the sugar factory now stands. Sometimes it would be high water, sometimes grasshoppers or crickets would take his crop; so he got discouraged with farming, sold his farm and put up a store. We had just got well started in the business and had got a bill of goods, when in the spring of 1875 my husband was called on another mission to England.

Before starting on his mission he sold his team and all available property, also mortgaged our home, for although he was called to travel without purse or scrip, he had to raise enough money to pay his passage and his expenses to his field of labor in Europe. He had too tender a heart for a merchant; he simply could not say no when people came to him with pitiful stories of sickness and privation. He would give them credit, and the consequence was that when he was suddenly called on a mission, the goods were gone and there were hundreds of dollars coming to us from the people, some of which we never got. Everything was left in my hands.

On the 24th of October 1875, after my husband's departure, our daughter Ada was born. . . . I nursed her, along with my little granddaughter Maud, as twins, kept all the books and accounts . . . and was sustained as President and Secretary of the Relief Society Teachers, which office I held through many re-organizations.

During my husband's absence, we had considerable sickness. My little daughter, Mary, came near dying with scarlet fever. To help out, our eldest daughter, Emma, got a position as clerk in the Co-op store. I appreciated that action of the Board very much, as before that time they had not been employing lady clerks and she was the first girl to work in the store. . . .

In 1877, my twelfth child was born. . . . I have had seven daughters and five sons. . . .

My husband's health was not good after his return from his mission. He had pneumonia twice. We sold our home on Main Street, paid off the mortgage and put up a little house on the five acres of land we had given his parents. They had left it to us when they died. We have some of our children as near neighbors and are quite comfortable in our new home.

PART FIVE

An Age of Reform

Rearranging Social Patterns

During the second quarter of the nineteenth century, new social forces swept through the American villages, farms, and regions that had once existed in near isolation, disrupting traditional ways of work and life. The transportation revolution overcame barriers of distance, as highways, canals, steamships, and railroads linked and transformed established communities and existing markets. Farmers and craftsmen, inventors and factory owners, learned new ways to shape and dominate the physical world. Enterprises like the Lowell Mills introduced new methods of work as well as novel forms of social organization that changed the lives of workers like Harriet Hanson Robinson. The growing public school system began to inculcate common ideas and goals in young American minds, while evangelical Protestantism labored to purify souls.

The numerous reform movements of the time also represented a determination to perfect the republic of the founding fathers and, if possible, the lands beyond the nation's borders. In their search for social perfection, a few reformers questioned the foundations of capitalism. Some turned to religious or social experiments designed to reshape society. Most aimed at correcting specific problems. Reformers sometimes disagreed on goals and methods because they responded to contradictory moods: Some feared what they saw as disorder in society, loss of community, and declining morality; others acted on an optimistic faith in the ultimate perfectibility of the world in general and American society in particular. More than a million Americans, for example, crusaded against the excessive use of alcohol, as documented in Timothy Shay Arthur's *Ten Nights in a Bar-Room, and What I Saw There*.

As the nation slid toward Civil War, however, the crusade against slavery came to dominate American reform. Slaves themselves generated much of the heat that ignited the fierce controversy. Nat Turner's rebellion in 1831 helped to usher in an angrier era. Charles Ball, Josiah Henson, Francis Henderson, Harriet Jacobs, and Jacob Stroyer were slaves who, after running away or purchasing their freedom, wrote accounts of their lives under slavery. Such writings provided the growing abolition movement with vivid testimonies that supported the arguments against the institution of slavery. White reformers like William Lloyd Garrison, whose newspaper *The Liberator* began publication in the same year as Nat Turner's rebellion, made Southern leaders fearful of economic disaster by insisting on immediate abolition. As antislavery sentiment grew in the North, images of slaves and of the institution of slavery assumed an increasingly stark character, as the visual portfolio "Slavery and Freedom" (page 257) illustrates. And most of the early leaders of the women's rights movement had their first taste of organizing, petitioning, and public speaking in the antislavery movement. From this beginning, Elizabeth Cady Stanton, Susan B. Anthony, and others pioneered a women's rights movement that over many years would powerfully affect the lives of American women.

POINTS OF VIEW

Nat Turner's Rebellion (1831)

29

A Slave Insurrection

Nat Turner

Slaveowners, especially those in areas with large slave populations, lived in dread of slave uprisings. Rebellions in 1739 in South Carolina, in 1800 in Virginia, in 1811 in Louisiana, and in 1822 in South Carolina kept such fears alive. Nat Turner (1800–1831), a slave in Southampton County, Virginia, led the most sensational rebellion in 1831. Beginning on August 21, Turner's rebellion lasted only five days, but it claimed the lives of fifty-one whites. In response, terrified white Southerners increased restrictions on slaves' education, marriage, and right to assemble. The rebellion also dealt a serious blow to any chance of the South's voluntarily emancipating its slaves.

The Confessions of Nat Turner was published in 1832 by Thomas R. Gray, who interviewed Turner shortly before he was tried and executed. How much of the language of these confessions is Turner's and how much is Gray's is impossible to determine. Gray's account was widely read throughout the South.

The Confessions of Nat Turner, Leader of the Late Insurrection in Southampton, Virginia, as Fully and Voluntarily Made to Thomas R. Gray (1832; New York, 1964), pp. 5–17.

BEFORE YOU READ

1. What was Nat Turner's revelation? What purpose did he consider himself destined to fulfill?

2. How well planned was the rebellion?

3. What do you think Turner and his compatriots expected to achieve by their rebellion?

Agreeable to his own appointment, on the evening he was committed to prison, with permission of the jailer, I visited Nat on Tuesday the first of November, when, without being questioned at all, he commenced his narrative in the following words:

Sir,

You have asked me to give a history of the motives which induced me to undertake the late insurrection, as you call it. To do so I must go back to the days of my infancy, and even before I was born. I was thirty-one years of age the second of October last, and born the property of Benjamin Turner, of this county. In my childhood a circumstance occurred which made an indelible impression on my mind, and laid the groundwork of that enthusiasm which has terminated so fatally to many both white and black, and for which I am about to atone at the gallows. It is here necessary to relate this circumstance — trifling as it may seem, it was the commencement of that belief which has grown with time, and even now, sir, in this dungeon, helpless and forsaken as I am, I cannot divest myself of. Being at play with other children, when three or four years old, I was telling them something, which my mother overhearing, said it had happened before I was born. I stuck to my story, however, and related some things which went in her opinion to confirm it. Others being called on were greatly astonished, knowing that these things had happened, and caused them to say in my hearing, I surely would be a prophet, as the Lord had shown me things that had happened before my birth. And my father and mother strengthened me in this my first impression, saying in my presence, I was intended for some great purpose, which they had always thought from certain marks on my head and breast.

My grandmother, who was very religious, and to whom I was much attached — my master, who belonged to the church, and other religious persons who visited the house, and whom I often saw at prayers, noticing the singularity of my manners, I suppose, and my uncommon intelligence for a child, remarked I had too much sense to be raised — and if I was, I would never be of any service to any one — as a slave. The manner in which I learned to read and write, not only had great influence on my own mind, as I acquired it with the most perfect ease, so much so that I have no recollection whatever of learning the alphabet — but to the astonishment of the family, one day, when a book was shown me to keep me from crying, I began spelling the names of different objects — this was a source of wonder to all in the neighborhood, particularly the blacks — and this learning was constantly improved at all opportunities. When I got large enough to go to work, while employed, I was reflecting on many things that would present themselves to my imagination. I was not addicted to stealing in my youth, nor have never been. Yet such was the confidence of the Negroes in the neighborhood, even at this early period of my life, in my superior judgment, that they would often carry me with them when they were going on any roguery, to plan for them. Growing up among them, with this confidence in my superior judgment, and when this, in their opinions, was perfected by divine inspiration, from the circumstances already alluded to in my infancy, and which belief was ever afterward zealously inculcated by the austerity of my life and manners, which became the subject of remark by white and black. By this time, having arrived to man's estate, and hearing the Scriptures commented on at meetings, I was struck with that particular passage which says: "Seek ye the kingdom of Heaven and all things shall be added unto you." I reflected much on this passage, and prayed daily for light on this subject. As I was praying one day at my plough, the spirit spoke to me, saying "Seek ye the kingdom of Heaven and all things shall be added unto you." *Question*—What do you mean by the Spirit? *Answer*—The Spirit that spoke to the prophets in former days—and I was greatly astonished, and for two years prayed continually, whenever my duty would permit—and then again I had the same revelation, which fully confirmed me in the impression that I was ordained for some great purpose in the hands of the Almighty. Several years rolled round, in which many events occurred to strengthen me in this my belief. At this time I reverted in my mind to the remarks made of me in my childhood, and the things that had been shown me. And as it had been said of me in my childhood by those whom I had been taught to pray, both white and black, and in whom I had the greatest confidence, that I had too much sense to be raised, and if I was I would never be of any use to anyone as a slave. Now finding I had arrived to man's estate, and was a slave, and these revelations being made known to me, I began to direct my attention to this great object, to fulfill the purpose for which, by this time, I felt assured I was intended. Knowing the influence I had obtained over the minds of my fellow servants, (not by the means of conjuring and such like tricks—for to them I always spoke of such things with contempt) but by the communion of the Spirit whose revelations I often communicated to them, and they believed and said my wisdom came from God.

And on the twelfth of May 1828, I heard a loud noise in the heavens, and the Spirit instantly appeared to me and said the Serpent was loosened, and Christ had laid down the yoke he had borne for the sins of men, and that I should take it on and fight against the Serpent, for the time was fast approaching, when the first should be last and the last should be first. *Question*—Do you not find yourself mistaken now? *Answer*—Was not Christ crucified? And by signs in the heavens that it would make known to me when I should commence the great work—and until the first sign appeared, I should conceal it from the knowledge of men—and on the appearance of the sign (the eclipse of the sun last February), I should arise and prepare myself, and slay my enemies with their own weapons. And immediately on the sign appearing in the heavens, the seal was removed from my lips, and I communicated the great work laid out for me to do, to four in whom I had the greatest confidence (Henry, Hark, Nelson, and Sam). It was intended by us to have begun the work of death on the fourth of July last. Many were the plans formed and rejected by us, and it affected my mind to such a degree that I fell sick, and the time passed without our coming to any determination how to commence—still forming new schemes and rejecting them when the sign appeared again, which determined me not to wait longer.

Since the commencement of 1830, I had been living with Mr. Joseph Travis, who was to me a kind master, and placed the greatest confidence in me; in fact, I had no cause to complain of his treatment to me. On Saturday evening, the twentieth of August, it was agreed between Henry, Hark, and myself to prepare a dinner the next day for the men we expected, and then to concert a plan, as we had not yet determined on any. Hark on the following morning brought a pig, and Henry brandy, and being joined by Sam, Nelson, Will, and Jack, they prepared in the woods a dinner, where, about three o'clock, I joined them. . . .

I saluted them on coming up, and asked Will how came he there; he answered his life was worth no more than others, and his liberty as dear to him. I asked him if he thought to obtain it? He said he would or lose his life. This was enough to put him in full confidence. Jack, I knew, was only a tool in the hands of Hark. It was quickly agreed we should commence at home (Mr. J. Travis') on that night, and until we had armed and equipped ourselves, and gathered sufficient force, neither age nor sex was to be spared (which was invariably adhered to). We remained at the feast until about two hours in the night, when we went to the house and found Austin; they all went to the cider press and drank, except myself. On returning to the house, Hark went to the door with an ax, for the purpose of breaking it open, as we knew we were strong enough to murder the family, if they were awakened by the noise; but reflecting that it might create an alarm in the neighborhood, we determined to enter the house secretly, and murder them while sleeping. Hark got a ladder and set it against the chimney, on which I ascended, and hoisting a window, entered and came down stairs, unbarred the door, and removed the guns from their places. It was then observed that I must spill the first blood. On which armed with a hatchet, and accompanied by Will, I entered my master's chamber; it being dark, I could not give a death blow, the hatchet glanced from his head, he sprang from the bed and called his wife, it was his last word. Will laid him dead, with a blow of his ax, and Mrs. Travis shared the same fate, as she lay in bed. The murder of this family, five in number, was the work of a moment, not one of them awoke; there was a little infant sleeping in a cradle, that was forgotten, until we had left the house and gone some distance, when Henry and Will returned and killed it. We got here four guns that would shoot, and several old muskets, with a pound or two of powder. We remained some time at the barn, where we paraded; I formed them in a line as soldiers, and after carrying them through all the maneuvers I was master of, marched them off to Mr. Salathul Francis', about six hundred yards distant. Sam and Will went to the door and knocked. Mr. Francis asked who was there, Sam replied it was him, and he had a letter for him, on which he got up and came to the door; they immediately seized him, and dragging him out a little from the door, he was dispatched by repeated blows on the head; there was no other white person in the family. We started from there for Mrs. Reese's, maintaining the most perfect silence on our march, where finding the door unlocked, we entered, and murdered Mrs. Reese in her bed, while sleeping; her son awoke, but it was only to sleep the sleep of death, he had only time to say who is that, and he was no more. From Mrs. Reese's we went to Mrs. Turner's, a mile distant, which we reached about sunrise on Monday morning. Henry, Austin, and Sam went to the still, where, finding Mr. Pebbles, Austin shot him, and the rest of us went to the house; as we approached, the family discovered us, and shut the door. Vain hope! Will, with one stroke of his ax, opened it, and we entered and found Mrs. Turner and Mrs. Newsome in the middle of a room almost frightened to death. Will immediately killed Mrs. Turner, with one blow of his ax. I took Mrs. Newsome by the hand, and with the sword I had when I was apprehended, I struck her several blows over the head, but not being able to kill her, as the sword was dull. Will turning around and discovering it, dispatched her also. A general destruction of property and search for money and ammunition always succeeded the murders. By this time my company amounted to fifteen, and nine men mounted, who started for Mrs. Whitehead's (the other six were to go through a byway to Mr. Bryant's and rejoin us at Mrs. Whitehead's). . . . As we pushed on to the house, I discovered someone running round the garden, and thinking it was some of the white family, I pursued them, but finding it was a servant girl belonging to the house, I returned to commence the work of death, but they whom I left had not been idle; all the family were already murdered, but Mrs. Whitehead and her daughter Margaret. As I came round to the door I saw Will pulling Mrs. Whitehead out of the house, and at the step he nearly severed her head from her body, with his broad ax. Miss Margaret, when I discovered her had concealed herself in the corner, formed by the projection of the cellar cap from the house; on my approach she fled, but was soon overtaken, and after repeated blows with a sword, I killed her by a blow on the head with a fence rail. By this time, the six who had gone by Mr. Bryant's rejoined us, and informed me they had done the work of death assigned them. We again divided, part going to Mr. Richard Porter's and from thence to Nathaniel Francis', the others to Mr. Howell Harris', and Mr. T. Doyle's. On my reaching Mr. Porter's, he had escaped with his family. I understood there that the alarm had already spread.

I proceeded to Mr. Levi Waller's, two or three miles distant. I took my station in the rear, and as it was my object to carry terror and devastation wherever we went, I placed fifteen or twenty of the best armed and most to be relied on in front, who generally approached the houses as fast as their horses could run; this was for two purposes, to prevent their escape and strike terror to the inhabitants—on this account I never got to the houses, after leaving Mrs. Whitehead's, until the murders were committed, except in one case. I sometimes got in sight in time to see the work of death completed, viewed the mangled bodies as they lay, in silent satisfaction, and immediately started in quest of other victims. Having murdered Mrs. Waller and ten children, we started for

Mr. William Williams'—having killed him and two little boys that were there; while engaged in this, Mrs. Williams fled and got some distance from the house, but she was pursued, overtaken, and compelled to get up behind one of the company, who brought her back, and after showing her the mangled body of her lifeless husband, she was told to get down and lay by his side, where she was shot dead. I then started for Mr. Jacob Williams', where the family were murdered. Here we found a young man named Drury, who had come on business with Mr. Williams. He was pursued, overtaken, and shot. Mrs. Vaughan's was the next place we visited—and after murdering the family here, I determined on starting for Jerusalem. Our number amounted now to fifty or sixty, all mounted and armed with guns, axes, swords, and clubs. On reaching Mr. James W. Parker's gate, immediately on the road leading to Jerusalem, and about three miles distant, it was proposed to me to call there, but I objected, as I knew he was gone to Jerusalem, and my object was to reach there as soon as possible; but some of the men having relations at Mr. Parker's it was agreed that they might call and get his people. I remained at the gate on the road, with seven or eight; the others going across the field to the house, about half a mile off. After waiting some time for them, I became impatient, and started to the house for them, and on our return we were met by a party of white men, who had pursued our blood-stained track and who had fired on those at the gate and dispersed them, which I knew nothing of, not having been at that time rejoined by any of them. Immediately on discovering the whites, I order my men to halt and form, as they appeared to be alarmed. The white men, eighteen in number, approached us in about one hundred yards, when one of them fired.

I then ordered my men to fire and rush on them; the few remaining stood their ground until we approached within fifty yards, when they fired and retreated. We pursued and overtook some of them who we thought we left dead; after pursuing them about two hundred yards, and rising a little hill, I discovered they were met by another party, and had halted, and were reloading their guns, thinking that those who retreated first, and the party who fired on us at fifty or sixty yards distant, had all only fallen back to meet others with ammunition. As I saw them reloading their guns, and more coming up than I saw at first, and several of my bravest men being wounded, the others became panic struck and squandered over the field; the white men pursued and fired on us several times. Hark had his horse shot under him, and I caught another for him as it was running by me; five or six of my men were wounded, but none left on the field; finding myself defeated here I instantly determined to go through a private way, and cross the Nottoway River at the Cypress Bridge, three miles below Jerusalem, and attack that place in the rear, as I expected they would look for me on the other road, and I had a great desire to get there to procure arms and ammunition. After going a short distance in this private way, accompanied by about twenty men, I overtook two or three who told me the others were dispersed in every direction. After trying in vain to collect a sufficient force to proceed to Jerusalem, I determined to return, as I was sure they would make back to their old neighborhood, where they would rejoin me, make new recruits, and come down again. On my way back, I called at Mrs. Thomas's, Mrs. Spencer's, and several other places. The white families having fled, we found no more victims to gratify our thirst for blood, we stopped at Major Ridley's quarter for the night, and being joined by four of his men, with the recruits made since my defeat, we mustered now about forty strong. After placing out sentinels, I laid down to sleep, but was quickly roused by a great racket. Starting up, I found some mounted, and others in great confusion; one of the sentinels having given the alarm that we were about to be attacked, I ordered some to ride round and reconnoiter, and on their return the others being more alarmed, not knowing who they were, fled in different ways, so that I was reduced to about twenty again; with this I determined to attempt to recruit, and proceed on to rally in the neighborhood I had left. Dr. Blunt's was the nearest house, which we reached just before day; on riding up the yard, Hark fired a gun. We expected Dr. Blunt and his family were at Major Ridley's, as I knew there was a company of men there; the gun was fired to ascertain if any of they family were at home; we were immediately fired upon and retreated leaving several of my men. I do not know what became of them, as I never saw them afterward. Pursuing our course back, and coming in sight of Captain Harris's, where we had been the day before, we discovered a party of white men at the house, on which all deserted me but two (Jacob and Nat), we concealed ourselves in the woods until near night, when I sent them in search of Henry, Sam, Nelson, and Hark, and directed them to rally all they could at the place we had had our dinner the Sunday before, where they would find me, and I accordingly returned there as soon as it was dark, and remained until Wednesday evening, when discovering white men riding around the place as though they were looking for someone, and none of my men joining me, I concluded Jacob and Nat had been taken, and compelled to betray me. On this I gave up all hope for the present; and on Thursday night, after having supplied myself with provisions from Mr. Travis's, I scratched a hole under a pile of fence rails in a field, where I concealed myself for six weeks, never leaving my hiding place but for a few minutes in the dead of night to get water, which was very near; thinking by this time I could venture out, I began to go about in the night and eavesdrop the houses in the neighborhood; pursuing this course for about a fortnight and gathering little or no intelligence, afraid of speaking to any human being, and returning every morning to my cave before the dawn of day. I know not how long I might have led this life, if accident had not betrayed me, a dog in the neighborhood passing by my hiding place one night while I was out was attracted by some meat I had in my cave, and crawled in and stole it, and was coming out just as I returned. A few nights after, two Negroes having started to go hunting with the same dog, and passed that way, the dog came again to the place, and having just gone out to walk about, discovered me and barked, on which, thinking myself discovered, I spoke to them to beg concealment. On making myself known, they fled from me. Knowing then they would betray me, I immediately left my hiding place, and was pursued almost incessantly until I was taken a fortnight afterward by Mr. Benjamin Phipps, in a little hole I had dug out with my sword, for the purpose of concealment, under the top of a fallen tree. On Mr. Phipps discovering the place of my concealment, he cocked his gun and aimed at me. I requested him not to shoot, and I would give up, upon which he demanded my sword. I delivered it to him, and he brought me to prison. During the time I was pursued, I had many hair breadth escapes, which your time will not permit you to relate. I am here loaded with chains, and willing to suffer the fate that awaits me.

[Gray:] I here proceeded to make some inquiries of him, after assuring him of the certain death that awaited him, and that concealment would only bring destruction of the innocent as well as guilty, of his own color, if he knew of any extensive or concerted plan. His answer was, I do not. When I questioned him as to the insurrection in North Carolina happening about the same time, he denied any knowledge of it.

30

Who Is to Blame?

William Lloyd Garrison et al.

Nat Turner's rebellion occurred just when slavery was under attack from other quarters. In 1829, a free black named David Walker published his incendiary Walker's Appeal in Four Articles, Together with a Preamble to the Colored Citizens of the World, But in Particular and Very Expressly to Those of the United States of America, *which quoted the Declaration of Independence in justification of a slave insurrection. Then William Lloyd Garrison (1805–1879), who would also cite the Declaration of Independence, broke with the tradition among white abolitionists of calling for gradual emancipation. From the first issue of the* Liberator, *published in Boston on January 1, 1831, Garrison demanded the immediate and unconditional abolition of slavery.*

The Southern states reacted viscerally to Nat Turner's rebellion. In the immediate hysteria, slaves and free blacks were gunned down. The ongoing debate in Virginia over gradual emancipation ended. Instead, the Southern states moved toward strengthening the slave system by restricting the rights of free blacks as well as the right of owners to free slaves, augmenting the patrols that constricted the mobility of the slave population, setting limits on black religious meetings, and ensuring that marriage did not restrict the slave trade. And they moved on many fronts to close the South to antislavery propaganda, even touching off a national debate by forbidding the federal post office to deliver such antislavery writings as the Liberator *in Southern states.*

BEFORE YOU READ

1. Did William Lloyd Garrison approve of Nat Turner's rebellion?
2. How did he explain its occurrence?
3. Did John Hampden Pleasants, editor of the Richmond *Constitutional Whig*, approve of the treatment of blacks in the wake of the rebellion?

William E. Cain, ed., *William Lloyd Garrison and the Fight against Slavery* (Boston: Bedford/ St. Martin's, 1995), p. 80; *Constitutional Whig*, Richmond, Virginia, September 3, 1831; the original of Floyd's letter to Hamilton can be found in the Manuscript Division of the Library of Congress.

4. How did he explain its occurrence?
5. How did Virginia governor John Floyd explain the rebellion?
6. What did he propose to avoid further uprisings?

WILLIAM LLOYD GARRISON

The Liberator, *September 3, 1831*

What we have so long predicted,—at the peril of being stigmatized as an alarmist and declaimer,—has commenced its fulfilment. The first step of the earthquake, which is ultimately to shake down the fabric of oppression, leaving not one stone upon another, has been made. The first drops of blood, which are but the prelude to a deluge from the gathering clouds, have fallen. The first flash of the lightning, which is to smite and consume, has been felt. The first wailings of a bereavement, which is to clothe the earth in sackcloth, have broken upon our ears.

In the first number of the *Liberator*, we alluded to the hour of vengeance in the following lines:

> Wo if it come with storm, and blood, and fire,
> When midnight darkness veils the earth and sky!
> *Wo to the innocent babe*—the guilty sire—
> *Mother and daughter*—friends of kindred tie!
> *Stranger and citizen alike shall die!*
> Red-handed Slaughter his revenge shall feed,
> And Havoc yell his ominous death-cry,
> And wild Despair in vain for mercy plead—
> While hell itself shall shrink and sicken at the deed!

Read the account of the insurrection in Virginia, and say whether our prophecy be not fulfilled. What was poetry—imagination—in January, is now a bloody reality. "Wo to the innocent babe—to mother and daughter!" Is it not true? Turn again to the record of slaughter! Whole families have been cut off—not a mother, not a daughter, not a babe left. Dreadful retaliation! "The dead bodies of white and black lying just as they were slain, unburied"—the oppressor and the oppressed equal at last in death—what a spectacle!

True, the rebellion is quelled. Those of the slaves who were not killed in combat, have been secured, and the prison is crowded with victims destined for the gallows!

> Yet laugh not in your carnival of crime
> Too proudly, ye oppressors!

You have seen, it is to be feared, but the beginning of sorrows. All the blood which has been shed will be required at your hands. At your hands alone? No—but at the hands of the people of New-England and of all the free states. The crime of oppression is national. The south is only the agent in this guilty traffic. But, remember! the same causes are at work which must inevitably produce the same effects; and when the contest shall have again begun, it must be again a war of extermination. In the present instance, no quarters have been asked or given.

But we have killed and routed them now—we can do it again and again—we are invincible! A dastardly triumph, well becoming a nation of oppressors. Detestable complacency, that can think, without emotion, of the extermination of the blacks! We have the power to kill *all*—let us, therefore, continue to apply the whip and forge new fetters!

In his fury against the revolters, who will remember their wrongs? What will it avail them, though the catalogue of their sufferings, dripping with warm blood fresh from their lacerated bodies, be held up to extenuate their conduct? It is enough that the victims were black—that circumstance makes them less precious than the dogs which have been slain in our streets! They were black—brutes, pretending to be men—legions of curses upon their memories! They were black—God made them to serve us!

Ye patriotic hypocrites! ye panegyrists[1] of Frenchmen, Greeks, and Poles! ye fustian[2] declaimers for liberty! ye valiant sticklers for equal rights among yourselves! ye haters of aristocracy! ye assailants of monarchies! ye republican nullifiers! ye treasonable disunionists! be dumb! Cast no reproach upon the conduct of the slaves, but let your lips and cheeks wear the blisters of condemnation!

Ye accuse the pacific friends of emancipation of instigating the slaves to revolt. Take back the charge as a foul slander. The slaves need no incentives at our hands. They will find them in their stripes—in their emaciated bodies—in their ceaseless toil—in their ignorant minds—in every field, in every valley, on every hill-top and mountain, wherever you and your fathers have fought for liberty—in your speeches, your conversations, your celebrations, your pamphlets, your newspapers—voices in the air, sounds from across the ocean, invitations to resistance above, below, around them! What more do they need? Surrounded by such influences, and smarting under their newly made wounds, is it wonderful that they should rise to contend—as other "heroes" have contended—for their lost rights? It is *not* wonderful.

In all that we have written, is there aught to justify the excesses of the slaves? No. Nevertheless, they deserve no more censure than the Greeks in destroying the Turks, or the Poles in exterminating the Russians, or our fathers in slaughtering the British. Dreadful, indeed, is the standard erected by worldly patriotism!

For ourselves, we are horror-struck at the late tidings. We have exerted our utmost efforts to avert the calamity. We have warned our countrymen of the danger of persisting in their unrighteous conduct. We have preached to the slaves the pacific precepts of Jesus Christ. We have appealed to christians, philanthropists and patriots, for their assistance to accomplish the great work of national redemption through the agency of moral power—of public opinion—of

1. **panegyrists:** people who celebrate a person, group, or deed.
2. **fustian:** pretentious, pompous.

individual duty. How have we been received? We have been threatened, pro-scribed, vilified and imprisoned—a laughing-stock and a reproach. Do we fal-ter, in view of these things? Let time answer. If we have been hitherto urgent, and bold, and denunciatory in our efforts,—hereafter we shall grow vehement and active with the increase of danger. We shall cry, in trumpet tones, night and day,—Wo to this guilty land, unless she speedily repent of her evil doings! The blood of millions of her sons cries aloud for redress! IMMEDI-ATE EMANCIPATION can alone save her from the vengeance of Heaven, and cancel the debt of ages!

JOHN HAMPDEN PLEASANTS

Constitutional Whig, *September 3, 1831*

We have been astonished since our return from Southampton (whither we went with Capt. Harrison's Troop of Horse) in reading over the mass of exchange papers accumulated in our absence, to see the number of false, absurd, and idle rumors, circulated by the Press, touching the insurrection in that county. Edi-tors seem to have applied themselves to the task of alarming the public mind as much as possible by persuading the slaves to entertain a high opinion of their strength and consequences. While truth is always the best policy, and best rem-edy, the exaggerations to which we have alluded are calculated to give the slaves false conceptions of their numbers and capacity, by exhibiting the terror and confusion of the whites, and to induce them to think that practicable, which they see is so much feared by their superiors.

We have little to say of the Southampton Tragedy beyond what is already known. The origin of the conspiracy, the prime agents, its extent and ultimate direction, is matter of conjecture.—The universal opinion in that part of the country is that Nat, a slave, a preacher, and a pretended prophet was the first [blurred word], the actual leader, and the most remorseless of the execu-tioners. According to the evidence of a negro boy whom they carried along to hold their horses, Nat commenced the scene of murder at the first house (Travis') with his own hand. Having called upon two others to make good their valiant boasting, so often repeated, of what they would do, and these shrinking from the requisition, Nat proceeded to dispatch one of the family with his own hand. Animated by the example and exhortations of their leader, having a taste of blood and convinced that they had now gone too far to recede, his followers dismissed their doubts and became as ferocious as their leader wished them. To follow the [blurred word] capture of Travis' house early that day, to their dispersion at Parker's cornfield early in the afternoon, when they had traversed near 20 miles, murdered 63 whites, and approached within 3 or 4 miles of the Village of Jerusalem; the immediate object of their move-ment—to describe the scenes at each house, the circumstances of the murders, the hair breadth escapes of the few who were lucky enough to escape—would prove as interesting as heart rending. Many of the details have reached us but not in so authentic a shape as to justify their publication, nor have we the time or space. Let a few suffice. Of the event at Dr. Blount's we had a narrative from the gallant old gentleman himself, and his son, a lad about 15, distinguished for his gallantry and modesty, and whom we take leave to recommend to Gen. Jackson, for a warrant in the Navy or at West Point. The Doctor had received information of the insurrection, and that his house would be attacked a short time before the attack was made. Crippled with the gout, and indisposed to leave, he decided to defend his home. His force was his son, overseer and three other white men. Luckily there were six guns, and plenty of powder and shot in the house. These were barely loaded, his force posted, and the instructions given, when the negroes from 15 to 30 strong, rode up about day break. The Doctor's orders were that each man should be particular in his aim and should fire one at a time; he himself reserved one gun, resolved if the house was forced to sell his life as dearly as he could. The remaining five fired in succession upon the assailants, at the distance of fifteen or twenty steps. The blacks, upon the fifth fire, retreated, leaving one killed (we believe) and one wounded (a fellow named Hark,) and were pursued by the Doctor's negroes with shouts and execrations. Had the shot been larger, more execution doubtless would have been done.

Mrs. Vaughan's was among the last houses attacked. A venerable negro woman described the scene which she had witnessed with great emphasis: it was near noon and her mistress was making some preparations in the porch for dinner, when happening to look towards the road she discerned a dust and wondered what it could mean. In a second, the negroes mounted and armed, rushed into view, and making an exclamation indicative of her horror and agony, Mrs. Vaughan ran into the house.—The negroes dismounted and ran around the house, pointing their guns at the doors and windows. Mrs. Vaughan appeared at a window, and begged for her life, inviting them to take everything she had. The prayer was answered by one of them firing at her, which was followed by another, and a fatal, shot. In the meantime, Miss Vaughan, who was upstairs, and unappraised of the terrible advent until she heard the noise of the attack, rushed down, and begging for her life, was shot as she ran a few steps from the door. A son of Mrs. Vaughan, about 15, was at the still house, when hearing a gun and conjecturing, it is supposed, that his brother had come from Jerusalem, approached the house and was shot as he got over the fence. It is difficult for the imagination to conceive a situation so truly and horribly awful, as that in which these unfortunate ladies were placed. Alone, unprotected, and unconscious of danger, to find themselves without a moment's notice for escape or defence, in the power of a band of ruffians, from whom instant death was the least they could expect! In a most lively and picturesque manner, did the old negress describe the horrors of the scene; the blacks riding up with imprecations, the looks of her mistress, white as a sheet, her prayers for her life, and the actions of the scoundrels environing the house and pointing their guns at the doors and windows, ready to fire as occasion offered. When the work was done they called for drink, and food, and becoming nice, damned the brandy as vile stuff.

The scene at Vaughan's may suffice to give an idea of what was done at the other houses. A bloodier and more accursed tragedy was never acted, even by the agency of the tomahawk and scalping knife. Interesting details will no doubt be evolved in the progress of the trials and made known to the public.

It is with pain we speak of another feature of the Southampton Rebellion; for we have been most unwilling to have our sympathies for the sufferers diminished or affected by their misconduct. We allude to the slaughter of many blacks, without trial, and under circumstances of great barbarity. How many have thus been put into death (generally by decapitation or shooting) reports vary; probably however some five and twenty and from that to 40; possibly a yet larger number. To the great honor of General Eppes, he used every precaution in his power, and we hope and believe with success, to put a stop to the disgraceful procedure.—We met with one individual of intelligence, who stated that he himself had killed between 10 and 15. He justified himself on the grounds of the barbarities committed on the whites; and that he thought himself right is certain from the fact that he narrowly escaped losing his own life in an attempt to save a negro woman whom he thought innocent but who was shot by the multitude in despite of his exertions. We (the Richmond Troop) witnessed with surprise the sanguinary temper of the population who evinced a strong disposition to inflict immediate death on every prisoner. Not having witnessed the horrors committed by the blacks, or seen the unburried and disfigured remains of their wives and children, we were unprepared to understand their feelings, and could not at first admit of their extenuation, which a closer observation of the atrocities of the insurgents suggested. Now, however, we feel individually compelled to offer an apology for the people of Southampton, while we deeply deplore that human nature urged them to such extremities. Let the fact not be doubted by those whom it most concerns, that another such insurrection will be the signal for the extermination of the whole black population in the quarter of the state where it occurs.

The numbers engaged in the insurrection are variously reported. They probably did not exceed 40 or 50, and were fluctuating from desertions and new recruits. About fifty are in Southampton jail, some of them on suspicion only.—We trust and believe that the intelligent magistracy of the county, will have the firmness to oppose the popular passions, should it be disposed to involve the innocent with the guilty, and to take suspicion for proof.

The presence of the troops from Norfolk and Richmond alone prevented retaliation from being carried much farther.

At the date of Capt. Harrison's departure from Jerusalem, Gen. Nat had not been taken. On that morning, however, Dred, another insurgent chief, was brought prisoner to Jerusalem, having surrendered himself to his master, in the apprehension, no doubt, of starving in the swamps or being shot by the numerous parties of local militia, who were in pursuit. Nat had not certainly been heard from since the skirmish in Parker's cornfield, which was in fact, the termination of the insurrection; the negroes after that dispersing themselves, and making no further attempt. He is represented as a shrewd fellow, reads, writes, and preaches; and by various artifices had acquired great influence over the minds of the wretched beings whom he has led into destruction. It is supposed that he induced them to believe that there were only 80,000 whites in the country, who, being exterminated, the blacks might take possession. Various of his tricks to acquire and preserve influence had been mentioned, but they are not worth repeating. If there was any ulterior purpose, he probably alone knows it. For our own part, we still believe there was none; and if he be the intelligent man represented, we are incapable of conceiving the arguments by which he persuaded his own mind of the feasibility of his attempt, or how it could possibly end but in certain destruction. We therefore incline to the belief that he acted upon no higher principle than the impulse of revenge against the whites, as the enslavers of himself and his race; that, being a fanatic, he possibly persuaded himself that Heaven would interfere; and that he may have convinced himself, as he certainly did his deluded followers to some extent, that the appearance of the sun some weeks ago, prognosticated something favorable to their cause. We are inclined to think that the solar phenomenon exercised considerable influence in promoting the insurrection; calculated as it was to impress the imaginations of the ignorant.

A more important inquiry remains—whether the conspiracy was circumscribed to the neighborhood in which it broke out, or had its ramifications through other counties. We, at first, adopted the first opinion; but there are several circumstances which favor the latter. We understand that the confessions of all the prisoners go to show that the insurrection broke out too soon, as it is supposed, in consequence of the last day of July being a Sunday, and not, as the negroes in Southampton believed, the Saturday before. The report is that the rising was fixed for the fourth Sunday in August, and that they supposing Sunday, the 31st of July to be the first Sunday in August, they were betrayed into considering the 3d Sunday as the 4th. This is the popular impression founded upon confessions, upon the indications of an intention of the negroes in Nansemond and other places to unite, and upon the allegation that Gen. Nat extended his preaching excursions to Petersburg and this city; allegations which we, however, disbelieve. It is more than probable, nevertheless, that the mischief was concerted and concocted under the cloak of religion. The trials which are now proceeding in Southampton, Sussex, and elsewhere, will develop all the truth. We suspect the truth will turn out to be that the conspiracy was confined to Southampton, and that the idea of its extensiveness originated in the panic which seized upon the South East of Virginia.

GOVERNOR JOHN FLOYD OF VIRGINIA

Letter to Governor James Hamilton Jr. of South Carolina

Richmond
November 19, 1831

Sir:

I received your letter yesterday and with great pleasure will give you my impressions freely—

I will notice this affair in my annual message, but here only give a very careless history of it, as it appeared to the public—

I am fully persuaded, the spirit of insubordination which has, and still manifests itself in Virginia, had its origin among, and eminated from, the Yankee population, upon their *first* arrival amongst us, but mostly especially the Yankee pedlers and traders.

The course has been by no means a direct one—they began first, by making them religious—their conversations were of that character—telling the blacks, God was no respecter of persons—the black man was as good as the white—that all men were born free and equal—that they cannot serve two masters—that the white people rebelled against England to obtain freedom, so have the blacks a right to do.

In the mean time, I am sure without any purpose of this kind, the preachers, principally Northern—were very assiduous in operating upon our population, day and night, they were at work—and religion became, and is, the fashion of the times—finally our females and of the most respectable were persuaded that it was piety to teach negroes to read and write, to the end that they might read the *Scriptures*—many of them became tutoresses in Sunday schools and, pious distributors of tracts, from the New York Tract Society.

At this point, more active operations commenced—our magistrates and laws became more inactive—large assemblages of negroes were suffered to take place for religious purposes—Then commenced the efforts of the black preachers, often from the pulpits these pamphlets and papers were read— followed by the incendiary publications of Walker,[3] Garrison and Knapp[4] of Boston, these too with songs and hymns of a similar character were circulated, read and commented upon—We resting in apathetic security until the Southampton affair.

From all that has come to my knowledge during and since this affair—I am fully convinced that every black preacher in the whole country east of the Blue Ridge was in the secret, that the plans as published by those Northern presses were adopted and acted upon by them—that their congregations, as they were called knew nothing of this intended rebellion, except a few leading and intelligent men, who may have been head men in the Church—*the mass* were prepared by making them aspire to an equal station by such conversations as I have related as the first step.

I am informed that they had settled the form of government to be that of white people, whom they intended to cut off to a man—with the difference that the preachers were to be their Governors, Generals and Judges. I feel fully justified to myself, in believing the Northern incendiaries, tracts, Sunday Schools, religion and reading and writing has accomplished this end.

I shall in my annual message recommend that laws be passed—To confine the Slaves to the estates of their masters—prohibit negroes from preaching—

---

3. **Walker:** David Walker, a free black whose published writing justified slave insurrection.
4. **Knapp:** Isaac Knapp, abolitionist editor and associate of William Lloyd Garrison.

absolutely to drive from this State all free negroes—and to substitute the surplus revenue in our Treasury annually for slaves, to work for a time upon our Rail Roads etc etc and these sent out of the country, preparatory, or rather as the first step to emancipation—This last point will of course be tenderly and cautiously managed and will be urged or delayed as your State and Georgia may be disposed to co-operate.

In relation to the extent of this insurrection I think it greater than will ever appear—the facts will as now considered, appear to be these—It commenced with Nat and nine others on Sunday night—two o'clock, we date it, Monday morning before day and ceased by the dispersion of the negroes on Tuesday morning at ten o'clock—During this time the negroes had murdered sixty one persons, and traversed a distance of twenty miles, and increased to about seventy slave men—they spared but one family and that one was so wretched as to be in all respects upon a par with them—all died bravely indicating no reluctance to loose [sic] their lives in such a cause.

> I am Sir,
> with consideration and respect
> Your obt Sevnt
> John Floyd

His Excy
James Hamilton, Jr.
Governor of South Carolina

FOR CRITICAL THINKING

1. Examine the language of *The Confessions of Nat Turner.* Can you identify parts that seem to be the language expected of a Virginia lawyer like Thomas Gray and parts that you might imagine to be Nat Turner's own words? Compose a defense of his actions as you think Nat Turner might have presented it.

2. Why do you think that many people linked Turner's rebellion with the writings of William Lloyd Garrison? What does that say about their view of the slaves? What was Garrison's response to this linking?

3. Compose a possible reply from South Carolina governor James Hamilton Jr. to Governor Floyd's letter.

31

Life of a Female Slave

Harriet Jacobs

Harriet Jacobs's Incidents in the Life of a Slave Girl *is only now emerging as the classic narrative of a woman slave, a work to rank with the several autobiographies of Frederick Douglass. Published under a pseudonym in 1861, edited by a white abolitionist, and borrowing form and rhetoric from sentimental novels such as Harriet Beecher Stowe's* Uncle Tom's Cabin, *the authenticity of the work remained suspect for 120 years. Only in 1981, when Jean Fagan Yellin published documentary evidence for Jacobs's authorship* (American Literature, *November 1981: 479–86), did recognition come that this is a major work of African American literature, as well as an essential document for the history of antebellum slavery. Her bold discussion of sexual relations between the races prepared her audience in the North for the images of slave and slaveholder families such as those of Plates 10 and 11 in the visual portfolio "Slavery and Freedom" (page 257).*

Jacobs (1813–1897), writing under the pseudonym of Linda Brent, emerges as a remarkably determined woman. To prevent the permanent enslavement of her children, she hid for seven years in the attic of her grandmother's house, a tiny space only three feet high, while deceiving her master into thinking she had escaped to the North by smuggling out letters to be mailed from New York City and Boston. Finally she and then her children escaped from slave territory to discover the ambiguities of freedom in the so-called free states.

BEFORE YOU READ

1. What does Harriet Jacobs's account of her experience add to our picture of slavery?

2. Does she picture herself as a victim? What does she emphasize about her reaction to the position her master placed her in?

3. How do you think readers of the time reacted to her picture of the experiences of young female slaves?

THE TRIALS OF GIRLHOOD

During the first years of my service in Dr. Flint's family, I was accustomed to share some indulgences with the children of my mistress. Though this seemed to me no more than right, I was grateful for it, and tried to merit the kindness

Harriet Jacobs, *Incidents in the Life of a Slave Girl* (Boston, 1861), pp. 44–49, 51–55, 57–67, 82–89.

by the faithful discharge of my duties. But I now entered on my fifteenth year
—a sad epoch in the life of a slave girl. My master began to whisper foul words
in my ear. Young as I was, I could not remain ignorant of their import. I tried
to treat them with indifference or contempt. The master's age, my extreme
youth, and the fear that his conduct would be reported to my grandmother,
made me bear this treatment for many months. He was a crafty man, and re-
sorted to many means to accomplish his purposes. Sometimes he had stormy,
terrific ways, that made his victims tremble; sometimes he assumed a gentleness
that he thought must surely subdue. Of the two, I preferred his stormy moods,
although they left me trembling. He tried his utmost to corrupt the pure principles my grandmother had instilled. He peopled my young mind with unclean
images, such as only a vile monster could think of. I turned from him with disgust and hatred. But he was my master. I was compelled to live under the same
roof with him—where I saw a man forty years my senior daily violating the
most sacred commandments of nature. He told me I was his property; that I
must be subject to his will in all things. My soul revolted against the mean
tyranny. But where could I turn for protection? No matter whether the slave
girl be as black as ebony or as fair as her mistress. In either case, there is no
shadow of law to protect her from insult, from violence, or even from death; all
these are inflicted by fiends who bear the shape of men. The mistress, who
ought to protect the helpless victim, has no other feelings towards her but those
of jealousy and rage. The degradation, the wrongs, the vices, that grow out of
slavery, are more than I can describe. They are greater than you would willingly
believe. Surely, if you credited one half the truths that are told you concerning
the helpless millions suffering in this cruel bondage, you at the north would not
help to tighten the yoke. You surely would refuse to do for the master, on your
own soil, the mean and cruel work which trained bloodhounds and the lowest
class of whites do for him at the south.

Every where the years bring to all enough of sin and sorrow; but in slavery
the very dawn of life is darkened by these shadows. Even the little child, who is
accustomed to wait on her mistress and her children, will learn, before she is
twelve years old, why it is that her mistress hates such and such a one among
the slaves. Perhaps the child's own mother is among those hated ones. She lis-
tens to violent outbreaks of jealous passion, and cannot help understanding
what is the cause. She will become prematurely knowing in evil things. Soon
she will learn to tremble when she hears her master's footfall. She will be compelled to realize that she is no longer a child. If God has bestowed beauty upon
her; it will prove her greatest curse. That which commands admiration in the
white woman only hastens the degradation of the female slave. I know that
some are too much brutalized by slavery to feel the humiliation of their position; but many slaves feel it most acutely, and shrink from the memory of it. I
cannot tell how much I suffered in the presence of these wrongs, nor how I am
still pained by the retrospect. My master met me at every turn, reminding me
that I belonged to him, and swearing by heaven and earth that he would compel
me to submit to him. If I went out for a breath of fresh air, after a day of unwea-
ried toil, his footsteps dogged me. If I knelt by my mother's grave, his dark

shadow fell on me even there. The light heart which nature had given me became heavy with sad forebodings. The other slaves in my master's house noticed the change. Many of them pitied me; but none dared to ask the cause. They had no need to inquire. They knew too well the guilty practices under that roof; and they were aware that to speak of them was an offence that never went unpunished.

I longed for some one to confide in. I would have given the world to have laid my head on my grandmother's faithful bosom, and told her all my troubles. But Dr. Flint swore he would kill me, if I was not as silent as the grave. Then, although my grandmother was all in all to me, I feared her as well as loved her. I had been accustomed to look up to her with a respect bordering upon awe. I was very young, and felt shamefaced about telling her such impure things, especially as I knew her to be very strict on such subjects. Moreover, she was a woman of a high spirit. She was usually very quiet in her demeanor; but if her indignation was once roused, it was not very easily quelled. I had been told that she once chased a white gentleman with a loaded pistol, because he insulted one of her daughters. I dreaded the consequences of a violent outbreak; and both pride and fear kept me silent. But though I did not confide in my grandmother, and even evaded her vigilant watchfulness and inquiry, her presence in the neighborhood was some protection to me. Though she had been a slave, Dr. Flint was afraid of her. He dreaded her scorching rebukes. Moreover, she was known and patronized by many people; and he did not wish to have his villany made public. It was lucky for me that I did not live on a distant plantation, but in a town not so large that the inhabitants were ignorant of each other's affairs. Bad as are the laws and customs in a slaveholding community, the doctor, as a professional man, deemed it prudent to keep up some outward show of decency. . . .

I once saw two beautiful children playing together. One was a fair white child; the other was her slave; and also her sister. When I saw them embracing each other, and heard their joyous laughter, I turned sadly away from the lovely sight. I foresaw the inevitable blight that would fall on the little slave's heart. I knew how soon her laughter would be changed to sighs. The fair child grew up to be a still fairer woman. From childhood to womanhood her pathway was blooming with flowers, and overarched by a sunny sky. Scarcely one day of her life had been clouded when the sun rose on her happy bridal morning.

How had those years dealt with her slave sister, the little playmate of her childhood? She, also, was very beautiful; but the flowers and sunshine of love were not for her. She drank the cup of sin, and shame, and misery, whereof her persecuted race are compelled to drink.

In view of these things, why are ye silent, ye free men and women of the north? Why do your tongues falter in maintenance of the right? Would that I had more ability! But my heart is so full, and my pen is so weak! There are noble men and women who plead for us, striving to help those who cannot help themselves. God bless them! God give them strength and courage to go on! God bless those, every where, who are laboring to advance the cause of humanity!

THE JEALOUS MISTRESS

I would ten thousand times rather that my children should be the half-starved paupers of Ireland than to be the most pampered among the slaves of America. I would rather drudge out my life on a cotton plantation, till the grave opened to give me rest, than to live with an unprincipled master and a jealous mistress. The felon's home in a penitentiary is preferable. He may repent, and turn from the error of his ways, and so find peace; but it is not so with a favorite slave. She is not allowed to have any pride of character. It is deemed a crime in her to wish to be virtuous. . . .

I had entered my sixteenth year, and every day it became more apparent that my presence was intolerable to Mrs. Flint. Angry words frequently passed between her and her husband. He had never punished me himself, and he would not allow any body else to punish me. In that respect, she was never satisfied; but, in her angry moods, no terms were too vile for her to bestow upon me. Yet I, whom she detested so bitterly, had far more pity for her than he had, whose duty it was to make her life happy. I never wronged her, or wished to wrong her; and one word of kindness from her would have brought me to her feet.

After repeated quarrels between the doctor and his wife, he announced his intention to take his youngest daughter, then four years old, to sleep in his apartment. It was necessary that a servant should sleep in the same room, to be on hand if the child stirred. I was selected for that office, and informed for what purpose that arrangement had been made. By managing to keep within sight of people, as much as possible, during the daytime, I had hitherto succeeded in eluding my master, though a razor was often held to my throat to force me to change this line of policy. At night I slept by the side of my great aunt, where I felt safe. He was too prudent to come into her room. She was an old woman, and had been in the family many years. Moreover, as a married man, and a professional man, he deemed it necessary to save appearances in some degree. But he resolved to remove the obstacle in the way of his scheme; and he thought he had planned it so that he should evade suspicion. He was well aware how much I prized my refuge by the side of my old aunt, and he determined to dispossess me of it. The first night the doctor had the little child in his room alone. The next morning, I was ordered to take my station as nurse the following night. A kind Providence interposed in my favor. During the day Mrs. Flint heard of this new arrangement, and a storm followed. I rejoiced to hear it rage. . . .

The secrets of slavery are concealed like those of the Inquisition. My master was, to my knowledge, the father of eleven slaves. But did the mothers dare to tell who was the father of their children? Did the other slaves dare to allude to it, except in whispers among themselves? No, indeed! They knew too well the terrible consequences. . . .

Southern women often marry a man knowing that he is the father of many little slaves. They do not trouble themselves about it. They regard such children as property, as marketable as the pigs on the plantation; and it is seldom that they do not make them aware of this by passing them into the slave-trader's hands as soon as possible, and thus getting them out of their sight. I am glad to say there are some honorable exceptions.

I have myself known two southern wives who exhorted their husbands to free those slaves towards whom they stood in a "parental relation;" and their request was granted. These husbands blushed before the superior nobleness of their wives' natures. Though they had only counselled them to do that which it was their duty to do, it commanded their respect, and rendered their conduct more exemplary. Concealment was at an end, and confidence took the place of distrust.

Though this bad institution deadens the moral sense, even in white women, to a fearful extent, it is not altogether extinct. I have heard southern ladies say of Mr. Such a one, "He not only thinks it no disgrace to be the father of those little niggers, but he is not ashamed to call himself their master. I declare, such things ought not to be tolerated in any decent society!"

A PERILOUS PASSAGE
IN THE SLAVE GIRL'S LIFE

Dr. Flint contrived a new plan. He seemed to have an idea that my fear of my mistress was his greatest obstacle. In the blandest tones, he told me that he was going to build a small house for me, in a secluded place, four miles away from the town. I shuddered; but I was constrained to listen, while he talked of his intention to give me a home of my own, and to make a lady of me. Hitherto, I had escaped my dreaded fate, by being in the midst of people. My grandmother had already had high words with my master about me. She had told him pretty plainly what she thought of his character, and there was considerable gossip in the neighborhood about our affairs, to which the open-mouthed jealousy of Mrs. Flint contributed not a little. When my master said he was going to build a house for me, and that he could do it with little trouble and expense, I was in hopes something would happen to frustrate his scheme; but I soon heard that the house was actually begun. I vowed before my Maker that I would never enter it. I had rather toil on the plantation from dawn till dark; I had rather live and die in jail, than drag on, from day to day, through such a living death. I was determined that the master, whom I so hated and loathed, who had blighted the prospects of my youth, and made my life a desert, should not, after my long struggle with him, succeed at last in trampling his victim under his feet. I would do any thing, every thing, for the sake of defeating him. What *could* I do? I thought and thought, till I became desperate, and made a plunge into the abyss.

And now, reader, I come to a period in my unhappy life, which I would gladly forget if I could. The remembrance fills me with sorrow and shame. It pains me to tell you of it; but I have promised to tell you the truth, and I will do it honestly, let it cost me what it may. I will not try to screen myself behind the plea of compulsion from a master; for it was not so. Neither can I plead ignorance or thoughtlessness. For years, my master had done his utmost to pollute my mind with foul images, and to destroy the pure principles inculcated by my grandmother, and the good mistress of my childhood. The influences of slavery had had the same effect on me that they had on other young girls; they had made me prematurely knowing, concerning the evil ways of the world. I knew what I did, and I did it with deliberate calculation.

But, O, ye happy women, whose purity has been sheltered from childhood, who have been free to choose the objects of your affection, whose homes are protected by law, do not judge the poor desolate slave girl too severely! If slavery had been abolished, I, also, could have married the man of my choice; I could have had a home shielded by the laws; and I should have been spared the painful task of confessing what I am now about to relate; but all my prospects had been blighted by slavery. I wanted to keep myself pure; and, under the most adverse circumstances, I tried hard to preserve my self-respect; but I was struggling alone in the powerful grasp of the demon Slavery; and the monster proved too strong for me. I felt as if I was forsaken by God and man; as if all my efforts must be frustrated; and I became reckless in my despair.

I have told you that Dr. Flint's persecutions and his wife's jealousy had given rise to some gossip in the neighborhood. Among others, it chanced that a white unmarried gentleman had obtained some knowledge of the circumstances in which I was placed. He knew my grandmother, and often spoke to me in the street. He became interested for me, and asked questions about my master, which I answered in part. He expressed a great deal of sympathy, and a wish to aid me. He constantly sought opportunities to see me, and wrote to me frequently. I was a poor slave girl, only fifteen years old.

So much attention from a superior person was, of course, flattering; for human nature is the same in all. I also felt grateful for his sympathy, and encouraged by his kind words. It seemed to me a great thing to have such a friend. By degrees, a more tender feeling crept into my heart. He was an educated and eloquent gentleman; too eloquent, alas, for the poor slave girl who trusted in him. Of course I saw whither all this was tending. I knew the impassable gulf between us; but to be an object of interest to a man who is not married, and who is not her master, is agreeable to the pride and feelings of a slave, if her miserable situation has left her any pride or sentiment. It seems less degrading to give one's self, than to submit to compulsion. There is something akin to freedom in having a lover who has no control over you, except that which he gains by kindness and attachment. A master may treat you as rudely as he pleases, and you dare not speak; moreover, the wrong does not seem so great with an unmarried man, as with one who has a wife to be made unhappy. There may be sophistry in all this; but the condition of a slave confuses all principles of morality, and, in fact, renders the practice of them impossible.

When I found that my master had actually begun to build the lonely cottage, other feelings mixed with those I have described. Revenge, and calculations of interest, were added to flattered vanity and sincere gratitude for kindness. I knew nothing would enrage Dr. Flint so much as to know that I favored another; and it was something to triumph over my tyrant even in that small way. I thought he would revenge himself by selling me, and I was sure my friend, Mr. Sands, would buy me. He was a man of more generosity and feeling than my master, and I thought my freedom could be easily obtained from him.

The crisis of my fate now came so near that I was desperate. I shuddered to think of being the mother of children that should be owned by my old tyrant. I knew that as soon as a new fancy took him, his victims were sold far off to get rid of them; especially if they had children. I had seen several women sold, with his babies at the breast. He never allowed his offspring by slaves to remain long in sight of himself and his wife. Of a man who was not my master I could ask to have my children well supported; and in this case, I felt confident I should obtain the boon. I also felt quite sure that they would be made free. With all these thoughts revolving in my mind, and seeing no other way of escaping the doom I so much dreaded, I made a headlong plunge. Pity me, and pardon me, O virtuous reader! You never knew what it is to be a slave; to be entirely unprotected by law or custom; to have the laws reduce you to the condition of a chattel, entirely subject to the will of another. You never exhausted your ingenuity in avoiding the snares, and eluding the power of a hated tyrant; you never shuddered at the sound of his footsteps, and trembled within hearing of his voice. I know I did wrong. No one can feel it more sensibly than I do. The painful and humiliating memory will haunt me to my dying day. Still, in looking back, calmly, on the events of my life, I feel that the slave woman ought not to be judged by the same standard of others.

The months passed on. I had many unhappy hours. I secretly mourned over the sorrow I was bringing on my grandmother, who had so tried to shield me from harm. I knew that I was the greatest comfort of her old age, and that it was a source of pride to her that I had not degraded myself, like most of the slaves. I wanted to confess to her that I was no longer worthy of her love; but I could not utter the dreaded words.

As for Dr. Flint, I had a feeling of satisfaction and triumph in the thought of telling *him*. From time to time he told me of his intended arrangements, and I was silent. At last, he came and told me the cottage was completed, and ordered me to go to it. I told him I would never enter it. He said, "I have heard enough of such talk as that. You shall go, if you are carried by force; and you shall remain there."

I replied, "I will never go there. In a few months I shall be a mother."

He stood and looked at me in dumb amazement, and left the house without a word. I thought I should be happy in my triumph over him. But now that the truth was out, and my relatives would hear of it, I felt wretched. Humble as were their circumstances, they had pride in my good character. Now, how could I look them in the face? My self-respect was gone! I had resolved that I would be virtuous, though I was a slave. I had said, "Let the storm beat! I will brave it till I die." And now, how humiliated I felt!

I went to my grandmother. My lips moved to make confession, but the words stuck in my throat. I sat down in the shade of a tree at her door and began to sew. I think she saw something unusual was the matter with me. The mother of slaves is very watchful. She knows there is no security for her children. After they have entered their teens she lives in daily expectation of trouble. This leads to many questions. If the girl is of a sensitive nature, timidity keeps her from answering truthfully, and this well-meant course has a tendency to drive her from maternal counsels. Presently, in came my mistress, like a mad woman, and accused me concerning her husband. My grandmother, whose suspicions had been previously awakened, believed what she said. She exclaimed, "O Linda! has it come to this? I had rather see you dead than to see you as you now are. You are a disgrace to your dead mother." She tore from my fingers my mother's wedding ring and her silver thimble. "Go away!" she exclaimed, "and never come to my house, again." Her reproaches fell so hot and heavy, that they left me no chance to answer. Bitter tears, such as the eyes never shed but once, were my only answer. I rose from my seat, but fell back again, sobbing. She did not speak to me; but the tears were running down her furrowed cheeks, and they scorched me like fire. She had always been so kind to me! *So* kind! How I longed to throw myself at her feet, and tell her all the truth! But she had ordered me to go, and never to come there again. After a few minutes, I mustered strength, and started to obey her. With what feelings did I now close that little gate, which I used to open with such an eager hand in my childhood! It closed upon me with a sound I never heard before.

Where could I go? I was afraid to return to my master's. I walked on recklessly, not caring where I went, or what would become of me. When I had gone four or five miles, fatigue compelled me to stop. I sat down on the stump of an old tree. The stars were shining through the boughs above me. How they mocked me, with their bright, calm light! The hours passed by, and as I sat there alone a chilliness and deadly sickness came over me. I sank on the ground. My mind was full of horrid thoughts. I prayed to die; but the prayer was not answered. At last, with great effort I roused myself, and walked some distance further, to the house of a woman who had been a friend of my mother. When I told her why I was there, she spoke soothingly to me; but I could not be comforted. I thought I could bear my shame if I could only be reconciled to my grandmother. I longed to open my heart to her. I thought if she could know the real state of the case, and all I had been bearing for years, she would perhaps judge me less harshly. My friend advised me to send for her. I did so; but days of agonizing suspense passed before she came. Had she utterly forsaken me? No. She came at last. I knelt before her, and told her the things that had poisoned my life; how long I had been persecuted; that I saw no way of escape; and in an hour of extremity I had become desperate. She listened in silence. I told her I would bear any thing and do any thing, if in time I had hopes of obtaining her forgiveness. I begged of her to pity me, for my dead mother's sake. And she did pity me. She did not say, "I forgive you;" but she looked at me lovingly, with her eyes full of tears. She laid her old hand gently on my head, and murmured, "Poor child! Poor child!"

The Lowell Textile Workers

Harriet Hanson Robinson

The transportation revolution made the movement of goods easier and cheaper, greatly expanding the potential market for manufactured products, particularly textiles. More-over, incorporation permitted manufacturing concerns and transportation projects to grow large. But where would the workers come from?

One early answer was the Waltham system, the brainchild of New England indus-trialist and reformer Francis Cabot Lowell. To recruit respectable young women from New England farms to work in his mills, he developed a highly organized paternal sys-tem. Lowell offered reasonable wages and working conditions as well as carefully chap-eroned boarding houses. He even sponsored literary journals to create a genteel atmosphere. But within a few years, under the pressure of business competition, work-ing and living conditions worsened, and eventually the farm girls were replaced by des-perately poor Irish immigrant workers.

As a young girl in the 1830s, Harriet Hanson Robinson (1825–1911) worked in the Lowell mills. She became deeply troubled by the deteriorating conditions under which many young women labored. This led her into reform movements, including woman suffrage. In 1898, more than sixty years after she worked in the mills, she pub-lished Loom and Spindle, *telling of her experience.*

BEFORE YOU READ

1. Why did Harriet Hanson Robinson work in the mills?
2. What did she like about life at the mills?
3. How did she think working at the mills affected the status of women?
4. Why did the young women strike?

CHAPTER II. CHILD-LIFE
IN THE LOWELL COTTON-MILLS

In 1831, under the shadow of a great sorrow, which had made her four children fatherless, — the oldest but seven years of age, — my mother was left to struggle alone; and, although she tried to earn bread enough to fill our hungry mouths, she could not do it, even with the help of kind friends. And so it happened that one of her more wealthy neighbors, who had looked with longing eyes on the

Harriet Hanson Robinson, *Loom and Spindle or Life among the Early Mill Girls* (New York: Crowell, 1898), pp. 16–22, 37–43, 51–53.

one little daughter of the family, offered to adopt me. But my mother, who had had a hard experience in her youth in living amongst strangers, said, "No; while I have one meal of victuals a day, I will not part with my children." I always remembered this speech because of the word "victuals," and I wondered for a long time what this good old Bible word meant.

That was a hard, cold winter; and for warmth's sake my mother and her four children all slept in one bed, two at the foot and three at the head,—but her richer neighbor could not get the little daughter; and, contrary to all the modern notions about hygiene, we were a healthful and a robust brood.

Shortly after this my mother's widowed sister, Mrs. Angeline Cudworth, who kept a factory boarding-house in Lowell, advised her to come to that city.

I had been to school constantly until I was about ten years of age, when my mother, feeling obliged to have help in her work besides what I could give, and also needing the money which I could earn, allowed me, at my urgent request (for I wanted to earn *money* like the other little girls), to go to work in the mill. I worked first in the spinning-room as a "doffer." The doffers were the very youngest girls, whose work was to doff, or take off, the full bobbins, and replace them with the empty ones.

Some of us learned to embroider in crewels,[1] and I still have a lamb worked on cloth, a relic of those early days, when I was first taught to improve my time in the good old New England fashion. When not doffing, we were often allowed to go home, for a time, and thus we were able to help our mothers in their housework. We were paid two dollars a week; and how proud I was when my turn came to stand up on the bobbin-box, and write my name in the paymaster's book, and how indignant I was when he asked me if I could "write." "Of course I can," said I, and he smiled as he looked down on me.

The working-hours of all the girls extended from five o'clock in the morning until seven in the evening, with one-half hour for breakfast and for dinner. Even the doffers were forced to be on duty nearly fourteen hours a day, and this was the greatest hardship in the lives of these children. For it was not until 1842 that the hours of labor for children under twelve years of age were limited to ten per day; but the "ten-hour law" itself was not passed until long after some of these little doffers were old enough to appear before the legislative committee on the subject, and plead, by their presence, for a reduction of the hours of labor.

I do not recall any particular hardship connected with this life, except getting up so early in the morning, and to this habit, I never was, and never shall be, reconciled, for it has taken nearly a lifetime for me to make up the sleep lost at that early age. But in every other respect it was a pleasant life. We were not hurried any more than was for our good, and no more work was required of us than we were able easily to do.

---

1. **crewels:** embroidery or embroidery yarn.

Most of us children lived at home, and we were well fed, drinking both tea and coffee, and eating substantial meals (besides luncheons) three times a day. We had very happy hours with the older girls, many of whom treated us like babies, or talked in a motherly way, and so had a good influence over us. And in the long winter evenings, when we could not run home between the doffings, we gathered in groups and told each other stories, and sung the old-time songs our mothers had sung, such as "Barbara Allen," "Lord Lovell," "Captain Kid," "Hull's Victory," and sometimes a hymn.

Among the ghost stories I remember some that would delight the hearts of the "Society for Psychical Research." The more imaginative ones told of what they had read in fairy books, or related tales of old castles and distressed maidens; and the scene of their adventures was sometimes laid among the foundation stones of the new mill, just building.

And we told each other of our little hopes and desires, and what we meant to do when we grew up. For we had our aspirations; and one of us, who danced the "shawl dance," as she called it, in the spinning-room alley, for the amusement of her admiring companions, discussed seriously with another little girl the scheme of their running away together, and joining the circus.

I cannot tell how it happened that some of us knew about the English factory children, who, it was said, were treated so badly, and were even whipped by their cruel overseers. But we did know of it, and used to sing, to a doleful little tune, some verses called, "The Factory Girl's Last Day." I do not remember it well enough to quote it as written, but have refreshed my memory by reading it lately in Robert Dale Owen's writings: —

The Factory Girl's Last Day

'Twas on a winter morning,
    The weather wet and wild,
Two hours before the dawning
    The father roused his child,
Her daily morsel bringing,
    The darksome room he paced,
And cried, 'The bell is ringing—
    My hapless darling, haste!'

The overlooker met her
    As to her frame she crept;
And with this thong he beat her,
    And cursed her when she wept.
It seemed as she grew weaker,
    The threads the oftener broke,
The rapid wheels ran quicker,
    And heavier fell the stroke.

The song goes on to tell the sad story of her death while her "pitying comrades" were carrying her home to die, and ends: —

That night a chariot passed her,
    While on the ground she lay;

> The daughters of her master,
> An evening visit pay.
> Their tender hearts were sighing,
> As negroes' wrongs were told,
> While the white slave was dying
> Who gained her father's gold.

In contrast with this sad picture, we thought of ourselves as well off, in our cosey corner of the mill, enjoying ourselves in our own way, with our good mothers and our warm suppers awaiting us when the going-out bell should ring.

CHAPTER IV. THE CHARACTERISTICS OF THE EARLY FACTORY GIRLS

When I look back into the factory life of fifty or sixty years ago, I do not see what is called "a class" of young men and women going to and from their daily work, like so many ants that cannot be distinguished one from another; I see them as individuals, with personalities of their own. This one has about her the atmosphere of her early home. That one is impelled by a strong and noble purpose. The other, —what she is, has been an influence for good to me and to all womankind.

Yet they were a class of factory operatives, and were spoken of (as the same class is spoken of now) as a set of persons who earned their daily bread, whose condition was fixed, and who must continue to spin and to weave to the end of their natural existence. Nothing but this was expected of them, and they were not supposed to be capable of social or mental improvement. That they could be educated and developed into something more than mere work-people, was an idea that had not yet entered the public mind. So little does one class of persons really know about the thoughts and aspirations of another! It was the good fortune of these early mill-girls to teach the people of that time that this sort of labor is not degrading; that the operative is not only "capable of virtue," but also capable of self-cultivation.

At the time the Lowell cotton-mills were started, the factory girl was the lowest among women. In England, and in France particularly, great injustice had been done to her real character; she was represented as subjected to influences that could not fail to destroy her purity and self-respect. In the eyes of her overseer she was but a brute, a slave, to be beaten, pinched, and pushed about. It was to overcome this prejudice that such high wages had been offered to women that they might be induced to become mill-girls, in spite of the opprobrium that still clung to this "degrading occupation." At first only a few came; for, though tempted by the high wages to be regularly paid in "cash," there were many who still preferred to go on working at some more *genteel* employment at seventy-five cents a week and their board.

But in a short time the prejudice against factory labor wore away, and the Lowell mills became filled with blooming and energetic New England women.

In 1831 Lowell was little more than a factory village. Several corporations were started, and the cotton-mills belonging to them were building. Help was in great demand; and stories were told all over the country of the new factory town, and the high wages that were offered to all classes of work-people,— stories that reached the ears of mechanics' and farmers' sons, and gave new life to lonely and dependent women in distant towns and farmhouses. Into this Yankee El Dorado, these needy people began to pour by the various modes of travel known to those slow old days. The stage-coach and the canal-boat came every day, always filled with new recruits for this army of useful people. The mechanic and machinist came, each with his homemade chest of tools, and often-times his wife and little ones. The widow came with her little flock and her scanty house-keeping goods to open a boarding-house or variety store, and so provided a home for her fatherless children. Many farmers' daughters came to earn money to com-plete their wedding outfit, or buy the bride's share of housekeeping articles.

Women with past histories came, to hide their griefs and their identity, and to earn an honest living in the "sweat of their brow." Single young men came, full of hope and life, to get money for an education, or to lift the mortgage from the home-farm. Troops of young girls came by stages and baggage-wagons, men often being employed to go to other States and to Canada, to collect them at so much a head, and deliver them at the factories.

[The] country girls had queer names, which added to the singularity of their appearance. Samantha, Triphena, Plumy, Kezia, Aseneth, Elgardy, Leafy, Ruhamah, Lovey, Almaretta, Sarepta, and Florilla were among them.

Their dialect was also very peculiar. On the broken English and Scotch of their ancestors was ingrafted the nasal Yankee twang; so that many of them, when they had just come *daown*, spoke a language almost unintelligible. But the severe discipline and ridicule which met them was as good as a school educa-tion, and they were soon taught the "city way of speaking."

Their dress was also peculiar, and was of the plainest of homespun, cut in such an old-fashioned style that each young girl looked as if she had borrowed her grandmother's gown. Their only head-covering was a shawl, which was pinned under the chin; but after the first payday, a "shaker" (or "scooter") sun-bonnet usually replaced this primitive headgear of their rural life.

But the early factory girls were not all country girls. There were others also, who had been taught that "work is no disgrace." There were some who came to Lowell solely on account of the social or literary advantages to be found there. They lived in secluded parts of New England, where books were scarce, and there was no cultivated society. They had comfortable homes, and did not perhaps need the *money* they would earn; but they longed to see this new "City of Spindles." . . .

The laws relating to women were such, that a husband could claim his wife wherever he found her, and also the children she was trying to shield from his in-fluence; and I have seen more than one poor woman skulk behind her loom or her frame when visitors were approaching the end of the aisle where she worked. Some of these were known under assumed names, to prevent their husbands from trusteeing their wages. It was a very common thing for a male person of a certain kind to do this, thus depriving his wife of *all* her wages, perhaps, month after month. The wages of minor children could be trusteed, unless the children (being fourteen years of age) were given their time. Women's wages were also trusteed for the debts of their husbands, and children's for the debts of their parents.

It must be remembered that at this date woman had no property rights. A widow could be left without her share of her husband's (or the family) property, a legal "incumbrance" to his estate. A father could make his will without reference to his daughter's share of the inheritance. He usually left her a home on the farm as long as she remained single. A woman was not supposed to be capable of spending her own or of using other people's money. In Massachusetts, before 1840, a woman could not legally be treasurer of her own sewing-society, unless some man were responsible for her.

The law took no cognizance of woman as a money-spender. She was a ward, an appendage, a relict. Thus it happened, that if a woman did not choose to marry, or, when left a widow, to re-marry, she had no choice but to enter one of the few employments open to her, or to become a burden on the charity of some relative.

In almost every New England home could be found one or more of these women, sometimes welcome, more often unwelcome, and leading joyless, and in many instances unsatisfactory, lives. The cotton-factory was a great opening to these lonely and dependent women. From a condition approaching pauperism they were at once placed above want; they could earn money, and spend it as they pleased; and could gratify their tastes and desires without restraint, and without rendering an account to anybody. . . .

Among the older women who sought this new employment were very many lonely and dependent ones, such as used to be mentioned in old wills as "incumbrances" and "relicts," and to whom a chance of earning money was indeed a new revelation. How well I remember some of these solitary ones! As a child of eleven years, I often made fun of them—for children do not see the pathetic side of human life—and imitated their limp carriage and inelastic gait. I can see them now, even after sixty years, just as they looked,—depressed, modest, mincing, hardly daring to look one in the face, so shy and sylvan had been their lives. But after the first pay-day came, and they felt the jingle of silver in their pockets, and had begun to feel its mercurial influence, their bowed heads were lifted, their necks seemed braced with steel, they looked you in the face, sang blithely among their looms or frames, and walked with elastic step to and from their work. And when Sunday came, homespun was no longer their only wear; and how sedately gay in their new attire they walked to church, and how proudly they dropped their silver fourpences into the contribution-box! It seemed as if a great hope impelled them,—the harbinger of the new era that was about to dawn for them and for all women-kind.

CHAPTER V.
CHARACTERISTICS (CONTINUED)

One of the first strikes of cotton-factory operatives that ever took place in this country was that in Lowell, in October, 1836. When it was announced that the wages were to be cut down, great indignation was felt, and it was decided to strike, *en masse*. This was done. The mills were shut down, and the girls went in procession from their several corporations to the "grove" on Chapel Hill, and listened to "incendiary" speeches from early labor reformers.

One of the girls stood on a pump, and gave vent to the feelings of her companions in a neat speech, declaring that it was their duty to resist all attempts at cutting down the wages. This was the first time a woman had spoken in public in Lowell, and the event caused surprise and consternation among her audience.

Cutting down the wages was not their only grievance, nor the only cause of this strike. Hitherto the corporations had paid twenty-five cents a week towards the board of each operative, and now it was their purpose to have the girls pay the sum; and this, in addition to the cut in wages, would make a difference of at least one dollar a week. It was estimated that as many as twelve or fifteen hundred girls turned out, and walked in procession through the streets. They had neither flags nor music, but sang songs, a favorite (but rather inappropriate) one being a parody on "I won't be a nun."

> Oh! isn't it a pity, such a pretty girl as I—
>   Should be sent to the factory to pine away and die?
> Oh! I cannot be a slave,
>   I will not be a slave,
> For I'm so fond of liberty
>   That I cannot be a slave.

My own recollection of this first strike (or "turn out" as it was called) is very vivid. I worked in a lower room, where I had heard the proposed strike fully, if not vehemently, discussed; I had been an ardent listener to what was said against this attempt at "oppression" on the part of the corporation, and naturally I took sides with the strikers. When the day came on which the girls were to turn out, those in the upper rooms started first, and so many of them left that our mill was at once shut down. Then, when the girls in my room stood irresolute, uncertain what to do, asking each other, "Would you?" or "Shall we turn out?" and not one of them having the courage to lead off, I, who began to think they would not go out, after all their talk, became impatient, and started on ahead, saying, with childish bravado, "I don't care what you do, *I* am going to turn out, whether any one else does or not"; and I marched out, and was followed by the others.[2]

As I looked back at the long line that followed me, I was more proud than I have ever been since at any success I may have achieved, and more proud than I shall ever be again until my own beloved State gives to its women citizens the right of suffrage.

The agent of the corporation where I then worked took some small revenges on the supposed ringleaders; on the principle of sending the weaker to the wall, my mother was turned away from her boarding-house, that functionary saying, "Mrs. Hanson, you could not prevent the older girls from turning out, but your daughter is a child, and *her* you could control."

---

2. I was then eleven years and eight months old. [Robinson's note.]

It is hardly necessary to say that so far as results were concerned this strike did no good. The dissatisfaction of the operatives subsided, or burned itself out, and though the authorities did not accede to their demands, the majority returned to their work, and the corporation went on cutting down the wages.

And after a time, as the wages became more and more reduced, the best portion of the girls left and went to their homes, or to the other employments that were fast opening to women, until there were very few of the old guard left; and thus the *status* of the factory population of New England gradually became what we know it to be to-day.

33

Life under the Lash

Charles Ball et al.

One of the great efforts of the current generation of American historians has been to capture the African American experience of slavery directly rather than from sources written by whites. As a result of this work, not only have new documents been unearthed, but a new appreciation has developed for those slave writings that have been long known to historians but that required verification of their reliability.

The authors of the more than one hundred extant book-length accounts of slavery were by no means typical former slaves. Most of them succeeded in gaining their freedom by escape or purchase, which was not the lot of their less fortunate brothers and sisters. Most were highly literate. Some had help in writing their accounts from abolitionists and other ghost writers and editors. Nevertheless, historians in recent decades have discovered how generally accurate — in fact, how indispensable — their narratives are for any serious understanding of the institution of American slavery.

The sampling of the literature presented here provides insights into the work regimen of a plantation, living conditions of slaves, and limits on parental authority. These accounts may be compared with some of the images in the visual portfolio "Slavery and Freedom" (page 257), particularly Plates 1 and 12.

BEFORE YOU READ

1. How did Charles Ball explain the differences among the plantations on which he labored as a slave?

2. What, according to Josiah Henson and Francis Henderson, were living conditions under slavery?

3. What was Francis Henderson's view of white Southerners?

4. What effect, as Jacob Stroyer described it, did slavery have on family relationships?

CHARLES BALL[1]

The Work Regimen of a Tobacco Plantation

In Maryland and Virginia, although the slaves are treated with so much rigour, and oftimes with so much cruelty, I have seen instances of the greatest tenderness of feeling on the part of their owners. I, myself, had three masters in Maryland,

[1]. Ball had been a slave in Maryland, South Carolina, and Georgia.

Steven Mintz, ed., *African American Voices: The Life Cycle of Slavery* (St. James, N.Y.: Brandywine Press, 1993), pp. 73–75, 78–79, 87–89, 111–13.

and I cannot say now, even after having resided so many years in a state where slavery is not tolerated, that either of them (except the last, who sold me to the Georgians, and was an unfeeling man,) used me worse than they had a moral right to do, regarding me merely as an article of property, and not entitled to any rights as a man, political or civil. My mistresses, in Maryland, were all good women; and the mistress of my wife, in whose kitchen I spent my Sundays and many of my nights, for several years, was a lady of most benevolent and kindly feelings. She was a true friend to me, and I shall always venerate her memory. . . .

If the proprietors of the soil in Maryland and Virginia, were skillful cultivators — had their lands in good condition — and kept no more slaves on each estate, than would be sufficient to work the soil in a proper manner, and kept up the repairs of the place — the condition of the coloured people would not be, by any means, a comparatively unhappy one. I am convinced, that in nine cases in ten, the hardships and suffering of the coloured population of lower Virginia, are attributable to the poverty and distress of its owners. In many instances, an estate scarcely yields enough to feed and clothe the slaves in a comfortable manner, without allowing anything for the support of the master and family; but it is obvious, that the family must first be supported, and the slaves must be content with the surplus — and this, on a poor, old, worn out tobacco plantation, is often very small, and wholly inadequate to the comfortable sustenance of the hands, as they are called. There, in many places, nothing is allowed to the poor Negro, but his peck of corn per week, without the sauce of a salt herring, or even a little salt itself. . . .

The general features of slavery are the same everywhere; but the utmost rigour of the system, is only to be met with, on the cotton plantations of Carolina and Georgia, or in the rice fields which skirt the deep swamps and morasses of the southern rivers. In the tobacco fields of Maryland and Virginia, great cruelties are practiced — not so frequently by the owners, as by the overseers of the slaves; but yet, the tasks are not so excessive as in the cotton region, nor is the press of labour so incessant throughout the year. It is true, that from the period when the tobacco plants are set in the field, there is no resting time until it is housed; but it is planted out about the first of May, and must be cut and taken out of the field before the frost comes. After it is hung and dried, the labor of stripping and preparing it for the hogshead in leaf, or of manufacturing it into twist, is comparatively a work of leisure and ease. Besides, on almost every plantation the hands are able to complete the work of preparing the tobacco by January, and sometimes earlier; so that the winter months, form some sort of respite from the toils of the year. The people are obliged, it is true, to occupy themselves in cutting wood for the house, making rails and repairing fences, and in clearing new land, to raise the tobacco plants for the next year; but as there is usually time enough, and to spare, for the completion of all this work, before the season arrives for setting the plants in the field; the men are seldom flogged much, unless they are very lazy or negligent, and the women are allowed to remain in the house, in the very cold, snowy, or rainy weather. . . .

In Maryland I never knew a mistress or a young mistress, who would not listen to the complaints of the slaves. It is true, we were always obliged to approach the door of the mansion, with our hats in our hands, and the most subdued and beseeching language in our mouths—but, in return, we generally received words of kindness, and very often a redress of our grievances; though I have known very great ladies, who would never grant any request from the plantation hands, but always referred them and their petitions to their master, under a pretence, that they could not meddle with things that did not belong to the house. The mistresses of the great families, generally gave mild language to the slaves; though they sometimes sent for the overseer and had them severely flogged; but I have never heard any mistress, in either Maryland or Virginia, indulge in the low, vulgar and profane vituperations, of which I was myself the object, in Georgia, for many years, whenever I came into the presence of my mistress. Flogging—though often severe and excruciating in Maryland, is not practiced with the order, regularity and system, to which it is often reduced in the South. On the Potomac, if a slave gives offence, he is generally chastised on the spot, in the field where he is at work, as the overseer always carried a whip—sometimes a twisted cow-hide, sometimes a kind of horse-whip, and very often a simple hickory switch or gad, cut in the adjoining woods. For stealing meat, or other provisions, or for any of the higher offences, the slaves are stripped, tied up by the hands—sometimes by the thumbs—and whipped at the quarter—but many times, on a large tobacco plantation, there is not more than one of these regular whippings in a week—though on others, where the master happens to be a bad man, or a drunkard—the back of the unhappy Maryland slaves, is seamed with scars from his neck to his hips.

JOSIAH HENSON[2]

"We Lodged in Log Huts"

My earliest employments were, to carry buckets of water to the men at work, and to hold a horse-plough, used for weeding between the rows of corn. As I grew older and taller, I was entrusted with the care of master's saddle-horse. Then a hoe was put into my hands, and I was soon ·required to do the day's work of a man; and it was not long before I could do it, at least as well as my associates in misery.

A description of the everyday life of a slave on a Southern plantation illustrates the character and habits of the slave and the slaveholder, created and perpetuated by their relative position. The principal food of those upon my master's plantation consisted of corn-meal and salt herrings; to which was added in summer a little buttermilk, and the few vegetables which each might raise for himself and his family, on the little piece of ground which was assigned to him for the purpose, called a truck-patch.

In ordinary times we had two regular meals in a day: breakfast at twelve o'clock, after laboring from daylight, and supper when the work of the remain-

2. Henson had been a slave in Maryland before he escaped.

der of the day was over. In harvest season we had three. Our dress was of tow-cloth; for the children, nothing but a shirt; for the older ones a pair of pantaloons or a gown in addition, according to the sex. Besides these, in the winter a round jacket or overcoat, a wool-hat once in two or three years, for the males, and a pair of coarse shoes once a year.

We lodged in log huts, and on the bare ground. Wooden floors were an unknown luxury. In a single room were huddled, like cattle, ten or a dozen persons, men, women, and children. All ideas of refinement and decency were, of course, out of the question. We had neither bedsteads, nor furniture of any description. Our beds were collections of straw and old rags, thrown down in the corners and boxed in with boards; a single blanket the only covering. Our favourite way of sleeping, however, was on a plank, our heads raised on an old jacket and our feet toasting before the smouldering fire. The wind whistled and the rain and snow blew in through the cracks, and the damp earth soaked in the moisture till the floor was miry as a pig-sty. Such were our houses. In these wretched hovels were we penned at night, and fed by day; here were the children born and the sick—neglected.

FRANCIS HENDERSON[3]

Living Conditions on the Plantation

Our houses were but log huts—the tops partly open—ground floor—rain would come through. My aunt was quite an old woman, and had been sick several years; in rains I have seen her moving from one part of the house to the other, and rolling her bedclothes about to try to keep dry—everything would be dirty and muddy. I lived in the house with my aunt. My bed and bedstead consisted of a board wide enough to sleep on—one end on a stool, the other placed near the fire. My pillow consisted of my jacket—my covering was whatever I could get. My bedtick was the board itself. And this was the way the single men slept—but we were comfortable in this way of sleeping, being used to it. I only remember having but one blanket from my owners up to the age of nineteen, when I ran away.

Our allowance was given weekly—a peck of sifted corn meal, a dozen and a half herrings, two and a half pounds of pork. Some of the boys would eat this up in three days—then they had to steal, or they could not perform their daily tasks. They would visit the hog-pen, sheep-pen, and granaries. I do not remember one slave but who stole some things—they were driven to it as a matter of necessity. I myself did this—many a time have I, with others, run among the stumps in chase of a sheep, that we might have something to eat. . . . In regard to cooking, sometimes many have to cook at one fire, and before all could get to the fire to bake hoe cakes, the overseer's horn would sound: then they must go at any rate. Many a time I have gone along eating a piece of bread and meat, or

3. Henderson escaped from slavery at the age of nineteen.

herring broiled on the coals—I never sat down at a table to eat except at harvest time, all the time I was a slave. In harvest time, the cooking is done at the great house, as the hands they have are wanted in the field. This was more like people, and we liked it, for we sat down then at meals. In the summer we had one pair of linen trousers given us—nothing else; every fall, one pair of woolen pantaloons, one woolen jacket, and two cotton shirts.

My master had four sons in his family. They all left except one, who remained to be a driver. He would often come to the field and accuse the slave of having taken so and so. If we denied it, he would whip the grown-up ones to make them own it. Many a time, when we didn't know he was anywhere around, he would be in the woods watching us—first thing we would know, he would be sitting on the fence looking down upon us, and if any had been idle, the young master would visit him with blows. I have known him to kick my aunt, an old woman who had raised and nursed him, and I have seen him punish my sisters awfully with hickories from the woods.

The slaves are watched by the patrols, who ride about to try to catch them off the quarters, especially at the house of a free person of color. I have known the slaves to stretch clothes lines across the street, high enough to let the horse pass, but not the rider; then the boys would run, and the patrols in full chase would be thrown off by running against the lines. The patrols are poor white men, who live by plundering and stealing, getting rewards for runaways, and setting up little shops on the public roads. They will take whatever the slaves steal, paying in money, whiskey, or whatever the slaves want. They take pigs, sheep, wheat, corn—anything that's raised they encourage the slaves to steal: these they take to market next day. It's all speculation—all a matter of self-interest, and when the slaves run away, these same traders catch them if they can, to get the reward. If the slave threatens to expose his traffic, he does not care—for the slave's word is good for nothing—it would not be taken.

JACOB STROYER[4]

Parents and Children

Gilbert was a cruel [slave] boy. He used to strip his fellow Negroes while in the woods, and whip them two or three times a week, so that their backs were all scarred, and threatened them with severer punishments if they told; this state of things had been going on for quite a while. As I was a favorite with Gilbert, I always managed to escape a whipping, with the promise of keeping the secret of the punishment of the rest. . . . But finally, one day, Gilbert said to me, "Jake," as he used to call me, "you am a good boy, but I'm gwine to wip you some today, as I wip dem toder boys." Of course I was required to strip off my only garment, which was an Osnaburg linen shirt, worn by both sexes of the Negro children in the summer. As I stood trembling before my merciless superior, who had a switch in his hand, thousands of thoughts went through my little

4. Stroyer, who grew up a slave in several Southern states, wrote *My Life in the South* (Salem, MA: Newcomb & Gauss, 1898).

mind as to how to get rid of the whipping. I finally fell upon a plan which I hoped would save me from a punishment that was near at hand. . . . I commenced reluctantly to take off my shirt, at the same time pleading with Gilbert, who paid no attention to my prayer. . . . Having satisfied myself that no mercy was to be found with Gilbert, I drew my shirt off and threw it over his head, and bounded forward on a run in the direction of the sound of the [nearby] carpenters. By the time he got from the entanglement of my garment, I had quite a little start of him. . . . As I got near to the carpenters, one of them ran and met me, into whose arms I jumped. The man into whose arms I ran was Uncle Benjamin, my mother's uncle. . . . I told him that Gilbert had been in the habit of stripping the boys and whipping them two or three times a week, when we went into the woods, and threatened them with greater punishment if they told. . . . Gilbert was brought to trial, severely whipped, and they made him beg all the children to pardon him for his treatment to them.

[My] father . . . used to take care of horses and mules. I was around with him in the barn yard when but a very small boy; of course that gave me an early relish for the occupation of hostler,[5] and I soon made known my preference to Col. Singleton, who was a sportsman, and an owner of fine horses. And, although I was too small to work, the Colonel granted my request; hence I was allowed to be numbered among those who took care of the fine horses and learned to ride. But I soon found that my new occupation demanded a little more than I cared for. It was not long after I had entered my new work before they put me upon the back of a horse which threw me to the ground almost as soon as I had reached his back. It hurt me a little, but that was not the worst of it, for when I got up there was a man standing near with a switch in hand, and he immediately began to beat me. Although I was a very bad boy, this was the first time I had been whipped by anyone except father and mother, so I cried out in a tone of voice as if I would say, this is the first and last whipping you will give me when father gets hold of you.

When I had got away from him I ran to father with all my might, but soon found my expectation blasted, as father very coolly said to me, "Go back to your work and be a good boy, for I cannot do anything for you." But that did not satisfy me, so on I went to mother with my complaint and she came out to the man who had whipped me; he was a groom, a white man master had hired to train the horses. Mother and he began to talk, then he took a whip and started for her, and she ran from him, talking all the time. I ran back and forth between mother and him until he stopped beating her. After the fight between the groom and mother, he took me back to the stable yard and gave me a severe flogging. And, although mother failed to help me at first, still I had faith that when he had taken me back to the stable yard, and commenced whipping me, she would come and stop him, but I looked in vain, for she did not come.

Then the idea first came to me that I, with my dear father and mother and the rest of my fellow Negroes, were doomed to cruel treatment through life, and was defenseless. But when I found that father and mother could not save

5. **hostler:** a person who takes care of horses.

me from punishment, as they themselves had to submit to the same treatment, I concluded to appeal to the sympathy of the groom, who seemed to have full control over me; but my pitiful cries never touched his sympathy. . . .

One day, about two weeks after Boney Young [the white man who trained horses for Col. Singleton] and mother had the conflict, he called me to him. . . . When I got to him he said, "Go and bring me the switch, sir." I answered, "yes, sir," and off I went and brought him one . . . [and] . . . he gave me a first-class flogging. . . .

When I went home to father and mother, I said to them, "Mr. Young is whipping me too much now, I shall not stand it, I shall fight him." Father said to me, "You must not do that, because if you do he will say that your mother and I advised you to do it, and it will make it hard for your mother and me, as well as for yourself. You must do as I told you, my son: do your work the best you can, and do not say anything." I said to father, "But I don't know what I have done that he should whip me; he does not tell me what wrong I have done, he simply calls me to him and whips me when he gets ready." Father said, "I can do nothing more than to pray to the Lord to hasten the time when these things shall be done away; that is all I can do. . . ."

34

A Pioneer for Women's Rights

Elizabeth Cady Stanton

The women's movement before the Civil War was among the most intensely unpopular of all the reform efforts of that era. The ideal of domesticity, which assigned to women a separate and less-powerful role in the family, made the reformists' claims for equal rights, especially the right to vote, a violation of social convention and of the religious beliefs of many. Friendships were enormously important in providing the courage and emotional support women needed to oppose the oppressive family, religious, and political institutions. Elizabeth Cady Stanton (1815–1902) was inspired by Lucretia Mott, whose Quaker practice had given her experience in public speaking that she applied to the antislavery cause. The two had met at an antislavery convention in London in 1840 and, as Stanton was to recall later, "resolved to hold a convention as soon as we re-turned home, and form a society to advocate the rights of women." Yet eight years elapsed before this resolve bore fruit in the Seneca Falls Woman's Rights Convention. In the interim, Stanton had settled in three different locations, bore three children (she would eventually have seven), and assumed all the other cares of a financially strapped, middle-class household.

Reflecting on the Seneca Falls convention in her autobiography, Eighty Years and More, *published in 1898 when she was eighty-three years old, Elizabeth Cady Stanton remained astonished at the avalanche of criticism and sarcasm provoked by the "Declaration of Sentiments." Commenting on the meeting, a Philadelphia newspaper asserted, "A pretty girl is equal to ten thousand men," and sneered, "The ladies of Philadelphia . . . are resolved to maintain their rights as Wives, Belles, Virgins and Mothers, and not as Women." But the women who met at Seneca Falls in 1848 had succeeded in launching a women's rights movement that would continue, and it would do so mainly by following Stanton's strategy of making suffrage the major objective until that goal was achieved in 1920 with the ratification of the Nineteenth Amendment to the Constitution.*

BEFORE YOU READ

1. Describe the impact of Elizabeth Cady Stanton's attendance at the World's Anti-slavery Convention in 1840.

2. What did Stanton do in the years between the World's Anti-slavery Convention in 1840 and the Seneca Falls Convention of 1848?

Elizabeth Cady Stanton, *Eighty Years and More: Reminiscences, 1815–1897* (London: T. Fisher Unwin, 1898), pp. 79–83, 143–50; Copy of the Declaration of Sentiments, courtesy of the Seneca Falls Historical Society, Seneca Falls, N.Y.

3. What does Stanton mean when she says that "if I had had the slightest premonition of all that was to follow that convention, I fear I should not have had the courage to risk it"?

4. Viewed more than a century and a half later, what relevance do you see in the Declaration of Sentiments?

EIGHTY YEARS AND MORE

Our chief object in visiting England at this time was to attend the World's Anti-slavery Convention, to meet June 12, 1840, in Freemasons' Hall, London. Delegates from all the anti-slavery societies of civilized nations were invited, yet, when they arrived, those representing associations of women were rejected. Though women were members of the National Anti-slavery Society, accustomed to speak and vote in all its conventions, and to take an equally active part with men in the whole anti-slavery struggle, and were there as delegates from associations of men and women, as well as those distinctively of their own sex, yet all alike were rejected because they were women. Women, according to English prejudices at that time, were excluded by Scriptural texts from sharing equal dignity and authority with men in all reform associations; hence it was to English minds pre-eminently unfitting that women should be admitted as equal members to a World's Convention. The question was hotly debated through an entire day. My husband made a very eloquent speech in favor of admitting the women delegates.

When we consider . . . [the] many remarkable women . . . [who] were all compelled to listen in silence to the masculine platitudes on woman's sphere, one may form some idea of the indignation of unprejudiced friends, and especially that of such women as Lydia Maria Child, Maria Chapman, Deborah Weston, Angelina and Sarah Grimké, and Abby Kelly, who were impatiently waiting and watching on this side, in painful suspense, to hear how their delegates were received. Judging from my own feelings, the women on both sides of the Atlantic must have been humiliated and chagrined, except as these feelings were outweighed by contempt for the shallow reasoning of their opponents and their comical pose and gestures in some of the intensely earnest flights of their imagination.

The clerical portion of the convention was most violent in its opposition. The clergymen seemed to have God and his angels especially in their care and keeping, and were in agony lest the women should do or say something to shock the heavenly hosts. Their all-sustaining conceit gave them abundant assurance that their movements must necessarily be all-pleasing to the celestials whose ears were open to the proceedings of the World's Convention. . . .

One of our champions in the convention, George Bradburn, a tall thick-set man with a voice like thunder, standing head and shoulders above the clerical representatives, swept all their arguments aside by declaring with tremendous emphasis that, if they could prove to him that the Bible taught the entire subjection of one-half of the race to the other, he should consider that the best thing he could do for humanity would be to bring together every Bible in the universe and make a grand bonfire of them.

It was really pitiful to hear narrow-minded bigots, pretending to be teachers and leaders of men, so cruelly remanding their own mothers, with the rest of womankind, to absolute subjection to the ordinary masculine type of humanity. I always regretted that the women themselves had not taken part in the debate before the convention was fully organized and the question of delegates settled. It seemed to me then, and does now, that all delegates with credentials from recognized societies should have had a voice in the organization of the convention, though subject to exclusion afterward. However, the women sat in a low curtained seat like a church choir, and modestly listened to the French, British, and American Solons for twelve of the longest days in June, as did, also, our grand Garrison and Rogers in the gallery. They scorned a convention that ignored the rights of the very women who had fought, side by side, with them in the anti-slavery conflict. "After battling so many long years," said Garrison, "for the liberties of African slaves, I can take no part in a convention that strikes down the most sacred rights of all women." After coming three thousand miles to speak on the subject nearest his heart, he nobly shared the enforced silence of the rejected delegates. It was a great act of self-sacrifice that should never be forgotten by women. . . .

As the convention adjourned, the remark was heard on all sides, "It is about time some demand was made for new liberties for women." As Mrs. Mott and I walked home, arm in arm, commenting on the incidents of the day, we resolved to hold a convention as soon as we returned home, and form a society to advocate the rights of women. At the lodging house on Queen Street, where a large number of delegates had apartments, the discussions were heated at every meal, and at times so bitter that, at last, Mr. Birney packed his valise and sought more peaceful quarters. Having strongly opposed the admission of women as delegates to the convention it was rather embarrassing to meet them, during the intervals between the various sessions, at the table and in the drawing room.

These were the first women I had ever met who believed in the equality of the sexes and who did not believe in the popular orthodox religion. The acquaintance of Lucretia Mott, who was a broad, liberal thinker on politics, religion, and all questions of reform, opened to me a new world of thought. As we walked about to see the sights of London, I embraced every opportunity to talk with her. It was intensely gratifying to hear all that, through years of doubt, I had dimly thought, so freely discussed by other women, some of them no older than myself—women, too, of rare intelligence, cultivation, and refinement. . . .

In the spring of 1847 we moved to Seneca Falls. Here we spent sixteen years of our married life, and here our other children—two sons and two daughters—were born. . . .

The house we were to occupy had been closed for some years and needed many repairs, and the grounds, comprising five acres, were overgrown with weeds. My father gave me a check and said, with a smile, "You believe in woman's capacity to do and dare; now go ahead and put your place in order." After a minute survey of the premises and due consultation with one or two sons of Adam, I set the carpenters, painters, paper-hangers, and gardeners at work, built a new kitchen and woodhouse, and in one month took possession.

Having left my children with my mother, there were no impediments to a full display of my executive ability. In the purchase of brick, timber, paint, etc., and in making bargains with workmen, I was in frequent consultation with Judge Sackett and Mr. Bascom. The latter was a member of the Constitutional Convention, then in session in Albany, and as he used to walk down whenever he was at home, to see how my work progressed, we had long talks, sitting on boxes in the midst of tools and shavings, on the status of women. I urged him to propose an amendment to Article II, Section 3, of the State Constitution, striking out the word "male," which limits the suffrage to men. But, while he fully agreed with all I had to say on the political equality of women, he had not the courage to make himself the laughing-stock of the convention. Whenever I cornered him on this point, manlike he turned the conversation to the painters and carpenters. However, these conversations had the effect of bringing him into the first woman's convention, where he did us good service.

In Seneca Falls my life was comparatively solitary, and the change from Boston was somewhat depressing. There, all my immediate friends were reformers, I had near neighbors, a new home with all the modern conveniences, and well-trained servants. Here our residence was on the outskirts of the town, roads very often muddy and no sidewalks most of the way, Mr. Stanton was frequently from home, I had poor servants, and an increasing number of children. To keep a house and grounds in good order, purchase every article for daily use, keep the wardrobes of half a dozen human beings in proper trim, take the children to dentists, shoemakers, and different schools, or find teachers at home, altogether made sufficient work to keep one brain busy, as well as all the hands I could impress into the service. Then, too, the novelty of housekeeping had passed away, and much that was once attractive in domestic life was now irksome. I had so many cares that the company I needed for intellectual stimulus was a trial rather than a pleasure.

There was quite an Irish settlement at a short distance, and continual complaints were coming to me that my boys threw stones at their pigs, cows, and the roofs of their houses. This involved constant diplomatic relations in the settlement of various difficulties, in which I was so successful that, at length, they constituted me a kind of umpire in all their own quarrels. If a drunken husband was pounding his wife, the children would run for me. Hastening to the scene of action, I would take Patrick by the collar, and, much to his surprise and shame, make him sit down and promise to behave himself. I never had one of them offer the least resistance, and in time they all came to regard me as one having authority. I strengthened my influence by cultivating good feeling. I lent the men papers to read, and invited their children into our grounds; giving them fruit, of which we had abundance, and my children's old clothes, books, and toys. I was their physician, also—with my box of homeopathic medicines I took charge of the men, women, and children in sickness. Thus the most amicable relations were established, and, in any emergency, these poor neighbors were good friends and always ready to serve me.

But I found police duty rather irksome, especially when called out dark nights to prevent drunken fathers from disturbing their sleeping children, or to minister to poor mothers in the pangs of maternity. Alas! alas! who can measure the mountains of sorrow and suffering endured in unwelcome motherhood in the abodes of ignorance, poverty, and vice, where terror-stricken women and children are the victims of strong men frenzied with passion and intoxicating drink?

Up to this time life had glided by with comparative ease, but now the real struggle was upon me. My duties were too numerous and varied, and none sufficiently exhilarating or intellectual to bring into play my higher faculties. I suffered with mental hunger, which, like an empty stomach, is very depressing. I had books, but no stimulating companionship. To add to my general dissatisfaction at the change from Boston, I found that Seneca Falls was a malarial region, and in due time all the children were attacked with chills and fever which, under homeopathic treatment in those days, lasted three months. The servants were afflicted in the same way. Cleanliness, order, the love of the beautiful and artistic, all faded away in the struggle to accomplish what was absolutely necessary from hour to hour. Now I understood, as I never had before, how women could sit down and rest in the midst of general disorder. Housekeeping, under such conditions, was impossible, so I packed our clothes, locked up the house, and went to that harbor of safety, [my parents'] home, as I did ever after in stress of weather.

I now fully understood the practical difficulties most women had to contend with in the isolated household, and the impossibility of woman's best development if in contact, the chief part of her life, with servants and children. Fourier's phalansterie[1] community life and co-operative households had a new significance for me. Emerson says, "A healthy discontent is the first step to progress." The general discontent I felt with woman's portion as wife, mother, housekeeper, physician, and spiritual guide, the chaotic conditions into which everything fell without her constant supervision, and the wearied, anxious look of the majority of women impressed me with a strong feeling that some active measures should be taken to remedy the wrongs of society in general, and of women in particular. My experience at the World's Anti-slavery Convention, all I had read of the legal status of women, and the oppression I saw everywhere, together swept across my soul, intensified now by many personal experiences. It seemed as if all the elements had conspired to impel me to some onward step. I could not see what to do or where to begin—my only thought was a public meeting for protest and discussion.

In this tempest-tossed condition of mind I received an invitation to spend the day with Lucretia Mott, at Richard Hunt's, in Waterloo. There I met several members of different families of Friends, earnest, thoughtful women. I poured out, that day, the torrent of my long-accumulating discontent, with such vehemence and indignation that I stirred myself, as well as the rest of the party, to do and dare anything. My discontent, according to Emerson, must have been healthy, for it moved us all to prompt action, and we decided, then and there, to call a "Woman's Rights Convention." We wrote the call that

1. **phalansterie:** a community of the followers of Charles Fourier, who advocated a society that was organized into small, self-sustaining communal groups.

evening and published it in the *Seneca County Courier* the next day, the 14th of July, 1848, giving only five days' notice, as the convention was to be held on the 19th and 20th. The call was inserted without signatures,—in fact it was a mere announcement of a meeting,—but the chief movers and managers were Lucretia Mott, Mary Ann McClintock, Jane Hunt, Martha C. Wright, and myself. The convention, which was held two days in the Methodist Church, was in every way a grand success. The house was crowded at every session, the speaking good, and a religious earnestness dignified all the proceedings.

These were the hasty initiative steps of "the most momentous reform that had yet been launched on the world—the first organized protest against the injustice which had brooded for ages over the character and destiny of one-half the race." No words could express our astonishment on finding, a few days afterward, that what seemed to us so timely, so rational, and so sacred, should be a subject for sarcasm and ridicule to the entire press of the nation. With our Declaration of Rights and Resolutions for a text, it seemed as if every man who could wield a pen prepared a homily on "woman's sphere." All the journals from Maine to Texas seemed to strive with each other to see which could make our movement appear the most ridiculous. The anti-slavery papers stood by us manfully and so did Frederick Douglass, both in the convention and in his paper, *The North Star*, but so pronounced was the popular voice against us, in the parlor, press, and pulpit, that most of the ladies who had attended the convention and signed the declaration, one by one, withdrew their names and influence and joined our persecutors. Our friends gave us the cold shoulder and felt themselves disgraced by the whole proceeding.

If I had had the slightest premonition of all that was to follow that convention, I fear I should not have had the courage to risk it, and I must confess that it was with fear and trembling that I consented to attend another, one month afterward, in Rochester. Fortunately, the first one seemed to have drawn all the fire, and of the second but little was said. But we had set the ball in motion, and now, in quick succession, conventions were held in Ohio, Indiana, Massachusetts, Pennsylvania, and in the City of New York, and have been kept up nearly every year since.

DECLARATION OF SENTIMENTS, 1848

When, in the course of human events, it becomes necessary for one portion of the family of man to assume among the people of the earth a position different from that which they have hitherto occupied, but one to which the laws of nature and of nature's God entitle them, a decent respect to the opinions of mankind requires that they should declare the causes that impel them to such a course.

We hold these truths to be self-evident: that all men and women are created equal; that they are endowed by their Creator with certain inalienable rights; that among these are life, liberty, and the pursuit of happiness; that to secure these rights governments are instituted, deriving their just powers from the consent of the governed. Whenever any form of government becomes destructive of these ends, it is the right of those who suffer from it to refuse allegiance to it, and to insist upon the institution of a new government, laying its foundation on such principles, and organizing its powers in such form, as to them shall seem most likely to effect their safety and happiness. Prudence, indeed, will dictate that governments long established should not be changed for light and transient causes; and accordingly all experience hath shown that mankind are more disposed to suffer, while evils are sufferable, than to right themselves by abolishing the forms to which they were accustomed. But when a long train of abuses and usurpations, pursuing invariably the same object evinces a design to reduce them under absolute despotism, it is their duty to throw off such government, and to provide new guards for their future security. Such has been the patient sufferance of the women under this government, and such is now the necessity which constrains them to demand the equal station to which they are entitled.

The history of mankind is a history of repeated injuries and usurpations on the part of man toward woman, having in direct object the establishment of an absolute tyranny over her. To prove this, let facts be submitted to a candid world.

He has never permitted her to exercise her inalienable right to the elective franchise.

He has compelled her to submit to laws, in the formation of which she had no voice.

He has withheld from her rights which are given to the most ignorant and degraded men—both natives and foreigners.

Having deprived her of this first right of a citizen, the elective franchise, thereby leaving her without representation in the halls of legislation, he has oppressed her on all sides.

He has made her, if married, in the eye of the law, civilly dead.

He has taken from her all right in property, even to the wages she earns.

He has made her, morally, an irresponsible being, as she can commit many crimes with impunity, provided they be done in the presence of her husband. In the covenant of marriage, she is compelled to promise obedience to her husband, he becoming to all intents and purposes, her master—the law giving him power to deprive her of her liberty, and to administer chastisement.

He has so framed the laws of divorce, as to what shall be the proper causes of divorce, and in case of separation, to whom the guardianship of the children shall be given, as to be wholly regardless of the happiness of women—the law, in all cases, going upon a false supposition of the supremacy of man, and giving all power into his hands.

After depriving her of all rights as a married woman, if single and the owner of property, he has taxed her to support a government which recognizes her only when her property can be made profitable to it.

He has monopolized nearly all the profitable employments, and from those she is permitted to follow, she receives but a scanty remuneration.

He closes against her all the avenues to wealth and distinction, which he considers most honorable to himself. As a teacher of theology, medicine, or law, she is not known.

He has denied her the facilities for obtaining a thorough education—all colleges being closed against her.

He allows her in Church as well as State, but a subordinate position, claiming Apostolic authority for her exclusion from the ministry, and, with some exceptions, from any public participation in the affairs of the Church.

He has created a false public sentiment by giving to the world a different code of morals for men and women, by which moral delinquencies which exclude women from society, are not only tolerated, but deemed of little account in man.

He has usurped the prerogative of Jehovah himself, claiming it as his right to assign for her a sphere of action, when that belongs to her conscience and to her God.

He has endeavored, in every way that he could, to destroy her confidence in her own powers, to lessen her self-respect, and to make her willing to lead a dependent and abject life.

Now, in view of this entire disfranchisement of one-half the people of this country, their social and religious degradation,—in view of the unjust laws above mentioned, and because women do feel themselves aggrieved, oppressed, and fraudulently deprived of their most sacred rights, we insist that they have immediate admission to all the rights and privileges which belong to them as citizens of these United States.

In entering upon the great work before us, we anticipate no small amount of misconception, misrepresentation, and ridicule; but we shall use every instrumentality within our power to effect our object. We shall employ agents, circulate tracts, petition the State and national Legislatures, and endeavor to enlist the pulpit and the press in our behalf. We hope this Convention will be followed by a series of Conventions, embracing every part of the country.

Firmly relying upon the final triumph of the Right and the True, we do this day affix our signatures to this declaration.

Ten Nights in a Bar-Room
Timothy Shay Arthur

From colonial days Americans had been heavy drinkers. Wine, hard cider, and whiskey were staples of both economic and social life. Before the advent of canals and railroads, farmers often sent their corn to market distilled in a jug or barrel: whiskey cost less than corn to ship over long distances and found a ready market. In many places, it was safer to drink than water. An early nineteenth-century traveler in Ohio found the use of alcohol nearly universal: "A house could not be raised, a field of wheat cut down, nor could there be a log rolling, a husking, a quilting, a wedding, a sheepwashing, or a funeral without the aid of alcohol."

Antebellum reformers mounted a determined attack on the evils of drink and were remarkably successful in reducing American consumption of alcohol. In the late 1830s a million people belonged to temperance societies. Timothy Shay Arthur's (1809–1885) Ten Nights in a Bar-Room, and What I Saw There, *published in 1854, was the most popular of all the attacks on the tavern and during the 1850s was a best seller second only to* Uncle Tom's Cabin. *Like Harriet Beecher Stowe's antislavery novel,* Ten Nights *became a widely performed stage melodrama.*

As is true of Uncle Tom's Cabin, Ten Nights *is a far more shrewd work than is sometimes thought. Simon Slade, Judge Hammond, Judge Lyman, and young Willy are people with whom respectable Americans could easily identify. The book is not an evangelical tract about the sin of drinking but an often subtle account of a tavern that corrupts the republican virtue of the town of Cedarville.*

BEFORE YOU READ

1. Who is the owner of the Sickle and Sheaf? How does the town regard him?
2. What types of people frequent the tavern?
3. According to the story of Willy Hammond, what does alcohol do to a man's ambitions, career, and health? Does it benefit him in any way?
4. How would you describe the effect of the tavern on the town of Cedarville? Why is the description so one-sided?

NIGHT THE FIRST

The "Sickle and Sheaf"

Ten years ago, business required me to pass a day in Cedarville. It was late in the afternoon when the stage set me down at the "Sickle and Sheaf," a new

Timothy Shay Arthur, *Ten Nights in a Bar-Room, and What I Saw There* (Boston: Crown, 1854), pp. 7–11, 153–68.

tavern, just opened by a new landlord, in a new house, built with the special end of providing "accommodations for man and beast." As I stepped from the dusty old vehicle in which I had been jolted along a rough road for some thirty miles, feeling tired and hungry, the good-natured face of Simon Slade, the landlord, beaming as it did with a hearty welcome, was really a pleasant sight to see, and the grasp of his hand was like that of a true friend.

I felt, as I entered the new and neatly furnished sitting-room adjoining the bar, that I had indeed found a comfortable resting-place after my wearisome journey.

"All as nice as a new pin," said I, approvingly, as I glanced around the room, up to the ceiling—white as the driven snow—and over the handsomely carpeted floor. "Haven't seen any thing so inviting as this. How long have you been open?"

"Only a few months," answered the gratified landlord. "But we are not yet in good going order. It takes time, you know, to bring every thing into the right shape. Have you dined yet?"

"No. Every thing looked so dirty at the stage-house where we stopped to get dinner, that I couldn't venture upon the experiment of eating. How long before your supper will be ready?"

"In an hour," replied the landlord.

"That will do. Let me have a nice piece of tender steak, and the loss of dinner will soon be forgotten."

"You shall have that, cooked fit for an alderman," said the landlord. "I call my wife the best cook in Cedarville." . . .

The arrival of a traveller called away the landlord, and I was left alone for observation and reflection. The bar adjoined the neat sitting-room, and I could see, through the open door, the customer upon whom the lad was attending. He was a well-dressed young man—or rather boy, for he did not appear to be over nineteen years of age—with a fine, intelligent face, that was already slightly marred by sensual indulgence. He raised the glass to his lips, with a quick, almost eager motion, and drained it at a single draught. . . .

"Who is that young man in the bar?" I asked, a few minutes afterward, on being rejoined by the landlord.

Simon Slade stepped to the door and looked into the bar for a moment. Two or three men were there by this time; but he was at no loss in answering my question.

"Oh, that's a son of Judge Hammond, who lives in the large brick house just as you enter the village. Willy Hammond, as everybody familiarly calls him, is about the finest young man in our neighbourhood. There is nothing proud or put-on about him—nothing—even if his father is a judge, and rich into the bargain. Every one, gentle or simple, likes Willy Hammond. And then he is such good company. Always so cheerful, and always with a pleasant story on his tongue. And he's so high-spirited withal, and so honourable. Willy Hammond would lose his right hand rather than be guilty of a mean action."

NIGHT THE SEVENTH

Sowing the Mind

The state of affairs in Cedarville, it was plain, from the partial glimpses I had received, was rather desperate. Desperate, I mean, as regarded the various parties brought before my observation. An eating cancer was on the community, and so far as the eye could mark its destructive progress, the ravages were fearful. That its roots were striking deep, and penetrating, concealed from view, in many unsuspected directions, there could be no doubt. What appeared on the surface was but a milder form of the disease, compared with its hidden, more vital, and more dangerous advances.

I could not but feel a strong interest in some of these parties. The case of young Hammond, had from the first, awakened concern. . . . The gentleman at whose office I met Mr. Harrison on the day before—the reader will remember Mr. H. as having come to the "Sickle and Sheaf" in search of his sons—was thoroughly conversant with the affairs of the village, and I called upon him early in the day in order to make some inquiries. . . .

"When Willy was eighteen—he was then reading law—I think I never saw a young man of fairer promise. As I have often heard it remarked of him, he did not appear to have a single fault. But he had a dangerous gift—rare conversational powers, united with great urbanity of manner. Every one who made his acquaintance became charmed with his society; and he soon found himself surrounded by a circle of young men, some of whom were not the best companions he might have chosen. Still, his own pure instincts and honourable principles were his safeguard; and I never have believed that any social allurements would have drawn him away from the right path, if this accursed tavern had not been opened by Slade."

"There was a tavern here before the 'Sickle and Sheaf' was opened," said I.

"Oh, yes. But it was badly kept, and the bar-room visitors were of the lowest class. No respectable young man in Cedarville would have been seen there. It offered no temptations to one moving in Willy's circle. But the opening of the 'Sickle and Sheaf' formed a new era. Judge Hammond—himself not the purest man in the world, I'm afraid—gave his countenance to the establishment, and talked of Simon Slade as an enterprising man who ought to be encouraged. Judge Lyman and other men of position in Cedarville followed his bad example; and the bar-room of the 'Sickle and Sheaf' was at once voted respectable. At all times of the day and evening you could see the flower of our young men going in and out, sitting in front of the bar-room, or talking hand and glove with the landlord, who, from a worthy miller, regarded as well enough in his place, was suddenly elevated into a man of importance, whom the best in the village were delighted to honour.

"In the beginning, Willy went with the tide, and, in an incredibly short period, was acquiring a fondness for drink that startled and alarmed his friends. In going in through Slade's open door, he entered the downward way, and has been moving onward with fleet footsteps ever since. The fiery poison inflamed his mind, at the same time that it dimmed his noble perceptions. Fondness for mere pleasure followed, and this led him into various sensual indulgences, and exciting modes of passing the time. Every one liked him—he was so free, so companionable, and so generous—and almost every one encouraged, rather than repressed, his dangerous proclivities. Even his father, for a time, treated the matter lightly, as only the first flush of young life. 'I commenced sowing my wild oats at quite as early an age,' I have heard him say. 'He'll cool off, and do well enough. Never fear.' But his mother was in a state of painful alarm from the beginning. Her truer instincts, made doubly acute by her yearning love, perceived the imminent danger, and in all possible ways did she seek to lure him from the path in which he was moving at so rapid a pace. Willy was always very much attached to his mother, and her influence over him was strong; but in this case he regarded her fears as chimerical. The way in which he walked was, to him, so pleasant, and the companions of his journey so delightful, that he could not believe in the prophesied evil; and when his mother talked to him in her warning voice, and with a sad countenance, he smiled at her concern, and made light of her fears.

"And so it went on, month after month, and year after year, until the young man's sad declensions were the town talk. In order to throw his mind into a new channel—to awaken, if possible, a new and better interest in life—his father ventured upon the doubtful experiment we spoke of yesterday: that of placing capital in his hands, and making him an equal partner in the business of distilling and cotton-spinning. The disastrous—I might say disgraceful result—you know. The young man squandered his own capital, and heavily embarrassed his father. . . .

"It seemed as if he could not stop. Some terrible necessity appeared to be impelling him onward. If he formed good resolutions—and I doubt not that he did,—they were blown away like threads of gossamer, the moment he came within the sphere of old associations. His way to the mill was by the 'Sickle and Sheaf'; and it was not easy for him to pass there without being drawn into the bar, either by his own desire for drink or through the invitation of some pleasant companion, who was lounging in front of the tavern." . . .

The man was strongly excited.

"Thus it is," he continued; "and we who see the whole extent, origin, and downward rushing force of a widely sweeping desolation, lift our voices of warning almost in vain. Men who have every thing at stake—sons to be corrupted, and daughters to become the wives of young men exposed to corrupting influences—stand aloof, questioning and doubting as to the expediency of protecting the innocent from the wolfish designs of bad men, who, to compass their own selfish ends, would destroy them body and soul. We are called fanatics, ultraists, designing, and all that, because we ask our law-makers to stay the fiery ruin. Oh, no! we must not touch the traffic. All the dearest and best interests of society may suffer; but the rum-seller must be protected. He must be allowed to get gain, if the jails and poor-houses are filled, and the graveyards made fat with the bodies of young men stricken down in the flower of their years, and of wives and mothers who have died of broken hearts. Reform, we are told, must commence at home. We must rear temperate children, and then we shall have temperate men. That when there are none to desire liquor, the rum-seller's traffic will cease. And all the while society's true benefactors are engaged in doing this, the weak, the unsuspecting, and the erring must be left an easy prey, even if the work requires for its accomplishment a hundred years. Sir! a human soul destroyed through the rum-seller's infernal agency, is a sacrifice priceless in value. No considerations of worldly gain can, for an instant, be placed in comparison therewith. And yet souls are destroyed by thousands every year; and they will fall by tens of thousands ere society awakens from its fatal indifference, and lays its strong hand of power on the corrupt men who are scattering disease, ruin, and death, broadcast over the land!

"I always get warm on this subject," he added, repressing his enthusiasm. "And who that observes and reflects can help growing excited? The evil is appalling; and the indifference of the community one of the strangest facts of the day."

While he was yet speaking, the elder Mr. Hammond came in. He looked wretched. The redness and humidity of his eyes showed want of sleep, and the relaxed muscles of his face exhaustion from weariness and suffering. He drew the person with whom I had been talking aside, and continued in earnest conversation with him for many minutes—often gesticulating violently. I could see his face, though I heard nothing of what he said. The play of his features was painful to look upon, for every changing muscle showed a new phase of mental suffering.

"Try and see him, will you not?" he said, as he turned, at length, to leave the office.

"I will go there immediately," was answered.

"Bring him home, if possible."

"My very best efforts shall be made."

Judge Hammond bowed, and went out hurriedly.

"Do you know the number of the room occupied by the man Green?" asked the gentleman, as soon as his visitor had retired.

"Yes. It is No. 11."

"Willy has not been home since last night. His father, at this late day, suspects Green to be a gambler! The truth flashed upon him only yesterday; and this, added to his other sources of trouble, is driving him, so he says, almost mad. As a friend, he wishes me to go to the 'Sickle and Sheaf,' and try and find Willy. Have you seen any thing of him this morning?"

I answered in the negative.

"Nor of Green?"

"No."

"Was Slade about when you left the tavern?"

"I saw nothing of him."

"What Judge Hammond fears may be all too true—that, in the present condition of Willy's affairs, which have reached the point of disaster, his tempter means to secure the largest possible share of property yet in his power to pledge or transfer,—to squeeze from his victim the last drop of blood that remains, and then fling him, ruthlessly, from his hands."

"The young man must have been rendered almost desperate, or he would never have returned, as he did, last night. Did you mention this to his father?"

"No. It would have distressed him the more, without effecting any good. He is wretched enough. But time passes, and none is to be lost now. Will you go with me?"

I walked to the tavern with him; and we went into the bar together. Two or three men were at the counter, drinking.

"Is Mr. Green about this morning?" was asked by the person who had come in search of young Hammond.

"Haven't seen any thing of him."

"Is he in his room?"

"I don't know."

"Will you ascertain for me?"

"Certainly. Frank,"—and he spoke to the landlord's son, who was lounging on a settee,—"I wish you would see if Mr. Green is in his room."

"Go and see yourself. I'm not your waiter," was growled back, in an ill-natured voice.

"In a moment I'll ascertain for you," said Matthew, politely.

After waiting on some new customers, who were just entering, Matthew went up-stairs to obtain the desired information. As he left the bar-room, Frank got up and went behind the counter, where he mixed himself a glass of liquor, and drank it off, evidently with real enjoyment.

"Rather a dangerous business for one so young as you are," remarked the gentleman with whom I had come, as Frank stepped out of the bar, and passed near where we were standing. The only answer to this was an ill-natured frown, and an expression of face which said, almost as plainly as words, "It's none of your business."

"Not there," said Matthew, now coming in.

"Are you certain?"

"Yes, sir."

But there was a certain involuntary hesitation in the bar-keeper's manner, which led to a suspicion that his answer was not in accordance with the truth. We walked out together, conferring on the subject, and both concluded that his word was not to be relied upon.

"What is to be done?" was asked.

"Go to Green's room," I replied, "and knock at the door. If he is there, he may answer, not suspecting your errand."

"Show me the room."

I went up with him, and pointed out No. 11. He knocked lightly, but there came no sound from within. He repeated the knock; all was silent. Again and again he knocked, but there came back only a hollow reverberation.

"There's no one there," said he, returning to where I stood, and we walked down-stairs together. On the landing, as we reached the lower passage, we met Mrs. Slade. I had not, during this visit at Cedarville, stood face to face with her before. Oh! what a wreck she presented, with her pale, shrunken countenance, hollow, lustreless eyes, and bent, feeble body. I almost shuddered as I looked at her. What a haunting and sternly rebuking spectre she must have moved, daily, before the eyes of her husband.

"Have you noticed Mr. Green about this morning?" I asked.

"He hasn't come down from his room yet," she replied.

"Are you certain?" said my companion. "I knocked several times at the door just now, but received no answer."

"What do you want with him?" asked Mrs. Slade, fixing her eyes upon us.

"We are in search of Willy Hammond; and it has been suggested that he is with Green."

"Knock twice lightly, and then three times more firmly," said Mrs. Slade; and as she spoke, she glided past us with noiseless tread.

"Shall we go up together?"

I did not object, for, although I had no delegated right of intrusion, my feelings were so much excited in the case, that I went forward, scarcely reflecting on the propriety of so doing.

The signal knock found instant answer. The door was softly opened, and the unshaven face of Simon Slade presented itself.

"Mr. Jacobs!" he said, with surprise in his tones. "Do you wish to see me?"

"No, sir; I wish to see Mr. Green," and with a quick, firm pressure against the door, he pushed it wide open. The same party was there that I had seen on the night before,—Green, young Hammond, Judge Lyman, and Slade. On the table at which the three former were sitting, were cards, slips of paper, an ink-stand and pens, and a pile of bank-notes. On a side table, or, rather, butler's tray, were bottles, decanters, and glasses.

"Judge Lyman! Is it possible?" exclaimed Mr. Jacobs, the name of my companion: "I did not expect to find you here."

Green instantly swept his hands over the table to secure the money and bills it contained; but, ere he had accomplished his purpose, young Hammond grappled three or four narrow strips of paper, and hastily tore them into shreds.

"You're a cheating scoundrel!" cried Green, fiercely, thrusting his hand into his bosom as if to draw from thence a weapon; but, the words were scarcely uttered, ere Hammond sprung upon him with the fierceness of a tiger, bearing him down upon the floor. Both hands were already about the gambler's neck, and, ere the bewildered spectators could interfere, and drag him off, Green was purple in the face, and nearly strangled.

"Call me a cheating scoundrel!" said Hammond, foaming at the mouth, as he spoke,—"Me! whom you have followed like a thirsty bloodhound. Me! whom you have robbed, and cheated, and debased from the beginning! Oh! for a pistol to rid the earth of the blackest-hearted villain that walks its surface. Let me go, gentlemen! I have nothing left in the world to care for,—there is no consequence I fear. Let me do society one good service before I die!"

And, with one vigorous effort, he swept himself clear of the hands that were pinioning him, and sprung again upon the gambler with the fierce energy of a savage beast. By this time, Green had got his knife free from its sheath, and, as Hammond was closing upon him in his blind rage, plunged it into his side. Quick almost as lightning, the knife was withdrawn, and two more stabs inflicted ere we could seize and disarm the murderer. As we did so, Willy Hammond fell over with a deep groan, the blood flowing from his side.

In the terror and excitement that followed, Green rushed from the room. The doctor, who was instantly summoned, after carefully examining the wound, and the condition of the unhappy young man, gave it as his opinion that he was fatally injured.

Oh! the anguish of the father, who had quickly heard of the dreadful occurrence, when this announcement was made. I never saw such fearful agony in any human countenance. The calmest of all the anxious group was Willy himself. On his father's face his eyes were fixed as if by a kind of fascination.

"Are you in much pain, my poor boy!" sobbed the old man, stooping over him, until his long white hair mingled with the damp locks of the sufferer.

"Not much, father," was the whispered reply. "Don't speak of this to mother, yet. I'm afraid it will kill her."

What could the father answer? Nothing! And he was silent.

Slavery and Freedom

The visual representations of African Americans in the nineteenth century varied considerably over time according to the presuppositions of the beholder. The growing controversy over the institution of slavery fostered new images of slavery that first appeared before the public in the 1830s. With the advent of photography in 1839, stills and daguerreotypes of slaves as well as of free blacks were developed for personal and public use. Magazines such as *Harper's Weekly* illustrated their stories with wood engravings made from photographs. Next, several commercial forms of photography evolved for sale to a mass market. One was the stereo card, a format that offered the illusion of three dimensions when two side-by-side images were seen through a viewer and that remained popular from the 1850s into the twentieth century. Another was the carte-de-visite. Originally a way to produce small portraits cheaply, it soon led to the sale of pictures of celebrities on a large scale. About the size of the visiting card used in social life—hence their name—cartes-de-visite consisted of an image on a thin piece of photographic paper that was pasted to thicker cardboard backing; messages could be inscribed on the back. Most of these texts were simple advertisements for the photographic studios, but some were used as conveyors of propaganda to represent people's political, moral, or aesthetic passions, much like we print messages on buttons, T-shirts, and bumper stickers today. People collected cartes-de-visite most commonly for celebrity worship, as hobbyists buy and sell sports figure cards today.

Early photographic processes set certain limits and created specific conventions about the images produced in this era. Bulky equipment, the time required for preparation of a photosensitive surface, and lengthy exposure times gave nineteenth-century portraiture a solemn character. Movement produced a blur, so people had to set their faces into an expression that they could hold for about thirty seconds, which is actually a long time. Smiling and saying "cheese" belong to a much later era when cameras had become easier to use and the portrait had evolved into the "snapshot"—a picture captured in an instant. Most photographs from the nineteenth century convey seriousness, with their subjects, even unwilling ones, striving for a dignified image.

Plate 1. Unknown artist, "United States: The South," from *Malte-Brun's School Geography*, 1836.

Plate 3. Brady & Co., "Interior View of the Price, Birch & Co. Slave Dealership, Alexandria, Va.," 1865

The plates on these pages offer sharply divergent images of slavery. Children throughout the nation learned to view the American South from images like the woodcut shown in Plate 1, taken from a widely used school geography book of the 1830s. The photographs in Plates 2 and 3 were made near the end of the Civil War by men who sold their work in various formats to a mass market. Some of these photographers were interested in reproducing the photos as testimonials to the need for the end of slavery. Plate 3, made by a photographer working for Brady & Company, famous for its depictions of the Civil War, is half of a set of stereo viewing images. How did the image of slavery change from the schoolbook image of 1836 to the photographs from 1865?

Left: Plate 2. Andrew J. Russell, "Price, Birch & Co., Dealers in Slaves, Alexandria, Va.," 1865

Plate 4. J. T. Zealy, "Jack (Driver), a Slave in Columbia, S.C., '... from the Guinea Coast,'" 1850

Plate 5. J. T. Zealy, "Delia, a Slave in Columbia, S.C., '... Country Born of African Parents,'" 1850

All the daguerreotypes on these pages were made for private enterprises or for personal reasons, not as public documents. One of the leading scientists in the United States, Louis Agassiz, used the images in Plates 4 and 5, which he instructed a South Carolina daguerreotypist to make, to demonstrate an anthropological theory of the "separate creation" of the different races. Plate 6 presents the image of a slaveholding family; note the position of the slave nanny within the picture. Plates 7 and 8 are representations of free African Americans choosing to be photographed at their own expense, just as middle-class whites of the period did. Plate 8, in fact, was made by Augustus Washington, an African American daguerreotypist who owned a studio in Hartford, Connecticut. What do these faces tell you about slavery and freedom?

Plate 6. Thomas M. Easterly, "Southern Man, His Two Daughters, and Nanny," St. Louis, Mo., 1848

Plate 7. Thomas M. Easterly, "Robert J. Wilkinson, Successful Businessman," St. Louis, Mo., c. 1860

Plate 8. Augustus Washington, "Portrait of an Unidentified Woman," Hartford, Conn., c. 1850

Plates 9 through 12 are all public representations of slaves from Northern sources. The photos were designed to make a particular point, as were the daguerreotypes that supposedly demonstrated racial theories for Agassiz. Plates 9 and 10 are from *Harper's Weekly*, a journal with a strong antislavery bias. What message does Plate 9 communicate? How do Plates 10 and 11 connect to Harriet Jacob's experiences (Selection 31)? The message on the back of Plate 12, a carte-de-visite portrait of Gordon, a slave who entered Union territory in 1863 and became a Union soldier, reads:

> "The Peculiar Institution" Illustrated. Copy of a photograph taken from life at Baton Rouge, La. Ap. 2, '63; the lacerated body—months after the brutal flogging had been inflicted—having healed in the manner represented. The alleged offense was a trifling one. How noble and benignant the countenance of the victim!

What message about slavery was each of these images delivering? How did the public debate over slavery influence the way African Americans were visualized in these images?

Left: Plate 9. Unknown artist, "The Africans of the Slave Bark 'Wildfire,'" *Harper's Weekly*, June 2, 1860

Above right: Plate 10. Unknown artist, "Emancipated Slaves—White and Colored," *Harper's Weekly*, January 30, 1864

Right: Plate 11. Charles Payson, "Freedom's Banner. Charley, a Slave Boy of New Orleans," 1863

Far right: Plate 12. McPherson & Oliver, "'The Peculiar Institution.' Gordon, Escaped from Mississippi," 1863

EX-SLAVES.   INQUIRING STRANGER.   EX-DOMINANT RACE.
"we's gwine to draw." "Draw what!" "Draw rations, Sir."   "Well, how the war is over, what are you people going to do for a living!"   "I reckon we'll run—" "Run! After what!" "Of we'll gon for offices of some sort—Congress, Legislature, Cons or Notary Public, or any thing!"

Plates 13 through 15 are images from late in the Civil War and from the Reconstruction era. What effect have these events had on photographers' perceptions of African Americans? Have the images become more positive? More realistic? More suggestive of people directing their own lives? Overall, in what ways has a generation of conflict over the question of slavery changed the way African Americans are portrayed?

Above left: Plate 13. Timothy O'Sullivan, " 'Contrabands.' Fugitive Slaves Crossing the Rappahannock River during Grant's Second Manassas Campaign," 1864

Left: Plate 14. Unknown artist, "Solution of the Labor Question of the South," *Harper's Weekly*, December 2, 1865

Below: Plate 15. Unknown artist, "The Ebony Bridal—The Wedding Ceremony," *Frank Leslie's Popular Monthly*, October 1877

PART SIX

Civil War and Reconstruction

The Price of War

During the thirty years leading to the Civil War, the United States' early nationalism gave way to antebellum sectionalism. Settlers from the North and from the South resolutely proceeded westward, but in economic and societal matters the rapidly growing Southwest, including Alabama, Mississippi, and Louisiana, differed greatly from the new Northwest of Ohio, Illinois, and Wisconsin. Though both regions were dominated by small farms, the South also cultivated large plantations. Slaves worked vast acreage in the South, while free labor developed the North. One society produced a rural gentry, and the other cities, entrepreneurs, and lawyers; one grew conservative and fearful of change, while the other spawned liberal religions and reforms. Beneath the expansion was a national antipathy to the black race that made Southerners fearful of the abolition of slavery and committed Northerners to halting the expansion of slavery in their own society, a commitment that in much of the North coexisted with a moral abhorrence of the institution of slavery.

The readings in this section reflect the crises the nation faced at midcentury. Cornelia Hancock's description of the battlefield and the accounts by George Ward Nichols and Pauline DeCaradeuc Heyward of the devastation wrought by William Tecumseh Sherman's march through Georgia and the Carolinas graphically illustrate the impact of war. Ellen Leonard's account of the New York antidraft riot exposes the dilemma of conflicting visions of the goals of the war. Victory for the Union did not answer all the major questions posed by the antislavery debate and the war.

"I have vowed that if I should have children—the first ingredient of the first principle of their education shall be uncompromising hatred & contempt of the Yankee," declared a white Southerner toward the end of the Civil War. You will read a similar response from another white Southerner, Caleb Forshey. "I'm free as a frog!" exulted one former slave, reacting like Felix Haywood and other black Southerners to the prospect of a future without slavery. Great hopes or extreme bitterness, more common than the philosophical resignation found in the journal of slaveowner Henry Ravenel, promised a painful future for the South.

In the months following Lee's surrender to Grant at Appomattox, the South was a landscape of abandoned fields, twisted rails, burned buildings, white men hobbling about on one leg or dangling an empty sleeve, and former slaves exploring their new freedom or searching for food, shelter, and work. Plates 11–13 in the visual portfolio "Civil War and Reconstruction" (page 322) demonstrate the extent of the destruction in many places. Some things the war had settled: secession was impossible, slavery dead, and the South desperately impoverished, its prewar agricultural, slave-based economy gone with the wind. Other outcomes the region and the United States struggle with still. In particular, victory for the Union did not resolve questions about the role that African American men and women were to play in American life. The first attempts to secure rights for the former slaves, known as Reconstruction (1865–1876), produced the Thirteenth, Fourteenth, and Fifteenth Amendments to the Constitution, which provided the legal basis for a revolutionary change in their place in American life. But determined opposition from white Southerners largely defeated Reconstruction. Emerging from the era of Civil War and Reconstruction neither slaves nor fully free, African Americans faced a civil rights struggle that would consume the next century and beyond.

POINTS OF VIEW

Sherman's "March to the Sea" (1863–1865)

36

Marching with Sherman's Army

George Ward Nichols

In 1864 the Union organized for final victory. General Ulysses S. Grant, in overall command of the Union Army, led his troops against Robert E. Lee in the east while his trusted subordinate William Tecumseh Sherman pressed into Georgia from the west. As Grant made his slow, bloody way through Virginia, Sherman was changing the rules of war. Hacking their way through the lower South, slashing to bits much of what remained of the

George Ward Nichols, *The Story of the Great March from the Diary of a Staff Officer* (New York: Harper & Brothers, 1865).

rebel heartland, Sherman's men burned and looted their way through Georgia and the Carolinas.

George Ward Nichols's The Story of the Great March *became one of the most popular accounts of Sherman's campaign. Within a year of its publication in 1865, the book sold sixty thousand copies, and it was reprinted in European newspapers. An aide-de-camp on the general's personal staff, Nichols depicted the public side of Sherman as he met with various groups—his field staff, his soldiers, and freed slaves. Nichols described as well Sherman's methods of warfare and the character of his famous "March to the Sea."*

Nichols (1831–1885), who had been active in the antislavery struggles in Kansas in the 1850s, settled in Cincinnati after the war and became a leading figure in developing that city's museum, art school, and orchestra.

BEFORE YOU READ

1. What did Nichols think of General Sherman and his strategy?
2. Why did the Union Army destroy Southern land and property?
3. What was Nichols's opinion of the Southerners he encountered along the way?
4. How intense was the fighting during the march? How would you generally characterize it?

PREPARATIONS FOR THE SEAWARD MARCH— THE BURNING OF ATLANTA

General Sherman at once made preparations to abandon all the posts south of Dalton [Georgia]. From Gaylesville and Rome he issued his orders concerning the new movement. The sick and wounded, noncombatants, the machinery, extra baggage, tents, wagons, artillery, ammunition stores, every person and every thing not needed in the future campaigns, were sent back to Chattanooga. The army was stripped for fighting and marching.

Let us for a moment look at General Sherman as he appeared at Gaylesville, seated upon a camp-stool in front of his tent, with a map of the United States spread upon his knees. . . . General Sherman's finger runs swiftly down the map until it reaches Atlanta; then, with unerring accuracy, it follows the general direction to be taken by the right and left wings, until a halt is made at Milledgeville. "From here," the general says, "we have several alternatives; I am sure we can go to Savannah, or open communication with the sea somewhere in that direction." After studying the map a while, tracing upon the tangled maze of streams and towns a line from Savannah north and east, at Columbia, South Carolina, General Sherman looks up at General Howard with the remark, "Howard, I believe we can go there without any serious difficulty. If we can cross the Salkahatchie, we can capture Columbia. From Columbia"— passing his finger quickly over rivers, swamps, and cities to Goldsboro, North Carolina—"that point is a few days' march through a rich country. When we reach that important railroad junction—when I once plant this army at

Goldsboro—Lee must leave Virginia, or he will be defeated beyond hope of recovery. We can make this march, for General Grant assures me that Lee can not get away from Richmond without his knowledge, nor without serious loss to his army."

To those who gazed upon the map, and measured the great distance to be traversed, from this quiet village away up in the mountains of Northern Alabama down to the sea, and thence hundreds of miles through a strange and impassable country away to the south again, and over wide rivers and treacherous bogs, the whole scheme, in the hands of any man but he who conceived it, seemed weird, fatal, impossible. But it was at that moment in process of operation. General Sherman at once communicated the first part of his plan to General Grant, subsequently receiving his hearty approval, with entire freedom to act as he should deem best. The army was at once set in motion; the numerous threads spreading over a wide field of operations were gathered up; out of confusion came exquisite order. Detachments guarding various dépôts were sent to their commands, outposts were withdrawn, the cavalry were concentrated in one division, under the lead of a gallant soldier. Compact, confident, and cheerful, this well-appointed host, guided by that master mind, moved grandly on to the fulfillment of its high mission. The field of operations now entered upon belonged, as has been said, to the genius of strategy. Those who have written of this campaign always date its commencement as from Atlanta. Inasmuch as we trod upon hitherto unconquered soil when we went out from Atlanta, this statement is true; but the march really began at Rome and Kingston, and it is from this point that we take up the diary of events which occurred within the experience and knowledge of the writer.

November 13th.—Yesterday the last train of cars whirled rapidly past the troops moving south, speeding over bridges and into the woods as if they feared they might be left helpless in the deserted land. At Cartersville the last communications with the North were severed with the telegraph wire. It bore the message to General Thomas, "All is well." And so we have cut adrift from our base of operations, from our line of communications, launching out into uncertainty at the best, on a journey whose projected end only the General in command knows. Its real fate and destination he does not know, since that rests with the goodness of God and the brave hearts and strong limbs of our soldiers. The history of war bears no similar example, except that of Cortés burning his ships. It is a bold, hazardous undertaking. There is no backward step possible here. Thirty days' rations and a new base: that time and those supplies will be exhausted in the most rapid march ere we can arrive at the nearest sea-coast; arrived there, what then? I never heard that manna[1] grew on the sand-beaches or in the marshes, though we are sure that we can obtain forage on our way; and I have reason to know that General Sherman is in the highest degree sanguine and cheerful—sure even of success.

As for the soldiers, they do not stop to ask questions. Sherman says "Come," and that is the entire vocabulary to them. A most cheerful feature of

---

1. **manna:** food that, according to the Bible, was miraculously supplied to the Israelites during their escape from Egypt.

the situation is the fact that the men are healthful and jolly as men can be; hoping for the best, willing to dare the worst.

Behind us we leave a track of smoke and flame. Half of Marietta was burned up—not by orders, however; for the command is that proper details shall be made to destroy all property which can ever be of use to the Rebel armies. Stragglers will get into these places, and dwelling-houses are leveled to the ground. In nearly all cases these are the deserted habitations formerly owned by Rebels who are now refugees.

Yesterday, as some of our men were marching toward the Chattahoochee River, they saw in the distance pillars of smoke rising along its banks—the bridges were in flames. Said one, hitching his musket on his shoulder in a free and easy way: "I say, Charley, I believe Sherman has set the river on fire." "Reckon not," replied the other, with the same indifference; "if he has, it's all right." And so they pass along; obeying orders, not knowing what is before them, but believing in their leader.

From Kingston to Atlanta the rails have been taken up on the road, fires built about them, and the iron twisted into all sorts of curves; thus they are left, never to be straightened again. The Rebel inhabitants are in agony of wonder at all this queer manœuvring. It appears as if we intended evacuating Atlanta; but our troops are taking the wrong direction for the hopes and purposes of these people.

Atlanta is entirely deserted by human beings, excepting a few soldiers here and there. The houses are vacant; there is no trade or traffic of any kind; the streets are empty. Beautiful roses bloom in the gardens of fine houses, but a terrible stillness and solitude cover all, depressing the hearts even of those who are glad to destroy it. In the peaceful homes at the North there can be no conception how these people have suffered for their crimes.

Atlanta, Night of the 15th November. A grand and awful spectacle is presented to the beholder in this beautiful city, now in flames. By order, the chief engineer has destroyed by powder and fire all the store-houses, dépôt buildings, and machine-shops. The heaven is one expanse of lurid fire; the air is filled with flying, burning cinders; buildings covering two hundred acres are in ruins or in flames; every instant there is the sharp detonation or the smothered booming sound of exploding shells and powder concealed in the buildings, and then the sparks and flame shoot away up into the black and red roof, scattering cinders far and wide.

These are the machine-shops where have been forged and cast the Rebel cannon, shot and shell that have carried death to many a brave defender of our nation's honor. These warehouses have been the receptacle of munitions of war, stored to be used for our destruction. The city, which, next to Richmond, has furnished more material for prosecuting the war than any other in the South, exists no more as a means for injury to be used by the enemies of the Union.

A brigade of Massachusetts soldiers are the only troops now left in the town: they will be the last to leave it. To-night I heard the really fine band of the Thirty-third Massachusetts playing "John Brown's soul goes marching on," by the light of the burning buildings. I have never heard that noble anthem when it was so grand, so solemn, so inspiring.

News came from General Howard that the advance of the 17th Corps had arrived, at nine o'clock that morning, at a point thirteen miles from Cheraw, and had found the enemy intrenched in their front. It was said that Beauregard, Johnston, Hardee, and Hampton, with the garrisons of Charleston, Wilmington, and other points, were in Cheraw, and that a great battle was probable. The Rebels had certainly gathered an array of talent, in the way of generals, enough to appal this little army! The presence of all these men and any large force is doubtless an exaggeration, although there can be no question but the delays of the last few days have given the enemy an intimation of our plans, which they have improved by guarding the important outlet at Cheraw.

We were inclined to believe that the Rebels, not liking our society, would not interfere with our movements; indeed, that they would assist our passage through the country. The care with which they have laid in plentiful supplies of corn, fodder, hams, beef on the hoof, and other supplies, would have indicated this. Again, our infantry have hardly seen a Rebel soldier since we left Columbia until this morning. Our route from the Catawba crossed several creeks where there were valuable bridges uninjured, the destruction of any one of which would have delayed our column a day or more. Certainly we had every reason to suppose that the Rebels wished us a good riddance, and offered no objections to our speedy passage to the sea, or wherever we chose to go. Only one other hypothesis remained, and the presence of an enemy in our front to-night is a cogent argument in its favor. It is that the Rebel leaders did not divine the real movement until the last moment, and are now throwing obstacles in the way of our passage over the Pedee. We estimate that, without assistance from Virginia, they can not concentrate more than twenty-five thousand men in our front, and we will undertake to start that force in two or three days. Within that time we shall have brought up all our troops, and it will go hard with the Rebels, but we will have a pontoon floating quietly from either bank of the Pedee. Of course the hope of saving the bridge at Cheraw must be abandoned, and we must depend upon other resources.

Although for the last three days we have not seen the sun, and the rain has fallen now and then, the left wing has made some fine marches. The 14th Corps yesterday traveled over eighteen miles of the road which had already been used by the 20th Corps, and to-day the 20th Corps has marched twenty-one miles since daylight. Fortunately the route has led along the high ridges and through the pine barrens, where the soil is sandy, and better for the light fall of rain. Thus we were able to reach this place early in the afternoon, driving before us, at a good marching pace, Butler's, or rather Hampton's cavalry, who opposed the advance.

During the skirmishing, one of our men, a forager, was slightly wounded; but the most serious accident of the day occurred to a negro woman in a house where the Rebels had taken cover. When I saw this woman, who would not have been selected as the best type of South Carolina female beauty, the blood was streaming over her neck and bosom from a wound in the lobe of her ear, which the bullet had just clipped and passed by.

"What was it that struck you, aunty?" I asked.

"Lor bress me, massa, I dun know; I just fell right down."

"Didn't you feel any thing, nor hear any sound?"

"Yes, now I 'member, I heerd a s-z-z-z-z-z, and den I just knock down. I drap on de groun'. I'se so glad I not dead, for if I died den de Bad Man would git me, cos I dance lately a heap."

To-day is the first time within a week when I have seen a household where the women are neatly dressed and the children cleanly. The people who have inhabited the houses along the roads for fifty miles behind us are among the most degraded specimens of humanity I have ever seen. Many of the families I now refer to do not belong to the class known as the "poor whites" of the South, for these are large landowners, and holders of from ten to forty slaves.

The peasantry of France are uneducated, but they are usually cleanly in their habits. The serfs of Russia are ignorant, but they are semi-barbarous, and have, until lately, been slaves. A large proportion of the working classes in England are debased, but they work. But the people I have seen and talked to for several days past are not only disgustingly filthy in their houses and their persons, but are so provokingly lazy, or "shiftless," as Mrs. Stowe[2] has it, that they appear more like corpses recalled to a momentary existence than live human beings, and I have felt like applying a galvanic battery to see if they could be made to move. Even the inroads of our foragers do not start them into life; they loll about like sloths, and barely find energy enough to utter a whining lamentation that they will starve.

During this campaign I have seen terrible instances of the horrors of slavery. I have seen men and women as white as the purest type of the Anglo-Saxon race in our army, who had been bought and sold like animals. I have looked upon the mutilated forms of black men who had suffered torture at the caprice of their cruel masters, and I have heard tales of woe too horrible for belief; but in all these cases I have never been so impressed with the degrading, demoralizing influence of this curse of slavery as in the presence of these South Carolinians. The higher classes represent the scum, and the lower the dregs of civilization. They are South Carolinians, not Americans.

The clean people whom I met this afternoon were a refreshing spectacle. Several of the young ladies—the men ran away at our approach—were attending school at this place, where a seminary has been situated for many years. One of these girls, in reply to my question why she had not gone to her home, forty miles down the river, answered:

"What is the use? Your people go every where; you overrun the state; and I am as well off here as at my father's house."

I acknowledged the wisdom of her action, for there is no doubting the fact that our presence is quite sensibly felt.

2. **Mrs. Stowe:** Harriet Beecher Stowe, author of *Uncle Tom's Cabin.*

I happened to be present this afternoon at one of those interviews which so often occur between General Sherman and the negroes. The conversation was piquant and interesting; not only characteristic of both parties, but the more significant because, on the part of the General, I believe it a fair expression of his feelings on the slavery question.

A party of ten or fifteen negroes had just found their way through the lines from Cheraw. Their owners had carried them from the vicinity of Columbia to the other side of the Pedee, with the mules and horses which they were running away from our army. The negroes had escaped, and were on their way back to find their families. A more ragged set of human beings could not have been found out of the slave states, or, perhaps, Italy. The negroes were of all ages, and had stopped in front of the General's tent, which was pitched a few feet back from the sidewalk of the main street.

Several officers of the army, among them General Slocum, were gathered round, interested in the scene. General Sherman said to them:

"Well, men, what can I do for you—where are you from?"

"We's just come from Cheraw. Massa took us wid him to carry mules and horses away from youins."

"You thought we would get them; did you wish us to get the mules?"

"Oh yes, massa, dat's what I wanted. We knowed youins cumin, and I wanted you to hav dem mules; but no use; dey heard dat youins on de road, and nuthin would stop 'em. Why, as we cum along, de cavalry run away from de Yanks as if dey fright to deth. Dey jumped into de river, and some of dem lost dere hosses. Dey frightened at de berry name ob Sherman."

Some one at this point said: "That is General Sherman who is talking to you."

"God bress me! Is you Mr. Sherman?"

"Yes, I am Mr. Sherman."

"Dat's him, su' nuff," said one.

"Is dat de grre-aat Mr. Sherman dat we'se heard ob so long?" said another.

"Why, dey so frightened at your berry name dat dey run right away," shouted a third.

"It is not me that they are afraid of," said the General; "the name of another man would have the same effect with them if he had this army. It is these soldiers that they run away from."

"Oh no," they all exclaimed, "it's de name ob Sherman, su'; and we hab wanted to see you so long while you trabbel all roun' jis whar you like to go. Dey said dat dey wanted to git you a little furder on, and den dey whip all your soldiers; but, God bress me! you keep cumin' and a cumin', an' dey allers git out."

"Dey mighty 'fraid ob you, sar; dey say you kill de colored men too," said an old man, who had not heretofore taken part in the conversation.

With much earnestness, General Sherman replied:

"Old man, and all of you, understand me. I desire that bad men should fear me, and the enemies of the government which we are all fighting for. Now we are your friends; you are now free ('Tank you, Massa Sherman,' was ejaculated by the group). You can go where you please; you can come with us or go home to your children. Wherever you go you are no longer slaves. You ought to be able to take care of yourselves. ('We is; we will.') You must earn your freedom, then you will be entitled to it, sure; you have a right to be all that you can be, but you must be industrious, and earn the right to be men. If you go back to your families, and I tell you again you can go with us if you wish, you must do the best you can. When you get a chance, go to Beaufort or Charleston, where you will have a little farm to work for yourselves."

The poor negroes were filled with gratitude and hope by these kind words, which the General uttered in the kindest manner, and they went away with thanks and blessings on their lips.

37

A Southern Woman's Wartime Journal
Pauline DeCaradeuc Heyward

The journal of Pauline DeCaradeuc Heyward (1843–1914) offers a spirited account of a slaveholding family's experience of Sherman's march. Union soldiers, in Heyward's account, were determined to penalize South Carolina, the original seat of secession, for starting the Civil War. That the DeCaradeuc women managed to limit the damage done to their plantation and property indicates that even angry Union troops approaching the end of a terrible war continued to pay some homage to the code requiring gentlemen to treat ladies courteously.

The war cost the DeCaradeuc family the lives of two sons as well as most of its wealth. After the war Pauline married Geurard Heyward. When he failed as a planter, Geurard, Pauline, and their growing family moved to Savannah, Georgia, where they modestly prospered and continued to enlarge their family. Until her death in 1914, Pauline maintained the standards of gentility required of a Southern wife and mother.

BEFORE YOU READ

1. What were the Union soldiers seeking at the Heyward plantation?
2. How did the DeCaradeuc women manage to keep possessions they valued and avoid sexual assault?
3. Why was Pauline DeCaradeuc Heyward so afraid for her father?

Mary D. Robertson, ed., *A Confederate Lady Comes of Age: The Journal of Pauline DeCaradeuc Heyward, 1863–1888* (Charleston: University of South Carolina Press, 1992), pp. 36–37, 65–69.

Feb. 14th, 1864

Carrie and I went over to Augusta yesterday, and really in spite of everything had a very amusing time. We bought several photographs of our most illustrious Gen's. I got Lee, Davis & Kirby Smith. John Cochran sent me word the other day that he had sent out to Richmond for Stonewall Jackson's for me, so that I'll have that too.

We visited Mr. Henry who is better, also Mrs. Foster, Mrs. Tubman & Mother's old friend, Mrs. Campbell. Then we tried to shop, but the only thing in the shape of a dress for myself that we saw, was a worsted stuff at $30.00 a yard.

I met Lieut. Col. Croft who stopped me & talked awhile on the street, he is most dreadfully, *agonizingly*, wounded in his right hand & looks very badly.

When we finished our business we sauntered round to the church yard & sat there 'till time to meet the train. When we reached the depot there was such a concourse of soldiers there that I begged an old lady who was going too, to let us remain with her. I was very uneasy as I never was in a crowd of men without a protector before, however, a young & handsome soldier came up & introduced himself, Major Beaufort of Va. and begged us to allow him to remain near us until the car was opened. When the doors were unlocked we got in & obtained good seats, some twenty-five ladies had to stand up & as many had to be left, & such crowds of soldiers!! An officer in front of us spread his blanket on the seat & begged us to keep it for him, but 'twas impossible & he couldn't even get in the car again. After a little while I heard a plaintive voice outside under the window, say: "Oh, Miss Pauline, ain't there any room in there for me?" I looked out & saw Col. Croft, of course, he couldn't get in our car; he asked me to look for his cousin in our car who was wounded & on crutches, but I couldn't even move, after talking a while he went into the conductor's car then I heard another voice say: "Miss Pauline, can't you get me a seat in front of you? I want to get in your car so much." What could I do? He was a very handsome Capt. I felt assured I knew him, his face & voice were perfectly familiar, but I could not remember his name, he conversed for awhile just like some old friend, seemed to know me well, but I don't yet remember who he is. Anyhow *he* too had to go off. Then our Va. Major came under the window to chat, & I gave him some cake I bought for the children, they would not allow soldiers to come in our car, without a lady; meanwhile a soldier on crutches stood near us looking sick & weak, he *stood* of course, & Carrie, noble as she always is rose & insisted on his taking her seat, but he would not hear of it, he then introduced himself, Captain Croft, the cousin, the Lieut. Col. asked me to look for, he remained with us the rest of the time & proved to be most agreeable.

After awhile we looked up & there was our kind Virginia Major standing by us, he pretended to the conductor that he had to see us out, & thus got into our car from which he did not again move, he is really quite charming & entertained us very nicely, two more Captains spoke to us & offered to assist us in any way, but our Va. friend didn't give them a chance, he saw us to the carriage at Johnston's & all but cried when we got off the car. I think somehow we will hear of him again, he was 'mazin kind & attentive to us, should like to return it.

May 23, 1864

I have no heart to keep this Journal or tell of the dreadful, fatal battles in Va. Oh my God! my heart is too heavy, I am entirely miserable. Many whom I know are killed & wounded. Robert Taft and Col. Shooter are killed. Capt. Barnwell killed. George Lalane wounded. Wise's Brigade was subjected to a fearful firing from the enemy at Druery's Bluff. I suppose John Cochran is wounded, from the moment I saw him I felt that his life would be given to this devouring war; and I am assured that he is dead or wounded, for I *feel it.*

Feb. 18th, 1865

The Yankees have come & gone. On the 10th Feb. they encamped at Johnstons. The whole of Kilpatrick's forces, they were turned on the country for forage, plunder, & provisions. The first we saw of them was about a dozen of them, dashing thro the gate shouting: "Here come the Yankees, look out now you d——d rebels." A moment after they were in the house, Mother & Grandmother met them at the door, but they didn't listen to a word they tried to say, but said, "Come give us your keys, where is your liquor? get your gold, get your silver, you old women, hurry yourselves, I say." I had a belt on under my dress, with my revolver, and a bag of bullets, caps & powder in my pocket, they rushed into the room, where all of us ladies were sitting, saying, "Give me your revolvers, d——d you, if we find them, you'd better look out, where are your pistols, we know you've got 'em." I felt it wouldn't do for them to find mine on me, infuriated as they were, so I took Tante's arm, hurried upstairs & threw the revolver between her sheets, hardly I had finished when the door burst open & the room was filled with them, they pulled the bed to pieces, of course.

We all went into the parlor, and by this time there were hundreds of them, in the house, upstairs, in the garret, in every chamber, under the house, in the yard, garden, &c., &c., some singing, shouting, whistling, and Oh, my God, *such cursing.* Both pianos were going at the same time, with axes they broke open every door, drawer, trunk that was locked, smashed a large French mirror, broke pieces of furniture, and flung every piece of clothing, that they didn't carry off, all over the floors, they got some of Fa.'s prettiest paintings and broke bottles of catsup over them, they carried off every piece of silver, every knife, jewel, & particle of possessions in the house & negro houses, every paper, letter, receipt, &c., they flung to the winds, all the roads are strewn with them. Mother and G. M. went among them like brave women, trying to save some few things in vain, at one time a horrid looking ruffian came into the parlor, seeing only women there, he entered shut both doors, & said in an undertone, "You cursed rebels, now empty your pockets." Ah, mon Dieu, mine had my bag of ammunition in it, I rose, & while he was grabbing Miss Hessie's pocket book, I dropped my bag in a corner & flung an old bonnet over it, in my pocket, he found my watch. "Ah," said he, "This is a pretty little watch, now where is the key, & does it go good?" & the villain put his hand on my shoulder, I rose & stood before him, with all possible dignity & he turned away. Then after taking Tante's watch and everybody's money, he walked up to Mother, grinding his teeth & looking her full in the face, said: "Now, you've just *got* to tell me where your gold & silver is buried, I know you've got it, and if you know what's good for yourself & all in this room, you'll tell me where it is." "I have no gold, my silver you have all taken with every other valuable in the house." "That's a d——d lie, now I'll burn your house this minute, if you don't tell me." "I have nothing more to tell, do you think I'd tell a lie?" "I don't know." Then he walked up & down the room cursing, swearing, threatening, & spitting on every side, then finding he could do nothing with us, took Solomon out, put a pistol to his head, saying he would blow his brains out, if he didn't tell. Solomon is as true to us as steel, so are they all, all faithful & friends to us.

About sundown, on the 10th they left off coming here. I then went to ascertain the fate of my revolver, there it was still rolled in the sheets, thrown on the floor with the chaos of clothing. I of course, sent it off. They took every blanket & pillow case & towel, the cases for bags to carry off what they took, & towels for handkerchiefs, they even made the servants get our chemises & tear them up into pocket handkerchiefs for them.

Well the next day, which was Saturday, they came just the same, hundreds of them, one of our villianous neighbors told them that our boys fired the first gun on Sumter, so they said this house was the root of the rebellion & burn it they would, but our good servants & Mother and G. Mother entreated in such a way that they desisted, then they said that they had to arrest and shoot every influential citizen in S.C., every mover of secession, & from the accumulation of wealth, the quantities of food, books & clothes in this house, the finest they had seen in these parts, that they knew Father was wealthy, literary, & influential, & they had heard enough of him, to make an example of him & catch him they would. We have no less than five large libraries of refugees, here, besides our own, & the accumulated clothing & valuables of four separate families, no wonder they found us so rich, & came here so often.

As to provisions, 'tis true, few was so bountifully supplied. We had 7 barrels of fine flour, 300 bushels of corn, 1 barrel & 1 box of nice sugar, &c., &c.

Out of that we have 15 bushels corn, 1 bag flour, 3 hams, they took all the wine & brandy. They had scouts out in every direction looking for Father. Thus passed Saturday, on Sunday morning they burned Uncle & Daughter's home *everything* & every building on their place, even the well, they are here with nothing but their clothes on, in the world, they searched uncle's person. After breakfast, 500 Yankees came here in a body & dispersed over the house & place, carrying off everything they could, they attempted to get into Aiken Saturday morning but were repulsed by Wheeler.

Well, on Saturday night, Father who was encamped in the woods, with the mules, horses & some provisions & one or two of the servants, sent us word that he could not evade the scouts longer & he was going to give himself up to K.ptr. [Gen. Kilpatrick] & demand protection, as a Frenchman, for himself & household, I went down in the swamp to see him & when half way between there & the house saw four Yankees entering the gate, my goodness didn't I run, it was a regular tug between them & me to see who could get to the house first, but I beat in safety, but I never ran so in my life.

Well, after Father went, we were filled with anxiety about him, knowing their threats about him, Oh, we were so frightened for him, when the door opened & a Yankee rushed in with a lit candle, he looked all 'round then ran into every room in the house to look for "that d——d rebel," he then went out saying he'd return during the night to fire the house,—pleasant intelligence— then he & two others asked the servants if there were any young ladies in the house, how old they were & where they slept, during all this I had on blue spectacles & my face muffled up, Carrie too.

When I heard of their questions to the servants I thought that burning the house was nothing; I was almost frantic, I sat up in a corner, without moving or closing my eyes once the whole night. My God! I suffered agony, I trembled *unceasingly* till morning; about eleven o'clock that night, two men went up the back stairs, we heard them walking over head, they went into the room over the parlour (we were in the parlour, of course, all together) and went to bed there, they stayed there all night.

Well, none of us undressed or went to bed for six nights. On Sunday, Mother & Grandmother determined to go out to the camp, to Kilpatrick & ask for protection & for Father's release, they went in the cart with a little blind mule, the only animal they left us, with pieces of yarn for bridle, as they carried off all the harness, &c., during their absence, quantities of Yankees came here, and walked in *every direction* sticking the ground with their swords, feeling for buried things. Wherever the ground was soft they dug, they found all Tante's silver, bonds & jewels, a quantity of provisions,—barrel of wine, one of china, a box of Confederate money & bonds, &c.

Fortunately, the bulk of our silver was sent off.

Mother returned from the camp, bringing Father and William whom they had captured.

Monday morning only a few Yankees came, about ten, I suppose, and then the entire force fell back, not wishing to engage our troops, the R.R., of course, cut & we knew nothing more of them.

Our own soldiers have been coming here constantly, these last two or three days. My goodness, how different they are to the Yankees, the commonest one is as gentle & respectful to us as can be.

Sherman was at Johnstons on Sunday. One dashing looking young officer entered the room where we were sitting on Saturday & Mother said, "Are you an officer, sir?" "I am Madam." "Then, sir, I entreat your protection for my helpless household." "I will, Madam, God knows I am disgusted with all this." He left the room, *we hoped*, to try to check the pillage, he walked into Miss Hessie's room, broke open her trunk and began stuffing his pockets.

They threw a good many shells at this house.

FOR CRITICAL THINKING

1. Was Sherman's policy of total war against the Confederacy justified? Compare the picture of the South's circumstances presented by George Ward Nichols with that presented by Pauline DeCaradeuc Heyward, and argue for one side or the other.

2. How sympathetic are you to Heyward's moral outrage over the treatment her household received from Union soldiers? Should the soldiers have left the family's property alone? Argue for either side.

3. How effectively does George H. Barnard, in Plates 8 through 13 of the visual portfolio "Civil War and Reconstruction" (page 322), capture the scenes and emotions presented in the writings of Nichols and Heyward?

38

Three Days of Terror

Ellen Leonard

*Rioting was an all too regular part of mid-nineteenth-century New York City life. Six-
teen major and many lesser riots erupted in the city between 1834 and 1874. Almost
any reason sufficed to bring out the clubs, guns, and paving stones: Protestants attacked
Catholics, Irish Catholics fought Irish Protestants, slavery-supporting mobs roughed up
abolitionists, partisans of one actor attacked the fans of another (in the infamous Astor
Place riot of 1849), rival fire companies and gangs started violence that simply spread.
Sometimes drunken brawls erupted into large-scale rioting with participants not quite
knowing the reason for their fighting. But mobs had made their feelings known this
way since the revolutionary era. In addition, municipal government was ineffective and
corrupt; the weak and unprofessional New York police often could not maintain order
without calling out the militia; alcohol was cheap, readily available, and habitually
drunk to excess; and vast numbers of new immigrants and unskilled laborers lived per-
petually on the edge of destitution. When the Civil War sharpened political conflicts
and war-induced inflation made the living conditions of the poor even worse than usual,
widespread rioting broke out in the great draft riot of 1863.*

*When the Civil War began, North and South fielded large armies of patriotic vol-
unteers, but as the war continued, both sides turned to conscription. Drafts were ineffective and demoralizing, although they did succeed in their main purpose of encouraging
more volunteers. Only about seven percent of those whose names were drawn in draft
lotteries actually served. Many simply refused or ran off to another district. And both
sides allowed those drafted to hire substitutes to fight in their place or to pay a fee of
$300 to avoid serving, arousing cries that the conflict was "a rich man's war, but a
poor man's fight." In fact, historians have found that draft districts regularly came up
with the money to exempt those who did not wish to serve or hired substitutes by offering bounties for enlistment so that roughly equal proportions of men in all classes served.*

*Still, the Union conscription law was vastly unpopular. The Democratic Party press
made the draft a major issue, fanning opposition particularly among urban Irish American populations who largely opposed the war and feared black competition for the unskilled
jobs that provided their meager livelihoods. One orator told a mass meeting in New York
City that "when the President called upon them to go and carry on a war for the nigger,
he would be d—— d if he believed they would go." As soon as actual conscription began
taking place in July 1863, rioting broke out in several cities. Most horrific was the one in
which Ellen Leonard found herself trapped from July 13 through 16 in New York City.*

Ellen Leonard, "Three Days of Terror," *Harper's New Monthly Magazine* 34 (January 1867):
pp. 225–33.

It remains, in fact, the worst riot in New York City history. Many of the federal troops usually stationed in the city were in Pennsylvania in pursuit of General Lee's retreating army after the battle of Gettysburg. Over one hundred people died, most of them rioters gunned down when troop reinforcements arrived to retake control of the streets. In addition to random looting and vandalism, the rioters lynched several blacks, burned down the Colored Orphan Asylum, and attacked Republican newspapers, the homes of prominent Republicans and abolitionists, and businesses that employed blacks. Ellen Leonard's article on the riot, published in 1867, offers a rare eyewitness account of an innocent visitor accidentally trapped in these dramatic and dangerous events.

BEFORE YOU READ

1. According to Ellen Leonard's account, what seem to have been the main motivators of the mob?
2. How much danger did the mob pose to the citizens of the city and to visitors like Ellen Leonard?
3. How did women behave during the riot? In what ways did they behave more assertively than demanded by the "separate spheres" ideology of the era?

THREE DAYS OF TERROR

On the tenth of July, 1863, my mother and myself arrived in the city of New York. We had set out on a grand tour of visitation. After vegetating year after year in a New England village, we had sallied forth in genuine country fashion to hunt up our kinsfolk in various parts of the land. We were in no hurry. We had the whole summer before us. . . . We hoped now to spend a few days quietly with my brother J., call on various friends and relatives, visit Central Park and a lion or so, shop a little, and move onward at our leisure.

But man proposes and Fate *disposes*, and nothing in New York turned out as we expected. Instead of visiting our friends and meandering leisurely about the city, we were caught in a mob and penned up in our first stopping-place. . . . The streets were dark, dirty, and crowded with ill-looking people. The whole city was enveloped in fog and gloom. The home regiments had gone to drive the rebels from Pennsylvania, and many hearts were trembling. The household which received us had its full share of anxiety. Its youngest member, a youth of seventeen, had gone with the volunteers, and other friends were in the Army of the Potomac. . . .

I [went] to Broadway. But even there I could see nothing attractive. Every thing looked hot, glaring, and artificial, and every body looked shabby, jaded, and care-worn. An overworked horse dropped dead in the street before me, and I was glad to take refuge for a time in the Astor Library.

Returning thence at mid-day I first saw signs of disturbance. A squad of policemen passed before me into Third Avenue, clerks were looking eagerly from the doors, and men whispering in knots all up and down the street; but I was too much a stranger to be certain that these appearances were unusual, though they annoyed me so much that I crossed at once to Second Avenue, along which I pursued my way peacefully, and once at home thought no more of it. We were indulging ourselves in siestas after our noonday lunch, when a great roaring suddenly burst upon our ears—a howling as of thousands of wild Indians let loose at once; and before we could look out or collect our thoughts at all the cry arose from every quarter, "The mob! the mob!" "The Irish have risen to resist the draft!"

In a second my head was out the window, and I saw it with my own eyes. We were on a cross-street between First and Second avenues. First Avenue was crowded as far as we could see it with thousands of infuriated creatures, yelling, screaming, and swearing in the most frantic manner; while crowds of women, equally ferocious, were leaning from every door and window, swinging aprons and handkerchiefs, and cheering and urging them onward. The rush and roar grew every moment more terrific. Up came fresh hordes faster and more furious; bareheaded men, with red, swollen faces, brandishing sticks and clubs, or carrying heavy poles and beams; and boys, women, and children hurrying on and joining with them in this mad chase up the avenue like a company of raging fiends. In the hurry and tumult it was impossible to distinguish individuals, but all seemed possessed alike with savage hate and fury. The most dreadful rumors flew through the street, and we heard from various sources the events of the morning. The draft had been resisted, buildings burned, twenty policemen killed, and the remainder utterly routed and discomfited; the soldiers were absent, and the mob triumphant and increasing in numbers and violence every moment.

Our neighborhood was in the greatest excitement. The whole population turned out at once, gazing with terror and consternation on the living stream passing before them, surging in countless numbers through the avenue, and hurrying up town to join those already in action. Fresh yells and shouts announced the union of forces, and bursting flames their accelerated strength and fury. The armory on Twenty-second Street was broken open, sacked, and fired, and the smoke and flames rolled up directly behind us. . . .

Bells were tolling in every quarter. The rioters were still howling in Twenty-second Street, and driving the firemen from the burning armory. The building fell and the flames sunk, and then darkness came all at once and shut out every thing. We gathered gloomily around my brother in the back-parlor. An evening paper was procured, but brought no comfort. It only showed more clearly the nature and extent of this fearful outbreak. It only told us that the whole city was as helpless and anxious as ourselves. Many were in far greater danger, for obscurity is sometimes safety; but the black, lowering night, and the disabled condition of our only male protector, oppressed us heavily. Our neighborhood was all alive. Men tramped incessantly through the street, and women chatted and scolded in the windows; children cried and cats squalled; a crazy man in the rear raved fiercely for Jeff Davis and the Southern Confederacy; but over every other sound every few moments the bells rang out the alarm of some new fire. Some were very near; some at a distance. . . .

As the clocks struck twelve a great shout startled me, and a light flamed right up before me. A huge bonfire had been kindled in the middle of the street not far below us. Wild forms were dancing about it, and piling on fresh fuel. Great logs and beams and other combustibles were dragged up and heaped upon it. Sleep, now, was of course impossible. From a seat in an upper window I saw it rise and fall, flame up and fade. . . .

[The next day] there was no milk, no ice to be had, and meat and bread were on the wane; and so I ventured out with my sister H. for supplies. We found our street full of people, excitement, and rumors. Men and boys ran past us with muskets in their hands. We heard that a fight was in progress above Twenty-second Street. The mob had seized a gun-factory and many muskets; but the police had driven them off and taken back part of their plunder. It was cheering to find that the police were still alive. . . . Men talked in low, excited tones, and seemed afraid of each other. The stores were mostly closed and business suspended. With difficulty we procured supplies of provisions and a newspaper; but percussion caps and ammunition were stoutly denied us. No one dared to admit that they kept any such articles lest the rioters should take them away by force. A friendly bookseller at last supplied us. He had been out in disguise, he said, and heard the rioters boasting among themselves. One said he had made a hundred dollars already, and now he had arms and meant to use them. All the shops on the avenue had been threatened. The mob were gathering in great force in our vicinity, and things looked every moment more threatening; so we hurried home as fast as possible, and I took my post again at the window.

New and strange sights met my eyes. Such multitudes of people every where; filling street and sidewalks, crowding all the doors and windows, the balconies and roofs of the houses. Many were merely spectators; some not far distant were *actors*. In the First Avenue the crowd was now very dense and clamorous. The liquor store on the corner was thronged with villainous-looking customers, and the women who had welcomed the mob on their first appearance were again talking loudly as if urging them on to action. "Die *at home!*" was the favorite watch-word which often reached our ears. Every thing indicated that a collision was approaching. We caught, after a time, a glimpse of soldiers, and heard the welcome rattle of musketry, distant at first, then nearer and nearer. The soldiers marched to and through Twenty-second Street and turned down First Avenue. The mob yelled and howled and stood their ground. Women from the roofs threw stones and brickbats upon the soldiers. Then came the volleys; the balls leaped out and the mob gave way at once and fled in every direction. A great crowd rushed through our street, hiding in every nook and corner. We closed doors and blinds, but still peeped out of the windows. The soldiers marched slowly back up the avenue, firing along the way; crossed over into Second Avenue, marched down opposite our street and fired again. Again the mob scattered, and scampered in droves through the street. Yet another volley, and balls came tearing down the centre of our street right before us, dashing along the pavements and carrying off frames from the trees. A boy on the sidewalk opposite was struck; he fell in a pool of blood, and was carried away to die. The streets were now cleared, the crowds had vanished, the soldiers withdrew, and the mob was quelled. For two hours peace and quiet prevailed. . . .

The papers brought no encouragement. Fearful deeds of atrocity were recorded. The mob were increasing in power and audacity, and the city was still paralyzed and panic-struck. The small military force available could only protect a few important positions, leaving the greater part defenseless. Our inflammable neighborhood was wholly at the mercy of the mob. . . .

Scarcely had my head touched the pillow when a new alarm of fire sounded. Lights streamed through the door of my room and illumined the houses opposite. "Another fire in Twenty-second Street!" was the cry. The police station had been set on fire, and volumes of smoke and flame were rising again very near us. From the rear windows we saw it all with the utmost distinctness; heard the roaring and crackling, and felt the heat of the flames. Soon they wrapped the house and caught the adjacent fire-tower, whose bell was clamoring even now for aid. The mob yelled with delight, and drove off the eager firemen. The flames soon wreathed the tower and rose in majestic columns. The whole neighborhood was flooded with light. . . . We heard [the mob] hurrying on to the gas-works, leaving the waning fires at last to the firemen. We could hear them pounding and shaking the gates, swearing at their inability to force them, and then rushing off again for some easier prey.

The fires were now quite subdued, and we ventured to return to our several rooms. It was past midnight, but the city was still wide awake. The streets were thronged, and the opposite houses were all open and brilliantly lighted. They belonged to the better class of tenement houses; and their occupants, though not themselves rioters, so far sympathized with them as evidently to feel no fear of them. Many were chatting at this time about the doors and windows with a careless merriment which I could not but envy. I gave a parting look up and down the street, and again sought my pillow . . . when a sudden rush and scream brought me again in an instant to my window. There was a spring and a chase, and then such piercing, thrilling cries as words can not describe. I could see nothing. Not a person was in sight; but from the vicinity of that wretched liquor store I distinctly heard dreadful cries, and caught these broken words: "Oh, brothers! brothers! Save me! save me!"

Another day had come, Wednesday, July 15th. . . . The city was not all burned down, we found. The newspapers were still alive, and insisting that more troops were on hand and the mob checked; but we saw no signs of it. The morning indeed passed more quietly. The rioters were resting from the labors of the night; but business was not resumed, and swarms of idle men still hung about the streets and stores. No cars were running in the avenues, no carts in the streets. No milkmen came, and no meatmen, and not a soldier or policeman showed his head. . . .

As night approached we heard drums beating, and gangs of rioters marched up their favorite avenue. . . . Then some one shouted, "They are coming!" and a small band of soldiers appeared marching up our street. The mob seemed to swell into vast dimensions, and densely filled the whole street before them. Hundreds hurried out on the house-tops, tore up brickbats, and hurled them with savage howls at the approaching soldiers. Shots were fired from secret ambushes, and soldiers fell before they had fired. Then they charged bravely into the mob, but their force was wholly inadequate. One small howitzer and a company of extemporized militia could do little against those raging thousands.

A fierce conflict raged before our eyes. With breathless interest we watched them from door and windows. We feared the soldiers would be swallowed up and annihilated. Some now appeared in sight with a wounded officer and several wounded men, looking from side to side for shelter. Their eyes met ours with mute appeal. There was no time to be lost; the mob might any moment be upon them. There was a moment's consultation, a hasty reference to J., an unhesitating response: "Yes, by all means;" we beckoned them in, and in they came. Doors and windows were at once closed, and the house became a hospital, and seemed filled with armed men. The wounded men were carried into my brother's room; the Colonel was laid on the bed, and the others propped up with pillows. There were a few moments of great commotion and confusion. We flew for fans, ice water, and bandages. Some of the soldiers went out into the fight again, and some remained with the wounded. A surgeon, who had volunteered as a private under his old commander, dressed the wounds of the sufferers. The Colonel was severely wounded in the thigh by a slug made of a piece of lead pipe, producing a compound fracture. The wounds of two others, though less dangerous, were severe and painful.

Twilight was now upon us, and night rapidly approaching. The soldiers had been forced to retreat, leaving the mob in great force and fury. We heard them shouting and raving on the corner, and knew that we were in great danger. Already they were clamoring for the wounded soldiers who had escaped them. We thought of Colonel O'Brien's fate, and could not suppress the thought that our own house might be made the scene of a like tragedy. Could we defend ourselves if attacked? A hurried consultation was held. We had arms and ammunition, and, including J. and the slightly wounded soldiers, half a dozen men able and willing to use them. But we could not "man our lines." We were open to attack at once from the front and rear, the roof, the front basement, and the balcony above it. We might, indeed, retreat to the upper stories, barricade the stairway, and hold it against all the assailants that could crowd into the hall. But if they chose to fire the house below we could not prevent it, and then there would be no escape either for our wounded or ourselves.

The Colonel promptly decided the question; resistance was hopeless, could only make the case worse, and must not be attempted. Not only so, but all signs of the presence of soldiers must be removed. Arms, military apparel, and bloody clothing were accordingly concealed. The Colonel was conveyed to the cellar and placed on a mattress. The young soldier, next to him most severely wounded, was assisted up to the rear apartment on the upper floor and placed in charge of my mother and myself. The soldiers who had remained were then ordered to make their escape from the house as they best could, and to hasten to head-quarters with an urgent request that a force might be sent to our relief. The surgeon was also requested to go, but would not listen to the suggestion. He had been regimental surgeon for two years under the Colonel, and insisted on remaining by his side, to take care of him, and to share his fate whatever it might be. He took his post, therefore, in the cellar, extemporizing as well as he could some scanty means of concealment for both from the boxes and bins which it contained. The remaining soldier, though severely wounded in the foot, could yet walk with pain and difficulty; and it was decided that, as soon as it should be safe or necessary, he should try the chances of escape through the scuttle and over the roofs of the adjoining buildings.

J., with his bandaged head and disabled arm, was liable to be taken for a wounded soldier, and his wife and her sister, Mrs. P——, insisted that he also should betake himself to the roof. He could render no material assistance if he remained; on the other hand, his presence might precipitate a scene of violence which would not be offered to ladies alone. They did not feel that they were personally in danger—so far there was no report that the lawless violence of the rioters had been directed against women; and if he could get away he might be the means of bringing speedier relief. Very reluctantly he yielded to these considerations, and prepared to accompany the wounded soldier. The mother of the household took refuge in her room on the second-floor. To her daughter-in-law, wife of an absent son, was assigned a post of observation at a front window. The two heroic women, H. and her sister, remained below to confront the mob.

Of all these arrangements, made mostly after we had assumed the charge assigned us, we at the time knew nothing. In utter darkness and desolation we sat above by the bedside of our young soldier, receiving his farewell messages for his mother and friends, and knowing not how soon he might be torn from us. There was no human power to help us in this extremity; we could only trust in Him "who stilleth the madness of the people." The suspense was terrible. In the rear, as we stole an occasional out-look through our closed blinds, we could see men here and there climbing the fences; they might be rioters breaking in, or residents breaking out. All was confusion and uncertainty. We knew not friends from foes.

In front the demonstrations were still more alarming. The rioters had taken possession of the street, stationed a guard on both avenues, and were chasing up and down for the soldiers. Then they were seen searching from house to house. . . . Then came a rush up the steps, and the bell rang violently. Not a sound was heard through the house. Again and yet again the bell rang, more and more furiously. Heart throbbed, nerves quivered, but no one stirred. Then came knocks, blows, kicks, threats, attempts to force the door. Come in they must and would; nothing could stay them.

Having gained for the retreating party all the time she could, Mrs. P—— at length unlocked the door, opened it, passed out, and closing it behind her, stood face to face with the mob, which crowded the steps and swarmed on the sidewalk and the adjacent street. What could she do? She knew that they would come in, that they would search the house, that they would find the men; but she was determined not to give them up without an effort to save them. Possibly, in parleying with them, she might at least calm somewhat the fury of the passion that swayed that howling mob; possibly in that brutal and maddened throng there might be a few with human hearts in their bosoms to which she might find a way, win them to her side, and enlist their aid in saving the lives of the intended victims. That was her only hope.

"What do you want?" she asked, while the air was yet ringing with the cry that came up from the crowd, "The soldiers! the soldiers!" "Bring out the soldiers!"

One who stood near and seemed to be a leader replied, "There were two soldiers went into this house, and we must have them. You must give them up."

"There *were* two that came in, but went out again. They are not here now."

She spoke in a low but perfectly clear and steady voice, that compelled attention, and the crowd hushed its ravings to catch her words.

"Let us see; if they are not here we will not harm you; but we must search the house."

"We can not let you in; there are only women here — some that are old and feeble, and the sight of such a crowd will frighten them to death."

"They shall not all come in," was the reply; and after some further parley it was agreed that half a dozen only should enter and make the search. The leader gave his orders, the door was opened, and the men detailed came in; but before it could be closed the mob surged up, pressed in, and filled the hall. Many of them were armed with the stolen carbines.

"Light the gas!" was the cry.

"My sister has gone for a light."

It came, and the parley was renewed. The leader again demanded the soldiers; insisted that they were there, and said it would be better for themselves if they would give them up. She persisted in the statement she had made.

"She is fooling us, and using up the time while they are getting away by the roof!" cried one, and pressing forward with his musket pointed at her, endeavored to pass her. Very deliberately she took hold of the muzzle and turned it aside, saying, "Don't do that. You know I am a woman, and it might frighten me."

The leader returned to the charge. "We know the men are here, and if you give them up to us you shall not be harmed. But if you do not, and we find them, you know what a mob is. I can not control them; your house will be burned over your heads, and I will not guarantee your lives for five minutes."

"You will not do that," was the reply. "We are not the kind of people whose houses you wish to burn. My only son works as you do, and perhaps in the same shop with some of you, for seventy cents a day."

She did not tell them that her amateur apprentice boy had left his place to go to Pennsylvania and fight their friends the rebels. A young man, whom she had noticed as one of the few of decent appearance, stepped to her side and whispered to her, advising her compliance with the demand, assuring her that the men could not be controlled. The tone more than the words indicated to her that she had made one friend; and she found another, in the same way, a moment later.

Meantime the leaders were consulting whether they should go first above or below, and decided on the latter. Stationing one man with a musket at the door, and one at the stairs, they proceeded, pioneered by H., first to the parlors, and then to the basement, thoroughly examining both. Most fortunately the sentinels were the two young men in whom Mrs. P—— felt she had found friends, and she was not slow to improve the opportunity to deepen the impression she had made. But now the crowd outside, thundering at the basement door, burst in the panels, and forcing it open, with terrible oaths and threats rushed in and filled the lower hall. Part joined the searching party, and some hurried up the first-floor. One, crowding past the sentinel, was striding up the stairs. We heard his call to his comrades, "Come on up stairs!" and our hearts sunk within us. But the sentinel's stern command, enforced by his leveled piece, brought him back.

The main party, having ransacked the basement rooms, now turned to the cellar. In a moment a loud shout announced that they had found a victim. The surgeon was dragged up, forced out at the lower door, and delivered over to the crowd outside. A blow from a bludgeon or musket felled him to the earth, inflicting a terrible wound on the head. "Hang him, hang him!" "To the post at the Twenty-second Street corner!" were the cries as they hurried him off. The search within proceeded; a moment more and they had found the Colonel. A new and fiercer shout was sent up. An order from a leader thrilled through the hall, "Come down here some of yees wid yer muskets!"

At the first cry from the cellar Mrs. P—— sprung for the basement, intending to make her way at any hazard. A sentinel stood at the head of the stairway; a stalwart brute, reeking with filth and whisky. He seized her, with both arms about her waist, with a purpose of violence quite too evident. She struggled to free herself without raising an alarm, but in vain; then a sudden and piercing shriek, which rung through the house, made him for an instant relax his hold, and, wrenching herself away, she hurried back and sought the protection of the friendly sentinel.

"He will not let me pass; I must go down."

"You must not," he replied; "it is no place for you." And then he added, looking sternly at her, "You have deceived us. You said there was no one here, and there is."

"I would have done the same thing for you if you had been wounded. Look at me; do you not believe me?"

He did look, full in her eye, for an instant; then said: "Yes, I do believe it. You have done right, and I admire your spirit."

"But I must go down. Go with me."

"No; it is no place for you."

"Then go yourself, and save his life."

And turning over his charge to the sentinel at the door, he did go. Meantime the searching party, having found the Colonel, proceeded to question him. He said he was a citizen, accidentally wounded, and had been obliged to seek refuge there.

"Why did you hide, if you are a citizen?"

Because, he said, he was afraid he should be taken for a soldier. They would not believe, but still he insisted on his statement. Then the muskets were sent for, and four pieces leveled at his head, as he lay prostrate and helpless.

"Fire, then, if you will, on a wounded man and a citizen. I shall die, any how, for my wound is a mortal one. But before you fire I wish you would send for a priest."

"What, are you a Catholic?"

"Yes."

This staggered them; and while they were hesitating the sentinel joined the group, and as soon as he looked on the Colonel exclaimed: "I know that man. I used to go to school with him. He is no soldier."

This turned the scale. The leaders were satisfied, and decided to let him go. But before leaving him they rifled his pockets; and here he narrowly escaped falling into renewed danger. While the parley was in progress his fingers had been busily occupied in quietly and coolly removing from his pocket a quantity of bullets which he had forgotten, and which, if they had been found, would certainly have betrayed him.

Those of the mob who had remained above, disappointed of their prey, with oaths and execrations protested against the action of their leaders, and sent the ruffian at the head of the stairway down to see if it was all right. But the positive statements of the friendly sentinel, which Mrs. P—— had the satisfaction of hearing him rehearse, as the two met in the lower hall, disarmed even his suspicions, and the rest could do no otherwise than acquiesce. So well satisfied, indeed, were the leaders, and, as it is not unreasonable to suppose, so impressed with the resolute bearing of the two ladies, that they volunteered to station a guard before the door to prevent the annoyance of any further search. As they had found the two men who had been reported to them as having entered the house, it did not seem to occur to them that there might be still others concealed; and so they took their departure, leaving the upper stories unvisited.

The surgeon in the mean time had been no less fortunate. In the crowd which hurried him off to death there happened to be one or two returned soldiers who had served in the same regiment with him, and when he came where it was light recognized him. They insisted on saving him, and, raising a party in their favor, finally prevailed, and having rescued him escorted him in safety to his home. . . .

It was now, we thought, past midnight. We had no hope of relief, no thought or expectation but of struggling on alone hour after hour of distress and darkness; but as I was listening in my window to some unusually threatening demonstrations from the mob, I heard the distant clank of a horse's hoof on the pavement. Again and again it sounded, more and more distinctly; and then a measured tread reached my ears, the steady, resolute tramp of a trained and disciplined body. No music was ever half so beautiful! It might, it must be, our soldiers! Off I flew to spread the good news through the household, and back again to the window to hear the tramp nearer and fuller and stronger, and see a long line of muskets gleam out from the darkness, and a stalwart body of men stop at our door. "Halt!" was cried; and I rushed down stairs headlong, unlocked the door without waiting for orders, and with tears of joy and gratitude which every one can imagine and nobody describe, welcomed a band of radiant soldiers and policemen, and in the midst of them all who should appear but my brother, pale and exhausted, who had gotten off the house-top in some mysterious way and brought this gallant company to our rescue! . . .

[They are taken to the Central Police Station.]

All now was life and animation. Well-dressed citizens were hurrying to and fro. Stalwart soldiers lined the street and guarded the steps and entrance, through which we were conducted to an inner apartment, and with much state and ceremony presented to the chieftains of civic power. Three days' experience of anarchy had made us feel the blessedness of lawful restraint, and surely no body of men ever looked so beautiful as these executives of law and government. Such fresh, radiant, energetic, clear-headed, and strong-hearted leaders looked able to conquer all the rioters in the land. Every body was wide-awake, dispatches coming and going, messengers flying about in all directions. . . .

Sleep was of course still impossible. The exciting scenes of the night, and the incessant roar and rumble of Broadway, kept all awake; and at four o'clock loud cheers brought us to the window to see the glorious returning "Seventh" marshaled before us, and with all our hearts and voices we joined in the welcome which greeted them. A brighter morning dawned upon the city; other regiments had arrived in the night, and we knew that it was now safe. Broadway was busy and noisy. Business was resumed, and the mob much subdued, though still rampant in our old neighborhood. A reconnoissance showed that it was still unsafe to venture there. We passed the morning comparing notes and considering what to do with ourselves. My only desire was to quit the city—to beat a retreat as soon as possible. . . . And so at three o'clock on Thursday afternoon, just three days from our first glimpse of the rioters, we shook the dust of New York from our slippers, and, trunkless and bonnetless, sped up North River.

39

Healing Wounds

Cornelia Hancock

Of about two million federal troops that served in the Civil War, three hundred-sixty thousand died. Among the more than one million who served in the Confederate military, some two hundred-fifty thousand also perished. Only one in three of these died of battle wounds; the others succumbed to disease or accident. There were also about a half million wounded, many of them severely.

A wounded man had only a precarious chance for survival. Little was known about infection, and military surgeons performed operations without sanitary precautions. Soldiers contracted gangrene and other deadly infections. Though anesthetics were known, doctors did not always have them on hand, and major surgery often resulted in shock, followed by death. Long delays occurred when transporting casualties to medical aid stations or hospitals. Soldiers suffered as well from the mosquitos, lice, and biting flies that infested the battlefront and that spread diseases such as malaria and yellow fever. Poor diet also undermined health, although the less well supplied Confederate soldiers suffered from malnourishment to a far greater degree than Union troops.

Cornelia Hancock (1840–1927), from a New Jersey Quaker family, was one of thousands of women who worked to improve health care for the Union Army. In 1863, she volunteered to be a nurse, but Dorothea Dix, then Superintendent of Female Nurses, rejected her application, disapproving of nurses who were attractive or under thirty. Cornelia, twenty-three and pretty, simply traveled to Gettysburg, arriving on the third day of the battle and going right to work helping the wounded. Her account vividly renders the many horrors of Civil War battles. It also illuminates the reactions of friends at home to her decision to strike out on such an unladylike course.

BEFORE YOU READ

1. How does Cornelia Hancock respond to the suffering around her?

2. Why do people at home complain about what Hancock is doing? What is her response to them?

3. How does Hancock respond to escaped slaves? How does her response compare to that of those around her?

Henrietta Stratton Jaquette, ed., *South after Gettysburg: Letters of Cornelia Hancock, 1863–1868* (New York: Crowell, 1956), pp. 6–11, 17–19, 42–45, 58–60, 73–77, 91–94.

HANCOCK'S ACCOUNT OF HER
FIRST DAY AT GETTYSBURG

We arrived in the town of Gettysburg on the evening of July sixth, three days after the last day of battle. We were met by Dr. Horner, at whose house we stayed. Every barn, church, and building of any size in Gettysburg had been converted into a temporary hospital. We went the same evening to one of the churches, where I saw for the first time what war meant. Hundreds of desperately wounded men were stretched out on boards laid across the high-backed pews as closely as they could be packed together. The boards were covered with straw. Thus elevated, these poor sufferers' faces, white and drawn with pain, were almost on a level with my own. I seemed to stand breast-high in a sea of anguish. . . .

Learning that the wounded of the Third Division of the Second Corps, including the 12th Regiment of New Jersey, were in a Field Hospital about five miles outside of Gettysburg, we determined to go there early the next morning, expecting to find some familiar faces among the regiments of my native state. As we drew near our destination we began to realize that war has other horrors than the sufferings of the wounded or the desolation of the bereft. A sickening, overpowering, awful stench announced the presence of the unburied dead, on which the July sun was mercilessly shining, and at every step the air grew heavier and fouler, until it seemed to possess a palpable horrible density that could be seen and felt and cut with a knife. Not the presence of the dead bodies themselves, swollen and disfigured as they were, and lying in heaps on every side, was as awful to the spectator as that deadly, nauseating atmosphere which robbed the battlefield of its glory, the survivors of their victory, and the wounded of what little chance of life was left to them.

As we made our way to a little woods in which we were told was the Field Hospital we were seeking, the first sight that met our eyes was a collection of semi-conscious but still living human forms, all of whom had been shot through the head, and were considered hopeless. They were laid there to die and I hoped that they were indeed too near death to have consciousness. Yet many a groan came from them, and their limbs tossed and twitched. The few surgeons who were left in charge of the battlefield after the Union army had started in pursuit of Lee had begun their paralyzing task by sorting the dead from the dying, and the dying from those whose lives might be saved; hence the groups of prostrate, bleeding men laid together according to their wounds.

There was hardly a tent to be seen. Earth was the only available bed during those first hours after the battle. A long table stood in this woods and around it gathered a number of surgeons and attendants. This was the operating table, and for seven days it literally ran blood. A wagon stood near rapidly filling with amputated legs and arms; when wholly filled, this gruesome spectacle withdrew from sight and returned as soon as possible for another load. So appalling was the number of the wounded as yet unsuccored, so helpless seemed the few who were battling against tremendous odds to save life, and so overwhelming was the demand for any kind of aid that could be given quickly, that one's senses were benumbed by the awful responsibility that fell to the living. . . .

I need not say that every hour brought an improvement in the situation, that trains from the North came pouring into Gettysburg laden with doctors, nurses, hospital supplies, tents, and all kinds of food and utensils: but that *first* day of my arrival, the sixth of July, and the third day after the battle, was a time that taxed the ingenuity and fortitude of the living as sorely as if we had been a party of shipwrecked mariners thrown upon a desert island.

LETTERS

Gettysburg, Pa. July 7th, 1863

My Dear Cousin

I am very tired tonight; have been on the field all day — went to the 3rd Division 2nd Army Corps. I suppose there are about five hundred wounded belonging to it. They have one patch of woods devoted to each army corps for a hospital. I being interested in the 2nd, because Will [her brother] had been in it, got into one of its ambulances, and went out at eight this morning and came back at six this evening. There are no words in the English language to express the sufferings I witnessed today. The men lie on the ground; their clothes have been cut off them to dress their wounds; they are half naked, have nothing but hardtack to eat only as Sanitary Commissions, Christian Associations, and so forth give them. I was the first woman who reached the 2nd Corps after the three days fight at Gettysburg. I was in that Corps all day, not another woman within a half mile. Mrs. Harris was in first division of 2nd Corps. I was introduced to the surgeon of the post, went anywhere through the Corps, and received nothing but the greatest politeness from even the lowest private. . . . To give you some idea of the extent and numbers of the wounds, four surgeons, none of whom were idle fifteen minutes at a time, were busy all day amputating legs and arms. I gave to every man that had a leg or arm off a gill of wine, to every wounded in Third Division, one glass of lemonade, some bread and preserves and tobacco — as much as I am opposed to the latter, for they need it very much, they are so exhausted.

I feel very thankful that this was a successful battle; the spirit of the men is so high that many of the poor fellows said today, "What is an arm or leg to whipping Lee out of Penn." I would get on first rate if they would not ask me to write to their wives; *that* I cannot do without crying, which is not pleasant to either party. I do not mind the sight of blood, have seen limbs taken off and was not sick at all.

It is a very beautiful, rolling country here; under favorable circumstances I should think healthy, but now for five miles around, there is an awful smell of putrefaction. Women are needed here very badly, anyone who is willing to go to field hospitals, but nothing short of an order from Secretary Stanton or General Halleck will let you through the lines. Major General Schenk's order for us was not regarded as anything; if we had not met Miss Dix at Baltimore Depot, we should not have gotten through. It seems a strange taste but I am glad we did. We stay at Doctor Horner's house at night — direct letters care of Dr. Horner, Gettysburg, Pa. If you could mail me a newspaper, it would be a great satisfaction, as we do not get the news here and the soldiers are so anxious to hear; things will be different here in a short time.

Cornelia

3rd Division—2nd Army Corps Hospital
Gettysburg, Pa. July 26th [1863]—Sunday

My Dear Mother

Today is Sunday but there is no semblance of it here. It is now about five o'clock in the morning. Our hospital has been moved and our stores have given out. There is nothing to cook with, hence I have nothing to do, and therefore, have time to write.

. . . I have eight wall tents full of amputated men. The tents of the wounded I look right out on. It is a melancholy sight—but you have no idea how soon one gets used to it. Their screams of agony do not make as much impression on me now as the reading of this letter will on you. The most painful task we have to perform here is entertaining the friends who come from home and see their friends all mangled up. I do hate to see them. Soldiers take everything as it comes, but citizens are not inured. You will think it is a short time for me to get used to things, but it seems to me as if all my past life was a myth, and as if I had been away from home seventeen years.

. . . What I do here one would think would kill at home, but I am well and comfortable. When we get up early in the morning, our clothes are so wet that we could wring them. On they go, and by noon they are dry.

From thy affectionate daughter—
C. Hancock

Jan. 1864

Dear William [Cornelia's brother]

Where are the people who have been professing such strong abolition proclivity for the last thirty years? Certainly not in Washington laboring with these people whom they have been clamoring to have freed. They are freed now or at least many of them, and herded together in filthy huts, half clothed. And what is worse than all guarded over by persons who have not a proper sympathy for them. I have been in the Washington Contraband Hospital for the past two months. It is in close proximity to the Camp of Reception [where the patients first arrived]—and I have had ample opportunity to see these people, the persons in charge of them, and the whole mode of proceeding with them. Their wants are great and appeal in every way for aid from the North.

. . . Smallpox has raged here to a great extent but a separate hospital has been established for that now. The order now is to remove all contrabands south of the Potomac. It may be better there than here, but we remain under the same authority and let me state emphatically that nothing for the permanent advancement of these people can be effected until the whole matter is removed from the military authority and vested in a separate bureau whose sole object is the protection and elevation of these people.

. . . There is much charity being extended to our poor soldiers and I would note that any one should withhold one mite from them, but I maintain that persons living in their comfortable homes in the North should give liberally to those so sadly situated as these forlorn contrabands, as well as to the soldiers.

A national Sanitary Commission for the Relief of Colored Persons of this class would save lives and a great deal of suffering. The slaves generally get free when our army advances; they come into our lines several hundred at a time, follow the army for a while, then come into Washington, some probably having walked 50 miles. One woman carried one child in her arms and dragged two by her side. Judge of the condition of that woman when she arrives. Should not some comfortable quarters await her weary body?

Thy sister,
Cornelia H.

[In February 1864 Cornelia became a nurse with the Army of the Potomac, then headquartered near Brandy Station, Virginia.]

2nd Corps, 3rd Div. Hospital
Feb. 24th, 1864

My Dear Sister
　　. . . I hope the army will stand still forever. . . . If it is not enough to sicken one to hear of the condition in which the officers lead our good men into these small fights. Gen. Warren's orderly is sick in hospital here, he says that he will not go on the field when he is drunk and the day of the last fight he could not get out of his Quarters until 4 o'clock. Gen. Hays meanwhile went splashing around on his own hook. I do not care what anyone says, war is humbug. It is just put out to see how much suffering the privates can bear I guess. . . .

from thy sister, C. Hancock

3 Div. 2nd Corps Hospt.
Near Brandy St., March 1st [1864]

My Dear Sister
　　. . . A colored man is now having both limbs amputated from the effects of small pox. Dr. Dudley says he will try my Abolitionism taking care of him. I think I will stand the test. He is down on the coloreds but always does his duty by his patients and will by him for the reason that he is a patient. He would not suit thee the way he talks, but he is young and may change before he dies.

from thy sister
Cornelia Hancock

3rd Div. 2 Corps Hospital
March 25, 1864

My Dear Sister
　　. . . On Wednesday we received orders to send all the sick and wounded to Washington, along with the order came a snow storm, along with the snow

storm came an orderly countermanding the previous order, along with him came a splendid morning, along with it, came another orderly ordering to move on Thursday; and at 8 o'clock we had them all loaded and on stretchers, and proceeded with the long train from the three hospitals to Brandy station. There the platform was strewed full of helpless men wounded at Morton's Ford. How like Gettys[burg] it seemed to me. I had all our worst cases put in a pile, took a whiskey bottle, and sat down and helped the poor souls to live while they were loaded. Two mortal hours we sat in the sun and heard the locomotive hiss, the cars back and go ahead, then back, etc., etc., etc., just what always happens at depots. One of our nice wounded wanted to give me some greenbacks right in the hubbub. There were two women who stay at the station with hot tea, etc. They supplied all hands and retired. There I sat, I suppose five hundred men staring at me, but Dr. Miller and our own steward and hospital boys were with me and I did not care. By dint of great perseverance a hospital car was provided for the worst cases and I went in and saw them lying comfortably upon the stretchers, saw the cars trudge off with their groaning load, and think I to my-self, the idea of making a business of maiming men is not one worthy of a civi-lized nation. By the time I got home over the corduroy [a bumpy road] had a headache of the first water, went to bed, and there could lay, as my occupation is nearly gone now. . . .

from thy affectionate sister
Cornelia Hancock

3rd Div. 2 Corps Hosp.
March 27, 1864

My Dear Mother
    . . . Our hospital will soon fill up with sick unless they move. Then what will become of us is unknown—Ellen is fretting for fear I shall go on a march. My only answer to all such worriments is you ought to have confidence enough in my judgment to think I will do the best thing. After campaigning successfully for 9 months I ought to have some experience. In regard to Salem people think-ing I ought to have a woman to sleep with me, I am much better guarded than the lone widows and maids at Isabell's. Another woman is not needed nor would be allowed here. Mrs. Lee is within sending distance if I was sick, so calm all your fears. I go to sleep just as quick as I touch the bed, am used to being alone, like it, and never feel lonely and would not sleep with Mrs. Lee if I could. I am sorry you have any distress on my account, but I cannot help you any and I assure you it is all unnecessary.
    . . . Sarah Sinnickson wrote me a letter expressive of great concern from my "way of living." I wrote her a letter that she will not forget soon. They can-not expect everyone to be satisfied to live in as small a circle as themselves in these days of great events. She expresses it as the great concern of the whole family and her approaching sickness made her bold to express it. . . .

from thy daughter
Cornelia Hancock

[May 1864]

Dear Ellen

... I am in Fredericksburg city. I do not know where Doctor is. On going ashore at Belle Plain we were met with hordes of wounded soldiers who had been able to walk from the Wilderness battlefield to this point. They were famished for food and as I opened the remains of my lunch basket the soldiers behaved more like ravenous wolves than human beings, so I felt the very first thing to be done was to prepare food in unlimited quantities, so with my past experience in arranging a fire where there seemed no possibility of one, I soon had a long pole hanging full of kettles of steaming hot coffee, and this, with soft bread, was dispensed all night to the tramping soldiers who were filling the steam boats on their return trip to Washington.

... when daylight came Dr. Detmold and Dr. Vanderpool, two eminent surgeons of New York, and I boarded [an ambulance] to go to Fredericksburg, where our hospital is established. On arriving here the scenes beggared all description and these two men, eminent as they are in their profession, were paralyzed by what they saw. Rain had poured in through the bullet-riddled roofs of the churches until our wounded lay in pools of water made bloody by their seriously wounded condition. On these scenes Dr. Detmold and Dr. Vanderpool gazed in horror and seemed not to know where to take hold. My Gettysburg experience enabled me to take hold. The next morning these two surgeons came to me and said: "If we open another church under better conditions than these, will you accompany us?" and I said "Yes." After they got their nerve their splendid executive ability asserted itself and they had the pews knocked to pieces; under the backs and seats put a cleat and made little beds to raise the wounded from the floor. 'Tis true the beds have no springs, but it keeps them from lying in the water. Here day by day things are improving. An amputating table is improvised under a tree in the yard where these two good men work indefatiguably.

[May 1864]

My Dear Mother

... I was the first and only Union woman in the city [Fredericksburg]. I believe today there were some of Miss Dix's nurses came thru. I have good quarters. We calculate there are 14,000 wounded in the town; the Secesh [rebel Southerners] help none, so you may know there is suffering equal to any thing anyone ever saw, almost as bad as Gettysburg, only we have houses and churches for the men. I am well, have worked harder than I ever did in my life. There was no food but hard tack to give the men so I turned in and dressed their wounds. It was all that could be done. I hear from my friends at the front one by one. Almost every one I knew was shot dead except the Doctor. Some of them are taken prisoners, Dr. Aiken for one. Dr. Dudley was safe last night. Lieut. Fogg was shot dead, so was Capt. Madison—this battle is still raging. I am glad I am here but I really thought my heart would break as one after another they told me was dead. If they only accomplish getting to Richmond. If not, it is a dear battle. There is very heavy firing today. I hope Dr. Dudley will get thru safe. He sent a Doctor to see me, told him he knew I would get thru. He is out on the front with his Regt. Oh, how awful, it seems as if the great judgment day was upon us now; the Secesh are still in town but we take possession of all churches and houses we want. I am well. Write to me in care of Dr. Davis, 1st Div. 2nd Corps. hospt., Fred'ksburg, Va. . . .

Thine in haste
Cornelia Hancock

40

A Slaveowner's Journal
at the End of the Civil War

Henry William Ravenel

In a letter of August 26, 1865, Henry William Ravenel (1814–1887) summarized the immediate effects of the collapse of the Confederacy as well as anyone ever has:

> *A new era opens before us, but alas! with what great changes. Our country is in ruins, and our people reduced to poverty. . . . We had no money but Confederate and that is now worthless . . . all our securities and investments are bankrupt. . . . There is little money in the country, little cotton and other produce, so there is no business or employment for those who are anxiously seeking to make a living. . . .*

Emancipation had altered social relations; the collapse of the Confederacy and then Reconstruction were transforming Southern politics; the war and emancipation had upset every economic arrangement, making currency worthless, land unsalable, and credit — previously based on chattel mortgages on slave "property" — scarcely to be obtained.

Ravenel was born to a prominent South Carolina slaveholding family. In addition to managing a plantation, he also became an important self-trained naturalist whose studies of American fungi achieved international renown. After the war he supported his family by selling seeds and parts of his collections of fungi to collectors and later worked as a naturalist for the U.S. Department of Agriculture. After his death, Ravenel's botanical collections were sold to the British Museum.

Ravenel began his journal in 1859 and continued it to within weeks of his death in 1887. The journal shows how one thoughtful and well-placed member of the Southern elite struggled to understand the collapse of his familiar world.

BEFORE YOU READ

1. How did Ravenel interpret the causes and outcome of the Civil War?
2. What did he expect to happen to former slaves, and how did he explain their behavior?
3. Are his reactions what you expected of a slaveholder, or do they surprise you?

November [1864]

F. 18 The Augusta paper of this morning has startling intelligence from Atlanta. There is no doubt that Sherman has burned Rome, Decatur & Atlanta, & has

Arney Robinson Childs, ed., *The Private Journal of Henry William Ravenel, 1859–1887* (Columbia: University of South Carolina Press, 1947), pp. 202–03, 206–07, 210–21 passim, 228–29, 237, 239–40.

commenced a move with 4 or 5 army corps (40 to 50,000) in the direction of Macon & Augusta. The Northern papers say his intention is to move through to Charleston & Mobile, destroy the rail road & bridges behind him & feed his army from the country. I have been apprehending just such a move since Hood's army was withdrawn. It is a bold stroke, & if successful, would bring untold evils upon us, in the destruction of property & the means of subsistance. . . .

Sunday 20 Beauregard telegraphs the people to be firm & resolute—to obstruct his passage by cutting the woods in his front & flank—to destroy all provisions which cannot be carried away—to remove all negroes, horses & cattle, & leave a scene of desolation in his front, instead of in his rear as it would be if he passed. . . . Should Sherman succeed in taking Augusta, his march will be onward toward Charleston, & his track will be a scene of desolation. I await the developments of the next few days with anxiety, chiefly on account of my negroes. If I send them away & the farm & house is left without protection, my house will be robbed & despoiled of every thing, whether the enemy passes here or not. I must wait before removing them, until I am very sure the enemy will succeed in his designs upon Augusta—& then perhaps it may be too late.

M. 21 I have had a talk with my negroes on the subject, & explained to them the true state of affairs—that should the enemy pass through this place they must escape & take care of themselves for a while until the danger is passed. I am well satisfied from their assurances, that they are really alarmed at the idea of being seized & taken off by the Yankees, & that they will not desert me.

F. 25 We are now at the gloomiest period of the war which for nearly four years has afflicted our land. I cannot conceal from myself the many discouraging features of our situation & the perilous straits in which we stand.

1st Our Finances are in such a condition that universal discontent & real suffering exists. The currency is so much depreciated, that for the ordinary & necessary articles of subsistance, it requires an outlay beyond the means of most people. This involves privation & suffering. There is a want of confidence in the ability of the Govt. to redeem its credits, founded partly on their great amount & partly on the precarious condition of our affairs. If our cause fails the whole Govt. credits are lost, & doubtless this consideration has its weight among capitalists in producing distrust.

Sunday 8 Samuel Ravenel at home on furlough from Measles was here this morning. He told me that the Post Surgeon had offered Harry & himself & three other boys, exemptions on account of their age & size, & that two had accepted. He & Harry & another had declined. I was gratified to hear that our boys took such high views of their duty. Sam says they have no tents, & have to lie on the bare ground, or with such protection as a few bushes or straw can give. They do picket & *vidette* [watch] duty in sight & hearing of the enemy, see them drill & enjoy the music from their bands every day. . . .

M. 9 Sent off two boxes bacon today to the Depot for Aiken via Charleston. I hope these supplies may not be caught in Charleston or intercepted by the enemy on the way. We are in a quandary what to do. I am buying hogs down here, & at the same time sending supplies hurriedly to Aiken. . . .

January [1865]

Sunday 15 My claim for compensation for slave (Jim) lost in Confed. service, has passed the Legislature & $2000 are allowed. I am to send James Wilson a power of attorney to receive it. They have commenced to fortify Columbia. . . .

M. 23 Our currency still continues to depreciate, as is shown by the increasing prices of all articles. . . .

February [1865]

S. 18 It is reported that Columbia has fallen - - - - No mail from Charleston. We are now closed in & cut off from all news from the outside world. . . . We are now virtually in the enemy's lines. I am in doubt what to do with Harry. He is very weak & just able to walk about. If he remains, he may be captured as prisoner of war — if I undertake to carry him away, I then leave my family never to see them until the war is over. I would not hesitate about leaving my family if they were in a region where they needed no protection & could get subsistance — but the thoughts of deserting them here is very distressing to me.

Sunday 19 Dr. Frank Porcher dined here today. He thinks we should remain where we are. The upper country is in danger of famine, & will soon be without salt, now the coast is given up. . . . Charleston was occupied by the enemy yesterday at 10 A.M. — Columbia has been captured. We hear of a great fire in Charleston yesterday, but no particulars yet. Exciting times!

M. 20 In a few days the last of our army will have crossed the Santee, the bridge burnt behind them — & we then become an evacuated & conquered region. We fall under Yankee rule & the laws & authority of the U. States are established during the continuance of the war. What new relations between us & our negroes will be established we cannot tell but there is no doubt it will be a radical change. I do not apprehend destructive raids, or personal violence to citizens who remain, but we will be compelled to conform to the new conditions under which we are placed, as a conquered people. I suppose all the cotton will be seized & confiscated to the use of the U. S. govt, — & probably a system of culture will be adopted & enforced the profits from which will accrue to them. I think it the duty of all slave owners & planters who remain, to be with their negroes. They have been faithful to the last, & they deserve in turn, confidence from him, protection, attention & care. . . .

T. 21 I think masters who are within these lines of the enemy, should remain on their plantations among their negroes; — the first change of conditions should not be volunteered by us. We have always believed we were right in maintaining the relation of master & slave for the good of the country & also for the benefit of the negro. If we have believed firmly in the Divine sanction which the Bible affords to this relation, we should not be the first to sever it, by abandoning them. They have grown up under us, they look to us for support, for guidance & protection—They have faithfully done their duty during this trying time, when the great temptations were offered to leave us. In the sight of God, we have a sacred duty to stand by them as long as they are faithful to us. We know that if left to themselves, they cannot maintain their happy condition. We must reward their fidelity to us by the same care & consideration we exercised when they were more useful. . . .

T. 28 David returned with a cart from PineVille last night, & said Rene told him the Yankees had been, or were, in PineVille, taking poultry & whatever they wanted. The negroes on many places have refused to go to work. . . . I have spoken to some of them here & intend to give them advice as a friend to continue on the plantation, & work—Of course there must be great care & judgement used in preserving discipline & I have advised with the overseer. I think for their own good & the good of the country, it would be best for the present organization of labor to go on, so that all may get a subsistance, the old & young, the sick & disabled, & the other non producers. . . . The freed & idle negroes who are not kept now under discipline or fear will give us trouble. I feel great anxiety for the future. . . .

March [1865]

Th. 2 Half past two o'clock A.M. Night of horrors! How can I describe the agonizing suspense of the past six hours! Thank God who has protected us all we are still alive & have lost nothing but property.—About half past 8 oclock I was standing in the back piazza, when I heard the discharge of 3 or 4 fire arms. The negroes soon came running up to inform us that the Yankees were in the negro yard. They soon after entered the house, (4 or 5 colored men) armed & demanded to see the owner of the house. I called to Pa & he walked up to the back door where they were. They told him that they had come for provisions, corn, bacon, poultry & whatever they wanted—demanded his horses & wagons, his guns, wine &c. That they had come to tell the negroes they were free & should no longer work for him. They used very threatening language with oaths & curses. They then proceeded to the stable & took my pair & Renes horse—Took the 2 sets harness & put in the horses, into the two wagons & Lequeax buggy. They then emptied the smoke house, store room & meat house, giving to the negroes what they did not want. They then took from the fowl house what poultry they wanted, took the two plantation guns, & used great threats about the wine & brandy. To our great relief they did not enter the house again, & at 1.30 A.M. drove off. They told the negroes if they worked for their master again they would shoot them when they came back. What the future is to be to us God only knows. I feel that my trust is still unshaken in his all protecting Providence. I have all confidance in the fidelity of the negroes & their attachment to us if they are not restrained from showing it. We are all up for the night as the excitement is too great to permit sleep - - - - - 9 A.M. at the usual hour this morning the house negroes came in—They seemed much distressed & said the troops told them last night if they came to the yard or did anything for us, they would shoot them—That a large troop would come today. We told them to go back & not bring trouble upon themselves, until we could see the Commanding officer. The fidelity & attachment of some who have come forward is very gratifying. The girls have been cooking our simple breakfast & we have taken our first meal under the new regime. I long for a visit from some officer in authority, that we may know our future condition & whether the negroes will be allowed to hire themselves to us or not. I know if they are not restrained there are many who would willingly & gladly help us. I had heard often of insurrectionary feelings among the negroes, but I never believed they would be brought to it of their own accord. The experience of this war, & especially of last night all tend to confirm that conviction. Even when compelled by intimidation, & fear of the consequences to their lives, many of them evince real distress, & not one has yet joined in any language or act of defiance. Their fidelity & attachment is amazing with the temptations before them. Those who were engaged in the sacking of the store room & meat house, did so stealthily & I believe not until they were commanded to help themselves.

S. 4 Inauguration of Presdt. Lincoln today for his 2d term of 4 years. Will any thing come out of it in respect to the war? The negroes are completely bewildered at the change of their condition. Many are truly distressed, some of the younger ones delirious with the prospect of good living & nothing to do. Some are willing to remain & work, but object to gang work,—all is in a chaotic state. When they were told that they were free, some said they did not wish to be free, & they were immediately silenced with threats of being shot. I fear this region will be a desolate waste in one year hence, if this state of things continue - - On Thursday night when the army was camped here, their troops were among our negroes, distributing sugar, coffee, meats & bread in profusion—they killed 8 or 10 of the sheep & had them cooked in the negro yard. This was all intended as an earnest of the good things which followed their freedom. . . .

M. 6 The events of the past week have brought up vividly before us the horrors of the French Revolution—& those startling scenes which Dickens describes in his "Tale of two cities." We are in a fearful & trying crisis. If those who had unsettled the present order of things in the name of Humanity, were consistent, they would make some effort to order the freed negroes for their good, & ought to take some steps toward restoring order & recommanding & enforcing some plan by which such a large number may escape the horrors of insubordination, violence & ultimately starvation. The negroes are intoxicated with the idea of freedom. Many of them are deluded into the hope that their future is to be provided for by the U S. Govt.—& hence they do not feel the necessity of work. Many are disposed to remain, but perhaps will insist on terms which are incompatable with discipline & good management. It is a fearful crisis.

T. 7 No disposition evinced among the negroes to go to work. There seems to be sullenness which I dislike to see. I think those who are disposed to work or to do for us, are restrained. I hear that many of the negroes are armed with pistols & guns. Some were at Black Oak last night firing off pistols. This is a bad feature in this fearful period. — Oh, Humanity! what crimes are committed in thy name. One week ago we were in the midst of a peaceful, contented & orderly population — now all is confusion, disorder, discontent, violence, anarchy. If those who up-rooted the old order of things had remained long enough to reconstruct another system in which there should be order restored, it would have been well, but they have destroyed our system & left us in the ruins — "God is our refuge & strength, a very present help in trouble" - - - - The negroes are rambling about the country. This morning 4 mounted on horses & mules rode through the negro yard, stopping for a while, & some have passed through in vehicles. It is said they were told to go to St Stephens for horses which the army left behind.

W. 8 We heard guns again last night, but cannot learn from the negroes who fired them. The disordered state of affairs keeps us anxious. . . . On this day a week ago the old system of slave labour was in peaceful operation. The breath of Emancipation has passed over the country, & we are now in that transition state between the new & the old systems — a state of chaos & disorder. Will the negro be materially benefitted by the change? Will the condition of the country in its productive resources, in material prosperity be improved? Will it be a benefit to the landed proprietors? These are questions which will have their solution in the future. They are in the hands of that Providence which over-ruleth all things for good. It was a strong conviction of my best judgement that the old relation of master & slave, had received the divine sanction & was the best condition in which the two races could live together for mutual benefit. There were many defects to be corrected & many abuses to be remedied, which I think would have been done if we had gained our independence & were freed from outside pressure. Among these defects I will enumerate the want of legislation to make the marriage contract binding — to prevent the separation of families, & to restrain the cupidity of cruel masters. Perhaps it is for neglecting these obligations that God has seen fit to dissolve that relation. I believe the negro must remain in this country & that his condition although a freed-man, must be to labour on the soil. Nothing but necessity will compel him to labour. Now the question is, will that necessity be so strong as to compel him to labour, which will be profitable to the landed proprietors. Will he make as much cotton, sugar, rice & tobacco for the world as he did previously? They will now have a choice *where* to labour. This will ensure good treatment & the best terms. The most humane, the most energetic & the most judicious managers have the best chances in the race for success. I expect to see a revolution in the ownership of landed estates. Those only can succeed who bring the best capacity for the business. Time will show. . . .

Sunday 12 Some of the very peculiar traits of negro character are now exhibited. John & Solomon left Morefield on Thursday with the black troops wild with excitement & probably drunk — In all this reign of disorder & anarchy I have not seen or heard of any violence or even of rudeness or incivility from the plantation negroes. Docility & submissiveness still prevail. There are two exhibitions of character which have surprised us, & which were never anticipated. 1st. On many places where there was really kind treatment & mutual attachment, the exciting events of the last week or two, & the powerful temptations brought to bear upon them, have seemed to snap the ties suddenly. Some have left their comfortable homes & kind masters & friends, & gone off with the army, thinking to better their conditions. We must be patient & charitable in our opinions—They are ignorant of what they have to encounter, mere children in knowledge & experience, excitable, impulsive & have fallen under the tempting delusions presented to them in such glowing terms—Some who are disposed to take a proper view of their condition, & to return to work, are intimidated & kept back by threats from the more strong & overbearing. They do not clearly comprehend this situation—they have been told they are free, & their idea of freedom is associated with freedom from work & toil. In many places there was bad discipline & little care for the negroes. These are generally the foremost in all the acts of disorder,—& their example & word keep back others. We are astonished at this defection when we do not expect it, but on reflection the causes at work are sufficient to account for it. 2nd. Had we been told four years ago, that our negroes would have withstood the temptation to fidelity which have been constantly before them during the war, we would have doubted the possibility—& had we been told further of the events of the last two weeks, the incitements to acts of violence both by the example & the precepts of the black troops all throughout this region, we would have shuddered for the consequences. Except from the black soldiers, I have not heard of a single act of violence, or even of rude or uncivil language. Their behaviour is perfectly civil so far, & I believe, with a judicous course on the part of the whites, will continue so. This whole revolution from its commencement has developed in its progress, a course of events which no human sagacity on either side, ever foresaw. We are carried along by an inscrutable providence to the consummation of great & radical changes,—we are the actors in a Great Revolution where, not civil institutions only, but social polity, must be reconstructed & re-organized. . . .

May [1865]

May M. 1   Gen Lees surrender took place on the 9th.ult, but it only reached us through our papers & the returning prisoners about a week ago. . . . [This] means the loss of our Independence for which we have been struggling for four years with immense loss of life & property. But the fate of nations is controlled & over-ruled by a wise Providence, which sees the end from the beginning, & orders all things in the highest wisdom. Whatever therefore may be the will of God regarding our destiny, I accept His decision as final & as eminently good. I have honestly believed we were right in our revolution, & would receive the divine sanction—if I have erred, I pray God to forgive me the error, & I submit with perfect satisfaction to His decree, knowing that He cannot err.

M. 22   We begin now to realize the ruin to property which the war has entailed upon us. All classes & conditions of men will suffer who had property, except the small farmers who owned no negroes. Confederate securities, I consider a total loss. Bank stock, confederation & private bonds, are all more or less dependent for their availability upon Confed securities, & upon the value of negro property; both of which are lost. The Rail road companies are nearly all ruined by the destruction of their roads & the heavy debt they must incur to rebuild. The only money now in possession of our people is coin in small quantities which had been hoarded through the war, & some bills of the local banks. There will be but little means of increasing this amount for some time to come, as provisions are scarce, & the cotton has been mostly burnt, captured or sold. The financial prospect is a gloomy one, & there will be much distress before our conditions can improve. . . .

M. 29 I went in to Aiken this morning & called at the hotel to inquire if any officer in Aiken was authorized to administer the Oath of Allegiance. They expected in a day or two to have it done here. It is necessary now in order to save property, have personal protection, or exercise the rights of citizenship, or any business calling. Every one who is allowed, is now taking the oath, as the Confederate govt. is annulled, the state govt. destroyed, & the return into the Union absolutely necessary to our condition as an organized community. As Gen. Gillmore's order based upon Chief Justice Chase's opinion announces the freedom of the negroes there is no further room to doubt that it is the settled policy of the country. I have today formally announced to my negroes the fact, & made such arrangements with each as the new relation rendered necessary. Those whose whole time we need, get at present clothes & food, house rent & medical attendance. The others work for themselves giving me a portion of their time on the farm in lieu of house rent. Old Amelia & her two grandchildren, I will spare the mockery of offering freedom to. I must support them as long as I have any thing to give.

T. 30 My negroes all express a desire to remain with me. I am gratified at the proof of their attachment. I believe it to be real & unfeigned. For the present they will remain, but in course of time we must part, as I cannot afford to keep so many, & they cannot afford to hire for what I could give them. As they have always been faithful & attached to us, & have been raised as family servants, & have all of them been in our family for several generations, there is a feeling towards them somewhat like that of a father who is about to send out his children on the world to make their way through life. Those who have brought the present change of relation upon us are ignorant of these ties. They have charged us with cruelty. They call us, man stealers, robbers, tyrants. The indignant denial of these charges & the ill feelings engendered during 30 years of angry controversy, have culminated at length in the four years war which has now ended. It has pleased God that we should fail in our efforts for independance—& with the loss of independance, we return to the Union under the dominion of the abolition sentiment. The experiment is now to be tried. The negro is not only to be emancipated, but is to become a citizen with all the right & priviledges! It produces a financial, political & social revolution at the South, fearful to contemplate in its ultimate effects. Whatever the result may be, let it be known & remembered that neither the negro slave nor his master is responsible. It has been done by those who having political power, are determined to carry into practice the sentimental philanthropy they have so long & angrily advocated. Now that is fixed. I pray God for the great issues at stake, that he may bless the effort & make it successful—make it a blessing & not a curse to the poor negro.

41

African Americans during Reconstruction
Felix Haywood et al.

The Thirteenth, Fourteenth, and Fifteenth Amendments to the U.S. Constitution decreed an equality between the races that did not become a reality in African Americans' daily lives. At first the federal government established the Freedman's Bureau and supported Reconstruction governments in Southern states, making vigorous efforts to help the freed slaves gain education, legal and medical services, reasonable employment contracts, and a measure of political power. But within about a decade those efforts were abandoned as the Northern public, tired of disorder in the South and wary of government intervention, abandoned the freed slaves to their former masters. African Americans were left to respond however they could to the social revolution brought about by emancipation, the war's impoverishment of the South, and the violence of groups like the Ku Klux Klan. Historians have pieced together the story of their actions from a multiplicity of sources. Interviews with former slaves collected in the 1930s, of which you will here read a sample, are one important source.

BEFORE YOU READ

1. What, judging from these accounts, were the major problems that former slaves faced after the war?
2. What did these former slaves expect of freedom?
3. What role did the Ku Klux Klan play in former slaves' lives?
4. Why did some freedmen continue to work for their former masters?

FELIX HAYWOOD

San Antonio, Texas. Born in Raleigh, North Carolina. Age at interview: 88.

The end of the war, it come just like that—like you snap your fingers. . . . How did we know it! Hallelujah broke out—

> Abe Lincoln freed the nigger
> With the gun and the trigger;
> And I ain't going to get whipped any more.
> I got my ticket,
> Leaving the thicket,
> And I'm a-heading for the Golden Shore!

"African Americans React to Reconstruction," from B. A. Botkin, ed., *Lay My Burden Down: A Folk History of Slavery* (Chicago: University of Chicago Press, 1945), pp. 65–70, 223–24, 241–42, 246–47.

Soldiers, all of a sudden, was everywhere—coming in bunches, crossing and walking and riding. Everyone was a-singing. We was all walking on golden clouds. Hallelujah!

> Union forever,
>   Hurrah, boys, hurrah!
> Although I may be poor,
>   I'll never be a slave—
> Shouting the battle cry of freedom.

Everybody went wild. We felt like heroes, and nobody had made us that way but ourselves. We was free. Just like that, we was free. It didn't seem to make the whites mad, either. They went right on giving us food just the same. Nobody took our homes away, but right off colored folks started on the move. They seemed to want to get closer to freedom, so they'd know what it was— like it was a place or a city. Me and my father stuck, stuck close as a lean tick to a sick kitten. The Gudlows started us out on a ranch. My father, he'd round up cattle—unbranded cattle—for the whites. They was cattle that they belonged to, all right; they had gone to find water 'long the San Antonio River and the Guadalupe. Then the whites gave me and my father some cattle for our own. My father had his own brand—7 B)—and we had a herd to start out with of seventy.

We knowed freedom was on us, but we didn't know what was to come with it. We thought we was going to get rich like the white folks. We thought we was going to be richer than the white folks, 'cause we was stronger and knowed how to work, and the whites didn't, and they didn't have us to work for them any more. But it didn't turn out that way. We soon found out that freedom could make folks proud, but it didn't make 'em rich.

Did you ever stop to think that thinking don't do any good when you do it too late? Well, that's how it was with us. If every mother's son of a black had thrown 'way his hoe and took up a gun to fight for his own freedom along with the Yankees, the war'd been over before it began. But we didn't do it. We couldn't help stick to our masters. We couldn't no more shoot 'em than we could fly. My father and me used to talk 'bout it. We decided we was too soft and freedom wasn't going to be much to our good even if we had a education.

WARREN McKINNEY

Hazen, Arkansas. Born in South Carolina. Age at interview: 85.

I was born in Edgefield County, South Carolina. I am eighty-five years old. I was born a slave of George Strauter. I remembers hearing them say, "Thank God, I's free as a jay bird." My ma was a slave in the field. I was eleven years old when freedom was declared. When I was little, Mr. Strauter whipped my ma. It hurt me bad as it did her. I hated him. She was crying. I chunked him with rocks. He run after me, but he didn't catch me. There was twenty-five or thirty hands that worked in the field. They raised wheat, corn, oats, barley, and cotton. All the children that couldn't work stayed at one house. Aunt Mat kept the babies and small children that couldn't go to the field. He had a gin and a shop. The shop was at the fork of the roads. When the war come on, my papa went to built forts. He quit Ma and took another woman. When the war close, Ma took her four children, bundled 'em up and went to Augusta. The government give out rations there. My ma washed and ironed. People died in piles. I don't know till yet what was the matter. They said it was the change of living. I seen five or six wooden, painted coffins piled up on wagons pass by our house. Loads passed every day like you see cotton pass here. Some said it was cholera and some took consumption. Lots of the colored people nearly starved. Not much to get to do and not much houseroom. Several families had to live in one house. Lots of the colored folks went up North and froze to death. They couldn't stand the cold. They wrote back about them dying. No, they never sent them back. I heard some sent for money to come back. I heard plenty 'bout the Ku Klux. They scared the folks to death. People left Augusta in droves. About a thousand would all meet and walk going to hunt work and new homes. Some of them died. I had a sister and brother lost that way. I had another sister come to Louisiana that way. She wrote back.

I don't think the colored folks looked for a share of land. They never got nothing 'cause the white folks didn't have nothing but barren hills left. About all the mules was wore out hauling provisions in the army. Some folks say they ought to done more for the colored folks when they left, but they say they was broke. Freeing all the slaves left 'em broke.

That reconstruction was a mighty hard pull. Me and Ma couldn't live. A man paid our ways to Carlisle, Arkansas, and we come. We started working for Mr. Emenson. He had a big store, teams, and land. We liked it fine, and I been here fifty-six years now. There was so much wild game, living was not so hard. If a fellow could get a little bread and a place to stay, he was all right. After I come to this state, I voted some. I have farmed and worked at odd jobs. I farmed mostly. Ma went back to her old master. He persuaded her to come back home. Me and her went back and run a farm four or five years before she died. Then I come back here.

LEE GUIDON

South Carolina. Born in South Carolina. Age at interview: 89.

Yes, ma'am, I sure was in the Civil War. I plowed all day, and me and my sister helped take care of the baby at night. It would cry, and me bumping it [in a straight chair, rocking.] Time I git it to the bed where its mama was, it wake up and start crying all over again. I be so sleepy. It was a puny sort of baby. Its papa was off at war. His name was Jim Cowan, and his wife Miss Margaret Brown 'fore she married him. Miss Lucy Smith give me and my sister to them. Then she married Mr. Abe Moore. Jim Smith was Miss Lucy's boy. He lay out in the woods all time. He say no need in him gitting shot up and killed. He say let the slaves be free. We lived, seemed like, on 'bout the line of York and Union counties. He lay out in the woods over in York County. Mr. Jim say all the fighting 'bout was jealousy. They caught him several times, but every time he got away from 'em. After they come home Mr. Jim say they never win no war. They stole and starved out the South. . . .

After freedom a heap of people say they was going to name theirselves over. They named theirselves big names, then went roaming round like wild, hunting cities. They changed up so it was hard to tell who or where anybody was. Heap of 'em died, and you didn't know when you hear about it if he was your folks hardly. Some of the names was Abraham, and some called theirselves Lincum. Any big name 'cepting their master's name. It was the fashion. I heard 'em talking 'bout it one evening, and my pa say, "Fine folks raise us and we gonna hold to our own names." That settled it with all of us. . . .

I reckon I do know 'bout the Ku Kluck. I knowed a man named Alfred Owens. He seemed all right, but he was a Republican. He said he was not afraid. He run a tanyard and kept a heap of guns in a big room. They all loaded. He married a Southern woman. Her husband either died or was killed. She had a son living with them. The Ku Kluck was called Upper League. They get this boy to unload all the guns. Then the white men went there. The white man give up and said, "I ain't got no gun to defend myself with. The guns all unloaded, and I ain't got no powder and shot." But the Ku Kluck shot in the houses and shot him up like lacework. He sold fine harness, saddles, bridles—all sorts of leather things. The Ku Kluck sure run them outen their country. They say they not going to have them round, and they sure run them out, back where they came from. . . .

For them what stayed on like they were, Reconstruction times 'bout like times before that 'cepting the Yankee stole out and tore up a scandalous heap. They tell the black folks to do something, and then come white folks you live with and say Ku Kluck whup you. They say leave, and white folks say better not listen to them old yankees. They'll git you too far off to come back, and you freeze. They done give you all the use they got for you. How they do? All sorts of ways. Some stayed at their cabins glad to have one to live in and farmed on. Some running round begging, some hunting work for money, and nobody had no money 'cepting the Yankees, and they had no homes or land and mighty little work for you to do. No work to live on. Some going every day to the city. That winter I heard 'bout them starving and freezing by the wagon loads. I never heard nothing 'bout voting till freedom. I don't think I ever voted till I come to Mississippi. I votes Republican. That's the party of my color, and I stick to them as long as they do right. I don't dabble in white folks' business, and that white folks' voting is their business. If I vote, I go do it and go on home.

I been plowing all my life, and in the hot days I cuts and saws wood. Then when I gets outa cotton-picking, I put each boy on a load of wood and we sell wood. The last years we got $3 a cord. Then we clear land till next spring. I don't find no time to be loafing. I never missed a year farming till I got the Bright's disease [one of several kinds of kidney ailments] and it hurt me to do hard work. Farming is the best life there is when you are able. . . .

When I owned most, I had six head mules and five head horses. I rented 140 acres of land. I bought this house and some other land about. The anthrax killed nearly all my horses and mules. I got one big fine mule yet. Its mate died. I lost my house. My son give me one room, and he paying the debt off now. It's hard for colored folks to keep anything. Somebody gets it from 'em if they don't mind.

The present times is hard. Timber is scarce. Game is about all gone. Prices higher. Old folks cannot work. Times is hard for younger folks too. They go to town too much and go to shows. They going to a tent show now. Circus coming, they say. They spending too much money for foolishness. It's a fast time. Folks too restless. Some of the colored folks work hard as folks ever did. They spends too much. Some folks is lazy. Always been that way.

I signed up to the government, but they ain't give me nothing 'cepting powdered milk and rice what wasn't fit to eat. It cracked up and had black something in it. A lady said she would give me some shirts that was her husband's. I went to get them, but she wasn't home. These heavy shirts give me heat. They won't give me the pension, and I don't know why. It would help me buy my salts and pills and the other medicines like Swamp Root. They won't give it to me.

TOBY JONES

Madisonville, Texas. Born in South Carolina. Age at interview: 87.

I worked for Massa 'bout four years after freedom, 'cause he forced me to, said he couldn't 'ford to let me go. His place was near ruint, the fences burnt, and the house would have been, but it was rock. There was a battle fought near his place, and I taken Missy to a hideout in the mountains to where her father was, 'cause there was bullets flying everywhere. When the war was over, Massa come home and says, "You son of a gun, you's supposed to be free, but you ain't, 'cause I ain't gwine give you freedom." So I goes on working for him till I gits the chance to steal a hoss from him. The woman I wanted to marry, Govie, she 'cides to come to Texas with me. Me and Govie, we rides the hoss 'most a hundred miles, then we turned him a-loose and give him a scare back to his house, and come on foot the rest the way to Texas.

All we had to eat was what we could beg, and sometimes we went three days without a bite to eat. Sometimes we'd pick a few berries. When we got cold we'd crawl in a brushpile and hug up close together to keep warm. Once in a while we'd come to a farmhouse, and the man let us sleep on cottonseed in his barn, but they was far and few between, 'cause they wasn't many houses in the country them days like now.

When we gits to Texas, we gits married, but all they was to our wedding am we just 'grees to live together as man and wife. I settled on some land, and we cut some trees and split them open and stood them on end with the tops together for our house. Then we deadened some trees, and the land was ready to farm. There was some wild cattle and hogs, and that's the way we got our start, caught some of them and tamed them.

I don't know as I 'spected nothing from freedom, but they turned us out like a bunch of stray dogs, no homes, no clothing, no nothing, not 'nough food to last us one meal. After we settles on that place, I never seed man or woman, 'cept Govie, for six years, 'cause it was a long ways to anywhere. All we had to farm with was sharp sticks. We'd stick holes and plant corn, and when it come up we'd punch up the dirt round it. We didn't plant cotton, 'cause we couldn't eat that. I made bows and arrows to kill wild game with, and we never went to a store for nothing. We made our clothes out of animal skins.

WHY ADAM KIRK WAS A DEMOCRAT

House Report No. 262, 43 Cong., 2 Sess., p. 106.
Statement of an Alabama Negro (1874)

A white man raised me. I was raised in the house of old man Billy Kirk. He raised me as a body servant. The class that he belongs to seems nearer to me than the northern white man, and actually, since the war, everything I have got is by their aid and their assistance. They have helped me raise up my family and have stood by me, and whenever I want a doctor, no matter what hour of the day or night, he is called in whether I have got a cent or not. And when I want any assistance I can get it from them. I think they have got better principles and better character than the republicans.

42

White Southerners' Reactions to Reconstruction

Caleb G. Forshey and Reverend James Sinclair

The Congressional Joint Committee of Fifteen, assembled to examine Southern represen-
tation in Congress, was named in December 1865 as part of the Republican Congress's re-
sponse to President Andrew Johnson's plan of Reconstruction. In 1866, the committee held
hearings as part of its effort to draft the Fourteenth Amendment. Despite the president's
veto, Congress had already enlarged the scope of the Freedmen's Bureau to care for displaced
former slaves and to try by military commission those accused of depriving freedmen of civil
rights. Republicans in Congress, in opposition to the Johnson administration, would con-
tinue to evolve a Reconstruction policy that attempted to protect the freedmen's rights.

Of the two white Southerners whose interviews with the committee you will read
here, Caleb G. Forshey had supported secession while James Sinclair, although a slave-
holder, had opposed it. A Scottish-born minister who had only moved to North Carolina
in 1857, Sinclair's Unionist sentiments had led to the loss of his church and then to his
arrest during the war. In 1865 he served on the Freedmen's Bureau.

BEFORE YOU READ

1. What effect did Caleb Forshey anticipate from military occupation of Southern
states?
2. How did he evaluate the effectiveness of the Freedmen's Bureau?
3. What were Forshey's beliefs about African Americans?
4. What were the strengths and weaknesses of the Freedmen's Bureau according to
James Sinclair?
5. How does Sinclair's view of Southern opinion differ from Forshey's?

CALEB G. FORSHEY

Washington, D.C., March 28, 1866

Question: Where do you reside?
Answer: I reside in the State of Texas.
Question: How long have you been a resident of Texas?

The Report of the Committees of the House of Representatives Made during the First Session, Thirty-Ninth
Congress, 1865–1866, vol. 2 (Washington, D.C.: Government Printing Office, 1866); Forshey:
pp. 129–32; Sinclair: pp. 168–71.

Answer: I have resided in Texas and been a citizen of that State for nearly thirteen years.

Question: What opportunities have you had for ascertaining the temper and disposition of the people of Texas towards the government and authority of the United States?

Answer: For ten years I have been superintendent of the Texas Military Institute, as its founder and conductor. I have been in the confederate service in various parts of the confederacy; but chiefly in the trans-Mississippi department, in Louisiana and Texas, as an officer of engineers. I have had occasion to see and know very extensively the condition of affairs in Texas, and also to a considerable extent in Louisiana. I think I am pretty well-informed, as well as anybody, perhaps, of the present state of affairs in Texas.

Question: What are the feelings and views of the people of Texas as to the late rebellion, and the future condition and circumstances of the State, and its relations to the federal government?

Answer: After our army had given up its arms and gone home, the surrender of all matters in controversy was complete, and as nearly universal, perhaps, as anything could be. Assuming the matters in controversy to have been the right to secede, and the right to hold slaves, I think they were given up teetotally, to use a strong Americanism. When you speak of feeling, I should discriminate a little. The feeling was that of any party who had been cast in a suit he had staked all upon. They did not return from feeling, but from a sense of necessity, and from a judgment that it was the only and necessary thing to be done, to give up the contest. But when they gave it up, it was without reservation; with a view to look forward, and not back. That is my impression of the manner in which the thing was done. There was a public expectation that in some very limited time there would be a restoration to former relations. . . . It was the expectation of the people that, as soon as the State was organized as proposed by the President, they would be restored to their former relations, and things would go on as before.

Question: What is your opinion of a military force under the authority of the federal government to preserve order in Texas and to protect those who have been loyal, both white and black, from the aggressions of those who have been in the rebellion?

Answer: My judgment is well founded on that subject: that wherever such military force is and has been, it has excited the very feeling it was intended to prevent; that so far from being necessary it is very pernicious everywhere, and without exception. The local authorities and public sentiment are ample for protection. I think no occasion would occur, unless some individual case that our laws would not reach. We had an opportunity to test this after the surrender and before any authority was there. The military authorities, or the military officers, declared that we were without laws, and it was a long time before the governor appointed arrived there, and then it was sometime before we could effect anything in the way of organization. We were a people without law, order, or anything; and it was a time for violence if it would occur. I think it is a great credit to our civilization that, in that state of affairs, there was nowhere any instance of violence. I am proud of it, for I expected the contrary; I expected that our soldiers on coming home, many of them, would be dissolute, and that many of them would oppress the class of men you speak of; but it did not occur. But afterwards, wherever soldiers have been sent, there have been little troubles, none of them large; but personal collisions between soldiers and citizens.

Question: What is your opinion as to the necessity and advantages of the Freedmen's Bureau, or an agency of that kind, in Texas?

Answer: My opinion is that it is not needed; my opinion is stronger than that—that the effect of it is to irritate, if nothing else. While in New York city recently I had a conversation with some friends from Texas, from five distant points in the State. We met together and compared opinions; and the opinion of each was the same, that the negroes had generally gone to work since January; that except where the Freedmen's Bureau had interfered, or rather encouraged troubles, such as little complaints, especially between negro and negro, the negro's disposition was very good, and they had generally gone to work, a vast majority of them with their former masters. . . . The impression in Texas at present is that the negroes under the influence of the Freedmen's Bureau do worse than without it.

I want to state that I believe all our former owners of negroes are the friends of the negroes; and that the antagonism paraded in the papers of the north does not exist at all. I know the fact is the very converse of that; and good feeling always prevails between the masters and the slaves. But the negroes went off and left them in the lurch; my own family was an instance of it. But they came back after a time, saying they had been free enough and wanted a home.

Question: Do you think those who employ the negroes there are willing to make contracts with them, so that they shall have fair wages for their labor?

Answer: I think so; I think they are paid liberally, more than the white men in this country get; the average compensation to negroes there is greater than the average compensation of free laboring white men in this country. It seems to have regulated itself in a great measure by what each neighborhood was doing; the negroes saying, "I can get thus and so at such a place." Men have hired from eight to fifteen dollars per month during the year, and women at about two dollars less a month; house-servants at a great deal more.

Question: Do the men who employ the negroes claim to exercise the right to enforce their contract by physical force?

Answer: Not at all; that is totally abandoned; not a single instance of it has occurred. I think they still chastise children, though. The negro parents often neglect that, and the children are still switched as we switch our own children. I know it is done in my own house; we have little house-servants that we switch just as I do our own little fellows.

Question: What is your opinion as to the respective advantages to the white and black races, of the present free system of labor and the institution of slavery?

Answer: I think freedom is very unfortunate for the negro; I think it is sad; his present helpless condition touches my heart more than anything else I ever contemplated, and I think that is the common sentiment of our slaveholders. I have seen it on the largest plantations, where the negro men had all left, and where only women and children remained, and the owners had to keep them and feed them. The beginning certainly presents a touching and sad spectacle. The poor negro is dying at a rate fearful to relate.

I have some ethnological theories that may perhaps warp my judgment; but my judgment is that the highest condition the black race has ever reached or can reach, is one where he is provided for by a master race. That is the result of a great deal of scientific investigation and observation of the negro character by me ever since I was a man. The labor question had become a most momentous one, and I was studying it. I undertook to investigate the condition of the negro from statistics under various circumstances, to treat it purely as a matter of statistics from the census tables of this country of ours. I found that the free blacks of the north decreased 8 per cent.; the free blacks of the south increased 7 or 8 per cent., while the slaves by their sides increased 34 per cent. I inferred from the doctrines of political economy that the race is in the best condition when it procreates the fastest; that, other things being equal, slavery is of vast advantage to the negro. I will mention one or two things in connexion with this as explanatory of that result. The negro will not take care of his offspring unless required to do it, as compared with the whites. The little children will die; they do die, and hence the necessity of very rigorous regulations on our plantations which we have adopted in our nursery system.

Another cause is that there is no continence among the negroes. All the continence I have ever seen among the negroes has been enforced upon plantations, where it is generally assumed there is none. For the sake of procreation, if nothing else, we compel men to live with their wives. The discipline of the plantation was more rigorous, perhaps, in regard to men staying with their wives, than in regard to anything else; and I think the procreative results, as shown by the census tables, is due in a great measure to that discipline. . . .

Question: What is the prevailing inclination among the people of Texas in regard to giving the negroes civil or political rights and privileges?

Answer: I think they are all opposed to it. There are some men—I am not among them—who think that the basis of intelligence might be a good basis for the elective franchise. But a much larger class, perhaps nine-tenths of our people, believe that the distinctions between the races should not be broken down by any such community of interests in the management of the affairs of the State. I think there is a very common sentiment that the negro, even with education, has not a mind capable of appreciating the political institutions of the country to such an extent as would make him a good associate for the white man in the administration of the government. I think if the vote was taken on the question of admitting him to the right of suffrage there would be a very small vote in favor of it—scarcely respectable: that is my judgment.

REVEREND JAMES SINCLAIR

Washington, D.C., January 29, 1866

Question: What is generally the state of feeling among the white people of North Carolina towards the government of the United States?

Answer: That is a difficult question to answer, but I will answer it as far as my own knowledge goes. In my opinion, there is generally among the white people not much love for the government. Though they are willing, and I believe determined, to acquiesce in what is inevitable, yet so far as love and affection for the government is concerned, I do not believe that they have any of it at all, outside of their personal respect and regard for President Johnson.

Question: How do they feel towards the mass of the northern people — that is, the people of what were known formerly as the free States?

Answer: They feel in this way: that they have been ruined by them. You can imagine the feelings of a person towards one whom he regards as having ruined him. They regard the northern people as having destroyed their property or taken it from them, and brought all the calamities of this war upon them.

Question: How do they feel in regard to what is called the right of secession?

Answer: They think that it was right . . . that there was no wrong in it. They are willing now to accept the decision of the question that has been made by the sword, but they are not by any means converted from their old opinion that they had a right to secede. It is true that there have always been Union men in our State, but not Union men without slavery, except perhaps among Quakers. Slavery was the central idea even of the Unionist. The only difference between them and the others upon that question was, that they desired to have that institution under the aegis of the Constitution, and protected by it. The secessionists wanted to get away from the north altogether. When the secessionists precipitated our State into rebellion, the Unionists and secessionists went together, because the great object with both was the preservation of slavery by the preservation of State sovereignty. There was another class of Unionists who did not care anything at all about slavery, but they were driven by the other whites into the rebellion for the purpose of preserving slavery. The poor whites are to-day very much opposed to conferring upon the negro the right of suffrage; as much so as the other classes of the whites. They believe it is the intention of government to give the negro rights at their expense. They cannot see it in any other light than that as the negro is elevated they must proportionately go down. While they are glad that slavery is done away with, they are bitterly opposed to conferring the right of suffrage on the negro as the most prominent secessionists; but it is for the reason I have stated, that they think rights conferred on the negro must necessarily be taken from them, particularly the ballot, which was the only bulwark guarding their superiority to the negro race.

Question: In your judgment, what proportion of the white people of North Carolina are really, and truly, and cordially attached to the government of the United States?

Answer: Very few, sir; very few. . . .

Question: Is the Freedmen's Bureau acceptable to the great mass of the white people in North Carolina?

Answer: No, sir; I do not think it is; I think the most of the whites wish the bureau to be taken away.

Question: Why do they wish that?

Answer: They think that they can manage the negro for themselves: that they understand him better than northern men do. They say, "Let us understand what you want us to do with [the] negro—what you desire of us; lay down your conditions for our readmission into the Union, and then we will know what we have to do, and if you will do that we will enact laws for the government of these negroes. They have lived among us, and they are all with us, and we can manage them better than you can." They think it is interfering with the rights of the State for a bureau, the agent and representative of the federal government, to overslaugh the State entirely, and interfere with the regulations and administration of justice before their courts.

Question: Is there generally a willingness on the part of the whites to allow the freedmen to enjoy the right of acquiring land and personal property?

Answer: I think they are very willing to let them do that, for this reason; to get rid of some portion of the taxes imposed upon their property by the government. For instance, a white man will agree to sell a negro some of his land on condition of his paying so much a year on it, promising to give him a deed of it when the whole payment is made, taking his note in the mean time. This relieves that much of the land from taxes to be paid by the white man. All I am afraid of is, that the negro is too eager to go into this thing; that he will ruin himself, get himself into debt to the white man, and be forever bound to him for the debt and never get the land. I have often warned them to be careful what they did about these things.

Question: There is no repugnance on the part of the whites to the negro owning land and personal property?

Answer: I think not.

Question: Have they any objection to the legal establishment of the domestic relations among the blacks, such as the relation of husband and wife, of parent and child, and the securing by law to the negro the rights of those relations?

Answer: That is a matter of ridicule with the whites. They do not believe the negroes will ever respect those relations more than the brutes. I suppose I have married more than two hundred couples of negroes since the war, but the whites laugh at the very idea of the thing. Under the old laws a slave could not marry a free woman of color; it was made a penal offence in North Carolina for any one to perform such a marriage. But there was in my own family a slave who desired to marry a free woman of color, and I did what I conceived to be my duty, and married them, and I was presented to the grand jury for doing so, but the prosecuting attorney threw out the case and would not try it. In former times the officiating clergyman marrying slaves, could not use the usual formula: "Whom God has joined together let no man put asunder"; you could not say, "According to the ordinance of God I pronounce you man and wife; you are no longer two but one." It was not legal for you to do so.

Question: What, in general, has been the treatment of the blacks by the whites since the close of hostilities?

Answer: It has not generally been of the kindest character, I must say that; I am compelled to say that.

Question: Are you aware of any instance of personal ill treatment towards the blacks by the whites?

Answer: Yes, sir.

Question: Give some instances that have occurred since the war.

Answer: [Sinclair describes the beating of a young woman across her buttocks in graphic detail.]

Question: What was the provocation, if any?

Answer: Something in regard to some work, which is generally the provocation.

Question: Was there no law in North Carolina at that time to punish such an outrage?

Answer: No, sir; only the regulations of the Freedmen's Bureau; we took cognizance of the case. In old times that was quite allowable; it is what was called "paddling."

Question: Did you deal with the master?

Answer: I immediately sent a letter to him to come to my office, but he did not come, and I have never seen him in regard to the matter since. I had no soldiers to enforce compliance, and I was obliged to let the matter drop.

Question: Have you any reason to suppose that such instances of cruelty are frequent in North Carolina at this time—instances of whipping and striking?

Answer: I think they are; it was only a few days before I left that a woman came there with her head all bandaged up, having been cut and bruised by her employer. They think nothing of striking them.

Question: And the negro has practically no redress?

Answer: Only what he can get from the Freedmen's Bureau.

Question: Can you say anything further in regard to the political condition of North Carolina—the feeling of the people towards the government of the United States?

Answer: I for one would not wish to be left there in the hands of those men; I could not live there just now. But perhaps my case is an isolated one from the position I was compelled to take in that State. I was persecuted, arrested, and they tried to get me into their service; they tried everything to accomplish their purpose, and of course I have rendered myself still more obnoxious by accepting an appointment under the Freedmen's Bureau. As for myself I would not be allowed to remain there. I do not want to be handed over to these people. I know it is utterly impossible for any man who was not true to the Confederate States up to the last moment of the existence of the confederacy, to expect any favor of these people as the State is constituted at present.

Question: Suppose the military pressure of the government of the United States should be withdrawn from North Carolina, would northern men and true Unionists be safe in that State?

Answer: A northern man going there would perhaps present nothing obnoxious to the people of the State. But men who were born there, who have been true to the Union, and who have fought against the rebellion, are worse off than northern men. . . .

Question: In your judgment, what effect has been produced by the liberality of the President in granting pardons and amnesties to rebels in that State—what effect upon the public mind?

Answer: On my oath I am bound to reply exactly as I believe; that is, that if President Johnson is ever a candidate for re-election he will be supported by the southern States, particularly by North Carolina; but that his liberality to them has drawn them one whit closer to the government than before, I do not believe. It has drawn them to President Johnson personally, and to the Democratic party, I suppose.

Civil War and Reconstruction

The Civil War was the first modern war. Guns with rifled barrels could send a bullet accurately for long distances, and cannons loaded with grapeshot could kill and maim many men at a time. Railroads enabled armies to transport troops and supplies over vast distances, greatly increasing the size of battles—and the number of casualties. Not simply fought between professional armies, the war scarred large proportions of the population on both sides.

The popular culture of the era, intensely romantic and heroic, only gradually began to reflect the reality of the war. The soldiers sang of "The Girl I Left behind Me," looked away to "Dixie land," and marched to the "Bonnie Blue Flag." The first visual images depicting the war were largely patriotic: wood engravings and paintings showing—as in Plate 1—soldiers grasping the flag as they fought. Photography, however, as modern as the war itself, eventually undermined this romantic vision of the war. Photographs of the litter of bodies strewn across battlefields and campsites forced the public to see some of the war's terrible realities.

As photographs came to dominate the public's vision of the war, the technical limits of what the camera could depict defined the way people imagined battle. The photographic process then in use was too cumbersome to allow "action" photographs: there are no Civil War photographs of actual battles. Nonetheless, skilled photographers such as Andrew J. Russell and James Gardner followed the Union Army closely, catching the preparations for battle, the sites where battles were fought, and the dreadful aftermaths of these events. The inability of the Confederacy to support a similar photographic industry has had a major impact on the way we visualize the war.

The works of George N. Barnard (Plates 8 through 13) show how photographic artists of the era selected subjects that might portray their own values. Barnard followed General Sherman's army as it fought its way through the South, photographing when the army paused long enough for him to take pictures, sketching when it moved too quickly for his bulky equipment. After the war, Barnard retraced the route of the army photographing "the principal events and most interesting localities" that he had not been able to capture during the actual march. Gathered together in *The Photographic Views of Sherman's Campaign*, a portfolio of views that Barnard published in 1866, these photographs suggest both the power and the limits of the era's photography for evoking a vision of war.

At first, images of the war kept a polite distance from the actual carnage of battle. Plate 1, the only image in this portfolio that is not a photograph, depicts men in battle. What picture of combat does it offer? What would the people who rioted against the draft (Selection 38) have thought of it? How does the mood of Plates 2 and 3 differ from that of Plate 1? Why do you think photographer Andrew J. Russell chose the scenes he did? What does he include, and what does he leave out?

Below: Plate 1. H. B. Hall from a drawing by F. O. C. Darley, "General Lyon's Charge at the Battle of Wilson's Creek," 1862

Above right: Plate 2. Andrew J. Russell, "Battlefield Aftermath at Chancellorsville," May 1863

Below right: Plate 3. Andrew J. Russell, "Battlefield Aftermath at Marey's Heights, Chancellorsville," May 1863

Plate 4. James F. Gibson, "16th N.Y. Infantry Wounded during Battle of Gain's Mill at Savage Station, Va.," June 28, 1862

Plate 4 is the first stereograph published that depicted wounded soldiers. Plates 5, 6, and 7 take us directly into the world of Cornelia Hancock (Selection 39). The images shown are of Fredericksburg, Virginia, in May 1864, when the entire town was converted to a makeshift hospital for those wounded in the battles of the Wilderness and of Spotsylvania Court House. Given the date and place, the woman sitting in the doorway in Plate 7 could indeed have been Cornelia Hancock herself—if she ever found time to sit. How do you think

Plate 5. Brady & Co., "Burying Union Soldiers at Fredericksburg Killed in the Battles of the Wilderness and Spotsylvania Court House," May 12, 1864

those back home reacted to these photographs, all of which circulated widely as cartes-de-visit or stereo views? What do the images suggest about the problems of caring for the wounded during the Civil War? How do they compare to Cornelia Hancock's descriptions of field hospitals?

Above: Plate 6. Brady & Co., "Wounded Indian Soldiers of the Union Army after the Battles of the Wilderness and Spotsylvania Court House," May 12, 1864

Right: Plate 7. James Gardner, "Soldiers from Grant's Army, Wounded at Battles of the Wilderness or Spotsylvania, at Fredericksburg, Va.," May 20, 1864

Plate 8. George N. Barnard, "Destroying the Railroad Just before the 'March to the Sea,'" Atlanta, November 1864

The photographs on this and the next three pages are part of a portfolio of images of Sherman's march by George H. Barnard, one of the best field photographers of the Civil War. The captions indicate—insofar as historians have the information—those plates taken at the time of the march and those completed after the war. Plates 8, 9, and 10 indirectly depict a climactic moment of Sherman's expedition: the capture of Atlanta. This Union victory, in which the Confederacy suffered 8,500 casualties and the Union 3,700, made certain Abraham Lincoln's reelection in 1864. One casualty came to symbolize that battle, the death of one of Sherman's leading commanders, General James Birdseye McPherson, on July 22, 1864. What mood is Barnard creating in these images? How does this mood compare to the accounts of Sherman's march that you have read? Do you think Northern audiences would have interpreted these images differently than would have Southern audiences? How would Pauline DeCaradeuc Heyward (Selection 37) react to these images? How would Ellen Leonard (Selection 38)?

Above: Plate 9. George N. Barnard, "Rebel Works in Front of Atlanta, Ga., No. 3," 1864

Below: Plate 10. George N. Barnard, "Scene of General McPherson's Death," 1864 or 1865

Above left: Plate 11. George N. Barnard, "Destruction of Hood's Ordnance Train," 1864

Left: Plate 12. George N. Barnard, "Ruins in Charleston, S.C.," 1865 or 1866

Above: Plate 13. George N. Barnard, "Ruins of the R.R. Depot in Charleston, S.C.," 1865

Plates 11 through 13 are images of the destruction and aftermath of war. How would you compare them to other images of the destruction of war with which you are familiar, such as Hiroshima and Nagasaki or the Vietnam War? In Plate 11, you can see the demolition of the rail lines that had brought food and supplies to Confederate troops; in Plates 12 and 13, Charleston, South Carolina, is reduced to a pile of rubble. Think again about how Northern and Southern audiences would interpret these images.

(*continued from page iv*)

Visual Portfolios